At the Crossroads

AT THE CROSSROADS

*Librarians on the
Information Superhighway*

Herbert S. White

1995

Libraries Unlimited, Inc.
Englewood, Colorado

Dedicated to the thousands of colleagues and students who have helped to shape my thinking, but most of all to my wife Virginia, who has played a role in this process for more than 40 years.

Libraries Unlimited, Inc.
P.O. Box 6633
Englewood, CO 80155-6633
1-800-237-6124

Production Editor: Kevin W. Perizzolo
Copy Editor: Tama J. Serfoss
Interior design and typesetting: Judy Gay Matthews

Library of Congress Cataloging-in-Publication Data

White, Herbert S.
   At the crossroads : librarians on the information superhighway / Herbert S. White.
   xviii, 422 p. 17x25 cm.
   Includes bibliographical references.
   ISBN 1-56308-165-2 (hardbound)
   1. Library science--United States. I. Title.
Z665.2.U6W48   1995
020'.0973--dc   95-18337
                                                            CIP

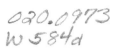

Contents

PART 2
Librarians, Their Self-Image,
and the Perceptions
That Define Their Preparation

PART 3
Librarians in the
Cruel World of Politics and Money

Foreword

In *At the Crossroads: Librarians on the Information Superhighway*, Herbert S. White has brought together 57 of his most trenchant, recent essays on the condition of our profession, its challenges, threats, and opportunities. Compiled from his "White Papers" published in *Library Journal* and numerous keynote addresses and other invitational writings, the essays in this work were written during the critical decade (early 1980s to 1994) that saw perhaps more change in librarianship than even the most radical futurist would have forecast. Readers already familiar with some of the essays in this collection or its predecessor, *Librarians and the Awakening from Innocence* (Boston: G. K. Hall, 1989), might fancy that they can skip those they have previously read. That would be a mistake: these essays sum up the experience and views of one of twentieth-century librarianship's keenest and most critically analytic minds. The advantage of absorbing an overview such a gestalt affords should not be carelessly discarded, for the present work forms a complete philosophy of modern librarianship.

A major characteristic of these essays is the series of unifying themes that run throughout. Over and over again one detects concepts central to White's philosophy of librarianship—the dangers inherent in what Drucker calls the "moral imperative," the unwillingness of some librarians to cope with either administration or politics (which are, of course, one and the same), the substantial differences between the oft confused concepts of education and training, the consequences of management styles that range from the abdicative to the autocratic, the interdependence of librarians and journal publishers, the political realities and rivalries inherent in the clashes over resources, and the paradoxical notion that "in the absence of money, there is money." Throughout, the discussion of these central concepts is as remarkably consistent as the author is insistent and persistent in broadcasting them.

Sometimes an essay focuses on a topic or principle that to casual readers might seem self-evident. Unfortunately, the reaction of our profession to some patently obvious contemporary issues is often deep denial; both practitioners and researchers can be unwilling to accept the reality of, or even to discuss, troubling concerns. If the emperor has no clothes, White will note that fact unhesitatingly, forthrightly, and unreservedly. We are fortunate indeed that White is catholic in his outlook, vociferous in his views, articulate in his writing, courageous in his approach to controversy, and generous with his deep knowledge of management. No one else has covered the manifold challenges of modern librarianship as broadly or as well.

If Herb White could function as a resident library consultant in each North American library, many of my anxieties about the future of our profession would be considerably reduced. Since this is not possible, the 57 essays presented in the current volume are surely the next best thing.

At the Crossroads: Librarians on the Information Superhighway is not a miscellany of armchair philosophizing; each critical essay is grounded in practicality yet based on sound theory. This work is an invaluable handbook that stresses management concepts and principles and the enduring aspects of personnel administration—all matters that remain independent of technological change. In short, this collection of "White Papers" and other writings is valuable precisely because it focuses on an abstract reality that changes very, very slowly, namely, human behavior. Herb White's work is both a wake-up call to contemporary library leadership and a clear beacon guiding those professionals who are committed to taking librarianship onto a twenty-first-century path.

Allen B. Veaner
Adjunct Assistant Professor
School of Library Science
University of Arizona
Tucson, Arizona

Introduction

The publication of this collection of writings is timed to coincide with the end of my formal career as a professional librarian. I began my career, after receiving my M.L.S. from Syracuse University, with the Library of Congress Special Recruit Intern Program in July 1950. I spent the next 25 years in increasingly significant management positions in government and corporate libraries and then in the corporate publications sector, providing products and services for the community of my fellow librarians. I became professionally active during this period, serving as president of two national library associations and on the board of several international ones.

I had participated as heavily as a speaker and writer during these years as my other activities permitted, but it has been during the last 20 years that I have done most of my writing and speaking. Asked to join the faculty of the Indiana University Graduate Library School (later the School of Library and Information Science) in 1975 as a faculty member, researcher, teacher, and dean, I entered an environment that not only encouraged writing and lecturing, but demanded it. That is when I began writing and speaking about issues in my field. I found to my great surprise not only that these endeavors came easily to me, but that I also had a great deal I wanted to say. Although my work has ranged from scholarly research to editorial exposition, I am probably best recognized for my regular column called "White Papers," which has been published 10 times annually in the pages of *Library Journal* since 1985. Prior to that time I wrote a regular column called "Research and Reality" for *American Libraries*, and before that for the British journal, *Information and Library Manager*. I have also written or co-authored seven monographs, including textbooks and collections of case studies. It might be assumed from this that writing short pieces (generally limited to 1,800 words) is an easy process for me. It is not, and cutting my columns from their original drafts is still my most difficult task. I identify completely with Mark Twain's written apology, "Please excuse this long letter, but I didn't have enough time to write a short one." Writing something longer is much easier.

At the same time, I am always surprised when individuals express admiration of my ability to find subjects about which to write. I don't look for subject matter, because I don't have to. The material comes to me primarily from what I have read and heard, and I usually have a supply of 10 or more columns waiting to be submitted to the editor. The hard part comes in deciding which column to publish when. Opportunities to speak and write about other subjects come in invitations from regional, national, and international organizations. I am grateful that the second stage of my career has not only allowed, but encouraged and credited, this part of my work. Nor can I promise (as perhaps some wish I would promise) to stop writing and speaking simply because I plan to retire from my faculty post at Indiana University. Academic faculty members are uniquely blessed in the fact that they never have to stop unless they want to. All of my colleagues at the Library of Congress in the 1950s or in the corporate environment in the 1960s and '70s are long gone, through voluntary retirement, or through early retirement "options" that may not be choices at all. Faculty members are fortunate in having real, ongoing options.

I have written hundreds of articles and given hundreds of talks, and while some were presented in a lighter vein, all were dead serious. Because I have been a manager and teacher of management for virtually all of my career, I am drawn to issues of management as they affect librarianship, probably because, like Peter Drucker, I have observed that the underlying measurement criteria (usually profits) that govern the management process in industry do not automatically apply to the not-for-profit service sector. I have never ceased to be amazed not only by how poorly many librarians manage, but more importantly, by the cavalier arrogance with which the nonlibrarians to whom all librarians ultimately report treat us. Why do they think they can get away with it, and how *do* they get away with it?

In my writings, I frequently refer to basic principles of management, which are generally known and available to any interested reader, and particularly easily available to librarians. Why then can't we find this information, or why don't we want to find it, or why don't we care? No higher-level manager is likely to offer more money, more support, or more staff to his or her subordinates. Instead, there is likely to be a plea of poverty, which may be real or contrived, but which is in any case irrelevant. The job of librarians is to run libraries effectively, the job of their bosses is to find the necessary funds, or to take full blame and responsibility for the results when the money is not provided. This is classic Management 101, and it is based on the principle that while responsibility can be delegated, it can never be abdicated. Managers receive either credit or blame for the actions of their subordinates, and act in accordance with their perception of whether they would rather provide needed funds and receive credit (even as they also get blamed for spending money), or whether the desire for frugality as a credit factor outweighs other variables. It is the job of all managers to make these tough decisions, and they make them all the time. Spend money for additional police protection? Or face a public angry about crime? Find the funds to repair highways devastated by earthquakes? Pump out the floodwaters under the city office buildings? They'd better, if they expect to further their careers. Support the continuation of library services?

The answer ought to be a resounding yes, because there are many factors in our favor. First, many surveys tell us that people like librarians, that they think librarians do a good job and that they are worthy of trust. The same cannot always be said of public perception of lawyers, doctors, and those we elect to public office.

Second, it is publicly accepted that education and literacy are important, and that information is key to the success of the individual, the community, and the corporation. Billions of dollars are being spent bolstering communications mechanisms through "superhighways" and other attractive-sounding and yet basically nonsensical terms. Society has developed, over a brief 20 years, a new profession called "information management," and a new industry that provides support services to a new generation of individuals who must access information sources, but who prefer to have others find information for them. So they delegate the process of information access to professionals and pseudo-professionals— qualified and unqualified.

The public might turn to librarians if they thought we were interested in providing information service rather than the educational preaching we call "bibliographic instruction." But there are too few librarians around, and those who are in view are always busy. This might be the fault of those who control resources, and we might expect librarians to complain loudly, as do police chiefs, traffic planners, and even teachers and nurses. However, librarians never seem to blame anyone. They instead thank profusely those who fail to support them, and only blame themselves for the poor quality of the library and its services. Is it perhaps the librarians' fault after all?

Fortunately for those in need of information, they have many options. If they have money, they can find someone to sell them services. They can dump the information search on their secretaries. If all else fails, they can pretend that they didn't need the information after all. It is a long-standing observation in academia that the more we learn, the more we become aware of how little we know. Those who know the least generally think they know everything. Is it only my observation that we librarians agonize far more about the growing numbers of adult functional illiterates than they themselves do? Do we have a workable strategy to counter the growing number of entertainment options that threaten to engulf the public, particularly television, all of which could be packaged under the marketing heading "How to enjoy life without funding annoying libraries and having to do something so unpleasant as reading?" Do we perceive the inconsistencies between the societal fascination with both education and indulgence, and what it means for us?

Because many of the articles included in this volume (and in my other writings) deal with our failure to articulate a winning strategy, let me restrict myself in this introduction to seven examples. I did not choose the number seven casually. Seven is frequently mentioned in the Bible, and it is believed to have particular power in the occult and at the gaming tables. Perhaps it will work here for me.

1. As I speak to groups of special and government librarians, I often find that the parent organization pays increasing lip service to the importance of information, to "linking into the superhighway," while at the same time, it cuts its own library budget. Does anyone notice, or point out, the absurdity in such inconsistency? Or don't they relate the two activities? Is it unfair to call those who cut our budgets while pretending to care about the importance of information hypocrites and liars?

2. Library education programs are continuing to close. That wouldn't bother me so much, because we undoubtedly acquired too many in the "anything is worth funding" 1960s, except that the schools being closed are not the weakest and least prestigious in the field. Some of the survivors are edging toward a strategy that completely eliminates the "l" word in favor of "information something-or-other." The two words—library and information—have coexisted comfortably in the names of most of our accredited programs for over 20 years, but now deans are perceiving a danger in the academic ranking system (which was fragile and arrogant at the best of times and is worse now) in retaining the word "library" in the title of a graduate education program. They still promise to educate librarians, because they don't want to lose those credit hours, but they'll presumably do it under the counter or in the back room. The university will still brag about its library as being the heart of the university, it will just get fuzzier about the need for librarians. What will this attitude mean to the self-esteem of those who still believe that they want to be librarians, or those who are librarians now? What will it do to our political assessment by outsiders?

3. Recently an American Library Association president brought an adorable little girl to the White House to present the president of the United States with a sweatshirt. White House staffers love such photo opportunities, but what's in it for us? The little girl urged the chief executive to increase funding for libraries, so that they could buy more books. I can hardly blame the child, but who told her that buying more books was the first priority of libraries today? Most likely book publishers, not librarians. Our own press releases report that the president was "sympathetic but noncommittal." Let me translate. That means that the president was totally unimpressed by the message. Presidents are not noncommittal when somebody points out an increase in crime, or even the need for an information superhighway or reinventing government, whatever that means. Couldn't we have used that opportunity to urge the president to support librarians, so as not to continue the disastrous current course (in fairness inherited from his predecessors) that is leaving this nation woefully unprepared for the global challenges of the twenty-first century? We might never have been invited to the White House again, but perhaps Wolf Blitzer would have commented on "CNN News" that evening.

And what is the point of opportunities such as this if not to invite comment?

4. In the national meetings of our major professional association, the American Library Association (ALA), we continue to be far more interested in bickering with one another on issues on which we have neither expertise nor acceptance (Middle-Eastern policies, the celebration of the landing of Columbus), rather than the issues for which, what we say, might have credibility. We move conferences from Phoenix and Cincinnati because we disapprove of the actions of local populations on nonlibrary issues. The Cincinnati boycott involved a legal issue already wending its way through the courts, in which voters had struck specific legislation to protect homosexuals. If we had waited just a few months, the issue would have resolved itself, because the courts overturned the vote. However, if the ban had been considered legal there still would have been no reason that was not simply censorious. If voters in Cincinnati do something they may not do, the courts will tell them. If they do something they do have a right to enact, do we librarians then become the judges over the social conscience of others? Indeed, that was the exact point in Phoenix, where the right of Arizona voters not to enact a specific holiday was never a legal question. Arizonans recanted their "sin," not because they were punished by losing an ALA conference, but because the Super Bowl was taken away. They have now been reinstated into the good graces of the National Football League, and perhaps soon also of the American Library Association. However, if we are to use whatever clout we might have to make political statements, why do we always restrict ourselves to nonlibrary issues? Have we ever threatened the state of California or the city of San Francisco with the loss of an ALA meeting until proper library funding is restored? Just a thought.

5. To enlarge on this last point, as California public library budgets are cut and reference service is decimated, have we developed a strategy for punishing those who made such stupid decisions in the face of the growing demand for reference services? Do we see this inconsistency as an opportunity, as certainly police chiefs would, to demand change or does it simply "challenge" us to absorb this problem as we've done in the past and try to do more with less?

6. At meetings of medical librarians, I ask if any of the attendees think that doctors do searches of medical databases three times as rapidly or three times as well as professional librarians. Everyone agrees they do not. My reason for asking is that doctors get paid at least three times as much. If this is so, why do we continue to train doctors to do anything other than specific item lookups? Many doctors must do their own searches because they have no access to reference librarians. But rather than forcing doctors to spend their more expensive time conducting their own searches, shouldn't the strategy be one of

insisting on an adequate supply of medical reference librarians? Shouldn't this solution be suggested to Mrs. Clinton as one of the cornerstones of any program to contain healthcare costs?

7. As we begin to discuss the implications of the virtual library, what is our strategy? Are we prepared to document that the virtual library will undoubtedly cost much more, but that it will be worth it? Is it illogical to suggest that, given this growth in both cost and importance, universities need information czars, formerly called librarians? Or, as I instinctively fear, do we see an "opportunity" for reducing the visibility of our own costs by distributing them into the budgets of user groups? Is that really an opportunity? In a political environment, isn't one of the clear sources of power the ability to control the money? As I ask my own management students, if in the concept of the virtual library, everything goes automatically to the terminal in the user's office, would anyone even notice if librarians ultimately went out on strike? Am I alone in believing that the source of political power is not making people independent of us, but rather dependent upon us? Do the people who redesigned automotive carburetors so that only specially qualified experts at the dealerships can work on them understand something we don't?

This book and its predecessor volume deal with issues such as these in a whole range of settings. The first collection of my writings, *Librarians and the Awakening from Innocence*, collected 37 research and argumentative pieces written between 1969 and 1988, out of a potential pool of about 100 articles. Its title was more optimistic than the present volume, *At the Crossroads: Librarians on the Information Superhighway*. Opportunities still exist for us to reestablish the importance of our field, at least in my judgment. However, I am not sure how much longer that will be true. Ours is an attractive piece of real estate, and others recognize it.

What I fail to see is the development of any sort of strategy that will allow librarians to win this fight. I am not even sure that we can agree on what it is we would like to achieve, and without that commitment to a direction, and to a ranking of priorities, even our would-be supporters are confused. What do we want from them? What do we expect, or even demand, of them? How is it possible that public libraries are deeply committed to serving the needs of senior citizens, while senior citizens routinely vote against library budgetary initiatives? If it is somehow assumed that library services are available without pain and without cost, who but we allowed that illusion to be created? Have we forgotten what an effective lobby the American Association of Retired Persons (AARP) is? Why haven't we made sure it understands the problem and the possible consequences to its members?

We still are fortunate in the fact that we do not face any sort of organized opposition. There is no anti-library lobby. However, there are anti-spending lobbies. Even more bedeviling are the lobbies in favor of spending, but only for their priorities. Drucker has made it clear that the "enemies" are not simply those who oppose us. Most people will at least state that they wish they had more money to give us. However, as Drucker tells us, in a political environment, an enemy is anyone who would rather not spend money at all or who thinks that funding us must come only after some other and higher priority. Those people are our enemies, even though we sometimes think they are our friends. Friends put our needs first, and that will explain why we have so few friends. We librarians simply refuse to understand the political process, in which one rewards for support and punishes for lack of support. Words are cheap, but words don't count. We could still build effective coalitions, but not without tough negotiation with our potential friends. I do not see that will or dedication in the field. It may even be, from the votes and discussions at our own "professional" meetings, that some of us agree that other people's needs come ahead of our own. I have no particular personal interest in either the National Rifle Association or the tobacco industry, but I think we could learn from their refusal to allow themselves to get sidetracked from their agendas. Just perhaps our definition of "enemy" can be found in the immortal words of Pogo Possum: "We have met the enemy, and it is us." At a minimum, in looking for the root causes of our problems, we might begin with introspection.

In planning this second collection of my writings, it was my intention to concentrate on material written between 1989 and 1994, and I have primarily done this. However, in looking over my files I found earlier works, particularly speeches presented at international meetings for limited audiences, that I consider worthy of inclusion. Ultimately the responsibility for selection and exclusion is mine. A number of individuals asked, after the first collection, why certain articles were not included. There really is no significant reason, except that some decisions had to be made, and my desire to keep overlap to a minimum. However, these words were spoken or written for specific and discrete audiences, so some repetition is inevitable. In academia we don't call that redundancy. We call it reinforcement.

The material in this collection is divided into three parts and arranged chronologically in each. The parts are "Librarians and Their Role as Defined by Themselves and by Others," "Librarians, Their Self-Image, and the Perceptions That Define Their Preparation," and "Librarians in the Cruel World of Politics and Money." These attempts at categorization are, I think, serviceable, but they are hardly perfect. A number of these articles could have been placed into more than one section. Problems, issues, and ideas frequently spill out of the boxes to which we might prefer to assign them, and have secondary impacts. To at least some extent our profession faces interrelated concerns that end up as a seamless continuum.

It is not my expectation that all readers, or for that matter, any readers, will agree with everything I have written. Indeed, there are things in this volume that, were I to write them today, I would write differently. It is certainly my hope that readers will agree with some of what I have said. However, my primary purpose in everything I have said to hundreds of audiences, written for publication, and taught in the classroom is to get people to think about their value systems, to assess and reassess their priorities, and to be aware that there are others who consider their own causes right and virtuous, who disagree with the priorities of librarians without automatically becoming evil people. I have become aware of the fact that there are individuals and groups of individuals who, in the pursuit of their own agendas in professional societies, find me threatening.

This disturbs me, but far more for its professional than its personal implications. I was initially trained as a scientist and I worked with the scientific literature. I realize that the scientific fields are replete with healthy and honest disagreements, sometimes expressed with white-hot anger, but always within the framework of scientific debate. Scientists, in their literature, have very little interest in discussing anything other than science. It appears to me that librarians, by contrast, often want to discuss everything but librarianship, and fail even to establish that the individuals we invite to our conferences should speak about librarianship and libraries. It is probably this perception of our failure to take ourselves seriously as a profession and as a potentially potent societal force that disturbs me most of all. It is this perception which has caused me to draw back from the optimism of my earlier collection. If the reader of this collection is forced to reexamine his or her own values, priorities, and strategies, I will have accomplished all that I can hope to do. I want the reader to think, and to think selfishly, about his or her profession, because that is the only way we can ever do anything for anyone else.

Finally, I must point out that any collection of articles and speeches, each originally prepared for a specific audience, will, when gathered together, inevitably produce both repetition and overlap. This affects all writers, because I am certain that any collection of Churchill speeches and articles during the Second World War would indicate a continuing preoccupation with Germany. In the selection process I have attempted to reduce such overlap, but I do not apologize for the fact that it certainly exists. I can only fall back on the standard explanation of any professor. We never repeat, we only reemphasize.

Part

1

Librarians and Their Role as Defined by Themselves and by Others

Introduction

I find it impossible to separate the introductory essay for this section from that of the next, "Librarians, Their Self-Image, and the Perceptions That Define Their Preparation." How librarians are perceived by others is largely determined by how they perceive themselves. Additionally, and unfortunately, how others expect us to behave often dictates the way we do act. We are perceived as great "copers," people who will make do with small resources without complaint or recrimination, and without making the kind of trouble that demands and often receives action, the kind that police chiefs make. As long as librarians are willing to allow others to define their roles and responsibilities, they will have difficulty in shaping their own futures, assuming that they can reach agreement on what that future should be. Indeed, the noncombative way in which we respond simply reinforces and validates the existing perceptions.

Two obvious and immediate examples come to mind. In the state of California, because of sweeping, draconian budget cuts enacted by the voters and the legislature, there is currently a movement to raise "temporary" funding so that public libraries can be kept open until funding can be restored through later legislation. The strategy assumes that public leaders are willing to find more money for libraries if given the chance to do so.

Is this in fact a good strategy? Is there likely to be more pressure to find funding if libraries are open or if they are closed? If libraries manage to fund themselves, even temporarily, isn't that likely to put the crisis on the back burner? Would we not be better off in exacerbating the crisis by wiping out library services until funds are restored? Are we certain that there is no way funds could be found, even today? Certainly funds are located, without a waiting period, to deal with an earthquake. A case can perhaps be made for any political strategy, and nobody can guarantee what would happen, but the point is that if librarians see their first responsibility as being not to their own careers and profession but to the institution, they may not only be wrong in terms of long-range impact, but more importantly they will have abdicated much of their professional control. Should keeping libraries open be our first priority? Isn't that supposed to be the governor's responsibility?

Another example, about which many, including myself, have written, concerns the continuing double-digit price increase of scholarly publications that academic libraries have faced for more than a decade, a price increase for which there are many explanations but really no legitimate rationale compared to the normal workings of inflation and currency exchange. It has been clear for some time that the primary reason for such price increases is that publishers perceive that the real decision makers about which publications to purchase are academic faculty members, who have authority but no responsibility for financial decisions.

This situation would suggest several alternative actions for academic library directors, but the first of these is clearly to state that such financial concerns are not their problem or responsibility. University administrators, whose responsibility it is, have several choices. They can find more money, a process literally without end, but with a clear understanding that the largesse being bestowed on publishers has nothing to do with the other priorities and budgetary needs of the library. They can put a ceiling on expenditures regardless of prices, and take responsibility for what happens to collection integrity. Or finally, they can look for ways to organize opposition to upwardly spiraling prices. The point is that academic librarians, like their public librarian colleagues, have demanded none of these things. They agonize, they complain, and they feel personally guilty and personally responsible. Can a profession so easily distracted from its own agenda by outside forces even find the time and energy to develop an agenda?

There are many definitions of professions, but perhaps the simplest and clearest of these is that professions control the interaction between themselves and their clients, who come to them as supplicants seeking advice, aid, and decisions from those acknowledged to have a greater level of expertise. Doctors and lawyers have been very successful in establishing this relationship between the ignorant and the (hopefully compassionate and helpful) knowledgeable. Is there even a glimmer of a chance, in this world of information superhighways, of librarians being accorded such a respectful status? Do we even aspire to it?

It is helpful to remember that there were people called librarians long before there were educational programs that promised to prepare them Initially, a "librarian" was a scholar who preferred to work with the literature rather than in the area of his or her expertise. Other "librarians" were teachers, or simply kind and caring people who wanted to help others. In many instances, and in many institutions called libraries, those definitions hold even today. Doctors and lawyers, by contrast, have moved well beyond that point. Doctors become doctors only when other doctors so proclaim them. Pretending to be a doctor can land you in jail.

The programs begun by Melvil Dewey and others around the start of the twentieth century were designed simply to formalize, standardize, and improve the training that had been carried out in libraries as part of a standard apprenticeship system, and, of course, that is how lawyers used to start. It was not until the work of C. C. Williamson that we began talking about the education rather than the training of librarians, and the conferring of a master's degree upon library professionals was instituted to confirm this. Doctoral programs in our own discipline, once restricted to the University of Chicago, were not slow in coming, and a dozen or more schools now prepare research scholars in our own discipline.

While we were perhaps able to convince others in the heady 1950s and '60s, when it was hard for a library or educational program not to grow, I am not sure that we ever convinced ourselves that we were truly a profession. And now, the hard times that came in the 1980s and '90s (as hard times always come cyclically), have caused us not to rally around our newly acknowledged professionals, but rather to seek ways to cut corners—or add water to extend the soup. We have been trying to find objectives that would fit budgets rather than demanding budgets that would fit objectives, and trying to avoid a public airing of the trashing of those objectives by those in power. Much of this preoccupation with what Peter Drucker calls "moral imperativism"—the belief that, with or without support, we must do everything or it will be our fault—has been well documented. We accept the language of the business schools that urge team-building and subordinate involvement in decision making, without necessarily understanding how these will impact the achievement of our own institutional objectives. While it seems a harsh and unfair generalization, it may be because many libraries, with declining budgets but without modified programs and strategies, have no goals other than survival.

All of this places a strain on the relationship between the institutions that prepare professional librarians and the employers who hire them, with students often unwitting pawns in the struggle. Perhaps the clearest difference comes in the emphasis placed on education (preparation for a career and a profession) and training (preparation for the requirements of a first job). In general, employers prefer the latter, at least in part because their own budget cuts have wiped out their own training and continuing education budgets. When the operative priority for a public library is nothing more than "keep the doors open," is it not then time to close the doors, to demonstrate that nothing of any uniquely significant value can now occur? What such a library has become is only a free bookstore. I suppose it is something, but not much.

It should be noted that practicing librarians and library educators have always eyed each other warily. My own columns on library research in *American Libraries* pointed out that practitioners rarely attend ALA conference programs with a research theme, even when the topic suggests findings that might be of value in an operational setting. In a study undertaken for the National Science Foundation (NSF) by the American Society for Information Science (ASIS) in the mid-1970s, practitioners barely acknowledged that publishing the results of library-related research studies might be valuable. Because the NSF has left the library research field (such results could hardly be encouraging), there is now very little funding for library research. The Department of Education Office of Library Programs defines its own research agenda, and it is my impression that the studies it funds search for an enabling rationale for conclusions already reached. Professions generally define their own research agenda, and then present that agenda to government agencies for funding. It still works that way in the hard sciences and in most of the social sciences.

The lack of academic rigor supporting research has not gone unnoticed in centers of academic administration. As a resident in a major research institution for 20 years, I never understood why the university library did not demand for itself laboratory status and research funding as well as operational funding, so it could study itself. Indeed, in most academic institutions control over library priorities rests with faculty committees, a situation that has no parallel elsewhere in the university. Sociologists do not make policy for biologists.

If, under the funding pressures that now plague academic institutions, largely caused by heady promises that were not kept and perhaps could not be kept about how an investment in higher education would solve the problems of the world, universities have looked for ways to eliminate library education programs, that action is not surprising. Library education programs are small, and their alumni have little political power and make relatively small financial contributions. As any student of management knows, and as library directors certainly should know, programs become vulnerable not because they are large and expensive, but because they are small and weak. Closing a library education program is at best a symbolic action. It gives the appearance of economy, without requiring the painful process of dealing with it. I can understand the process, but I would have felt more comfortable if the administrators at Columbia and Berkeley had simply acknowledged a pragmatic decision, without attempting to rationalize an intellectual base that was never there.

How librarians react to this frontal assault on their educational credentialing process is crucial. I am convinced that without the credibility brought about by an accredited educational degree, which at least some employers now demand as a hiring qualification, the profession would be left to whatever interpretations those doing the hiring would place on "qualifications." The result would be a dilution of professionalism and expertise and it is disturbing that the attempts to bypass stated educational qualifications (which are fundamental in the status of doctors and lawyers) come not only from nonlibrarians, but also from library professionals who pay low salaries or waive specializations spelled out in the job description because "they don't have the money." However, the suggestion that in such circumstances it might be better not to have a children's librarian than to have an unqualified one does not register very well with moral imperativists.

While it might be expected that, in these times of danger and stress, educators and practitioners might finally have banded together to present a united front, I have seen no such indication, and I am tempted to echo Mercutio's line in *Romeo and Juliet*, "a plague o' both your houses." However, I can't afford the luxury.

From my own experience as dean I know that practitioner groups are still pressuring library education for more specific courses—a second course in government publications, or a course in community college library administration or research library administration as opposed to a general course in academic librarianship. What these individuals are looking for is instant training, so that they can be hired at 9:00 A.M., processed at 9:30 A.M., and put to work attacking the backlog at 10:00 A.M. They forget that *professionals*, as that term is widely understood, are not only initially unproductive, they are initially negatively productive, because a senior professional has to train them. They are only educated. Training an educated professional is an investment by the employer. DuPont understands this when it hires chemists, and Price

Waterhouse understands it when it hires accountants. The doctors and lawyers who serve on public library boards understand it, at least as it applies to their own professions. If they don't make the connection to library professionals, it may explain why they consider the primary virtue of librarians that of unlocking the door.

I know that statement will make people angry, but it never ceases to amaze me to what extent public librarians are willing to adapt their agendas to the priorities of others—service to the homeless, service to latchkey children. They are worthy priorities, but they are not ours. Our goals are to match information with clients, at least that is what we know how to do better than anyone else. The availability of computer technology makes that job more complex, but much more important. Readers of this book and of my other writings know I have my own definition of bibliographic instruction. I define it as allowing individuals to find what they want or need, either on their own or through the intercession of a reference librarian. If, as a result of this instruction, a student writes an A paper that is partially plagiarized, that may indeed be a problem for the teacher, but it is not a problem for librarians. We can and do teach, but we are not simply semi-teachers, as an article in the second section suggests. Librarians and teachers are presumably partners of equal value, each with unique and nonduplicated expertise to bring to the process. When this is not understood, when librarians serve only as teachers' assistants, it is not surprising that teachers choose cutting the school library budget as their first option to save money. It is certainly easier for teachers to suggest terminating librarians than to volunteer for termination. If we look for friends and supporters, we must look first to ourselves, because many teachers and school administrators do not consider the contributions of librarians equal to (let alone superior to) their own.

When library practitioners demand more specialized courses, their requests fly in the face of study evidence (I know they don't read things in *Library Quarterly*) that demonstrates clearly that many graduates end up in positions other than the ones for which they prepared themselves. The issues that need to be stressed in the curriculum are not *how* we do something, because that can be taught specifically by the employer. We need to stress instead what we all do, and *why* we do it. As a teacher of management, I am aware of how little we prepare students for what is an intensely people-interactive profession. While I welcome the exposure to technology, again I think the emphasis should be not on how, but rather on why, and most specifically on the options that technology presents for our assessment and decision. I know that students need to understand the principles of online searching, but they can learn the nuances of specific databases later, once they know what databases the employer wants them to search. Of course, that won't happen by 10:00 A.M. on the first day.

When I read in the literature that some professional leaders suggest that we ought to abandon library schools and return to in-house training, or that the problems of library education are not the profession's problems, I find such utterances to be suicidal. Not only because of the decreased quality of our professionals, but because of the consequent decrease in status for our profession.

Library educators develop their own survival strategies. Such strategies as abandoning the "l" word and changing a program's title from "library and information science" to "information management," might initially seem harmless. However, the parent institution approving (or perhaps demanding) this change still has a massive investment in something called "library." What is the message about the importance of our profession, when the educators turn tail and run? It is a special annoyance when, after abandoning the word "library," deans hasten to assure us that despite the name change, they will still be educating librarians. They are not totally stupid. For much of the foreseeable future, prospective librarians will comprise a significant and perhaps major part of the student body. However, what does it suggest when academic administrators hire "professional" librarians without caring about or insisting on their academic preparation?

It is obvious that much is changing in this profession. The impact of technology, and the growth in the availability of information and its options for presentation, all make this inevitable. However, I would argue that this change is no more dramatic than the change from illuminated manuscripts to print, or from full-size text to microform. It is not formats that matter. It is not even the institutions called libraries, difficult as it may be to argue this to people who annually celebrate a building but never themselves, and whose slogan is not even *LEARN* but simply *READ*. What this profession does may change in specific emphasis, but never in concept. Computers are appropriate both because we are inundated with material, and because they can be (but are not automatically) cost-effective and useful. However, if we see this technology as an abdicative opportunity to dump more stuff on clients, who want not more but less and more relevant, then we don't understand our jobs. Perhaps because I am a special librarian, I see nothing new in the phrase "information management." Good librarians have always been information managers, but dubbing someone else "information manager" alone does not promise even poor librarianship.

However, the process of defining ourselves, and then insisting on that definition and on control over our professional priorities, cannot be fragmented either by type of library, or differences between educators and practitioners. I am not suggesting that we stop listening to our clients, because what they have to say is important. But the value of what they can tell us is limited simply because their knowledge base is limited. Perhaps before we embark on another White House Conference in which we solicit 100 recommendations from others, we need to come to grips with our own dilemma and our own opportunities, and in a process that rigidly excludes all distractions, reach consensus on what will then be a unified professional and political strategy. The two cannot be separated. I wish I could be more confident that this will happen, but the leadership for this difficult journey has yet to emerge.

Another characteristic of a profession is that it controls its own credentialing process. The Council on Post-Secondary Accreditation (COPA) understands this when it places with each profession, including ours, the authority and responsibility for what it takes to become a member. However, the process does not work very well when the ALA refuses even to defend the importance of its own monitored degree in the Merwine case (a

Mississippi legal claim to a position clearly advertised as requiring an ALA-accredited education), or when librarians allow nonlibrarians to fill jobs because it is inconvenient or more expensive to insist on accredited librarians, and ultimately because it might endanger "the library." Perhaps there are times when, for the achievement of larger objectives, the risk of closing libraries is worth taking. Only moral imperativists believe that the quality of service we provide is primarily our responsibility. It is, in fact, the primary responsibility of our bosses, and it is my personal observation that we already run libraries that are much better than their funding deserves—unfortunately without any real credit.

The problems of educators and practitioners are a seamless continuum, and it should be obvious that academic administrators are not going to be impressed with the rigor of an educational process unless they are first impressed with the academic rigor of the librarians they have hired, and that employers are not going to be concerned about the absence of a nearby accredited program if nonaccredited personnel are accepted by the State Library.

The process of credentialing begins at the top. Therefore, who gets hired to administer the accrediting program or administer our research libraries ought to be crucial to us, because virtually everything else follows from this. Why is it suggested that engineers can supervise the preparation of librarians, or that sociologists or historians can administer a research library, when it would never be suggested that librarians serve as the deans of engineering schools and of history departments? What then is our strategy for punishing such transgressions, and making sure they never recur? What would be the reaction of the American Bar Association if a children's librarian were nominated for the Supreme Court? It is issues such as these with which the first two sections deal, and if my ebbing optimism and growing anger are discernible, perhaps that should be understandable.

Let me state now, although I will be elaborating on this theme in the third section, that the presence or absence of money has nothing to do with these issues. The availability of funds is never admitted in any sort of management setting, but money is always found if it is necessary to find it. Our problem is one of making libraries a priority to decision makers. In the overall context of any larger organization, what is spent in support of our programs is truly trivial. Perhaps, as C. Northcote Parkinson has noted, the small amount of money involved is our first problem.

The Role of Reference Service in the Mission of the Academic Library

I accept my topic as somewhat tongue-in-cheek, because I assume that there is no one here who would argue that academic libraries should *not* perform reference service. However, the level of that service as provided in academic libraries, and particularly large academic libraries, varies substantially from that in public libraries and special libraries. Some librarians would argue that the only point in having a collection at all is for the use to which it is put, and a few would even argue that material that is not used is therefore wasted. Operations research people would probably agree with this, as it is harder to find things in a large collection than in a smaller one, and that unused material therefore inhibits the location of desired material. They would argue that we should weed continuously and ruthlessly, even if we have plenty of space.

While these are not necessarily generally held sentiments, I do recall the statement made, not by an academic librarian, but by a library school dean, that our job is to provide the material in the collection. Whether or not it is used is not our problem. We also have the rather famous quote attributed to one of our revered academic library leaders (a quote that I first thought a joke until assured of its accuracy) that "we will be remembered not for the service we gave but for the collection we left behind us." Exaggerated as some of these expressions may be, they are nevertheless based on some level of acceptance. There are clear indications that the academic library, unlike the special library, does not consider active or even aggressive service from the collection as a primary goal, or perhaps even as a goal at all.

Speech presented at a meeting of the College and University Libraries Section of the Kansas ACRL Chapter, Manhattan, Kansas, October 14, 1982.

11

It is argued that the academic library is primarily geared to be a self-service library, that for students this is desirable or expected, and that faculty insist on doing their own work. Therefore, even when we perform reference services for students, the main intent is to avoid having to do it in the future. We teach them so that they can serve themselves. Much of the emphasis on bibliographic instruction is to develop library users who can function on their own.

Special librarians, whose own contribution to the objectives of the organization may be measured more tangibly, complain that their users, who come to them largely from the academic community, are passive, accept low levels of service without complaint, and have no expectation of professional interaction. Their only expectation is for the development of a collection, and that the library purchase materials not for the library but for immediate transfer to their own offices. It is a concept of library service that I, perhaps simplistically and uncharitably, have termed the "free bookstore" as one of the fringe benefits to offset low salaries.

It can be argued, and frequently is, that whether or not this emphasis on collection instead of on service from the collection is the best approach, it is the approach upon which the academic community insists. However, that argument can be probed, and under intense scrutiny, it begins to show cracks.

It has been my observation, and I am sure that of others, that the individuals in the library accorded the highest level of professional recognition and regard by faculty are not the specialists who acquire and process, but those who actually work with the material. These individuals are the subject specialists or bibliographers and the branch librarians who frequently work as special librarians, doing what Grieg Aspnes would describe as taking the burden of the work off the user's shoulders. Just leave me the problem, and I will get back to you. Aspnes would state that this is in fact what most library users (including faculty) would really prefer if they thought it were acceptable to ask for it—that for most faculty members there is no particular thrill in digging in the library, and so the task is frequently shunted to graduate students.

Aspnes and other special librarians would argue that their clients, who are frequently academic degree holders at various levels, only one stage removed from the academic library experience, come to the special library expecting nothing more than the ordering of material on request, and must be weaned to a higher level of expectations. They would further state that once they recognize that librarians can and will do reference work, that they can do it better, and that it is not immoral or unethical to have this work done for them, they become addicted. Some of them continue to demand reference service well beyond retirement.

There is growing evidence that the so-called Madame Curie model of research, trying to learn everything on a subject and then sorting it out to determine where the truth lies, is not the way most research is conducted. Most library work is not in support of the search for knowledge, it is in support of evidence to further conclusions (or if you prefer, paradigms) already reached. This kind of applied research actually resembles much of what happens in special libraries. Osburn has argued that this change has even affected humanities researchers, who don't really want to be pointed at stacks of raw materials but the specific page or chapter or article or book that proves their point. Osburn[1] argues, and I would concur, that academic library operational philosophies are not geared to this kind of library use at all, except perhaps in some branch libraries.

The widespread belief that we don't help students very much because faculty don't want them helped is not really borne out by observation and experience. If this were true, faculty would assure that the materials necessary for the self-education process were available, and they would coordinate with the library to map out a program of student library education for the course in question. In reality, faculty frequently make assignments without bothering to determine whether or not the material is available. Like the law professor played by John Houseman in "Paper Chase," they may even consider it a part of the learning experience to cast the student adrift to shift for him- or herself, and any method of obtaining the answer is acceptable as long as it is obtained. Most would not condone outright plagiarism, but there are certainly enough known and acknowledged activities in cooperation, the use of test files, term paper models, coaching sessions for athletes and others, and a variety of other tactics, to convince at least me that for most academicians the accomplishment outweighs the concern about the process.

As a final point, and perhaps the most sensitive one, I would argue that it is simply not true that faculty members are experts who fully know their own literature. There is really no way that they could, given its growth both in size and interdisciplinary characteristics. At the same time, faculty can hardly admit to themselves, let alone others, that they don't keep up, or that there are things they should know which they don't know. And so *their* ignorance is the most dangerous of all, an ignorance that masquerades as knowledge. We can't really blame them for this, because they see no choice. An admission of a knowledge gap is not acceptable if there is no way that the gap can be closed. It only leads to an admission of permanent incompetence. I have had Ph.D. scientists doing industrial research tell me quite straightforwardly that the five journals they read contain everything they need to keep abreast of. How could they say anything else?

This narrow focus on the function of academic libraries, as orderers, arrangers, and distributors of requested material, causes particular problems. These problems began to emerge in the mid- and latter 1970s. Until then, the historical emphasis on the library as a self-service collection to be made as complete as possible had served at least some of us reasonably well. There was money for collections, there was money for new library buildings. Innovative and entrepreneurial administrators could not only keep pace with the literature growth, but they could score coups through the acquisition of a special collection or the development of a national or international unique strength. Satisfaction could be gained from statistics of growth, and from impressive new buildings and offices. Despite this general feeling of euphoria, in which library administrators did what they wanted to do, in which faculty were calm if not totally content (are they ever?), and in which academic administrators bragged about the value of the library as much as about the record of the football team, we paid a price.

That price came because what we did in acquiring, tagging, and processing (what Fairthorne[2] calls marking and parking) was not clearly understood, particularly in terms of its intellectual component and therefore faculty equivalence. Librarians may have faculty status, but except for a very few, perhaps not even the director, acceptance into full faculty collegiality is not generally extended. This may be partly our own fault, because the mysteries of the bibliographic and analytical rites that result in occult marking on cards have never been understood by, nor has their relevance been made clear to the general faculty. This is particularly true when faculty read in the *Chronicle of Higher Education*, their professional journal, or even the local newspaper, that the Library of Congress makes all bibliographic information available to all libraries, and that anything can be identified and obtained from anywhere via satellite.

However, recent history only provides a sharper focus for what has really plagued us all along. I recall repeated battles in special library settings with personnel administrators and wage analysts, who could easily understand why reference and bibliographic work required professional education and training, but who did not comprehend why cataloging or the adaptation of other cataloging could not be done by a clerk or a paraprofessional. And, of course, judging by staffing changes in academic libraries in the 1970s they may have been prophetically correct.

As a sidelight, it is startling and perhaps refreshing to hear of some of the changes in emphasis in our field. In a retreat sponsored by the Council on Library Resources that I attended in June 1982, I heard Robert Vosper, certainly one of our most distinguished leaders in research librarianship, stress that the greatest need in academic library administrators was now for individuals who are strong in areas of business management, conversant with publishing and legal ramifications, who understand national and international systems and technological implications, and are sensitive to people and issues of personnel administration. If Vosper is correct, it is not surprising that there has been so much turnover in academic library directorships.

However, there are other and perhaps more pressing reasons to change, and for embracing reference activities at the highest level—what I like to call information intermediation. These needs come primarily from an impossibility to meet present faculty expectations of what a library should be. I addressed some of these in my article "Between Scylla and Charybdis" in the *Journal of Academic Librarianship*[3] and will not repeat them here. My main reason for stating that we need to change the direction of academic libraries from a passive to an active role, convincing or overriding the conservative faculty, comes from a less scholarly source—my old tennis coach, who said "Always change a losing game. Try something." Providing more interactive information services, or just providing some interactive information services, may be the something we need to try. We may not yet be facing match point, but we've lost at least a set by now. There are several factors that must be incorporated into the need to change. All of these have really been noted before, by a variety of writers and speakers:

It will be impossible in the future, if indeed it ever was possible, to keep up with materials demand as our primary emphasis. The growth in the literature, estimated at between 2 percent and 8 percent per year (and it should be noted that journal publishing, unlike monographic publishing, is fairly impervious to the economic crunch because of the peculiarities of cash flow), must be multiplied by the price increases of materials, which are accelerated both by the rapid growth in labor, paper, and postage costs, and by the virtual disappearance of individual subscribers to scholarly journals to help defray the cost. Despite overall reductions in academia, new programs get started, and old ones hardly ever die. Maintaining collection equivalence would probably require an annual material budget increase of about 15 percent. That's a doubling every five years. It isn't going to happen. We must shift the emphasis away from collection as the sole or primary value of the library, because we aren't going to be able to keep pace.

There are also substantial changes taking place in the structure of the literature with which we deal. I have already mentioned that it becomes more complex as it becomes more interdisciplinary. There are also substantial changes in access to information. The most obvious one is the proliferation of machine-readable databases, at first in the physical sciences, then in the social sciences, now in the humanities, soon everywhere. There is no consistency in the structure of databases and in the search strategies needed to access them. To some extent, there probably will never be nor should there necessarily be, unless we are prepared to trade sophistication for ease of searching. The programs that attempt to provide a unified search approach to a variety of databases invariably must reduce these systems to a common denominator, and common denominators are usually small.

Database searching is a skill that can be developed at a variety of levels, and it is important that we understand the differences. I can drive a car, but I am not ready to drive at Le Mans, Daytona, or Indianapolis. It is important that we understand, and that users understand, that even a knowledge of the literature (and I have some doubts about that) does not automatically bring with it a knowledge of how to access that literature. We have consistently railed against the inability of university graduates to use the indexing tools of their own disciplines. In large part this is because nobody taught them how, and this is because their own professors did not think it important enough.

We have always assumed that academics wanted to search their own literature, despite the evidence that indicates that for most of them it isn't true. Project INTREX as designed by MIT, MEDLARS as developed by the National Library of Medicine, the NASA Information Facility, that I headed and that has become the DIALOG search system, all were based on the premise that researchers were just dying to get at those terminals. With rare and specialized exceptions, it just isn't true.

Searching is keying, and keying is a clerical task. Faculty will delegate it if they can, particularly if they don't know how to use the databases and don't want to admit it. But we have to let them know it is all right to delegate this task. That is the special library experience: freer bibliographic access to virtually any file through any terminal, and rapid document delivery systems for a fee—and who can doubt that these options will get more rapid, cheaper, and better as we improve the technology of satellite and telephone communication—have lost us our monopoly for bibliographic access. Until now, until we cataloged it and put it into the file, no one was even allowed to know it existed. That is a distinction we have now lost, but it is a distinction that wasn't really worth having in the first place.

We can and must establish a new level of expertise, one that concentrates on the literature of a discipline. The argument is that you may be a renowned anthropologist but you are not necessarily an expert in the rapidly changing literature of your field or of allied fields. This is our expertise, and working together we can achieve maximum results. Telling the faculty all this may have some value, but many won't believe us. Their idea of what librarians are and do is too ingrained. It is better to show them, and this is why any library policy that thwarts the already low level of demand for reference work, particularly in the use of computer-aided systems, is unthinkable, because it is so self-defeating.

Of course there are problems. The most significant of these, as I attempted to show in a column in *American Libraries*,[4] revolves around the nature and inflexibility of budgets in general, and library budgets in particular. The historic nature of most academic library budgets, as we have identified them through our studies for the National Science Foundation, effectively pre-commits the entire budget and leaves nothing to the initiatives of entrepreneurial decisionmaking. Between 60 percent and 70 percent of the budget is committed to ongoing staff salaries, and there are few options here except through resignation and retirement, and these fall not where we plan them but where happenstance places them. Most of the rest of the funds, perhaps between 20 percent and 30 percent, are allocated to the purchase of materials, and few options exist here as well.

Periodical expenditures, except where cancellations are forced down unwilling throats, are pre-committed, and so to an increasing extent are book expenditures when we recognize that the political process requires that "key" or "senior" faculty members be heeded at least part of the time, and that many libraries in fact allocate their materials budgets by funds or departments. This is not necessarily bad, but it trades the perception of equity (or perhaps even the reality of equity) against the loss of maneuverability. Collection development officers have told me that as budgets get tight, decisions actually get fewer, because little remains after we have bought what must be bought. I hadn't thought about it that way, and that's certainly not the way we teach collection building, but I am sure it is true.

We don't have enough money for people, and we don't have enough money for material. That is a harsh truth, but it has always been true, even in the more affluent 1960s. Our appetites, or perhaps I should say faculty appetites, have always exceeded our capability. Given the reality of academic funding, the chances of securing additional funds for the personnel necessary to continue to do what we presently do is nil. Problems of backlogs and even of a lack of support personnel have no real significance to academic administrators, who have no plans or expectations for the library except the hope that it will stay within the allocated budget and that the faculty and the students, in that order, won't complain too strenuously about it.

When you argue that you need more people because circulation has grown or because backlogs have doubled, those arguments are meaningless. Only the size of the collection, as related to that of other institutions or other academic programs, has significance, because deterioration at that point can be seen as directly threatening the individual's own peer evaluation. It is for these reasons that money to supplement the library materials budget can sometimes be cadged from reluctant administrators, either in the form of special allocation or through year-end funds. Personnel funds, on the other hand, are never supplemented, and neither is the catch-all category called "all other," that covers such a multitude of programs as photocopying, postage, travel, telephone, and supplies. If there are library expenditures in such areas as interlibrary borrowing or online search charges, they must be funded from this already impoverished category, and Parkinson as well as practical experience tell us that it is this "all other" category that, in any organization, be it the private, academic, or government sector, is in the worst shape. Not only don't we have any money with which to do *new* things. We don't have any money to do *any*thing in these budget categories.

Libraries have had some success in reducing technical processing labor costs, but they have not reallocated these resources. For the most part the savings have gone to pay salary increases to retain present positions, to supplement the inadequate original budget, and in a few cases to the materials budget.

We therefore must face the unpleasant truth that we will not get more money, and undoubtedly not enough money, to maintain the present level of operations except perhaps, and only perhaps, for materials. University administrators have no objectives for academic libraries except to avoid trouble. In one library with which I am well familiar, the suggestion that additional funds be allocated to provide an online circulation system was met with the answer that the faculty should be consulted as to whether they would rather have this or additional funds for the materials budget. If that sort of question is appropriate, then so is the question, "Would you rather have money for the library materials budget or as highly paid a university president?" and the answer is probably just as predictable.

Despite this depressing observation, there are some basic management truths we must bear in mind, and in my experience they are just as valid in academia as in industry and government. 1) in the absence of money there is always some money around, and 2) it is usually easier to get a lot of money than a little bit of money. Money is provided for those things that people really need or at least say they really need. The proven tactic of confrontation and assertive management is to offer a service, make it wanted, and then make sure the blame is properly allocated if that service is curtailed. The risk of confrontation and assertive management is that you can get fired. But there are worse things, and in some academic situations they can't even fire you—just shuffle you around.

Faculty pressures are the most effective in producing results, but even student concern can help. In one Big 10 university, a new undergraduate library, actually nothing more than an undergraduate reading room, became the campus number one priority when student groups broached the subject to the state legislature. At another university, this one in the southeast, additional funds to expand undergraduate library services were somehow found when students began dropping in at the president's home on campus to inquire politely if they could study at his house because the library was so crowded and noisy.

And so I would argue that libraries need to direct their resources to highly visible public services, particularly intellectual services, and most particularly services to faculty and administration. Reference services provide, in my judgment, the one great potential opening for the academic library—because there is so little of it done at present, at least as compared to other types of libraries, and because needs for it are almost open-ended. Once people become addicted to this service, they can't get enough.

This should not surprise us. We are a service-oriented society. We have not only a profusion of automotive services to fix our cars and to advise us specifically about our mufflers and our transmissions, we also have tax return services that prepare forms that practically anyone could do themselves in about 10 minutes. We have analysts on sports telecasts who explain to us what we just saw, and analysts after presidential speeches who tell us what we just heard. The rapid growth of the information service sector is a clear indication that people are willing to spend money for information services.

This would be expected naturally enough in industry, but we also find academicians buying information services, sometimes from grant and contract funds, sometimes with organizational overhead funds. We already know that even if we charge for online search services and interlibrary loan services, some individuals will pay. However, I think that such charges, although perhaps politically attractive, are the wrong direction in which to head, in part because it develops even on the campus an elite of information rich and of information poor (frequently humanists), but perhaps even more importantly, because it would lower our collegial esteem. Academicians deal with those who deal with money because they must, but they don't consider it a proper academic activity.

Even if I were to have convinced you up to now, you would still face the additional problem of how your budget is put together. It is a line item budget, and it allocates dollars not in terms of the services they provide but in the way the checks are written. What little money available for reference services is in the people budget. Therefore, assuming you already have reference librarians bought and paid for, they can happily run through the stacks answering reference questions, as long as they use material already there, because that category has already been expensed. It would be preferable if, in doing reference work, they not have to use the long distance telephone, because although that use might save hours of work, the telephone call is not budgeted for and the hours of work are. Similarly, online search costs are incremental charges, and they are not budgeted. This makes them expensive, even in those instances in which it can be proven that a machine search would be in fact cheaper to perform. It doesn't matter, because the one search is prepaid and the other isn't.

It is yet another indication of the passivity (or perhaps indifference) of the library users that they accept our explanation of having to pass along to them the cost of machine searches, or even the cost of interlibrary loan, because our budgets are not designed to absorb them. Sometimes we do this under the premise that these are "nontraditional" services, when in fact they are simply variants in the information supply business and the only thing that is nontraditional is the budget approach.

You may be glad that you don't have me in your academic community when I tell you that I refuse to accept pass-along charges in either the area of interlibrary loan or of online searching. I suspect that I have gotten away with this in part because I use neither of these services very extensively, because as a dean I pose something of a threat, or perhaps because I am considered something of an eccentric who should be humored as long as the cost is not prohibitive. However, I consider the issue anything but trivial, and it is my contention that by refusing to accept these transfer costs, I am according the library staff the professional respect that it deserves as expert in its own field, and then making it bear the responsibility for its professional decisions. My arguments run along relatively simple lines.

Interlibrary borrowing is a reasonable alternative to purchase. No library can afford to buy everything, but the determination of what it purchases and what it does not, and therefore has to borrow, is one that the library staff is supposed to make. I would prefer, ideally, that the library anticipated all of my needs and purchased everything I plan to request in the future. Failing that, I refuse to be doubly penalized, first by the time delay in their failure to have the material, and second, because they plan to make me pay the charges that their decision has incurred. Interlibrary borrowing is a materials cost and should be budgeted accordingly. Doing this would provide some easy crossover points between repeated borrowing and purchase, and almost automatically wipe out violations of the copyright law, because items borrowed frequently, if the same budget had to pay for them, would become quickly unattractive as candidates for borrowing and would probably be purchased.

With regard to online searching, my response to the question "Would you like to have an online search?" (although I am no longer asked that question) is "Why are you asking me? You are the reference librarian, use whatever approaches you consider most appropriate in your professional judgment." A number of libraries, both special and academic, have established their machine search operations as separate from their reference departments, to separate the accounting costs. I think it is a big mistake, because it establishes online searching as some sort of hothouse exotic plant rarely found in libraries. It is not difficult to predict that in the very near future, online searching will be the bread and butter of library reference, because in many cases it will be more complete, faster, and less expensive. All we have to do is figure out how to budget it. That is not an easy task, but it is the most fundamental issue we have to solve if we are going to do anything even remotely innovative.

The present line item expenditures that identify labor costs by individual salary, and materials costs not only by type of material (book, serial, microform) but also by subject discipline, leave us no options and no flexibility. What we need is program budgeting, and the program category we need to establish is something called information access, instead of materials purchase. Information access consists of a variety of things— most obviously the purchase of material, but also interlibrary borrowing and online access charges to databases that contain reference tools we didn't buy. Glyn Evans at SUNY Albany has been able to do something like this in his budgeting process, but there aren't many others of whom I am aware.

It obviously isn't easy. It requires wresting control over the library decision processes away from the faculty, and centralizing it in the library. It will not be easy to do, because campus administrators have no interest in antagonizing the faculty on our behalf, and because faculty have no expectations beyond the emphasis on size as a measure of quality and no real appreciation of the librarian's role in the intellectual processes of academia. When the president of the United States, the secretary of the Department of Education, and university presidents appoint nonlibrarians to key library posts it is a clear indication of that lack of perception. They wouldn't do this for appointments in the legal or medical fields. And yet, at the same time, we see examples of librarians who are accorded respect and status by their faculty colleagues. Invariably, it is not the keepers and processors of the warehouse. It is those individuals who work with them, and who assist them directly, in work with content and analysis, in problem solving.

My conclusion then is that academic librarians need to do reference work, and a lot more reference work than they presently do. How much? For starters, we could look at special libraries, which have transferred many of the acquisitions and processing costs to clerks and paraprofessionals, and which now expend at least twice the professional effort on user services as on technical services.

Academic libraries have also reduced the professional level of technical services, but those saved funds have not been identified and transferred, they have been gobbled up in the daily struggle to survive. Even in public services, we run the risk of falling into a trap. The most visible activity in libraries is clerical routine, and the danger is that in the absence of adequate budgets, clerical services will drive out professional services, unless we establish value systems and priorities to prevent this from happening.

I could argue with some assurance that for academic libraries the ratio of professional service activities should be even greater, because of the complexity, bulk, and interdisciplinary nature of the resources, and because there are fewer tools, particularly in the humanities. I would suggest that at least some, although certainly not all, of our academic scholars slog through the research process not because they want to but because they have to. They have no one to whom to delegate it, and they consider it imprudent to even think about whether they would like to be able to delegate it. One of my most interesting conversion projects in industrial consulting activities is to remind researchers in such organizations as chemical companies that they are not being paid to undertake research, they are being paid to produce research results. There is nothing immoral in delegation, if this process is effective and if you can find someone competent to whom to delegate. That competence, I also remind them, extends beyond an understanding of the subject field. It includes an understanding of the literature of that field, the literature of allied fields, and a comprehension of the skills necessary to access that literature through increasingly complex databases and search protocols. By that time, they are usually prepared to concede not only that there are some things that librarians could do as well, but even that there are some things librarians could do better than they.

That is the industrial model, but does it differ so greatly from the academic model? Not according to researchers such as Ladd and Lipseth, who report their findings in the *Chronicle of Higher Education*. According to them, even in major universities the faculty undertaking broad exploratory research is less than 10 percent of the total. The rest are either looking for proofs or solutions (just as their industrial brothers and sisters are), or are really doing no research at all.

And so we need to do much more reference work—and by reference work I have already stated that whether we approach it through a database, a published handbook, the card catalog, or a directory, it is an internal decision we don't even need to broach with the client. We need to do it because the public needs it. We also need to do it because we need it. An emphasis on collection rather than on service is for the present and the foreseeable future a no-win game, bound to lose us status and friends. It will ultimately get us bypassed by other services. Needs stimulate services, and not just in the for-profit sector. A class project by one of my colleagues at Indiana University to identify the number of information centers on campus unearthed more than 40, and that wasn't a complete list. Most of them did not know of the existence of others in overlapping areas, and many were unknown to the library. They sprang up because there was a need that was not being filled. What these information centers do is in most cases relatively simple. It includes screening the larger mass of literature for items of more specific interest, usually on fairly broad topical areas such as diabetes or railway transportation. When done by computer we now call this function SDI (selective dissemination of information), but alert and aggressive librarians were doing it long before then, if only by flagging specific items for the attention of readers. Some of these information centers publish newsletters and bulletins, most do reference work, many compile bibliographies. They do this for the same academic faculty members we presumably serve, in part because they want it done, and in part because nobody else, certainly not the academic library, has stepped forward to do it. And there is money available for these operations, some externally and some internally supplied. There is usually money for what is wanted badly enough.

Let me leave you with a few simple, if perhaps startling, statistics. Lee Burchinal,[5] former head of the National Science Foundation Office of Science Information Services, has estimated that the number of online searches grew from a start in 1968 to about 1 million per year in 1975, with a quadrupling to 4 million by 1980. If he is correct, we may be well beyond 5 million as I talk. If you think that's a lot of searches, please recognize that even if all of the searches had been performed for scientists and engineers, which they obviously weren't, it still only adds up to one search per technical professional every six months. The future growth of online searching is virtually beyond our ability to estimate. There can be little doubt that it will represent much of the substance, if not the backbone, of the use of library materials.

If libraries in general, and academic libraries in particular, refuse to accept their roles in aggressive reference service (and whether it is done by computer or not is really irrelevant) in the process of information intermediation, and I have already pointed out that this is a need increasingly filled by others on the campus, then I cannot feel encouraged about the importance and role of the future library. Not because I accept Lancaster's view of a paperless society. I don't. Computers are great producers of paper. I am concerned because if we refuse to become involved with the interpretative use of information files, and restrict our activities to document acquisition, document processing, document storage, document lookup, and document delivery and recall, then new technology will almost certainly lessen our role. Document lookup will not require use of a library card catalog, or even a library terminal. It can be done at home or at the office. Similarly, specific document delivery can be initiated directly at the same source. Teletransmittal and telecopying are still fairly expensive and of poor quality, but rapid progress is being made in both areas, and it does not take a wild-eyed radical to predict a throw-away copy technology by the year 2000, or perhaps much sooner.

That means nobody will care about local inventory, except perhaps senior faculty insecure about their department's ranking among peer institutions. The junior and rising faculty won't care. Nobody will care about circulation and material recall. I suspect that at least some of you still expect to be around and professionally active 18 years from now. If you are not prepared by then, or well before then, to support reference service and information intermediation as a prime priority, certainly as a higher priority than specific local collection development, and to make the adjustments in the library budgetary process to make this possible, then there may not be much else of professional consequence left for us to do.

Notes

1. Osburn, Charles B. *Academic Research and Library Resources: Changing Patterns in America.* Westport, Conn.: Greenwood Press, 1979.

2. Fairthorne, Robert A. *Towards Information Retrieval.* London: Butterworths, 1961.

3. White, Herbert S. "Library Materials Prices and Academic Library Practices: Between Scylla and Charybdis." *Journal of Academic Librarianship* 5 (March 1979): 20-23.

4. White, Herbert S. "Who Pays for 'Peripheral' Services, and What Are They Anyway?" *American Libraries* 13 (January 1982): 40, 44.

5. Burchinal, Lee G. "The S&T Communication Enterprise in the United States. Status and Forecasts." *Library Science with a Slant to Documents* (India) 14 (June 1977): 53-61.

Personal Information Needs in a Democratic Society

In approaching this talk, I also have taken some liberties in dealing with the issue of personal information needs within the context of the library profession and how we interact with individual personal information needs. At the same time, I am very, very pleased—I am not sure whether this was intentional, but I will pick up on it anyway—that the topic deals with personal information *needs* not with personal information *wants*, or personal information *requests*. Although you might assume that those are the same things, they indeed are not.

What people *need* is not necessarily what they *request*. What they ask for is, in fact, already filtered by what they think the system is geared to provide. In large part this is because the expectation for library service is largely that of self-service. Part of the reason, of course, is that libraries operate almost totally within the framework of the educational process. There is, I stress, a very clear contradiction between the library's role in the education process and the library's role in the information process. I am not saying that one is more important than the other. I am saying they constitute very, very different approaches in terms of service attitudes. I will give you an example which is, typically for me, a very garish, outrageous example. I tend to operate with outrageous examples, particularly in my classroom, because students tend to remember outrageous examples.

The example of the difference between an educational approach and an informational approach is that of the high school student who comes to the library for help because he has been assigned by some unreasonable teacher the responsibility of doing a book report. He wants help from the library. The library's basic approach, inevitably, is to find the student a book to read, so he can do a book report. But that does not deal with the

Paper presented at the 12th Annual Colloquium on Intellectual Freedom, Graduate School of Library and Information Science, UCLA, May 6, 1986.

23

student's information need, which is to figure out a way to write a book report without having to read a book. Therefore, if we wanted to deal with information needs, we would figure out a way for the student to fake this process by finding him something he could copy out of the *New York Times Book Review.*

I am not suggesting that we do that, but that would be, in fact, dealing with the student's information need, at least as the student perceives it. He did not ask for a book. The student said he needed to write a book report. Special librarians understand what I am talking about here; public librarians sometimes do not.

Library users have come to expect a low level of information service. What they expect is a document service. Providing documents is not the same thing as providing information. By and large, though, documents are what they get. Librarians, in turn, justify this low level of service in terms of their own limited budgets, sometimes not recognizing the cause and effect relationships: we have low budgets, we spend low budgets, and we don't make an issue of what is not being done because of low budgets. Unless problems are spotlighted and identified, they are never going to be solved.

Our approach then to these so-called needs—because in fact we are not dealing really with needs at all, we are dealing with requests that have been through a filter process—is a highly passive one that allows the user or client to interpret the need in terms of a request. Rather than focusing on the need, we allow the user to interpret for himself what the need is. The perceived need is in turn filtered to some extent by his assumptions of what we are willing and able to do and what is a reasonable thing to ask us.

I hear a lot of discussion in university libraries concerning what is a reasonable and what is an unreasonable request. I am a special librarian. When I go to the university library, I am a totally unreasonable library user. I expect to leave my questions, and I expect the reference librarian to find the answers. That is how I use libraries. That is how I have always used libraries. That is how I wish everybody used libraries. I do not want to do my own reference work. That is why we have librarians.

There are many examples of this, but this is the most obvious one. Those of you in library school know a great deal about the whole process of question negotiation, of trying to figure out what it is that people really want, because they will try their very best to hide that from you. They tend to oversimplify their requests, because they feel uncomfortable and want to get the whole thing over with. Going to the library for some people is like going to the dentist, because they do not think we would understand the question if they really told us what it was they want, and in part, because we give the appearance of being very, very busy and difficult to interrupt. That is not true of everybody, clearly, but that is the public perception.

I find that curious, because we are presumably a service profession. However, our greatest drive is toward self-service. I do not have time to discuss this in detail, but I have a great deal of ambivalence about the whole process of bibliographic instruction. I am not sure at all that it is a good idea. That is the value system we have imposed on the user. We insist that the user wants to do his own information work and should do his own information work, rather than recognize that as soon as he or she is able to change that relationship, many will prefer assistance or delegation. By the way, this number, I am quite positive, would include university professors if given half a chance.

So, this suggests that we already have placed boundaries on what we call reasonable needs on the part of users, while at the same time taking whatever the user says he or she wants or requests as an assumption of what he needs. Many information needs, therefore, may not be met because they are never identified, even if the question is answered. That is as true in the university environment as in the ghetto. Some requests for documents may be satisfied, and we think we do a pretty good job when we do that much.

Now, this is in turn a curious contradiction about what we know about professions. One definition of *profession* is that it controls its client interaction relationships. The professional is the expert in dealing with the client. Good doctors and good lawyers do not do this manipulatively, because they do indeed want to involve the client in the discussion of options; but ultimately, it is the professional who decides. That is the issue of professional turf that I have written about before, and part of that turf is helping the user identify his or her information needs.

We place other barriers before the process of properly fulfilling the information need simply by what we do or do not have available. Some of the material that we do not have available is a function of what government agencies do or do not furnish, but some of it is what we do or do not decide to acquire ourselves. Not even Harvard gets everything!

We fight censorship when it is imposed by others. But studies, for example by Judy Serebnick, a faculty member at Indiana University, indicate that our personal value systems influence selection and only give users access to what we think they ought to have access to. The selection process is highly unstructured. We buy to a large extent what others buy. We buy what is reviewed in the literature, even if it is negatively reviewed. We buy something that received rotten reviews rather than something that has no review at all. In other words, we censor ourselves.

Before we can come to grips with issues involving fulfilling individual information needs, we are going to have to deal with the question of our own roles. Are we educators? Certainly in the public school system we are. In the university library? In part. But the role of the educator is somewhat contradictory to that of the information professional, both because of the profession's emphasis on self-service and education's emphasis on a value system that has nothing to do with information. Are we social workers? Is our concern for the betterment of society an individual concern or a professional concern? Many finite priorities must be set. We establish these priorities based on perception of social good.

I will give you another garish example. Clearly we recognize our responsibility toward tenants who are about to be evicted and who have an information need. What is our responsibility toward landlords looking for loopholes so they can evict tenants? Is that a role for the library as well, as an information professional environment?

What I am suggesting to you is that our approach to serving information needs is neither unstructured nor unrestricted. We immediately enter the process, as Serebnick has shown, when we decide what to buy. Selection is hard to prove as censorship. All the issues of censorship, as they have come up, deal with removing something from the shelf and destroying it. I had a long discussion on this with Robert O'Neill, a constitutional lawyer who was at Indiana University and is now president of the University of Virginia. The simplest way to avoid the charges of censorship is to not buy a thing in the first place. No one can possibly chase you into that morass, because you cannot buy everything. O'Neill cannot imagine somebody being sued on censorship grounds for not having bought something. Burning it, of course, is a very clear case of censorship.

I need to refer to at least one more dilemma that confronts us: the conflict between freedom of information and personal privacy. We see this most directly in requests for access to historic library circulation records. Who borrowed what over what period of time? The question, of course, for me is, why do we keep this stuff around in the first place? Why on earth do we keep historic circulation records? In part it is because we are great savers of things that might be of some use to us sometime in the future.

However, as the information files grow, the ability to access those files in concert provides tremendous opportunities to paint composite pictures. We take a whole bunch of files in a computer search by using the social security number that they told us in the 1930s would never be publicly available to anyone. We are concerned about privacy, but probably as librarians we tend to be more overwhelmingly desirous of more information.

This fact struck me in a meeting with the Census Bureau as a special librarian. Most of my colleagues in the Special Libraries Association were thrilled at all the questions the Census Bureau was asking, because of all this marvelous information that they as business librarians would be able to have! I found myself all alone in arguing that what kind of refrigerator I bought last year is none of anyone's business. I do not want to answer that question. It is not likely that I am going to be called before a Senate committee for a confirmation hearing, but I doubt very much that I would be willing to answer any questions about myself that the senators would not be willing to answer themselves. Not because I have anything to hide, but because I do not think it is anybody's business. So there is that issue clearly.

Personal information needs are highly individualized. They probably defy categorization. I suspect we are dealing with something like Maslow's hierarchy of needs. It is a displacement process: as we fulfill one need, a new need is created. Information needs will grow as they are satisfied, and I suspect they will never be totally filled. That does not bother me because it provides great opportunities for us. It also places considerable responsibilities on us. The first, of course, is to resist the desire to define what is or is not a reasonable information need or a reasonable request. Many of my requests for the university library at Indiana are considered by some librarians to be unreasonable in terms of library resources. I do not think they are unreasonable. I think figuring out how to fill them is their problem not mine. I give them that professional courtesy.

Our second responsibility is to make sure that individuals know what the options available to them are. This requires that we take the professional responsibility of interpreting and interacting, responding to what people tell us they want. The important question is not what they think they want; it is what issue they need to deal with. These range from the informational, to the educational, to the very quality of life issues that have become central for survival. It seems almost certain that the amount of information necessary for personal decisionmaking is going to continue to grow.

We are an increasingly complex society in which we tend to know more and more about less and less. The great danger is in not knowing what it is we do not know. We also are increasingly willing to delegate to specialists in our society—car mechanics, lawn care specialists, investment advisors. The concept of the information specialist is not an unreasonable extension of this process.

As more information is available, we understand less and less of it. I was struck by something I read on the plane this morning. I now have a telephone bill eight pages long that I cannot understand. I used to be able to understand my telephone bill, but somebody in Congress was trying to do me a favor, and now it is all spelled out in such tremendous detail that I cannot make head nor tail of it. I was delighted to have an author writing in a national magazine say basically the same thing. Sometimes an overload of information can destroy you just as easily as not having enough information.

Ultimately then, I would have to agree both with Yehoshua Bar-Hillel and Donald Urquhart. Bar-Hillel argued that our professional responsibility is to maximize the availability of information and not to worry about the interpretation of what use is made of it. Some people have difficulty with that, but the alternative of having us decide individually or collectively what constitutes a worthy or even worthier demand on our time is even more intolerable.

Our business, Bar-Hillel argued, is to market the value of information. I stress to you that marketing is getting people to want things they do not even know they want. It is not to respond. It is to generate. Marketers generate information needs and information requests. The best example of what we were talking about is the telephone company. The telephone company's initial marketing approach was for everyone to have one telephone. They did that. Now they have to have everybody have two telephones, and three telephones, and cordless telephones, and call waiting, and Mickey Mouse telephones. That is marketing. Marketing is creating a need—hopefully a useful need, but not necessarily—in the minds of people who did not even know that they had a need until you told them.

Urquhart, a retired director of the British Lending Library at the Boston Spa, argued that we could exhaust ourselves and our resources if we market foolishly or stubbornly. He says that the most obvious and direct clients for information services are those who already have a predisposition for information services. This means it will be difficult to serve illiterates with reading materials until they know how to read and what to read. Nobody is quite sure where that border lies. How many of the people who cannot read want to learn? We have learned some very startling information. For example, we have always assumed that illiterates are the people who never went past the first grade, or second grade, or third grade. We now find that a great many illiterates are high school graduates. That is a remarkable fact. It has nothing to do with level of education; it has to do with quality of education.

Now, I am not insensitive to that issue in this country, but we know that in general massively funded programs to fight illiteracy have failed in this country and in others. I am concerned that if we librarians adopt this as our number one priority, it will swallow all of our energies and resources without leaving a trace, and probably without making a difference.

Urquhart, in a talk to the ALA about 10 years ago, put it very, very succinctly:

> McDonald's did not become wealthy trying to sell hamburgers to vegetarians. It marketed hamburgers first of all to those predisposed to hamburgers and fast food, tried to sell good and reasonably priced hamburgers and then depended on satisfied customers to tell the others.

It is a tactic that appears to work, at least for McDonald's.

The fulfillment of individual and for that matter organizational information needs, I suggest to you, is a never-ending process, because having information always leads to a need for more information. The more we know, the more we become aware of what we do not know. Information will not be an equally distributed resource because, if for no other reason, some people have a greater interest in information and a greater understanding of its value.

Our most significant contribution as librarians is to use our expertise, our education, and our training as information professionals to maximize the process for everyone, so that we do not put barriers or limits in the way: the barrier of preconception of what constitutes a proper level of information service; a sociological barrier in determining who should or should not be helped; an economic barrier in suggesting we have no money and do not know how to get it.

I do not wish to trivialize the process, but to me the question of whether an information service is free or whether we charge for it is secondary to the absolute insistence that we provide it. To me, the suggestion that we not provide it because we have not figured out how to provide it for free is an unacceptable approach. We have to figure out a way to provide it because we cannot back away from providing it. So, all of these barriers, it seems to me, are very real causes for concern. None of them are acceptable to us as professionals.

Librarians and the FBI

At this moment the argument between an FBI asking librarians to keep an eye out for suspicious-looking library users, particularly those with "foreign" names, and a library community for once pretty well united in opposition is very much in the news. The FBI initiative was a badly thought out one. The confrontation between librarians who seek to assure the maximum use of information and security officials for whom the ideal state may be one in which material is destroyed before anyone can read it is as natural and instinctive as that between the mongoose and the cobra.

Those Silly Feds

It is not only a natural conflict but perhaps a necessary one. There are issues of freedom of access, and there are issues of government security, and both are important. However, this particular battle makes the FBI look not so much nasty as silly, and that is bad for the country. We need an effective FBI, one we can rely on.

I think I understand the importance of government security. For much of my professional career as a special librarian I cataloged Navy reports at the Library of Congress, worked as a technical librarian for the Atomic Energy Commission, supervised the library of an aerospace company that produced fighter planes and guided missiles, worked with classified contract documents for the IBM Federal Systems Division, and ran the Technical Information Facility for NASA, an agency that houses classified material despite the overall peaceful thrust of space exploration. I had clearance for and access to highly classified information. I knew how to safeguard it, and I know why it is important to do so.

Reprinted, with changes, by permission of the author and *Library Journal* 113, no. 17 (October 15, 1988): 54-55. Copyright © 1988 Reed Publishing, U.S.A.

During all of this time it was a routinely accepted premise that just about every piece of classified knowledge could be reconstructed, even if slowly and laboriously, from information available in the open literature. The Soviet embassy was, and I suspect remains, one of the best customers of the National Technical Information Service, and the CIA Library did (and perhaps still does) provide interlibrary loan materials to that same embassy.

Espionage Exists

We knew all of this, and we accepted it because we recognized that piecing together military intelligence from unrestricted information takes a great deal of time, and ultimately military engineering superiority deteriorates over time and must be replaced. That, of course, is why weapons research is necessarily continuous, not invariably to build and stockpile better weapons, but to be able to build them.

I accept all of this. I also accept the premise that espionage exists throughout the world to shortcut this process, by stealing information that is legitimately classified. We knew that eventually the Soviet Union would be able to build an atomic bomb on its own. Espionage allowed them to build it much faster, and that was an unforeseen imbalance to our national game plan. I expect that my country will participate both in the stealing and in the defense against stealing, as all countries do. However, clandestine activities are the purview of professionals who have both the training and the stomach for it. It is not an activity in which we enlist volunteers at random.

The Intelligence Gold Rush

The diligent search of the unclassified literature for potential nuggets has been an old game, and generally an acknowledged one. Many of the attachés in embassies are charged precisely with the task of finding out what they can find out, and this is practiced not just in unfriendly countries but in allied nations. It has always amazed me that the present Iranian government can say the outrageous things it says without either choking or blushing, and that must require a special skill. It made the startling accusation that the American embassy in Tehran was a "nest of spies."

All embassies are nests of spies, that is part of their job. The FBI seems concerned that, for example, the Bulgarian agricultural attaché might be doing library research on high-energy technology. Perhaps I am not so naïve as the bureau, but I would hardly expect him to be spending his time checking price fluctuations in soybean futures. All attachés from any embassy deserve some attention, because they are not here for Monday night football. As long as they just use libraries we can relax. All of this has been understood for a long time. Anything one could find in an academic or public library was certainly fair game.

Our military, industrial, and political establishment had the confidence that if we could assure that only we knew it when it was classified, and others knew it only after it was declassified, we were still ahead and safe. The present paranoia, which appears to reflect a weakening in our own self-confidence as the leader, was crafted by such individuals as Richard Allen, former national security advisor to President Reagan, who in 1983 argued that national security was what the president said it was.

Scientists and scholars who participate in internationally known paranoia can be taken to extremes that only can prove embarrassing for our nation. The concern by FBI Deputy Assistant Director DuHadway that suspicious agents with foreign-sounding names have been combing our libraries for information follows naturally enough. In point of fact, this has gone on all along and may simply be an indication of growing national uncertainty that we have just begun to notice.

The Legal Steps

If the president and his advisors are concerned, there are enough legal steps that can be taken. Congress can be asked to impose tighter restrictions on the movements and access of foreigners, or on what can be exported and to whom. Properly trained and empowered security officers could implement these legal changes after enaction. However, the current vogue of implementing security through innuendo is both dangerous and silly. The issues that librarians have been fortunate enough to confront early—fortunate because it can raise our status and our image if we stand tall to protect what needs to be protected for all Americans—transcends the issue of whether we report odd-looking people in our libraries to the FBI. If we really reported all such people, the FBI would have to double its staff just to follow all the false leads.

The issue is silly because, for some reason, the FBI itself has chosen to trivialize it by making it appear to be just another normal little exercise. In that regard the bureau, which is just recovering its reputation after J. Edgar Hoover, is poorly advised. National Commission on Libraries and Information Science (NCLIS) Chair Newman has suggested that the quarrel is with only a small band of radical librarians as represented by the Office of Intellectual Freedom. The FBI surveillance program is not a lunatic left-fringe political issue. It should unite all librarians regardless of other ideology. Stupidity should not be allowed to masquerade as security.

Faraway Places?

It has been suggested that librarians be especially on the lookout for suspicious-looking individuals with foreign-sounding names. All that is left to complete the screenplay for a 1930s grade B movie is the injunction that we also look for individuals wearing beards. If access to the "security riches" contained in our public and academic libraries is really that important to our potential enemies, they will presumably take pains to send people searching who look like All-America halfbacks.

What is a foreign "sounding" name, anyway? The two individuals most recently convicted of espionage were named Walker and Pollard. My historical recollection of "American" names begins with Sitting Bull and Crazy Horse, and they were not heavy library users. Roosevelt, Truman,

Eisenhower, Kennedy, Johnson, Nixon, Ford, Carter, Reagan, DuHadway, and Newman are all foreign names. They come from various parts of Europe, and that is also where most of the spies come from. Why does the FBI engage in such silliness that only trivializes its own important role? Eliot Ness would never have asked librarians to look over the shoulders of library users.

The danger of the direction taken here, in alarming the country to gigantic conspiracies presumably all around us even in peacetime (we have seen from the illegal internment of Americans of Japanese extraction what can happen in wartime) is that it will turn us into a nation suspicious of its own citizens. One of the characteristics of totalitarian governments of both the left and the right (ultimately they are exactly the same) is that they breed fear and suspicion among their citizens, and they do so on purpose. Neighbors are asked to spy and report on other neighbors, children are encouraged to report their own parents to the government. It is only one step from reporting a stranger to reporting a friend or a relative without proof, and the first step is already the longest.

What Class Classified?

If the danger of being militarily and economically overrun is as great as some presidential advisors have argued, then that case should be made publicly and openly, and laws enacted to close whatever loopholes exist. This nation is a nation of laws and not of executive policy directives; if we ever lose that then whatever we have left won't be worth protecting because we'll be just like the totalitarian dictatorships.

Security classifications are a legitimate part of a nation's self-protection. But if things are unclassified then they are presumably available to anyone, and everything in the general collections of public and academic libraries is unclassified. Phrases such as "unclassified but sensitive" are oxymorons comparable to George Carlin's giant shrimp, or perhaps in our field to library administration. If things are unclassified then they are presumably not "sensitive." When these individuals say sensitive, do they mean security or merely embarrassment? The concern for an unfettered press certainly also extends to libraries. If something is so sensitive as to concern national security, then classify it if you can justify doing so

The recent *New York Times* report that the University of California canceled library subscriptions to NASA unclassified databases because the agency sought to place on librarians the responsibility for seeing to it that foreigners did not have access to this information gives us just one example of the extremes to which paranoia can drive us. Unlike the FBI's concern with strangely named foreigners plundering our journals for military secrets, the issue here is the worry about technological drain.

Shifting Responsibility

However, the problem for librarians is exactly the same. In both cases, a federal agency is trying to shift responsibility to librarians for a preference that has absolutely no legal standing. If it is classified, then classify it and restrict it accordingly. If legal constraints permit further actions, then do it. However, the NASA directive is not a legal directive from a government agency, it is a private contract. The FBI action is a "request for cooperation." Libraries can, as the University of California did, refuse to accept such NASA material.

However, such an action not only deprives the suspected foreigners but everyone else as well, and leads to the question of why NASA bothered to spend government funds to do the work in the first place. My preferred reaction would simply be to cross out the offending sections of the contract, sign it, and return it. It would help if the Association of Research Libraries urged such a consistent approach on all of its members. Here, as with journal publishers, librarians could exercise tremendous power if they acted in concert rather than allow themselves to be pressured individually.

Perhaps the saddest note in all of this is sounded by NCLIS Chair Newman, who weighs in on the side of the FBI with a number of sweeping generalizations about individuals who might dare to refuse to cooperate, although he acknowledges that "he is supposed to be neutral." No, he isn't supposed to be neutral. He is supposed to be on our side, on the side of the free and open use of unclassified information, and in opposition to anything that would constrain that use. That, I have long thought, is what libraries are supposed to do, and what NCLIS was established by Congress to support and defend.

"Send These, the Homeless, Tempest-Tost to Me"

Because I sailed as an immigrant child into New York harbor, the words of Emma Lazarus on the Statue of Liberty have always had a special significance for me. And yet, even then I probably realized that while we might have meant it in the 19th century, we don't mean it now. I knew that how long we had to wait was a subset of what country we were coming from, and the result of a value judgment as to the kinds of immigrants this country really wanted and needed.

This is not intended as an ugly American statement but as an observation of the world. We pick our immigrants in part to fit our needs and not theirs. So do other countries, and sometimes it may not be an issue of whether they let people in but rather whether they let them out. The recognition that individuals, organizations, corporations, and countries do what they think is best for them and then develop tortuous rationales for "proving" that what is most convenient is also most correct has been with us for some time.

Serving Tenants and Landlords

Almost 40 years ago public librarians resoundingly and angrily rejected the recommendation by Robert Leigh that they concentrate their services on those in the best position to use, appreciate, and support libraries. It is irrelevant at this point to argue with that decision, but one must nevertheless speculate on what it might have cost us.

Reprinted, with changes, by permission of the author and *Library Journal* 114, no. 3 (February 15, 1989): 146-147. Copyright © 1989 by Reed Publishing, U.S.A.

The importance given by public libraries in the days of John Cotton Dana to business service as a major if not primary emphasis has not entirely disappeared but has certainly receded. It appears to have been replaced by a mind set that looks at librarianship as a social service rather than as an educational or information profession.

We know, of course, that in public libraries tenants and landlords have equal status and deserve equal help. Is it just my imagination that some public libraries would rather serve tenants?

Whether or what this decision has cost us is pure conjecture. We know that libraries are poorly funded, generally loved but trivialized, and frequently overlooked even by the groups they serve so loyally. But we don't know what would have happened had we followed Leigh's advice that we seek and nurture a narrower but more proprietary turf.

Old Folks at Libraries?

It is perhaps a generalization and approximation to believe that the general public sees public libraries as primarily for children and the elderly, but I have seen those very arguments used in support of bond vote drives.

If these are among our major priorities, we are remarkably inept in securing loyalty and support in return for that which we provide. There is perhaps no more potent a political body than retirees, particularly as represented by the American Association of Retired Persons (AARP). When they unite on a political issue, such as Social Security benefit cuts, even the most secure and seasoned politicians quake. Where is support for libraries on the political agenda of the AARP? We are not even mentioned.

A similar point can be made about the education of school children. Public librarians often make the case to me of their crucial role in supporting the educational curriculum, and suggest that without them the school system would be badly crippled. Sometimes they say it proudly, sometimes angrily because of all of the extra work it creates. However, where is the recognition? Libraries were never even mentioned in *A Nation at Risk*. If we are so crucial to educators, how come they don't notice?

If we have chosen to concentrate on the priority of children and the elderly perhaps even to the exclusion of other clients whose cultivation might have brought us more political power, recognition, and funding, then that is certainly our right. We can even fall, as Peter Drucker suggests, into the service professional's value trap of accepting what he calls the "moral imperative": agree to do everything even without resources and then blame ourselves if we can't get it all done. Perhaps some librarians even enjoy the benign neglect and genteel poverty that have become our niche, and would feel uncomfortable clipping bond coupons or sanding the keels of their yachts.

Librarians, Not Pressure Groups

However, there is one point at which I draw the line. We can set such agendas for ourselves, but they are our decisions. That is true for any profession or it ceases to be a profession. It is librarians who must decide what libraries do, and not the collective ignorance or bias of outside pressure groups.

Politically this is true because without that insistence we have no power at all, but there is a better and less self-serving reason. It is because librarians are the only ones competent to decide. Few outsiders know what libraries do; fewer still what they ought to do; and virtually none what they could so. The manual "Planning and Role Setting for Public Libraries," prepared by a group of distinguished educators and researchers, suggests that we should do exactly that, and I agree.

I nevertheless suspect that in implementation this has become nothing more than a rationalization for justifying whatever it is we already do. That is, we do what engineers call retrofitting: making the "needs" match the resources rather than identifying needs in total independence of resources. If we do this then the exercise becomes pointless. If not, I would expect to see far more public library annual reports and other documents that charge that the library is inadequate to the needs because the support is inadequate, and, in some cases, that the public library in the community is a disgrace and a disaster. I am still looking for such documents.

Two New "Priorities"

It is within that overall context that I want to mention two new "priorities" for public libraries. Of course, new priorities automatically elbow their way to the front of the line precisely because they command attention through their novelty. They are programs for eliminating adult illiteracy and concern about latchkey children. They are major societal problems, but are they particularly ours? Or do we adopt them simply because they are there?

Adult illiteracy has many root causes, and suggests a complex array of strategies. Some of it comes from a failure to have a school to attend, some from excessive truancy, some from the failed experiment of social promotion on which some parents and some politicians still insist, some from a lack of desire to learn to read, some from a failure to exercise a skill once learned. Anyone will forget how to read when only watching reruns on TV. Whatever the cause, it is a problem for the educational community.

While we rail against the evil of adult illiteracy our school systems turn out yet more functional illiterates. We haven't yet figured out a way to make kids learn. Perhaps we never will until we can figure out a way to make children care and take responsibility, or at least have their parents care and take responsibility. We create new illiterates faster than we eliminate old ones. Our strategy appears as ineffective here (although as politically attractive) as our futile struggle in the drug arena. It might be better if society concentrated on *preventing* illiteracy.

There are things librarians can do to help educators attack their mess, and if they ask us and offer to fund what we do, we can talk about it. However, the problem is immense and certainly beyond the range of our poor, starved little budgets. It requires additional funding before we touch it, and if we can't get money for this, we can't get it for anything. If we offer to "absorb" it, we do nothing more than steal from our other patrons. If we let this camel into our tent, you ain't seen nothing yet.

One Hump or Two?

There is yet another camel in view. The societal problem of working parents, single parents, and after-school care for children is monumental. I have to give credit to the school systems for being smart enough to understand that they want no part of it.

What after-school programs there might be are offered strictly on a cost-recovery basis. Such supervised study or play can be expensive, and so some of these kids gravitate to the library. As often as not, it is the parents who send them there. Why? Because we are easy marks. It is perhaps part of our image.

Corporate libraries frequently serve as the personnel department dumping ground, the place to stash unproductive employees who cannot be, or perhaps ought not to be, fired. Why do they do this? For two very simple reasons. They don't know what libraries do and why good staff are important. And they know that librarians are suckers for a sob story and will take them. Nobody else will.

Latchkey kids bring out all of our instincts to tackle the world's problems, and the fact that this issue has nothing to do with us is somehow lost. When did we become social workers rather than or in addition to librarians? Is our social responsibility outside our discipline somehow greater than that of other citizens?

Two reasons for our concern in this instance are frequently heard. The first is simply that it is there, and that argument is so fuzzy as to defy discussion. Accept this premise and you have no agenda at all. The second reason is more subtle. Libraries, we are reminded, are for kids. Indeed they are, as they are for adults, for the elderly, and for the business community. But they are there *to be used as libraries,* and we have to determine what that means.

Are libraries for reading, for studying, for playing, for resting, for sleeping, for anything at all or nothing at all as long as you are quiet? Do people have to have an acceptable reason for being there, or can latchkey kids and homeless people simply be stashed in libraries because the door is open? In most places you need a better reason than that. The police station used to be the place for leftover kids, as dozens of 1930s films with gruff Irish cops demonstrate. Cops are too smart for that now, as are school teachers. Police are law enforcement agents, and this would be bad for their professional image.

A Mandate of Odds and Ends?

We might get some credit and some funding by acting as contractors to an educational community trying to clean up its own mess of adult illiteracy, but we must never accept as our own a problem that is not ours. The second camel is even more troublesome. We will get nothing at all for serving as baby-sitters besides more trivialization.

There are elected and appointed government officials whose problem this is. Just perhaps, if we refuse to touch it, they will do what they are supposed to do. The 1988 Public Library Association meeting ultimately worked its way to the conclusion that homeless people and children left without care or concern in the library's custody are community problems, not library problems. Exactly. Our problems concern the need to serve people who can use libraries as libraries, and that problem will require all of the energy and resources we can muster.

All we accomplish in following the suicidal path of allowing the library to become a parking lot is to alienate those who came to use the library as a library, and who find it impossible or unpleasant because of the noise of playing children or the aroma of vagrants looking only for a place to sleep. Are our priorities so easily manipulated and subverted into doing what nobody else wants to do, simply because they don't want to do it? Is our mandate nothing more than odds and ends?

The future for librarians, if we are to have a future, is in doing what we do uniquely and doing it well. There is plenty of that to be done, and it is important work, but our clients won't necessarily know until we tell them. It always seems to come back to that issue, whether we are talking about a role with latchkey kids that someone is trying to dump on us; or amateurs serving as directors of our research libraries; or the "competencies" invented by bureaucrats in creating pseudo-librarians by writing irrelevant job descriptions to fit the people they would like to put into them. The examples change, but the problem remains the same.

Pseudo-Libraries and Semi-Teachers

Because librarians cannot or will not define their own mission, public libraries fluctuate with society's whims, academic libraries serve as warehouses, and school libraries exist in never-never land.

Part 1

If we were to play word association games, I suspect the word "library" would trigger the response "books." The word "hospital," by contrast, would elicit "doctor" or "nurse," not "bed," "ward," or "hospital gown." When the public thinks of libraries it thinks of the collection of materials, and not of librarians.

This is easy to understand when we consider that even our profession itself does not know how many libraries are staffed by professionally educated librarians. One survey in a Canadian province concluded that less than half of the public libraries were professionally staffed, but we don't know in total, and certainly the public doesn't know. Nor does it care.

The word librarian is subsumed by the word library. In academia, even highly educated faculty members consider student circulation clerks to be "librarians." Librarians are the people who work in libraries. Such is not the case in hospitals, where confusion between doctors, nurses, orderlies, and candy stripers is rare. There are uniforms and apparent dress codes to accentuate the difference. I have found that in large hospitals I am frequently addressed as doctor, perhaps because I meet the perception of what a doctor looks like—if I am wearing a suit and not an old sweatshirt. I am convinced that in a large enough hospital my suit plus a stethoscope would allow me to sit in on staff meetings. Everybody would assume everybody else knew

Reprinted, with changes, by permission of the author and *American Libraries* 21, no. 2 (February 1990): 103-106; 21, no. 3 (March 1990): 262-266.

me. In hospitals the charade takes effort. In libraries it takes none at all. There is no need for a stethoscope or a lab coat. If you work in a library, you are a librarian.

Having made no attempt to differentiate between the people who work in them, how then has our profession defined libraries? What must all libraries be or do to qualify for the term "library" as opposed to "book room?"

Libraries are defined by the name over the door. What is called a library *is* a library. We are so much in favor of libraries that we willingly give the name to anything that claims it. In the public mind the library is the place that has the books. How many books, what kinds of books, for what purpose?

It might be interesting to have a contest for the greatest trivialization. In my experience, it may be what happens on cruise ships, where the "library" is a collection of old novels and mysteries that are never weeded and never replaced. Because the presumed purpose is to help people fall asleep, the more boring the better. It is open two hours a day and staffed by the most junior member of the cruise director's staff, the one who can't be trusted to manage shuffleboard tournaments. Sometimes it is the cruise singer or dancer, who unfortunately has only one skill but can certainly serve as the "librarian."

If I am on a one-week cruise, I no longer bother to tell these people that I am a librarian; there simply isn't enough time to explain the nuances. Besides, everybody already knows what a library is and what librarians do: They do what the cruise ship dancer does for two hours every day. I suspect that the cruise line does all this to claim some veneer of culture for its enterprise, and, of course, that tactic works. We are in favor of libraries, even if they serve only to induce sleep. It disturbs and angers me that we are so easily and willingly trivialized by the thousands of pseudo-libraries on ships and in small communities. We certainly "understand" that they can't afford a librarian, so we willingly help prepare pseudo-librarians— except that they are called librarians, just like me.

The danger in this for us is best described in the oft-cited Gresham's Law in economics: Bad money drives out good money. Bad library education can certainly endanger good library education—as long as both are equally accepted by the profession and by accrediting bodies because bad library education is cheaper. Similarly, the "standard" for libraries is the weakest thing you can think of called a library. Everything beyond that is grandiose, and may be unnecessary in the eyes of those who watch budgets—and their tribe increases.

Bigger, Not Better

Our response has been to try to make libraries bigger, on the presumption that bigger means better. More holdings, more circulation, more emphasis on getting people in and on giving them what they want. I am still confidently waiting for the first library McDonald's or pizza outlet. One of our most persuasive library columnists argues that the job of librarians is to select the books that people want to read. How then do we differ from the local supermarket manager, whose job is to stock merchandise that will move off the shelves, and who has no responsibility for nutritional content? I know why he does this. The store makes money when people buy, and he gets fired when they don't. Our comparable strategy is to increase circulation. For the same purpose, and without worrying about what people get out of the books they carry away?

Is "read" really the battle cry of our profession? As I have noted in other writings, even the promulgators of National Secretaries Week have not suggested that we celebrate by typing. If it is important to increase circulation, then we could hire people to charge out 20 books, keep them for an hour, bring them back, and charge out 20 more. A grotesque exaggeration? Sure, but I have known librarians who waved their hands in front of the electric eye because they were concerned about usage statistics.

Is This What Concerns Us?

In our frenzy to promote libraries, we have lost sight of whatever purpose we once had. We want lots of things called libraries so that everybody can have access to one. To accomplish this, we will tolerate and even encourage libraries without adequate funding, and sometimes without any funding. We run them without professional staff, and sometimes without any staff. Some individuals have reported proudly that as the only professional, they run ten libraries. Not without *Star Trek* technology, they don't.

The idea of the circuit-riding librarian is apparently back in style. I am talking about school districts, in which the number of librarians has been halved but the number of libraries remains the same. With half the librarians, the school board still claims that each school has a library, and we silently participate in the fraud perpetrated on the parents, who cannot *care* if they do not *know* that their children are now served by a pseudo- or a semi-library. And we are the only ones who can tell them.

School boards and school superintendents don't discuss the issue because it means money, and teachers don't discuss it because they consider it far less important than their other priorities. And that, of course, is why education organizations, which may do a reasonable job of monitoring their own educational preparation, cannot possibly monitor the education of school librarians with anything that resembles sense. They have only a binary model—teachers and nonteachers—and nonteachers represent the potential enemy. There is no room for librarians as an entity in this scenario. If we are lucky, they will allow us to be semi-teachers.

Library as Warehouse

The situation in university libraries invites comparison to hospitals. In hospitals, professional administrators run the place on a day-to-day basis but serve at the pleasure of the doctors who are ultimately the source of all power concerning the institution's value systems. Finally, there are the patients, who have no voice at all in the process. In university libraries we are the hired administrators, the faculty are the doctors, and, of course, you recognize the role of the students. Like patients they get to do and pay what they are told.

The difference in the two models is in the fact that doctors are, through their education, qualified to judge what happens in hospitals, while professors do not study the information process. They just "know" it, at least as it applies to them. The result is a balkanized approach, in which the quality of the library is not measured by overall holdings, but by the holdings in the professor's own field. That academic libraries provide little of the reference service and personal bibliographic interaction found in good corporate special libraries is not surprising, as the role of the librarian is primarily that of acquiring and enabling readiness for use.

With a continued absence of delineation of who does what—and more importantly who does not do what—it is not surprising that the staffing of academic libraries is considered unimportant, and that services are poorly developed. The emphasis on the library as a warehouse is, however, something we have helped perpetuate. It explains the transfer of funds from all other sources to the academic library materials budget over the last 15 years, and it explains how we could possibly have tried to meet 20 percent annual price increases, rather than simply tell the publishers to get real! The answer is simple. Like hospital administrators, we don't get to make these important decisions.

In public libraries the librarians do indeed run the library but have not attempted to establish ground rules about what the library's priorities are, and what it takes to fulfill them. Objectives and resources then become independent variables, because the library's job is to do everything the community needs with whatever funds are available. When there is a crunch, it affects the people who work there. We all know of library directors who have ordained that because of a budget cut, and because services must be protected, there would be no salary increases. Clearly the emphasis here is on the library and not on the librarians.

The word "library" has become a largely amorphous term that changes meaning based on societal values and pressures. Public librarians in particular accept the moral imperative ascribed to service professionals by management expert Peter Drucker: We must do everything, regardless of resources, or it will be our fault. The "everything" is then controlled by larger society issues rather than priorities as established by the library.

Library as Shelter

ALA's Public Library Association, together with the Association for Library Service to Children, has just published a work entitled *Latchkey Children in the Public Library*. The title suggests a study of what library policies toward this issue should be. However, that question never arises, because the manual, correctly subtitled "Resources for Planners" never deals with the whether, only the how. It notes an increase in children using the public library for shelter, and why this has occurred. It goes on to "suggest programs to meet the needs of this new clientele." Clientele? Is the library's role the provision of shelter? It is as if we simply assumed that we do for anyone what they came to have us do, that any professional decision making by librarians is really incidental to a changing set of circumstances we do not control. In fact, the manual warns that we better not try, lest "public libraries risk destroying a long and noble history of serving children."

Are public libraries so vulnerable as to be endangered by policies that delineate what are and what are not their appropriate roles in serving children? Hospitals also serve children; why don't the kids go there after school? Certainly in part because hospitals won't have them, because hospital policy is made by their professionals. And just perhaps in part because the public recognizes that the professionals in hospitals are busy people with much important work to do. Because we have allowed ourselves to be so trivialized, the library can be seen simply as a handy place to come in out of the rain. It is, of course, possible, as the manual suggests, that such a new open policy for the library might attract new converts to the opportunities that libraries offer. Possible, but I think not likely.

The library should be used on its professionals' terms or not at all, as indeed hospitals and even shopping malls are used. Even McDonald's knows better than to permit loitering. If we continued to apply such criteria and shaped our clients to the existing system, we wouldn't need a new handbook. However, if we are willing to accept any clients on any terms, we may need a new one every six months. I even have what may be the next clientele group to suggest. I understand there is a real shortage of golf courses, and waits for tee times, particularly on the weekend, can be many hours. Is there a potential role here for the library lawn?

Can those of you eager to accept one nontraditional clientele but repulsed by the thought of the other then explain what it is the library does? Historically, it provides books, and we generally agree on this. We also believe strongly in free access to information, and we define that in two ways. First, everything we provide must be free, and we deal with that quite neatly by not providing at all anything we haven't figured out how to provide from within the budget. Second, we insist that the library become the proper repository for all available information, and in particular the government documents that some administration is trying to suppress. However, our concern is curiously limited to assuring that the information is in our files so that our clients *could* use it. Whether or not they are *able* to use it is not considered.

When government agencies block access to information by trying to withhold it, that is a violation of freedom of information. When our governing boards accomplish the same thing by a failure to fund catalogers and reference librarians, we fail to see the connection. This curious value system protects "the library," whatever it is and whatever it does. It is that protection, which concentrates completely on appearance and never on results, that forms the focus of most ALA debate, energy, and fury.

No Change in Sight

What changes can we expect? Really very few. We have established some criteria that tend to be quantitative (holdings for academic libraries, circulation for public libraries) but we make no attempt to explain what these numbers mean, except that higher numbers are good and lower numbers are bad. We occasionally express other concerns—about hiring only graduates of accredited programs, paying certain minimum salaries, providing support for professional participation and continuing educa-tion—but we enforce none of these. How would we enforce them? Well, perhaps by mass protests that blocked the doors, or by barring miscreant libraries from participation in our networks and exchanges. Could we do it, either legally or effectively? I don't know. However, the question is irrelevant. We don't *want* to do it because any library is better than no library. This is an act of faith, and I am sure the suggestion that in some circumstances no library is better than some libraries sounds strange, but I do suspect that some communities would be better served in the knowl-edge that they had no real library, accompanied with strategies for getting one.

We categorically refuse to define library, or to define nonlibrary, and so anything called a library becomes a library—thus the fact that reductions in the number of school librarians do not necessarily relate to a reduction in the number of school libraries. Would a strategy of confrontation alert parents and taxpayers that while some kids had libraries, theirs didn't, despite the school superintendent's fraudulent argument that they did? Perhaps not, but I think it would be a fun effort in any case. I also know we won't do it. Saving the library, whatever it is, for that small town or for that small school seems to be our primary concern. All of this is based on the article of faith that any library is better than no library, and whether or not libraries accomplish certain objectives is secondary to this concern. We can see this exemplified in the concentrated fury with which public librarians (who muster little fury toward their governing bodies) have fought against any suggestion of externally imposed standards for their libraries. This allows them to select "community standards"—an oxymoron because com-munity standards are not standards at all. The standards are written to fit whatever happens.

Harsh and unfair?

Can We Have "Libraries" and Not Librarians?

How many public libraries fail their own standards and report that failing in local newspapers and in annual reports? Can we have "libraries" whether or not we have librarians? We have lots of them, and there is virtually nothing in our professional literature to suggest that there is anything wrong or strange about it. National Library Week invariably features something called "the library," otherwise undefined. The one time NLW actually suggested the theme of "Ask a professional, ask a librarian," some within our own ranks accused us of narrow selfishness. We have already been cautioned that the next White House Conference, like the first one, must only champion libraries and not librarians.

Part 2

In part 1 of this article, I commented on the user-dominated agendas of academic libraries, but what do public libraries do? Basically they dispense books to children and senior citizens. They also try very hard to do other things, so hard that their staffs often suffer from job burnout. For many, the largest responsibility of the public library is dealing with whatever wrongs need righting. Social activists in our profession insist that they are not really social workers. Maybe not, but they sure act as though they wish they were.

It is this acceptance of the moral imperative, of tackling problems because they are there—the same reason Hillary climbed Mount Everest—that has now caused us to accept at least two new responsibilities, adult illiteracy and latchkey children. Both are huge social problems that are getting worse every day. Our efforts are at best a token of goodwill.

I will not, at least for the moment, ask whether or not we should take on these responsibilities at all, but I will question whether we should do so without additional funds. When we do, we must surely realize that there are other things we will not do or not do as well.

What are those things, and whom have we told? If we refuse to confront this question, or even worse allow others to think that the good old library has simply "absorbed" this—just as it absorbed the budget cut and the staff cut—then, of course, the library becomes even more self-defined. What is the library? It is whatever goes on in the building (or shack, or room, or ocean liner card salon) with "Library" on the door. This argument of the primacy of libraries as visible ends in themselves allows no room for discussion of the rights and privileges of librarians.

I recall having this debate with another library school dean before a rather bewildered group of international students. He insisted that, if necessary, librarians mop the floor. I countered that librarians should mop the floor if the custodian is sick, but if a custodian has been requested and not provided it is absolutely essential that the floor be as filthy as possible, and to invite a visit from the Board of Health. Doing this endangers "the library," but failing to do it turns librarians into clerks and custodians, and keeps them from providing what their clients have every right to expect.

Split over Values

The value struggle between libraries and librarians has been going on for a long time. In the early 1900s special librarians, medical librarians, and law librarians packed up and left the American Library Association. The reasons were complex, but at least one of them was a conflict of emphases and value systems. The people who left were more interested in what librarians would *do*. Those who remained in ALA represented largely the "library lovers." The splinter group has been the far more rapidly growing and now comprises probably at least half of the profession.

There is now a more recent development, which throws the equation into disarray. We have long had libraries without librarians, because we have created definitions of libraries that allow them. The new and interesting switch is that we can now have librarians without libraries, and I am not certain how the library lovers will react to individuals who have no institutional loyalties at all, and no appreciation for either holdings or circulation, because they have nothing to hold or circulate.

The special librarians who left ALA placed less emphasis on the library as such and more on what the people in the library did. As these special associations have evolved their literature also shows more of an emphasis on what librarians do. Other libraries, most notably public and academic, have continued to concentrate on the library as an institution, giving people what they "want." This is not necessarily what they need, the far more proactive role of the professional.

The delineations are not uniform. There are special librarians who just sit there and wait for individuals to ask for interlibrary loan, while there are wonderfully proactive school and children's librarians. Nevertheless, the differentiations in emphasis can be seen in a variety of value systems.

Many libraries insist on ownership—a complete set of journals in academia or a complete set of government documents in academic or public libraries, but they don't worry particularly about whether ownership assures access—through the elimination of cataloging backlogs, through the decision not to catalog at all, through the development of a backup system if copies are out. If we own it, we have done our job. Whether you can get it on the day you request it is something we don't keep records about. This narrows the effectiveness of academic libraries, and as a result we see the springing up of campus pseudo-libraries. Sometimes they are called information services departments headed by a vice president, sometimes they aren't called anything at all, and the staff selection for these entities is completely haphazard. They may include a professionally educated librarian, or some clerk either not too busy or considered worthy of promotion.

In old aircraft companies it was fashionable to turn library administration over to the widows of test pilots killed while flying company experimental models. These were generally young mothers, educationally prepared for nothing except marriage and early motherhood, who now needed a job, and the company thought it ought to be a "nice" job in a dignified office setting that didn't require any particular skills. Aerospace companies have moved beyond this, but public libraries are still run by "nice ladies."

Universities have lots of pseudo-libraries, and in many cases the "real" librarians are totally oblivious of their existence, because they are swamped doing what the faculty "want," buying books and journals that are aimed at classic researchers who comprise perhaps 10 percent of faculty at research institutions. The other units presumably give people what they "need," but we don't even know that. All we really know is that we have left a vacuum, and a vacuum in information work as in nature tends to be filled.

The emphasis of even these new entities, however, is still traditional, even if perhaps the staffing and the collection are not. They are still libraries, and the emphasis is still on what the library does. In general that

is characterized by goals but an absence of objectives, and by task assignments for which there are no resources, simply because the library does
"what needs to be done." We accept budget and staff cuts in academic
libraries, but we don't insist that the faculty understand there must therefore be cuts in their conveniences, for which the university president is to
blame.

When in public libraries we accept the problems of adult illiteracy or
latchkey children without additional support simply because these problems are there, we carry on the tradition in which the library does whatever
needs to be done, and therefore the librarians obviously become secondary.
Although we try to do everything, we inevitably have to reorder priorities.
When we do so, we come down on the side of the people who "need" us
more, as opposed to those who may have alternatives for service and
therefore don't need us as much. We may call ourselves librarians, but we
really wish we were in the Peace Corps.

There is nothing wrong with this value system, except for the fact that
it has nothing to do with a profession called "librarianship," for which
people go to school and get master's degrees. That may explain why not
everybody considers the degree important or relevant. My own viewpoint
as an educator is, of course, quite clear. I teach management, and I think it
is the most important course in library education. Teaching collection
development is significant, but I consider it more significant to teach you
how to make others give you the resources you need to perform collection
development.

Librarians have a superb ability to rationalize, to explain why something is not possible. Teachers, in their rather strident and belligerent
reaction to *A Nation at Risk*, took the surprising position that the school
system was indeed in terrible shape, but that this was not their fault but
rather the fault of those who refused to listen to and support qualified
professionals. In a more specific application, teachers are pointing out that
while indeed some students learn little, this is related to the fact that in the
home environment there is no emphasis on kids doing their homework.

If education is largely a home responsibility, as teachers now claim,
then can it not be claimed that the quality of libraries is a community
responsibility? It is then the responsibility of professional librarians to
point out how terrible some of these libraries are, and how citizens of some
communities are being defrauded under the convenient guise of pseudo-
economy. Pseudo-economy in this context means that anything we don't
want to pay for we claim we can't afford to pay for.

Library as Good Thing

The assumption that libraries are good things—without any qualitative judgments and without even an insistence on librarians—has been
with us, as I have noted, for virtually the entire 20th century. It appears to
me that our strategies have worked better in some time periods, such as the
1960s, than in others, and they have not worked at all for the last 15 years.

We have strategies for a favorable and growing climate, but not for
an unfavorable and shrinking one, and what we have been forced to do is

defend the library at whatever level it is allowed to exist, because the premise of the library as an institution is more important to us than what it does. Thus, if public libraries find that they cannot recruit qualified children's librarians at starting salaries of $18,000 a year, the solution is to hire whomever we can get at $18,000 because we "must" have a children's librarian, at whatever qualitative level we can muster. Unfortunately, we can get away with this because we have never been willing to consider a scenario in which children's service is so bad that we urge parents to keep their kids at home and let them watch TV. If anything is better than nothing, then you get anything.

A Warm and Fuzzy Quality

The new phenomenon of librarians without libraries, or at least without a physical proximity to libraries, has developed in part from the value that has been assigned to information by companies such as AT&T and IBM. Libraries always stressed the value of information as a warm and fuzzy quality without defining it, but the new advocates are talking about information as return on investment and as a profitable commodity for a community seeking industrial development. However, the biggest reason we are now doing all this as a nation is because we can. Technology allows us bibliographic access and document delivery both rapidly and cheaply, and it's going to get faster and cheaper.

One would assume that our profession is embracing this new development as an opportunity to implement the egalitarianism we so fervently embrace. Physical isolation is no longer an excuse for poor service, and the developers of the MEDLARS system were talking directly about adequate information for doctors in isolated regions of Alaska. I tried to pick up on this theme in speaking at the annual meeting of the Alaska Library Association last year. I suggested that there was no longer any reason for citizens in small communities in Alaska to expect and receive public library service any less adequate than that provided to citizens of Boston and Chicago. We could not match browsing and serendipity, but we could give them 24-hour access to an 800 number staffed by reference librarians, with document delivery within 72 hours. There is no reason why we can't do this today. The only obstacle is a lack of money, and that excuse, which we have accepted so passively for so long, is really irrelevant. If it is worth doing, it is worth paying for. Certainly the citizens of Alaska understand that for the privilege of living in that great state they must accept that everything costs more, and that includes library service.

Librarian by Any Other Name

Information intermediaries work from offices and even their homes, using terminals, telephones, and fax machines to tap into major collections. Some of our graduates enter this field, but most of these new practitioners have no training in information work and think that what they do is a subsidiary of either business administration or computer science. They couldn't be more wrong. They are functioning as librarians. But my opinion alone will not change their minds.

These new opportunities should excite and challenge all of us, but strangely they do not even seem to interest many of us. Much of our discussion still centers on the unchanged library, and our strategies still concentrate on providing "library service" as our users "need" it. However, we cannot really respond to this need because we make no attempt to determine it. We take the easy way out and assume need is defined by request. I am not sure why we ignore this potential approach to a national service, except that it requires a shift in emphasis from the local library as a good thing, regardless of quality and professional interaction, to a concentration on librarians (or whatever we want to call information people) who see resources as a means to an end rather than as an end in itself.

Libraries without librarians, and librarians without libraries are two conditions that can co-exist, even if warily, within our professional bodies. But it won't happen if the librarians without libraries don't even know they are librarians, or don't want to admit it. That will easily be the case unless we stop defining the profession in terms of the institution. Libraries are the things anyone says they are, and we have no definitions that exclude any claimant from the use of the word. Librarians are the people who work in libraries. Which of the people who work in libraries? Unfortunately, in the public perception and perhaps in our own egalitarian value system, all of them. But it doesn't work. It has never worked for us, and it doesn't really work for professions that are assertively proactive, which now includes teaching and nursing. We may soon be the only ones left playing moral imperative games and climbing mountains simply because they are there.

We Hurt Ourselves

If we continue on our present course we will continue to hurt ourselves. The insults and trivializations—from "librarian jokes" to low status, low salaries, and lack of legal protection—will also continue. As a teacher of future librarians as well as a long-time practitioner, I might be forgiven for making a selfish plea to look out for librarians even at the expense of libraries. However, there is no such dilemma for us to face in my judgment, because we cannot have good libraries without first having strong, competent, and respected librarians to run them.

Users "invent" their libraries, both in terms of their expectations, which are small and narrow, and in the ignorance of what they might have. This narrowness is as true for the users of small public libraries as for distinguished academicians. Each simply assumes that a "good" library has the material they request, although what that material may be differs widely. However, the expected action of "acquire and furnish as requested" is the same, and what a waste of potential service it is.

We can never have good libraries to serve the information needs of our clients without first having librarians qualified to assess those needs and determined to market the resources that fill them. To suggest that only professionals can establish the bounds for professions is not elitism, it is for us the same common sense as it is for other professions whose professionals are now engaged in the desperate struggle for meaningful quality that we have thus far avoided. I am not sure why we want to continue to avoid it, because the present scenario does not work either for us or for our clients, and therefore it really works for nobody.

When we agree that the coming White House Conference on Library and Information Services can deal with "information needs of society" without first insuring the professionals to assess those needs, it makes as much sense as talking about medicine without considering whether there are doctors. When we graciously acquiesce in the nomination of "scholars" to direct research libraries and then clasp them to our bosoms because they use libraries, that makes as much sense as my being named to quarterback the San Francisco 49ers because I watch a lot of football on television.

I am constantly amazed at our failure to recognize that the game of favoring "libraries," whatever they might be, rather than establishing rules for professional assessment has never worked and will never work. It is simply an exercise in rationalization, primarily financial rationalization. We talk about this occasionally among ourselves, but we do not present the strong and combative front that other professions learned long ago. If they hadn't done it, doctors might still be barbers.

Managers and Leaders: Arc There More Differences Than Similarities?

Whenever I write about issues of management I catch some flak, and I prefer to think it comes largely from individuals who evaluate management by style rather than by results. Thus, when I wrote in these pages that participative management seemed to be the generally accepted answer but that I hadn't yet heard the question (White Papers, *Library Journal*, August 1985, p. 62-63), reactions suggested that participative management was "a good thing," and that I shouldn't be playing clever semantic games with it.

If participative management is a good thing, and for some issues it would seem clearly to be, then within the framework of management this is true because it produces positive results for the organization the manager is committed to keep or make effective, or at least efficient.

My Management Musings

My musings and writings on this issue do not come from the groves of academe. My thoughts come from the 25 years I spent managing, most of them in the corporate sector where one is supposed to be measured by results.

I understand that it is essential that communication with subordinates (yes, subordinates—the next time your boss tells you that you are really co-workers suggest a swap of offices and paychecks) is essential, because people cannot be coerced into working, and will only cooperate if they see doing it in their own best self-interest.

That connection can be made and indeed must be made by competent managers, and we can learn a great deal from the Japanese, who have perfected getting people to care by giving them a stake in their own work and how they do it. However, no two individuals, and certainly not the manager and the subordinate, automatically bring the same value system to the analysis of a problem.

The trick is to make disparate value systems blend into a confluence that serves us both. This is particularly true if we don't have finite objectives and battle plans for accomplishing them, and most libraries don't. We tend to have goals that are idealistically warm and fuzzy and that also can be revered without having to be funded.

Let's Examine Backlogs

One simple distinction between management and subordinate value systems comes in the examination of backlogs. Backlogs are bad and should be reduced or eliminated, right? Not necessarily! Backlogs are clearly understood by workers to represent job security.

Workers may or may not earn a little paid overtime, but at least they protect against either termination or a transfer into a less attractive assignment because they are now no longer busy enough, and people who are not busy are usually given what nobody else wants to do.

If you want me to work hard to eliminate my backlog, what will you do for me in return? Are we talking raise, promotion, compensatory time off, even just a little public praise? Don't let the fact that your subordinates don't ask you fool you; we are all acclimated to the desirability of acting "nice." However, they are thinking about it.

Leadership Is an "In" Word

All that is management. What about leadership, which we also espouse? Here, especially, we are vulnerable to the deceptive lure of language that tells us what we want to hear. As Tom Cosgrove notes in the September 1988 issue of *Campus Activities Programming*, leadership is an "in" word. Political candidates claim to have it. Centers are created to study it. Books written about it are almost certain to be best-sellers. And yet newspaper headlines chronicle the failings of people in power, and as a nation we lament the lack of leadership.

The cry for leaders in the library field demands some scrutiny. Where do we want to be led? Do we want excellent library education programs? Or do we primarily prefer geographically convenient ones? Or do we want to retain the luxury of hiring a cheap and available local candidate without interview and relocation expenses, even if that person doesn't meet the requirements you expect others to enforce? Make up your minds, because those are contradictory values.

As early as 1978, in his classic book called *Leadership*, James MacGregor Burns noted that part of the problem was conceptual, and that we know perhaps too much about our leaders and almost nothing about leadership.

Burns, who won the Pulitzer Prize for his efforts, suggested that "leadership over human beings is exercised when persons with certain motives and purposes mobilize, in competition or conflict with others, institutional, political, psychological, and other resources so as to arouse, engage, and satisfy the motives of followers."

By sharp contrast, management has been defined as the process by which a group called managers coordinate the activities of other people, while seldom performing them. Managers are concerned with specific and detailed decision making, organizing, staffing, planning, controlling, communicating, and directing.

In other words, leaders create mechanisms so that their creation endures. They develop, persuade, or hypnotize people who will share the vision and who will see to its continued implementation. And this is where management comes in. Leaders need managers to make their vision work. Managers do the donkey work.

A Confusion in Terms

Despite this earlier book, and the later writings of Peters and Waterman, we still get the two confused. Cosgrove reports that when individuals are asked to list characteristics of leaders, words such as visionary, enthusiastic, powerful, energizing, decision[making], political, inspirational, doer, and fighter emerge.

When these same people are asked what leaders should be taught or trained to do, the words are goal setting, communication, time management, stress management, and delegation. That's pretty tame stuff compared to the intuitively generated list of earlier adjectives.

The confusion is perhaps most closely etched in the way we use the word consensus, without ever knowing what we mean. Many managers "seek" consensus, which is a determination of what the group wants; what the group wants is assumed to be good even though history tells us that consensus is usually safe and free of innovative ideas. The joke that a camel is a horse built by a committee isn't quite as humorous when we are talking about *AACR* rules or insufferably complex interlibrary loan codes.

As Samuel Johnson noted that patriotism is the last refuge of the scoundrel, so it seems that sometimes consensus seeking is the last refuge of the designated manager who will avoid making decisions or accepting responsibility at any price.

Sometimes consensus seeking is an appropriate management tactic and sometimes not: certainly not when it conflicts with the manager's own responsibilities. "I know it was stupid, but it was what *they* decided" deserves to get any manager fired instantly, but rarely does. Leaders, by contrast, do not *seek* consensus. They *build* it, by persuading others to share their goals and their dreams.

Do Opposites Attract?

Cosgrove lists other major distinctions, almost oppositions in character traits, between managers and leaders.

Managers concentrate on problem solving, leaders on purposes and causes.

Managers are production driven and are fascinated by statistics, leaders are driven by values.

Managers seek conflict avoidance, in particular with other and higher-level managers. Leaders not only accept but also invite conflict.

Managers thrive on predictability, leaders are ambiguous.

Managers are good soldiers who assure that the organization's objectives are achieved even if they disagree with them. Leaders concentrate on assuring that their objectives become the organization's objectives.

Can we create competent managers? Of course we can, because managers operate within prescribed frameworks, and competence is usually all we ask for. Outstanding managers can be almost as troublesome as leaders because they test organizational tenets.

"I know that it's policy, but in this case the implementation of policy would be wrong" is something good managers are supposed to be willing to say, and that borders on leadership. However, we don't expect it of managers, and we settle for people who at least understand the policy and can explain its stupidity sympathetically.

Can We Create Leaders?

The nonsense that we can accomplish almost anything with enough goodwill and hard work goes all the way back to *The Little Engine That Could*, although the laws of physics tell us what engines can or cannot do.

So we have leadership conferences galore. If they spot and nurture potential leaders, that's fine. If they simply send individuals out into the world to battle the dragons of complacency and disavowal of responsibility armed with nothing but goodwill and good intentions, then we have learned nothing from Laurence Peter's work.

Many people could probably manage, but a lot of them don't want to, and shouldn't be pressured to do it. Even worse is pressuring people disinclined to lead into that role. Those who seek to be leaders might find their own mechanisms, but you can help those whom you find impressive or all that leadership potential might go down the drain. That is sometimes called mentoring, but sometimes it is just protecting those who look odd, just perhaps because they are smarter or more assertive.

How Do We Find Leaders?

You don't have to find leaders, they will find you. There is at least one thing we don't have to worry about. The process is self-weeding. Failed leaders are former leaders. By contrast, failed managers hang around our necks forever.

Does librarianship need leaders? Can there be any doubt? One look around at all the missed opportunities, unmet priorities, and lost turf should be enough to persuade. I think we all recognize this, and that is why books on leadership are instant best-sellers and why all professions, including our own, put a premium on "leadership development."

However, if we need and want leadership and leaders, that doesn't necessarily mean that we want what leaders do. Are we willing to accept the pain, the work, the risks, and the challenges to passivity and rationalization that leaders would try to make us face?

I'm not at all sure. It is certainly much easier for the profession to preach leadership than to embrace it.

Getting into This Mess Wasn't Easy! It Took a Lot of Effort on Our Part

The article traces the history of escalating prices for scholarly journals purchased by U.S. research libraries, and notes the various strategies employed over the past 15 years or longer not to solve this problem, but to deflect its impact. These strategies have included funding shifts from other library priorities, appeals to administrators for additional funds for this particular purpose, and outside fund raising uniquely aimed at paying these escalating periodical prices. The author argues that these strategies have not worked, and will not work as long as publishers simply take advantage of recognizing a scenario created for them by the academic publish-or-perish syndrome, a mechanism that rewards quantity even more than it rewards the quality it is intended to recognize.

We have been discussing the problems caused by runaway periodicals budgets for a long time. In style perhaps reminiscent of a Chekhov play, we bemoan our fate, rail against the rascals who are doing this to us, resolve to do something about this outrage, and ultimately adjourn to reconvene the following year to repeat the process. My own awareness of this crisis (can something this old still be called a crisis?) goes back to a study completed in 1976 for the National Science Foundation by the Indiana University Graduate Library School Research Center.[1] In that report we noted a massive shift since the early 1970s in academic and special libraries from the purchasing of monographs to the buying of serials. The reasons given to us by both publishers and librarians at that time suggested that there were not more titles, that the page counts in each issue had increased, that publication costs had grown beyond the level of inflation, and the charge by librarians that they were the victims of discriminatory pricing, both as against individual subscriptions and as against the prices charged to non-U.S. libraries. All of this, we should recall, happened at a time of a healthy dollar, a happy coincidence that was simply absorbed by the publishers of international scholarly journals who nevertheless increased the U.S. dollar price of their exports by a routine annual 15 percent or more.

In our analysis of these findings we concluded that serials subscriptions were impervious to the laws of supply and demand, since they represent front end cash flow for a period of as long as 18 months, and because for serials, unlike monographs, the publisher has your money before he spends any of his. Therefore, even if the journal doesn't make a lot of money, the money makes a lot of money. We also speculated that librarians had been willing to transfer money so readily from the monographic to the serials budget for largely political considerations. Cancellation of a periodical title is a highly visible and confrontational tactic. A reduction in the monographic budget only becomes an issue when the library refuses to purchase a book requested by a faculty member or other user. Librarians were able to defer this problem by reducing instead their own selection options, and buying largely faculty requests, even if this created imbalances in the collection. The users don't know, and wouldn't care in any case about titles other than those that interest them.

In reacting to our observations, a number of librarians acknowledged at the time that this was indeed true, but that the game had come to an end. Duplicate subscriptions had been canceled, the monographic budget had been milked dry, and henceforth both they and the rapacious publishers would have to live with the reality of "normal" 5 percent annual increments. We now of course know that the bleeding did not stop. It may even have accelerated. Periodicals costs are still rising at an annual rate of 15 percent or more (in some disciplines more than 20 percent). Periodical titles continue to proliferate, with larger issues, special issues, spin-off publications, and other tricks devised to entrap the librarians that publishers know to be preoccupied with keeping sets complete and avoiding gaps. What we have now plundered is everything else we do, perhaps not yet directly, although there are indications of libraries accepting substantial increases in the materials budget tied to decreases in everything else.

There is only so much money that a university is able to raise, and only so many priorities it is willing to support for any one supplicant. When librarians respond to inquiries asking them to list their priorities in case there is additional money by providing an agenda on which the first item is inevitably the materials budget, and when moreover the amount asked for in just that one category exceeds the total funds that might be available, then the fact that we also ask for money for additional staff, for automation, for clerical support, and perhaps even for professional travel or continuing education is seen as pious nonsense, and it will certainly never be funded. If you get anything at all, it will be for your first priority, particularly if it is also perceived by them as their first priority. If our and their priorities were to conflict, such as if we were to argue that materials budget increases are *not* our primary priority, then we would have a good old-fashioned fight for control over the library between the professionals and the kibitzers, but this has not happened. Is it because we are afraid to fight or because we genuinely agree? Perhaps a mixture of both. While there are librarians who have noted that the preoccupation with the periodicals budget deprives us of other initiatives (and Peter Drucker has stated that managers never get credit for the status quo, only for innovation), there are other librarians who have suggested we could help this process along by transferring money from the staff budget to the materials budget. It is difficult to react to such suggestions in the recognition that materials "needs" can never be satisfied[2] and that the library is a clerical trap for which the clerical work will always take precedence. A shortage of staff makes us all clerks. Perhaps the only realistic comment is to note, as Pogo Possum did some years ago, that our enemy usually turns out to be us.

What are we today? There is no indication that the problem has either changed or diminished, despite the certainty expressed by some of our librarian survey respondents more than 10 years ago that "this could not go on." It has gone on, if anything it has gotten worse. Furthermore, within the scenario in which we operate there is no reason for the present system to change. It works too well for the publishers, and it works quite well for the scholars/authors/editors/reviewers/users, who are really the same people wearing a variety of hats. Although they can be expected to continue to complain loudly about the "inadequacies" of the materials budget (people don't really have to be hurt to complain), these faculty members all share the characteristic of having lots of authority and little if any responsibility. They certainly have no sense of responsibility of what other effects this might have in libraries, such as forcing librarians to do clerical work because of inadequate clerical staffing, or having librarians forego employer-supported research or continuing education.

It would be naive to expect commercial publishers to change a system that works so well, in carving out an additional 15 or 20 percent in funds from an otherwise totally static market, and in developing such revenue growth without the need to increase either subscribers or readers. Commercial publishers are in the business of making money, and if we can find that money on an annual basis there is no reason for change in what is obviously a winning tactic. Librarians obviously now occasionally (and only as a last resort) cancel sole subscriptions, but publishers are confident it is never *their* journals because theirs are indispensable. Some are wrong, but they don't know that. Are we expecting these publishers to decide that they are really making enough money? Does anyone in the business of making money ever make enough money? Ultimately, of course, whether they can make enough profit or not is not even our problem, is it? In a true vendor/customer relationship, the customer determines whether or not to buy something at an offered price on the basis of value perceived and value received. Whether General Mills makes or loses money on the cereal they sell me is not my concern. I will buy the product if I like it, and if I believe that this purchase makes sense in view of my other alternatives and other priorities. The maker of cereal knows that I have both other alternatives and priorities, and adjusts to this.

And that, of course, represents the problem in our dealings with publishers. We are not treated as customers because we are not perceived as customers. We are perceived as purchasing agents or sometimes even purchasing clerks acting as directed, and the real "customers" are seen to be the faculty members of our institutions. Unfortunately, faculty are not required to justify what they "need" (something that cannot be defined except in terms of what they "want") against anything else *they* might want, such as higher salaries, better laboratory facilities, or improved travel budgets, and they don't need to balance this list against what *we* might need or want. This issue never arises, because we spare them the process through the simple expedient of never telling them what else we might need, perhaps to spare ourselves the humiliation of being told that what we need or profess to need is not important.

I will discuss a little later why faculty act as they do, but the point I want to make at this stage is that it is our relationship with faculty and not our relationship with publishers that represents the problem. Publishers cannot really be blamed for taking advantage of a phenomenon they recognize quite clearly. If they can create a sufficiently attractive journal— by giving it a title that strikes a responsive chord with at least one key faculty member because one will suffice, by creating a prestigious editorial advisory board for the masthead, which is easy to do as long as you don't ask them to do much work, and by the promise of being hospitable to submitted manuscripts in this discipline—then their work is done. We will be forced to buy the title by the pressures thus created. They exercise this strategy, we have noted, by targeting not us but the ultimate "customer" with their literature, something they started doing a long time ago by readvertising old monographs that happened to be plentiful in stock, while forgetting to mention the date of publication. We can rail that the practice is unethical. Perhaps it is, but it is certainly legal. Caveat emptor is still the underlying principle of the free enterprise system.

This perception by publishers also explains why libraries are charged higher prices than individual subscribers, and why American libraries are charged higher prices through manipulated exchange rates. These are marketing strategies, and they will work unless the fury of customer retribution forces a change, which would then come quickly enough. For the present, publishers believe, and have data to support that belief, that with the duplicate subscriptions already canceled, the survival of journals perceived to be of high quality is not price dependent in libraries, although it clearly is for individual subscriptions. A later study we undertook, also for the National Science Foundation,[3] clearly indicated that these publishers were correct. The price of canceled journals was consistently lower than the price of retained journals, and a price increase only made a journal vulnerable to cancellation if it was already vulnerable for reasons that might include librarian evaluation but were largely based on the absence of key faculty support. In other words, librarians cancel journals they think they need less, but primarily they cancel journals they think they can get away with canceling. If a "key" journal increases in price, the library action may be to cancel a title that did not increase in price at all. As Dr. Eugene Garfield of the Institute for Scientific Information once put it, accurately if wistfully: "Every time *Chemical Abstracts* increases its price some libraries cancel the *Science Citation Index.*"

All of this describes characteristics of a problem that has been with us for considerably more than a decade. What have we done about it? Basically, very little. We began by transferring funds from the monographic to the journals budget to buy time, and our NSF studies indicated that in a period of only six years major academic libraries had reversed a ratio of 2:1 in dollars spent on monographs versus dollars spent on serials. A quick exercise on the calculator will demonstrate the process. When your materials budget increases 5 percent in total, but the serials part increases 20 percent, the shift out of monographs doesn't take long. There was no indication in our studies that we did this because we had concluded we were spending too much on monographs. We shifted the dollars because it avoided an ugly scene, and because faculty only understand monographic budgets in terms of our willingness or unwillingness to buy the next title they suggest (or demand). We accomplished this balancing act by salvaging our own monographic collection decisions, even when this destroyed balance or the capability to buy interdisciplinary or general items so important to any library.

However, this strategy did not serve us for long. Some monographs we must buy, particularly in new fields for which there are no old monographs, and because not all major authors are dead. Some continue to write, even on our own faculties. However, this tactic, while it held sway, even had faculty approval, and some departments even voted to forego all monographic purchases to "save" the journals. Our next tactic was the elimination of duplicate subscriptions, and we really even did this in parallel with monographic dollar shifts, as though duplicates did not matter. We, of course, knew, or should have known, from the work of Trueswell[4] and later interlibrary borrowing studies that confirm the same premise,[5] that it is duplicates that form the heart of information service, and that our major problem in document supply is not with esoteric titles but with things we already own but are unable to supply within a convenient time frame. The individuals most vulnerable to this process of opting for collections over access are students, but students have no political clout and can usually be ignored until they have graduated and are replaced by other students who will take several years to figure out what is going on. It may even be that students do not care, but perhaps we should care about the needs of our diverse constituencies.

As a sidelight to the tactic of cutting duplicates we also tended to eliminate foreign language titles. This was a pragmatic decision, as so many of our decisions here have been. Most Americans, including our scholars, can only function comfortably in their own language. This is not a new phenomenon. While I served as head of the NASA Scientific and Technical Information Facility in the mid-60s, I noted that almost half of the individuals who had SDI (selective dissemination of information) profiles in our system had specified that they did not want to be notified about any publication not written in English, no matter what the subject. They already had more than enough to read, and didn't care for the additional guilt of being told about things they ought to read but were not going to read.

By the early or mid-1980s we had run out of all of these options, confronted by a steady drumbeat of journal publisher actions that, through a combination of new titles, special issues, more pages, spinoffs, Festschrifts, and just plain inexplicable increases, added up to price growth of 20 percent in a 5 percent economy. It is interesting that all of these actions were accompanied by carefully devised publisher rationales that argued that all of this made sense. In a true vendor/customer relationship, such arguments would have been irrelevant. We would simply have informed the publishers that the overall price we were willing to pay for all journals was only going up 5 percent, and left to them the decision of what to do.

Options would certainly have included controlling both page counts and the birth of new journals, but none of this was done because none of it was perceived, and correctly perceived, by publishers as necessary. By the mid-1980s we had also begun to experience a weakening U.S. dollar, and both publishers and librarians have occasionally found it useful to single out this cause as the culprit. This may be convenient but it is also inaccurate, because the same percentage price increases also took place during the strong dollar era. If the dollar were once more to gain in strength, publishers would simply factor that new reality into their equation, so that the total would still come out to whatever it was planned to come out.

I realize that this makes publishers out to be calculating villains, but that is not my intent. Publishers are simply astute businessmen and women operating in a laissez-faire environment, and we cannot expect them to be concerned by our problems unless they believe these affect them, and clearly at present they don't. My anger is only directed at the rationalizations they feed us, because this is an indication of how weak or stupid they think we are. One example will suffice. Does anyone (except perhaps a few librarians) really believe that a profit-oriented commercial publisher cannot control the size of each journal, even each issue, if only through the simple expedient of giving the editor a budgeted number of pages to allocate on the basis of ranked quality? They don't because they don't need to, and if they don't need to they have no reason to want to. Subscription agencies, while usually more sympathetic to our plight, are unfortunately for us also the beneficiaries of this same value system. Their service charge is usually a percentage of the total price, and higher library serials budgets make money for them as well. In any case, it would be unrealistic for us to expect subscription agencies to fight our battles for us. Publishers are not the cause of our problems. They are only the opportunistic beneficiaries.

The options we now exercise are three in number, and to some extent we use all three:

1. We beg for more money. We have been remarkably successful in this process as long as the money we beg for coincides in priority with what the faculty wants. Librarians have over many years been considered more adept as mendicants than as managers, although in all fairness many have not been allowed to manage. Our strategies of indicating that the periodicals budget represented a crisis of major proportions has been successful. Universities otherwise strapped for funds have made the library materials budget second in priority only to the faculty salary budget. We have in library after library and in year after year, received double the normal targeted increase, which would translate to 10 percent, and sometimes we have been given even more.

    The strategy has its shortcomings. First, it can't work in the long term, simply because publishers can find ways to spend our money faster than we can obtain it. Second, even administrators weaned on the premise that the value of the library and its only value is in the integrity or size of the collection will eventually get tired of making what are for them real and continuing sacrifices to no apparent end, because indeed this process never does end. And so, at least, some administrators are beginning to get angry, or at least testy. They are not certain at whom, but we are certainly the handiest targets. Perhaps they feel they are being ripped off, and that we should somehow have prevented this. However, even though librarians are genuinely angry at what they perceive as manipulation by publishers, they have not come up with any sort of effective counter-strategy, and our administrators sense it. More about this later. The most common way for administrators to vent their frustrations on us is to fund none of our other initiatives. To the extent to which these involve more professional staff, more clerks to free the professional staff, more automation, more investment in systems and resource sharing, a beginning investment in research into library operations, or a modest investment in continuing education and training, they are priorities that have never been in high favor in large part because they have not achieved faculty recognition, and administrators have abdicated the direction of library policy to the faculty. Fundamentally, faculty care about only two things: (1) the collection (specifically their part of it), and (2) hours of convenient opening, including liberal borrowing privileges, study carrels, etc. They don't need us for much library work involving their discipline, because they have their own supply of cheap student labor for this purpose.

2. We transfer money on our own. Of course, we were doing this in the 1970s, but here the transfers were within the materials budget. We now have suggestions that we have too many librarians and need to eliminate some to provide more materials dollars. We would expect and indeed have had such suggestions from faculty, and the only appropriate response is still to tell them to stop making suggestions in areas about which they know nothing at all. However, it is the fact that such suggestions are coming from some librarians that revives the specter of Pogo Possum. I will grant that in a library in which 60 percent of the budget is spent for salaries this would give us some leeway. To be exact, in a scenario of 5 percent budget and 20 percent price increase for the 30 percent that represents the materials budget, it would give us about 10 years before all the staff dollars were gone. Then, of course, the problem would return, but at least it wouldn't worry us because there wouldn't be any of us left to worry about it. It is interesting to see what would be next to be sacrificed, probably something affecting students—academic advisors or financial aid counselors. Just about anything except the collection (which would antagonize the faculty) or athletic teams (which would antagonize both alumni and students).

3. We go out for fund raising. Fund raising from alumni and friends has become an academic way of life. As the administrator of an academic program I don't much enjoy it, but I understand its necessity. At the same time, I practice the self-discipline of recognizing that my fund raising must only be for things I cannot expect the university or state legislature to support, and never just to let them off the hook. I therefore raise funds for academic equipment, for faculty research, and for student financial aid. I would assume that university libraries could do something similar—raise funds for librarian research, for continuing education, for scholarships for staff members, for professional involvement. What do we emphasize in fund raising? The one thing, perhaps the only thing for which the administration will give us money of its own accord. The collection budget! Publishers must wonder how they get this lucky.

Our political strategies, if they can be called this, have not been particularly effective. We have expressed our anger at publisher prices in resolutions passed in large assemblies and small committees, and these have had the effect such actions have always had. We have sent delegations to talk to publishers, who have explained to us patiently as one would to any child that we are all victims of circumstances and none of this is their fault. At one time some publishers were genuinely concerned that library groups might take some concerted action. Two obvious possibilities come to mind. First, we could unanimously cancel all ARL subscriptions to the most offensive journals, inform our own academic colleagues that this journal would be henceforth unavailable through libraries in the United States, and ask them to alert their colleagues and in particular their overseas colleagues not to waste their energies on publishing articles in journals nobody would be able to read. Second, we could cancel all but one subscription of the most offending journal most particularly in the tactic of discriminatory pricing, and make enough photocopies from that one subscription for every other library. We would then invite the publisher to sue us, of course, in recognition that this would have to be heard in a United States Court before a U.S. jury that would undoubtedly find all of this fascinating. If the publishers were ever worried about either possibility, they are worried no longer.

A few librarians, who must at least be given credit for courage, have sought to involve their own faculty colleagues, and particularly those who serve as editors or as members of advisory boards, in the problem. They have found, really not surprisingly, that these faculty members do not want to be involved. Why should they? The system works for them.

We come then, ultimately and circuitously, to an examination of the real forces that drive this out-of-control engine. Publishers, I have already noted, are not the instigators of this process, they are only the beneficiaries of a publish/perish syndrome that is based on the premise that much is good and more is better, and that completely frees faculty from the financial responsibility for their actions. The premise of academic publications is based on a peer review process in which articles are written to report on research findings or on original thought, and are then presumably judged stringently by a jury of academic peers. Worthy publications are accepted, unworthy publications are rejected, and all of this is then reflected in the appropriate decisions concerning promotion, tenure or banishment from the groves of academe. The system works in principle but not in practice, because the stakes are too high, and the evaluation and appeal procedures have become too legalized. The process still professes to evaluate quality, but to a larger extent it evaluates quantity. Individuals therefore write, whether they have anything to say or not, and whether or not the piece is original or simply another regurgitation. The peer review system as we know it broke down some time ago. Conscientious reviewers can still keep unworthy articles out of a major and prestigious journal, but they cannot keep it from being published somewhere. As a sometime reviewer I am well aware of this phenomenon in our field, which is no different from others. Every article I have rejected has later appeared in another publication. This then even creates a dilemma for the commercial publishers for whom I have expressed little sympathy up to now. They must indeed publish everything that "the system" tells them they ought to publish. If they don't, they leave materials that have been judged as publishable, and they don't like to leave room for a competing journal. For us the result would be no more pleasant. It would just create another journal, which we would be expected to buy. Starting a new journal, I would remind the reader again, is easy. It requires very little capital because the customers provide the capital. It also involves very little risk, because you know the success of much of your marketing efforts before you produce your first issue.

What drives this process is then not just scholarly communication but scholarly credit, and that is a far different and far more emotional issue. The journal that carries my article, or in which I might want to publish as a safety valve strategy, must therefore be purchased by my library, and, of course, that decision to buy the journal in turn "proves" it a high quality journal. The studies by Kent and Galvin[6] noted that there were journals residing in the University of Pittsburgh Library that were never touched, let alone read, by anyone, and it is not surprising that this finding was attacked with fury by the Pittsburgh faculty and others, not necessarily because it was wrong, but because it was very dangerous. Our own NSF studies had discovered that there were a considerable number of journals that had virtually no individual subscriptions. All of the customers were libraries. What if some of the journals bought only in libraries are also the ones never read in libraries, does this really matter? Not really, if the purpose is not communication but credit, because credit has already been reflected in the decision to publish and the inclusion in the curriculum vitae.

We don't know to what extent this level of "publication padding" takes place, but I don't think anyone can doubt its existence. For proof we need only look at our own discipline, which is probably not atypical. We know that the number of library schools has declined, the number of graduates produced has declined, the number of faculty members to whom considerable research is attributed has declined. How come we have the continuing increase in library publications? Who is writing all that stuff? And why?

If we deal with publications growth in both size and cost as an issue of academic credit rather than just scholarly communication, we deal with a far different and far more emotional issue. I am not certain a solution is even possible for me. As a manager I know well enough that not all problems have solutions. However, we should at least communicate to both faculty and administrators that we understand what is really happening here. How much does the budget in support of scholarly acquisition (real scholarly acquisition that reports something new) need to grow? We can never know with certainty, but we can make some educated guesses. Some disciplines grow as others decline, and therefore shifting would be inevitable. However, we know there has been no particular growth in the size of academics as such. We have no new universities, and most faculties are being held at zero growth. Perhaps we can therefore tolerate a 2 percent growth in genuine publication, and combine that with a 4 percent growth in the cost of publication, and 4 percent comes from inflation figures provided by the Federal government. If publishers in general or those in a particular country have special problems either with higher inflation or a weakening dollar, then I would wish them luck with *their* problem of cost reduction, but this has nothing to do with us, any more than the sudden price unattractiveness of Japanese cars as the American dollar weakened became a problem for anyone but the Japanese. I would then suggest that we ask for only, and accept no more than, 6 percent in support of increased materials costs. That should in turn allow us to implement some of our other long-sublimated needs, sublimated so long that nobody even knows what they are. Perhaps even we have forgotten.

If the university wants to fund materials budget increases above 6 percent, and certainly the academic credit system will demand it, then this additional cost should be properly labeled for what it is, a faculty fringe benefit designed to keep them happy and content, and not as a library operational cost. It can then compete with salaries and medical insurance for priority. Let us also not forget that the implementation of this fringe cost has additional costs for us that must be added to our budget, costs in labor, materials, and space storage. This last could be saved if it is agreed that buying is enough, and that after purchase it can be discarded.

Would any of this work? Perhaps not. Perhaps even probably not or certainly not. However, I know of no other approach, because the present system not only affords us no relief, but it also affords us nothing but blame and recrimination. If all else fails, let us at least stop being willing conspirators in our own destruction. Let us at least make clear that simply buying more and more expensive journals is not our first priority, and that this need, at whatever level it needs to be funded for whatever scholarly or humanitarian reason, cannot be allowed simply to erase what is for libraries a complex and multifaceted agenda of needs. This oversimplification comes into play when university administrators decide (and perhaps librarians agree) that buying journals is a "normal" expense (at whatever the level), while the implementation of technology is some sort of special hot-house exotic flower that requires special recognition and funding from other outside bodies. As surely we have learned by now, with special appropriations also come special constraints and controls, if and when the appropriations come at all.

There is, of course, total irony in all of this. The development of advanced systems of bibliographic access and document delivery make specific ownership far less important than it once was, certainly for much of the material we are expected to provide to faculty and students. Ownership is not the over-riding issue, the issue is access, and I congratulate those ARL libraries that have stopped reporting holdings counts as the truly irrelevant numbers they are. What we need instead are service measurements—in units of time and in units of accuracy. All of this suggests a shift away from rather than to the materials budget, and toward two other budgets, the access budget which is largely technology and delivery cost, and the people budget for individuals smart enough to run it. And, of course, we still have a long way to go before we provide our clients with proactive and interactive information service rather than just reactive materials service.

The problem for us is a faculty value system encrusted by years of decision making by individuals who don't know what is really possible and whom we have never told they don't know. How would they react to such a newly expressed librarian assertiveness? By a new understanding of a potentially exciting relationship between equal academic colleagues? Perhaps. By having us drawn and quartered and thrown to the dogs? Perhaps. I am quite sure that the quality of faculty and administrator perception will vary, and that some will welcome and others reject a new wave of assertive leadership. Much, I am sure, would depend on the skills and eloquence of the librarians. However, there are two things about which I am sure. One is that the present scenario as it is playing itself out cannot work for us, and cannot work for our institutions. The second is that faculty also recognize, perhaps only instinctively but nevertheless realistically, that the value systems governing library acquisitions for the last decade and longer have not worked for them, and will work even less in the future. They just don't know what the other alternatives are, and they only can decide on the basis of what they do know.

Notes

1. White, Herbert S. "Publishers, Libraries, and Costs of Journal Subscriptions in Times of Funding Retrenchment." *Library Quarterly* 46, no. 4 (October 1976): 359-77.

2. Munn, Robert F. "The Bottomless Pit; or the Academic Library as Viewed from the Administration Building." *College and Research Libraries* 29 (January 1968): 51-54.

3. White, Herbert S. "Factors in the Decision by Individuals and Libraries to Place or Cancel Subscriptions to Scholarly and Research Journals." *Library Quarterly* 50, no. 3 (July 1980): 287-309.

4. Trueswell, Richard W. "Some Behavioral Patterns of Library Users: The 80/20 Rule." *Wilson Library Bulletin* 44 (January 1969): 458-61.

5. Stewart, Blair. "Periodicals and the Liberal Arts College." *College and Research Libraries*, vol. 36, no. 5 (September 1975): 371-78.

6. Kent, Allen, and others. *Use of Library Materials; the University of Pittsburgh Study.* New York: M. Dekker, 1979.

Technology—A Means to an End
Only If You Can Agree on the End

Let me begin with a story that dates back almost 30 years, to the time I served as program manager of the IBM Corporate Technical Information Center, a job that despite its grandiose title meant that I was responsible for a number of libraries. A librarian and computer analyst approached the summit of a mountain from opposite sides. The librarian said, "What can you do for me?" The computer analyst responded, "What would you like to have done?" After that they looked at each other in silence for several minutes, and then each descended down his side of the mountain.

Of course, we in libraries are now much more heavily involved with the use of computers, but do we yet know what we want from them? Are we simply looking for easier and perhaps less expensive (although that is always doubtful) ways to do what we have always done? Are we satisfied with what we have always done or could we do more, or something else? More importantly for a service profession, does it work for our users? Who are our users? Are they just the individuals who use our institutions under the terms that we, and perhaps they together with us, have developed? Or does it include the people who do not use our libraries, in part perhaps because we have never asked them what they need or what they want (those are not the same things)?

Peter Drucker, with his Churchillian gift for coming to grips with an issue immediately and in few words, has postulated that automation is not about machines at all, but rather about how people work. How do librarians, and the people who depend on librarians, and the people who ought to depend on librarians, work? How would they want to work if they knew all their options? It is not an easy question to raise, even if we should care to raise it. I served for six years as a member of the

Speech presented at the 1990 Winsor Lectures, University of Illinois, Urbana, November 29, 1990.

Board of Directors of the American Federation of Information Processing Societies (AFIPS). That body was divided into two groups. One was made up of representatives of the computer societies, IEEE-CS, ACM, and DPMA, whose primary concern always appeared to be making computers more effective and efficient, and adapting people to them. The other group contained everyone else, from librarians to sociologists to historians to teachers, who insisted stubbornly that our convenience was more important than the efficiency of the computer system. It was a polite struggle, but it went on without end in a thousand little skirmishes, and I doubt that it has been resolved yet.

What this suggests is that as organizations in industry and government, and lastly but inevitably in academia, move toward the implementation of the ideas espoused by Daniel Bell, that we are an information society, and that information is the primary source of both power and correct decisions, we have and will have chief information officers or information vice presidents. Logically, that individual should be the librarian, if the librarian understands how to use computers *for a purpose*. That individual should, under no circumstances, be the chief computer professional in the organization, because that individual will, instinctively and without rancor, see to it that people adapt to the computer's purpose. Unfortunately, in some corporations and some countries, that has already started to happen. In academia, within 15 years, there will be a vice president for information sources and services, and the librarian will either be that person or report to that person. If, as an alternative, the library is somehow considered to be something other than an information source and service organization—just somehow the library, a collection of things for self-service—then our prospects would be bleak indeed, and precisely because of an inability or an unwillingness to harness technology to our objectives, and to reassess those objectives in light of what is possible.

I am now asked to speak increasingly about my vision of libraries in the twenty-first century. Futurists tell us that we overestimate change in the short term, because we fail to factor inertia into the equation. It will take a committee at least six months to report, whether it really ought to take six months or not, and it will take another six months to circulate and discuss the committee's report. By contrast, we underestimate what will happen over the longer term (10 years or more) simply because we cannot predict how changes outside our own field will affect us. The impact of technology raises huge questions, because we can be certain that developments in technology will not cease. We can also be certain that these breakthroughs will not be engineered specially for us. They will be developed for other reasons. We can adapt them to our needs, we can adapt ourselves to them (which is a less attractive alternative), or we can ignore them entirely. However, if we do this we run the real risk that others will harness what we choose not to consider because it does not meet our preconceptions.

The development of decentralized database searching is the most obvious example that comes to mind. Because central processing units work more rapidly than the input-output devices attached to them, it was found that one CPU could handle many external access devices, a process that is indeed sequential but appears simultaneous because we cannot recognize nanoseconds. This has revolutionized banking and airline reservations, and it has revolutionized the process of seeking information in libraries, because that process is no longer dependent on local holdings or the maintenance of a local laboriously filed catalog. What you have within your own four walls is ultimately irrelevant. The question is what can I access from a bibliography (or what can you access for me), and what sort of document delivery can I then get, from the shelves upstairs or from some collection several thousand miles away. The distance does not matter, only time does. Further developments in the application of this technology are already beginning to appear. We already know they include CD-ROM and file downloading. What else they will include I am loath to predict, but whatever they are, they will be tools for librarians to use, or perhaps for those who replace us because we stubbornly refuse to even consider using them.

Some changes brought about by technology are easy to enumerate, without the need for a crystal ball. We will have, and already have, increased and improved bibliographic access, no longer limited to the holdings of any particular library. That bibliographic access can be and we would hope frequently would be in and through the library and through the experts in bibliographic access, the librarians, but it does not have to be if we don't want to play. The game can be moved to another stadium. One of the things that this means immediately is that processing backlogs in any one library become highly visible, and therefore intolerable. Will any of us really have the nerve to suggest that what we own and have in the building will not be available for another nine months? I pray we will not be that foolish.

It also means improved document delivery, in part because the technology exists (we now have fax, satellite, and 24-hour messenger service and we will have more) and will get better, and because the absurdity of waiting several weeks for something identified in minutes will be striking. Lest we forget, we have no exclusive in the area of document delivery. Others already do it, and they will certainly do what we refuse to do or argue we cannot do. It amounts to the same thing.

Formats are changing, and will continue to change as they have throughout time. We need to remind ourselves that libraries existed long before the invention of movable type, and that stone tablets, papyrus scrolls, incunabula, hardcover books, paperbacks, journals, technical reports, microforms, and computer-generated and computer-stored information are part of the same continuing process. It is our job to assess the options and select the range most appropriate. If we are fascinated by formats, we could become the buggy whip manufacturers of the twenty-first century, and we could repeat the fatal mistakes of the American railroads in the 19th century, who thought they were in the railroad business when in fact they were in the transportation business. What business are we in? Let me give you a hint. It begins with the letter "I."

There is still indication that we are fascinated by formats. World War II spawned the technical report as a rapid means of scholarly communication, in response to the observations of Vannevar Bush, George Kistiakowsky, and others that the "traditional" means of communication, books (at least six years) and journal articles (at least two years), are simply too slow for some needs and for some disciplines. They work better for researchers into the look of minnesingers than for high-energy physicists. There is still some evidence that we decide on what to do with material based on its format rather than its content, and that we will routinely catalog a trivial book in preference to a breakthrough technical or business report held together by staples. Is it only my imagination that we prefer things that stand up by themselves, and will therefore routinely buy hardcover over softcover monographs at a much greater price even when expected use does not forecast wear and tear, or that catalogers still get more satisfaction from processing larger rather than smaller books?

There are imbedded in technology some great potential advantages for us. Holdings of a particular library will be less crucial, because our concern will be with delivery. We already know from the works of Trueswell that ownership is not an automatic predictor of access, but we have historically been fascinated with ownership as though it mattered. What matters to me as a user is whether or not I can get what I want or think I need, and when. It is a binary process, in which the reason I can't get what I want really doesn't matter very much, although we insist on explaining it as though it did matter. Technology is a great equalizer, if used properly, and the National Library of Medicine has already justified its activities on the premise that doctors in remote regions of Alaska should not be penalized by a lack of access to good medicine. Is there then any reason why any resident of that area of Alaska should have library information services any less adequate than those provided a citizen of Cleveland or Boston? Only the bibliographic access and delivery mechanisms change. Have we thought about 24-hour-a-day, seven-day-a-week 800 telephone numbers to individuals who might have a question for which they might need either an answer or a document? American Express offered that service to its customers a long time ago. The technology exists, the issue is "only" money, and it was again Peter Drucker who reminded us that in a provision of a service that people consider essential, cost becomes irrelevant. We have seen this in society repeatedly. We even, as a nation, spend $50 billion a year on processed pet food, and one could question how essential that might be. It does not matter, it is seen as essential by those who buy the pet food, after having been convinced that they should. The question that I see is not whether or not the money will be spent for bibliographic access and document delivery, but rather whether it will be spent through or around us.

I am concerned for my profession in an age of technology because we are still fascinated by format rather than content. We are also somewhat unwilling to reexamine our premises. Mortimer Taube noted in 1965 just before his death that technology allowed us to rethink all of our processing conventions, in particular those that suggested that we had to limit subject analysis because of the cost of filing 3 x 5 inch cards. Taube argued that it would be a serious mistake simply to put the Anglo-American Cataloging Rules on a computer. However, that is exactly what we have done, in this application and in others. To a great extent, when libraries have "computerized" they have simply moved their manual processes from quill pens to fountain pens to typewriters to computers. It has some advantages, but it misses most of the opportunities.

We seem still unwilling to recognize the diverse roles that most libraries (and certainly academic and public libraries) are required to play. Libraries in support of education and libraries in support of information have rather antithetical value systems, but we assume that everyone is here to be educated. That may be true for students, although I would argue that even bibliographic instruction should include a segment on what you can expect to get from a librarian. However, when we insist that faculty members and administrators in our institution should be trained to perform end user searching, what evidence do we have that the majority want to do it, or that they will do it better and cheaper if indeed they do it at all? There are always examples of basic scientists and scholars who want only raw material, but Ladd and Lipseth have written in the *Chronicle of Higher Education* that increasingly our research has become applied research, and that university faculty are looking either for specific answers to specific questions or for evidence to support the conclusions they have already transmitted to the funding agency. What does it tell us if faculty offered the opportunity for end user searching send their graduate assistants or even their secretaries?

Our failure to even evaluate how technology affects us can lead to a lose-lose environment, because what we get otherwise is unresponsive to our clients, and more expensive for the organization that ultimately pays all of the bills, theirs and ours. In addition we fail to realize that the provision of information, and not the gathering up of a huge warehouse, is where the academic credit of the future lies. Document delivery, which is the essence of our present value system even as we do it poorly (we measure ownership rather than access) will become in any case increasingly routine and clerical through the use of computers. Computer reproduction services will also lead us, and indeed already has for government technical reports, to a throw-away technology in which documents obtained and no longer needed will presumably be disposed of in an environmentally appropriate manner, but will not be returned to the dispensing organization. Think of it! No circulation control, no overdue notices. Can anyone among us mourn the loss of this incredibly annoying and clerically draining activity? I can't.

It goes almost without saying that the application of various options requires a restructuring of the library budget, but why haven't we all done it? Online searching is an alternative to manual searching. The first is accrued incrementally (unless we use CD-ROM and file downloading), the other is prepaid through the salaries of reference librarians (unless you are so busy paying journal invoices that you have forgotten to hire librarians who actually answer reference questions). Manual versus machine searching are then options, and both should be budgeted, so that a user's response to the question "Would you like me to do a computer search?" is "Why are you asking me?" It is the reference librarian's responsibility to select the most likely solution to a search problem, as under similar circumstances it is the responsibility of the doctor to suggest a treatment. In an extension of the same argument, interlibrary loan (or what I choose to call extended access) is simply an alternative to purchase. We purchase permanently those things that will probably be used often, at a greater initial but a smaller amortized cost. We purchase specifically and in response to a request those books or articles (rather than the whole journal) that in our judgment it would have been unwise to purchase in advance and in its entirety. That is our decision. Do we have the right to penalize the user because of our professional decision to purchase something in advance or not? I don't think so, and those options will continue to increase as material grows, as costs exceed budgets for initial purchase, and as technology allows us to bridge the gap. We need only budget appropriately.

There are other opportunities that automation provides to this profession and that I have not addressed directly in what has been largely a politically oriented discussion. Nevertheless, the opportunities are there. Technology promises a significant release from drudgery and from the clerical routines that engulf us today, precisely because librarians get caught in the clerical trap in which they are performing clerical duties over professional ones. This means that all of us become clerks, and people see us as clerks. I am not suggesting that technology will save a library money, but rather that it will shift the costs from clerical labor to clerical computer operations, and introduce new items into the equation. Some of these, and I have already mentioned them, are still basically clerical. I have already also mentioned the potential that technology provides for improvement in information access. As I see it, the question will not be whether the library is large or small, but whether the information system is adequate and sufficiently imaginative.

The use of online bibliographic searching provides Boolean options of and/or/not, as well as combined term searching of which the devotees of the manual catalog are not even aware. Why haven't we told them how much better this is? Is it perhaps because we are reluctant to note that the manual catalog was really all along a rather pedestrian approach to a small fraction of our collection, and that it worked as a document locator far better than as a subject analysis tool? Isn't it true? Isn't it also true that one of the reasons that faculty (or more likely their graduate assistants) have to spend so much time digging is because the tools are so antiquated? Will anyone complain if they get better?

There are, of course, other services we can offer through computerization, and most of them suggest personalized services geared not to the whole but to the individual researcher, from personalized bibliographies to SDI services. Even the traditional manual tools get better. Cumulative indexes prepared by shingling cards (and some of us remember using shingling cards to produce camera-ready pages) routinely took as long as a year to produce. The annual cumulative index for the 24 issues of the *NASA STAR*, which I produced, was at the Government Printing Office in camera-ready form before the end of January.

For librarians the large question concerns our ability and willingness to recognize and grasp the opportunity to shift from a collection, storage, and maintenance culture to an information intermediation culture. What librarians have traditionally prided themselves on doing (large collections, unique acquisition) will become largely routine through a combined process of technology and economy of cost. Stand-alone self-sufficiency is no longer affordable. We have stubbornly, certainly in academic libraries, insisted on teaching the student and providing the raw materials to the scholar. In doing this we may have failed to notice that teaching has never been the highest priority in major universities, and that fixation with imbuing the student with self-sufficiency is primarily ours and not the faculty's. As for the researching faculty, have we failed to keep track of their dwindling number, and of the change in the way they want to work?

Herbert Brinberg has suggested that professional information use ranges from pure scholars who want only raw material, to applied researchers and development people who want specific answers to specific questions, to managers who need to know what their options are. All three groups are located in universities, and academic observers like Ladd and Lipseth have suggested that the number of basic researchers is small and shrinking compared to the individuals who are working on contracts, grants, and timetables (it may be the tenure timetable) and want what specifically fits that model. Charles Osburn has noted that even humanistic work begins to resemble the work model of the physical and social sciences, as grants and contracts intrude into their value system. We seem hardly to have taken account of the change, and the results can be seen in part in the development of nonlibrary (informal and perhaps illegitimate) information collections in universities that meet the real needs of faculty and researchers, rather than what we tell them they want. Technology will accelerate this process of moving to alternatives if we fail to survey and monitor what is happening. And what about university administrators who need a business information system similar to any special library, and who will certainly ultimately get whatever they want, whether from us or not? What is the political price of wasting this opportunity?

There are some broadly developing pictures beginning to take shape. Ours is an information conscious society, even if not an information adept society. We can try to teach users self-service so that professional duties won't get in the way of our clerical activities, but even that won't work. Ours is also a service-based society, and the bottom line is that if we insist users do it themselves and they don't want to, they will find somebody else. That somebody else will undoubtedly base the process on the pure convenience of the technology, and will do what we refuse to do, less effectively and more expensively.

I can't predict what technology will bring to librarians in the next 20 years with any specificity, any more than we could have known 20 years ago what we have now. We do know that the opportunities for change will be continuous, and that they will be substantial. We also know that we are not the exclusive masters of our fate, and that if we refuse to make assessments and decisions, others will make them.

These changes can be a wonderful and an exciting opportunity, or a terrible disaster for those who refuse to deal with new realities. I know that we still have catalogers and reference librarians who hate and fear what technology has done to their jobs, failing to recognize that nobody is ever promised careers that are frozen in a time warp. I would hope that the students now graduating from library schools understand that we are preparing them for the jobs of today, and for the assessment of changes that are undefined but nevertheless certain. I am not really worried about the students, and we must deal humanely and yet firmly with those who are now obsolete, as any field must deal with them. I am not really worried about that process naturally reshaping itself. I am only concerned if the Luddites are our managers.

Technology can be a wonderful servant. Technology can be a terrible master. And the genie is long since out of the bottle.

Professional Librarians
and Professionals in Libraries

Individuals who aspire to the title of librarian must meet qualifications that are undoubtedly going to be largely educationally prescribed. To do otherwise is not only to forfeit our "turf," but it is also to abandon our clients.

If anyone may define librarian and library, then some rather awful things can pretend to either title; our publics are not even aware of how they are being cheated by the pretense that they really have a library. The medicine I prescribe is bitter for some; it suggests that in some cases no library is better than a pseudolibrary, always assuming that we have a strategy for providing a real library.

In none of my writings have I suggested that librarians are the only kind of professionals that can be found in libraries. Therefore it was surprising to find in the Professional Views column in the July/August 1990 *Public Libraries* (p. 209) an item titled "Non-M.L.S. Professionals in the Library" in which it was proposed that only librarians can fill professional posts in their libraries.

Library Is a Library Is a . . .

The point has always been that there could easily be other professional skills represented in large and complex organizations. After all, DuPont doesn't just have chemists and Price Waterhouse doesn't just have accountants. I served as director of the NASA contract-operated central library more than 25 years ago. NASA insisted and still insists on referring to itself as a scientific and technical information facility, presumably to get congressional funding; as its director, I knew it was a library.

Reprinted, with changes, by permission of the author and *Library Journal* 116, no. 1 (January 1991): 74-75. Copyright © 1991 by Reed Publishing, U.S.A.

My staff of 300 professionals and nonprofessionals included—in addition to M.L.S.-credentialed librarians—accountants, systems analysts and programmers, micrographic engineers, and scientifically trained abstractors and indexers.

In the complexity of life today, public and academic libraries can also make good use of accountants, public relations specialists, employment and benefits experts, fundraisers, and remedial reading specialists, in addition to the group of systems analysts found just about anywhere. All of these professions have educational and training programs of their own. Our question is whether or not these individuals are able to perform their jobs as we librarians have outlined and to our expectations.

Librarians and Nonlibrarians

This last sentence defines the issue for me. There is nothing wrong with having nonlibrarian professionals work under the overall direction of librarians. Indeed, in the time-honored tradition of using the number and type of individuals supervised as part of the wage and salary analysis process, such a scenario can only help us.

It is, of course, possible that some librarians would also have these specialized skills, but it isn't likely and it isn't necessary. Buying or renting specialized skills and services has become a routine process, and we use it all the time, from insurance agents to automobile mechanics, and, of course, for those most obvious of service professions, lawyers and doctors. We hire these people all the time, depending on the relationship, for a fee or for a salary.

The Uniqueness of Librarians

What then is it that librarians do uniquely, based on preparation as specific and unduplicated as for any other profession? There are two things. The first, of course, is represented by the range of specialized talents of our profession: reference work (manual or online) to collection development and acquisitions to cataloging; the applications areas in service to children, senior citizens, and the business community; and so on.

What librarians do uniquely is something we have to determine. Then we face the additional requirement of developing first educational and later training programs to meet those needs, and protecting those requirements from those who would prefer pragmatic cheapness. Reading that Library A hired somebody who didn't meet requirements because "they couldn't afford" somebody who did is almost guaranteed to drive me up the wall. Organizations afford what they consider worth affording.

We Run the Library

If librarians do uniquely what only they know how to do, and if we hire other professionals to perform those specialized tasks not encompassed in our own narrow and brief educational programs, what is the second thing that librarians have to do? Librarians have to run the library, or information center, or information facility, or whatever it is that the political process urges us to call it. Only librarians can manage the whole operation because only competent librarians understand why the fundraisers and systems analysts and budget specialists do what they do.

Many of the nonlibrarians spotlighted in the *Public Libraries* column understand and stress this point. However, as a special librarian I also encounter situations in which abstractors or literature searchers or programmers who work *in* the library do not want to report to a librarian, because they somehow consider it "beneath their dignity."

That point, in my view, is simply not open to negotiation. There are still choices in a democratic society. Individuals who find their management reporting line to be "demeaning" are certainly free to resign; if their view is that narrowly bigoted, I will shed no tears. There are other systems analysts, other accountants, and other fundraisers, as there are other librarians.

The incentives usually revolve around a meaningful challenge, an assignment that can be fulfilled (given the proper initiative, time, and resources), and a competitive salary. That matters even to librarians, and I hope it will matter more. It is always my hope that librarian jobs that pay too little remain vacant, or the whole point is lost.

If libraries are to be managed by librarians, then this suggests some level of management preparation in library school for everybody, and a good deal of management preparation for those really interested in management as a career direction within the library field.

Teaching Librarians to Manage

There seems to be a growing appreciation for the teaching of management in library schools, and that developing awareness certainly pleases me. My colleagues and students know that I teach just about everything as a management course. I insist with a lonely stubbornness that the teaching of management should precede the teaching of collection development, because without an understanding of the management process you will never get the money with which to do collection development at all, never mind doing it well.

Some practitioners, and certainly recent students, agree on the need for a greater emphasis on management education (see the White/Mort study of library school graduates nine years later in *Library Quarterly*, July 1990, and White Papers, *Library Journal*, October 15, 1990, pp. 61-62), but there is still little indication of a willingness to forgo the teaching of specific job-related training skills that make a new hire productive on the first day on the job. If students perceive that a familiarity with more databases is more impressive than a seminar in personnel administration in applying for the first job, they are unfortunately correct.

Finally, what of the nonlibrarians appointed as "heads" of major libraries? The *Public Libraries* item mentions Vartan Gregorian and Timothy Healy, and quotes Richard De Gennaro in defending these appointments. I quarrel with De Gennaro infrequently and then always reluctantly, and I am not even sure we disagree here. It depends on what these individuals do.

Do they really run the library on a day-to-day basis, or do they concentrate their skills on public relations and fundraising, leaving the running of the library to the librarians? If the latter case is so, I really have no problem with the process, because the relationship is in truth inverted. Super politicians, fundraisers, and public relations experts really work for the librarian in charge, even when they carry more grandiose titles.

For many years it was understood by all of us that the Library of Congress was really being run by librarians such as John Lorenz and Bill Welsh (I know Bill doesn't have a library degree but he's paid his dues); whoever trotted up to Capitol Hill didn't really matter as long as he or she got the money. I started at LC under Luther Evans. He lent prestige, but his energies were devoted to UNESCO; Verner Clapp ran the library.

The Power Behind the Throne?

There are many models for this, but unfortunately they tend to exist outside the United States. Constitutional monarchies free the prime minister for serious duties while the king or queen cuts ribbons; in the absence of a monarch, a ceremonial president takes care of these duties.

Only in the United States do we expect the president to welcome the champion hog grower as well as develop foreign policy alternatives. There is even an example, at least in recent history, from our own profession. The president of ASLIB was not a librarian, but rather a prominent or titled citizen who could put the best light on what the professionals did. However, the president of ASLIB also understood his or her role, which was to promote British special libraries but not to make decisions about them.

I have no problems with any of this, because I am enough of a pragmatist to favor that which works. I have only two rules. Only librarians can be allowed to do that which librarians are educated uniquely to do, and, like any profession, we get to decide what that is. And librarians run all libraries. Especially the big ones. Beyond that, I'll take all the help from other professionals that I can get, as long as they understand what they are qualified to do, and what they are not qualified to either do or decide. Then we'll get along just fine.

Librarians vs. Computer Professionals

As a practicing librarian, I worked with computer professionals during virtually all of my management career—starting at IBM, and then at both the NASA Scientific and Technical Information Facility and the Institute for Scientific Information, where both the systems and computer operations people reported to me. I never experienced any difficulties in this process, largely because I never lost sight of the fact that computer people are highly skilled and knowledgeable specialists.

But like any service professionals (and as librarians we certainly understand the role of service professionals in relationship to those whom they serve), computer people have to work to parameters and specifications established by library managers in those instances in which we consider computer approaches to information work. This makes sense particularly if you accept without question Peter Drucker's premise that automation is not about machines but rather about how people work.

The Technology Option

Thus the consideration of technology in libraries is always a subset of the question of what librarians need to do to serve their customers. In many cases the application of technology provides the only option for what would otherwise not be possible, often it is more rapid or of higher quality. Occasionally but rarely it is cheaper, and sometimes there is no reason to mechanize something that works well.

However, a comparison between an automated and a manual library service is frequently a comparison between apples and oranges, because technology in both internal operations and in bibliographic access and document delivery allows us to do things we could otherwise not do at all. Therefore, while cost is always a concern it is not the primary concern, which is still need

Reprinted, with changes, by permission of the author and *Library Journal* 116, no. 5 (March 15, 1991): 64-65. Copyright © 1991 by Reed Publishing, U.S.A.

and purpose. Again, as Drucker has reminded us, in the provision of products and services that people really want, cost ultimately becomes irrelevant.

Humpty Dumpty and Ideals

It did not take long for cracks to develop in my idealization of this relationship. I learned during my six years on the Board of the American Federation of Information Processing Societies that there are computer professionals who put the efficiency of the system ahead of the needs of the users; not only the librarian but also the educator, mathematician, and sociologist representatives on the board felt frustrated by this attitude. The realization that there are also librarians who put their internal rules and procedures ahead of the needs of their clients was not helpful, because two wrongs do not make a right.

I also began to learn that computer professionals were not long satisfied with that nomenclature, and began to clamor for job titles that incorporated the word "information," perhaps after realizing from the writings of Daniel Bell and the advertisements of AT&T and IBM that this was the new "in" word.

All of this caught me a little off guard. I had always assumed that information was a term subsumed in what librarians did. However, we have learned that not only do many public definitions of libraries and librarians exclude the information process and particularly the computerized information process, but some librarians are also happy to rid themselves of such unpleasant distractions as database searching.

If, in a concentration on purchase and circulation, libraries are simply defined by the parameters of book supply, then this certainly makes our job simpler but unfortunately also steadily less significant. I have already suggested that document access and even document control will become increasingly clerical routines. The question is not whether we have the documents, but what we do with them to help others deal with concerns in which the physical book or article is only a transitory vehicle of communication. In a talk to British librarians almost 20 years ago I borrowed the term information intermediation. It was and remains a rather pompous phrase, but somehow it seems apt.

At Arms Over "Information"

The battleground has come to center on the word "information," and the M.B.A.s and computer types seem to understand this better than we do. We wouldn't need to fight turf battles for that word if we had taken better care of the earlier word "library" and not allowed it to mean anything anyone wants it to mean.

Library is still worth fighting for, but we probably need more than one arrow in our quiver. Even William Tell carried a spare. The phrase "library and information science" used in so many library education programs may mean nothing at all beyond what the school has done quite correctly all along. Or conversely, it may mislabel a very traditional, narrowly focused program, but it protects the territory better than the phrase "library science" because we have allowed others to define the word library and it is hard to find science in programs if they are seen as training exercises.

The phrase "information science" is for us a territorial stake, and we certainly have at least as much right to it as some of the others who use it. In academia in particular, good fences make good neighbors.

Librarian/Computernik Relations

Librarians and computer professionals could certainly work together in a relationship in which the latter understand that they provide important skills to allow us to carry out our defined and described objectives, but the alliance is not really a natural one. As librarians and security officers are almost instinctively enemies (one wants to expand access to information preferably without limit and the other wants to limit access to the extent of preventing it), so librarians and computerniks may march to the sound of different drummers if one group seeks to provide maximum human results and the other maximum machine efficiency. And that is not even the worst scenario, because when computer experts start dabbling in human efficiency they are in an area for which they have neither academic preparation nor instinct.

When librarians work under the supervision of computer professionals (and the scenario is increasingly found in special libraries and government agencies), the result may not be a happy one, not just because they don't know but because they don't know what it is they don't know.

More ironically, reporting to a management of computer specialists doesn't even assure the library of hardware and software support. Frequently, in a repetition of the old saw about the shoemaker's children lacking shoes, libraries may have the least priority because they have no bargaining leverage, and because the systems and computer people are swamped. They always are. Little wonder that many librarians have welcomed stand-alone micros that they can run and program without outside "help." That can work in small special libraries, but not in larger academic ones.

In academia, the issue of developing an accommodation between librarians and computer people must be faced rapidly, and indeed it may already be late in the game. The premise persists that information access is nothing more than computer access (incorrect and simplistic though it is). As some of us insist that our concern is only with acquisition and readiness and not with interpretation, and as we limit our emphasis to researchers to the exclusion of a whole cadre of academic managers, we will find ourselves on a collision course.

Corporations long ago began creating the position of vice president for information, and universities usually follow industrial trends, even if more slowly. In academia, librarians and computer professionals will both report in the empire of the VP for information, and if one of them has that title, the other one obviously does not. Indeed, the trend has started.

Battle Stations

The issue deserves serious analysis and the development of battle strategies, and it is therefore disturbing to see very little of either. The report of the Association of College and Research Libraries (ACRL) Task Force on Libraries and Computer Centers chaired by Richard Boss reported back in the September 1987 issue of *C&RL News* that even when library directors and computer facility directors report to the same immediate manager (true in half the cases), 38 percent of the responding libraries mentioned little or no cooperation or coordination, a figure that rose to 58 percent when all institutions were counted.

Eighty-six percent predicted that an administrative merger in the near future was highly unlikely, but that dropped to 64 percent when the time frame was extended to the next decade. We are now a good way into that decade since the publication of the survey. How are the 22 percent who consider an administrative merger likely in the future planning for this eventuality? And what have the 14 percent who expect it to happen momentarily done? Are they planning to be the bosses or the subordinates?

Three Years After

The ACRL survey is now over three years old, and it might be interesting to determine whether academic librarian perceptions of the relationship have changed. Perhaps, but I suspect not.

We librarians are often accused of lacking political sophistication, and we may be too preoccupied with the next round of scholarly journal invoices to find time for political bargaining. Nor is this really an issue of heroes and villains. Computer people are not evil manipulators, but they understand better than we that academia has no respect for what it considers service professionals (be they accountants, purchasing agents, computer center managers, or librarians).

The Road to Academic Acceptance

The only road to academic acceptance requires the seizing of the toll bridges that lead to information access for decision-making, because neither the faculty nor administrators can function without that. If they really understand that they need your unique expertise, they can learn to love you and even respect you.

Librarians and computer professionals are, in my view, on an inevitable collision course in academia, and there can only be one eventual boss. Computer professionals started in universities with even less of a respect base than librarians, because their field is younger. However, time is on their side.

Given that warning, perhaps librarians should recall Ann Landers's frequent counsel that it is time to wake up and smell the coffee.

Diversity Is Not Fragmentation: Building a Strong Whole from Many Parts

There is a tendency not only in industry but throughout society to adopt catchy and positive-sounding phrases without necessarily knowing what we mean by them. "Participative management" is such a phrase, and it has not been clearly defined, but is used as the speaker however chooses to interpret it. In the more recent management literature, TQM, or Total Quality Management, is the "in" phrase. It is a "good" phrase, in the sense that total, quality, and management are all words with positive connotations. What does it mean? Whatever the one who uses the phrase means for it to mean!

Diversity, the subject of this conference, runs the danger of becoming such a word, well received but inexactly defined. I have no desire whatsoever to demean or trivialize the intent. Both as a process of democracy and as a tactic for achieving national strength, the word touches on important, indeed crucial, issues and values. Any failure to protect individuals because they fail to resemble an accepted and expected norm deprives all of us of talents we cannot afford to waste, whether those talents are brought to us by women, by Hispanics, by Asians, or by individuals whose ancestry lies in sub-Saharan Africa.

However, the issue is, at least for me, larger than that. An insistence on diversity means an acceptance of the premise that others might approach issues differently, or might bring a different perspective to the issue, probably from a different original value system. As a manager for over 25 years, I know that a coterie of sycophant subordinates who constantly tell me how right I am are totally useless to me. I already know I am correct.

Keynote address at the 1991 Washington Library Association conference, Spokane, Washington, April 26, 1991.

What a manager needs are individuals who will dare to disagree and can explain why.

Thomas Watson, Jr., in his book *Father, Son, and Company*, wrote frankly about the problems created when people were reluctant to disagree with his father, who had founded and developed IBM. The son noted that the comfortable assistant or the nice person one likes to go to lunch with is a great pitfall in management. He was always looking for sharp, scratchy, harsh, almost unpleasant people who could see and tell him about things as they really were. The younger Tom Watson attempted throughout his own career as IBM president to urge a protection of "wild ducks," individuals who disagreed with the group conclusions. They might be wrong and often unpleasant. However, they might also be right, and their obnoxiousness might stem from the fact that they see truths that others do not. Watson knew, as indeed just about all of us know, that many great ideas come from people considered by others wild-eyed, impractical, and even crazy. No great new ideas have ever come from the committee process. Only safe and comfortable ones. However, safety and comfort are not the main objectives for the organization, even as they might be for individual members of the group, or even for the group itself.

And so, as I speak about the importance of diversity, and perhaps the pitfalls of misunderstanding what diversity means, in society at large, let me postulate first of all that we are ruthless squashers of diversity in our own libraries.

No, I don't mean diversity of cultural background, sexual preference, religious upbringing, and color of skin. These are, of course, important issues and problems, but I need not discuss this larger framework here, because I would be preaching to the converted and wasting our time. I am talking instead about our lack of tolerance for diversity of viewpoints in our libraries. We think that we strengthen the process of democracy through committees, but committees can be even more intolerant than the most intolerant individual. They steamroll their way over recalcitrants by labeling those who don't agree as uncooperative, unreasonable, and unhelpful, and these are far more damning indictments than the word "stupid." We have a great acceptance for "stupid," or "always late," or even "strung out on drugs." We have little acceptance for "does not get along well with others," and although a case can be made against needless obstinacy, we don't have any real way to differentiate that from obstinacy based on convictions or even based on facts.

Committees have both their uses and their misuses, and the obvious misuse is as a way to avoid decisionmaking and the taking of responsibility. In the short film *Meetings, Bloody Meetings*, John Cleese deliciously dissects the absurdities to which this exercise can degenerate. Librarians laugh at the film, which is still a favorite at our conferences, and then go home to do exactly what the film warns us about. There are all sorts of reasons for this in the way we were educated, trained, and dare I say brainwashed? Both the general management literature and the library management literature present to us the assumption that similarity of interests breeds contentment in the workplace. Perhaps it does, but in any case the price is too high, both in what we achieve for society and the organization, and in what we do to the individual in this coercement and regimentation we call the group process. It is interesting to note that as management writers speculate about the workplace beyond the year 2000, they stress not group empowerment but individual empowerment, with individuals possessing both authority and responsibility. It is then expected that these individuals will form themselves *voluntarily* into groups to allow them to do what it is that they as *individuals* need to do. These groups will not be edicted by management. They will be self-formed and self-disbanded when the need no longer exists.

There is danger in this process as we seek to be fair and to encourage diversity, but the danger is no greater, and perhaps less great, than it was under the old "group" process. We could rationalize, and did rationalize, under the "group" process, not hiring older people into a group of predominantly younger employees, not hiring women to interact with men or men to interact with women, or not hiring blacks or Hispanics into predominantly white groups. It was equally likely not to hire whites for what was seen as predominantly black groups. The possibilities are endless in all directions, although it is certainly true that some groups were more penalized than others. However, the potential for antagonizing somebody will always be there as long as group collegiality is somehow considered as a virtue beyond its contribution to the workplace. We must be careful about how we select and legitimize teams. The Ku Klux Klan is certainly a team of like-thinking individuals, and it wouldn't be nearly as united in its thinking if it promoted diversity.

The great enemy of diversity is the insistence on comfort and pleasantness, even to the extent of ignoring real reasons for being in the workplace. Responses to the case studies published in *Library Journal* by my colleague A. J. Anderson almost automatically focus on group happiness, or even the boss's happiness, and almost never on why we are here. The great hope, as we move toward the twenty-first century, is that worker teams will be selfish enough to accept personal violation of our preconceptions (and that means biases) if we perceive that the end result will be worth it.

The great enemy of diversity in libraries that I see is not blatant bigotry (although that can certainly still surface—and no race, religious group, economic group, or sex is exempt from potential bigotry), but rather our insistence on comfort and pleasantness for ourselves. Diversity, as I choose to define it, is not counted in numbers. It is tolerance (and I use the term in its broadest Unitarian sense, to mean not just toleration but acceptance as equally valid). Most of us are perhaps more committed to the principle than to its individual implementation, because we still argue that homogeneity of viewpoint is somehow good for the group. I would argue, and I suspect that Thomas Watson, Jr. would agree from looking at the present-day IBM, that homogeneity and happy consensus can be very dangerous.

Let me turn to the specific issues involving diversity, particularly as it applies to libraries and librarians. I will postulate first of all that part of diversity is simply a process of fairness and decency, of judging individuals based on their personal merits and not because of some preconceptions we have about groups. Are there generalized preconceptions about blacks, about working mothers, about WASPS, about suburbanites, about just about any group we can name? Of course there are, and we all harbor at least some, because we are not a blank piece of paper. Our friends, relatives, our readings, and our experiences have all created perceptions and expectations. Rather than deny them, it might be better if we guarded against using such ugly irrelevancies as the basis of what are likely to be stupid decisions.

However, diversity is a great deal more than that, particularly in this country that is composed of so many different groups unlike some other nations. That, I would argue, is really their loss and our strength. "Political correctness" is an ugly phrase, no matter by whom applied, because it seeks to coerce through guilt and intimidation. It has made the phrase "melting pot" an outmoded term, perhaps because it assumed that it somehow made everyone conform to an existing norm. However, in my experience that is simply not true. What has shaped this country is the fact that it has absorbed and assimilated a whole stream of immigrants. It has, to some extent, shaped them, but it has also been shaped by them.

My personal commitment is very strong here, because I am one of the contributors to the process of diversity, although my contributions may not be fashionable to acknowledge. I believe fervently that I learned a great deal from coming to this country at the age of 11 without any knowledge of American culture or English language, and I will be forever grateful. It is said that naturalized citizens have a greater appreciation of this nation than those who were lucky enough to be born here, and perhaps it is true. At the same time, I also believe with equal fervor that in some tiny way I also helped shape this country into something slightly different, and perhaps even better, than it would have been without me. I hope you will not begrudge me that belief, because it is a tenet of my faith that this is not only important, but also possible for everyone.

When I first came to America, I found no real tolerance for diversity and multiculturalism. As I gained a new identity as an English-speaking American (and I understood that living here obligated me to that effort), I also lost my identity as a German-speaking Austrian. Certainly I was right in understanding which of the two was more important, but I should not have had to choose. What I have kept, if you will allow a slight biographical diversion, is my love for classical music, so natural to any Viennese kid of my generation.

The process of diversity, as I would have preferred it for myself and now try to insist on it for others, is a process of both keeping the old and learning the new. Not one instead of the other. Both. Governor Mario Cuomo, a second-generation American, and a number of eloquent Hispanic American writers, have dealt with this dilemma. And, of course, much of it centers on language. I am sorry to have lost my proficiency in German, but I am immensely grateful that I was given no excuse for not learning English. If I had been offered an excuse, I might have taken it. My parents, to a large extent, decided that they did not really have to learn English, although they understood clearly that I did. And here the politicization of the process of language education threatens, in my view, to destroy the hopes and aspirations of newer Americans.

As I have said, I believe in biculturalism, as I believe in diversity of background. Diversity of background is important because it helps strengthen the whole. Diversity is not fragmentation. It still results in the building of a unified American whole, although different from what it would have been without the mix of contributions. I have very little patience with the political slogans that are sometimes foisted off on us. Is this a "white country" with "white values"? Statistically undoubtedly more so than anything else, but it is certainly a different white country from Sweden, as Sweden differs from Luxembourg. And, of course, our own country is changing, as the number of nonwhites increases. It is certainly different even now in its ethnic mix than it was 20, 50, or 100 years ago. It will be different in the future. Does that worry me? Not unless we try to bend it out of shape. Is my campus at Indiana University a "white" institution? Statistically, that is undoubtedly true, but what does it mean? What do I share with my fellow "whites" on the campus who are not of my religious and ethnic background, who are not naturalized citizens, who do not enjoy classical music, and who enjoy (as students may) cruising in cars on a Friday evening? I suspect that students, regardless of race, share much more with each other than they do with me, and I know that I share nothing with the individuals whose concept of culture is sitting at home in their undershirts guzzling beer. Those come in all nationalities, and I share nothing with them. I have not asked his permission for this comparison, but I am sure that I share a great deal with Bob Wedgeworth. Does that make Bob somehow a pseudo-white? How arrogant and how bigoted such an assertion would be!

As I believe in diversity and multiculturalism, I believe strongly in the advantages of bilingualism. Please notice that I said bilingualism, the luxury I was never afforded. I was forced to accept monolingualism, and, of course, that language was English. If I had to make a choice here that was the right choice, as Spanish would have been the right choice in San Juan and French the right choice in Paris. I don't think we should have to choose, but we do have to insist that all Americans learn English, no matter what else they speak and read. Not to please me. To ensure for them the economic opportunities to which they are entitled. Parents who deny their children the opportunity to learn English in this country are selfishly hindering their chances of success. I find that sad.

I learned English cold turkey, and I can attest that it is a painful way to learn a language. Certainly there are easier ways, and libraries can help immigrants learn English, because that is probably the best help we can give them. Because English is the most important language in the world? No, of course not, but because it is the operative language in this country, as Spanish is in Mexico and English is not. The process of learning a language is relatively easy for kids (who will learn it despite what may be their parents' insistence that they speak the "old" language at home), it is more difficult for older people. Here as well libraries can help, and the point we must make to immigrants is that learning the primary language of their new country is not an act of disloyalty to the old one.

As anyone who went through the process personally would, I have strong feelings about how a language can be learned. If it is learned simply as a "foreign" language, our new immigrants will speak English as poorly as those for whom English is the primary language learned French and Spanish. Berlitz learned a long time ago that the way to teach a language is by immersion. You don't just study English in English. You study math, history, and art in English. As a college teacher I see the difficulty foreign students have when they take remedial English classes, and then immediately revert to the more comfortable language when they congregate in the cafeteria. And they learn very slowly. I have been tempted to suggest that international students should never be allowed to room with other international students who speak the same language. It is amazing how rapidly you learn English when you are 11 years old and want to play baseball with the other kids.

Why am I so emphatic on the insistence that bilingualism not be allowed to become a form of substituted monolingualism? Because I know that without the common thread of a language we all speak, our diversity will avail us little, and we will become a Tower of Babel. Because I see examples of fragmentation all around us. I see it in Canada, where the issue of language has become a politically divisive distraction, a problem that is not getting better. My Canadian friends know that Canada is not a bilingual country. It is a series of monolingual sections, certainly in Quebec. In any case, bilingualism would not suffice if we speak only of English and French, because in Manitoba the second language might be German or Ukrainian, in Toronto it might be Korean, Chinese, or even Hungarian.

It would be presumptuous for me to suggest to my colleagues to the north that every Canadian should be required to be fluent in English as a price of citizenship, because the majority still does rule, regardless of what other language one might speak (and French is still the preferred language for poetry and love if not for international diplomacy). However, I need not look outside our own country to show what horrors fragmentation can bring when it is not diversity. I need only point to Miami. Miami has a white community (whatever unity that suggests); it has several black communities, including an American black and a Haitian, French-speaking black; and it has at least two distinct Hispanic communities, one distinctly Cuban, and that group closes ranks against other Hispanics. I think that if we are wise we can learn something from the way these groups now dislike and mistrust each other, although it may be too late for Miami itself.

Why am I so passionate about this issue? You already know it is in part because I consider myself a product of diversity, even as that diversity is not what present advocates have in mind. Nevertheless, I would insist that both from my background and the uniqueness of my views, I represent a tower of diversity for this profession. Think about it!

However, my greater concern is that terms like diversity, just as terms such as bilingualism and racism (a pernicious disease from which I have suffered, although I have heard it suggested that there can be no such thing as black racists), can become twisted and used for meanings that can even be the reverse of what was intended. I teach management, and I stress to my students that terms such as fairness, reasonableness, and cooperation are defined by each of us to mean exactly what we want them to mean. Diversity, and the strength through unity that diversity brings, are too important to allow us to play games with the terminology.

Let me give you an example of what I mean from my own experience with the bureaucracy of my own institution, which, I suspect, differs very little from many others. Indiana University, for many reasons including geography, has very few Hispanic faculty members. In order to help redress this inequity, the university set aside some funds that could be used for recruiting individuals who could help bridge that cultural and linguistic gap. I set myself the task of finding such an individual, and I found one—linguistically and culturally Hispanic, and a qualified teacher and scholar to boot. I was told that my candidate did not qualify, because he was Peruvian. Only Puerto Ricans and Mexicans counted as Hispanics. The individual who informed me of this ruling was the Dean of Latino Affairs, and he was Argentinean. Do we need to play these games? Can we afford to play these games?

This, then, is my message. Jesse Jackson has made the case for diversity eloquently. He stated at a Democratic national convention that America is not a blanket woven from one thread, one color, one cloth. He is absolutely correct. However, it is also important that what must result is a blanket, or we will be very cold indeed. Jackson did not stress this, so allow me to do so. The various threads must be woven into a blanket, and that requires both hard work and a plan. Otherwise, we have simply a basketful of multicultured threads. As we stress our diversity, it is also important that we identify and stress our unity. What is it that Americans share, and share uniquely, and that differentiates us from Swedes, Austrians, Mexicans, and Nigerians? There had better be something, or we will have no blanket and no country at all. There are examples to frighten us.

Librarians are wonderful weavers. In the March 1991 issue of *American Libraries*, Deanna Marcum and Elizabeth Stone describe the crucial role that librarians played at the turn of the century in teaching new immigrants about their new country and its values.[1] I came later, but I was a beneficiary of that library acculturation role, and I am grateful. I grew up in a city with population centers that were heavily Jewish, Italian, Irish, and black. That mix in New York City has now shifted, but the issues remain the same, and the library is the same. If I now see more blacks, far more Hispanics, and a more recent influx of Asians, does that really make a difference? I think not. The library system was wonderful to me, but I will argue, perhaps ungratefully, that it could have done more. It impressed on me the importance of English and taught me to function in it, and the books on the shelves taught me about the Civil War and the Chicago Black Sox baseball scandal, and all of that was crucial to my becoming an American. I even remember exactly when I stopped being a European and became an American. It was when I had my first English language dream. It was after I had been here three months, and exposed to my new language for three months. But I worked at it. I compare that to the chambermaids in Los Angeles whose English is worse than my Spanish, and I find by conversing with them in Spanish that they have been here 15 years. We have failed these people as a society by sentencing them to second-class jobs, no matter how willing they might be to be sentenced. Libraries have a role to play here, and perhaps they fail to aggressively pursue that role because they perceive it as somehow improper, although turn-of-the-century librarians had no such qualms. What I wish the library had done for me when I was a child was, ironically, something libraries now do much better. I wish it had also allowed me to keep up with my readings in German. If we are serious about diversity we must do both.

My concern and my emphasis is that there is no contradiction between a celebration of diversity and multiculturalism, and the recognition that from all of this we must create a unified whole that is uniquely American. I have no patience with terms such as white society and black society, because there are many different blacks and many different whites, and they have the right to be judged as individuals and not as members of some larger and irrelevant group label. Perhaps paradoxically, there was a time when other liberals believed this, too. I had no patience then with government-edicted segregation, and I have just as little patience with self-segregation. Quotas are evil, because quotas judge the irrelevant and not the individual. That was true then and it is true now, regardless of all the tortuous rationalizations.

Perhaps we can see what fragmentation leads to from one small country, Switzerland. Switzerland has three languages (four if you count Romansch). Despite the fact that any part of Switzerland can be reached from any other part by train in three hours, most Swiss are not bilingual let alone trilingual. They are stubbornly monolingual, because the education system requires very little more. However, there is a difference. The German speakers run the country, and the Italian Swiss, stubbornly locked into their customs and language in the canton of Ticino, pay a terrible economic price for refusing to learn German. What all of this means for us should be obvious. English, if I can finish with a terrible pun, will be the *lingua franca* for this country for as far as anyone can see. English varies from region to region, but correct English as used in business and universities has a common thread. Those who do not speak English, who speak it poorly, or who rationalize that some form of English such as "black English" is an acceptable substitute, will pay a terrible economic price.

And, even if they are willing to stumble into that trap without knowing, it would be unthinkable for us as a nation, and for us as librarians, to allow them to suffer such a sentence without at least speaking up. It is only when we accept that further responsibility that diversity becomes more than a gimmicky slogan, and a real strategy for strength and empowerment.

Notes

1. Marcum, Deanna B., and Elizabeth W. Stone. "Literacy, the Library Legacy." *American Libraries* 22, no. 3 (March 1991): 202-5.

Off-Campus Education
and Library Service—
Experiences and Observations

I am honored to have been asked to speak at your conference, and I am fully cognizant of the fact that many of you have far more experience in the distance delivery of library services than I have. My own involvement in this process is limited to library education. I will therefore talk primarily about that topic, and will attempt to generalize from my experiences and observations in this area to look at opportunities as well as potential concerns in the larger area of the delivery of all kinds of information services, certainly including but not limited to documents. Document delivery, as I'm sure we all recognize, is only the last and really the most simple and straightforward of the information flow processes, even as we frequently have difficulty in bringing it to fruition.

I came to Indiana University in 1975, after a 25-year career that encompassed special libraries, corporate and government information systems, including national information delivery systems, and the information industry. Except as a guest speaker, I had not really experienced the academic campus. I came to Indiana as a professor and as director of the Research Center for Library and Information Science, and later, from 1980 to 1990, I served as dean of the school. I think I can state without contradiction, because the statistics are there to support the claim, that during this period the Indiana University School of Library and Information Science had the most highly developed system of delivering educational materials to students not located on the main residential campus, through a combination of off-campus teaching by regular faculty members, the use of

Reprinted, with changes, by permission of the author and Central Michigan University from *The Fifth Off-Campus Library Services Conference Proceedings: Albuquerque, New Mexico, October 30-November 1, 1991*, pp. 311-317, compiled by C. J. Jacob, © 1991, Central Michigan University Press.

adjuncts, and the use of the Indiana Higher Education Television System (IHETS).

Much of this, of course, came from initiative and planning, but it also resulted from fortuitous circumstances. The Indiana University library education program is the only accredited one in the state of Indiana. Bloomington, as a residential campus, is located at some distance from where many of the citizens live. It is ideal for full-time residential attendance, but that does not work for all students, and it was quickly apparent that not only the present reality in 1980 but also developing demographic trends were shifting away from this form of educational delivery. And, of course, what applies to library science education also applies to the use of academic libraries.

Indiana University is fortunate that its structure consists of eight separate campuses that cover most of the state, and that it is a centralized administration under one president. This is not true of all states, where there may be many small but totally separate institutions that compete with each other. The operating philosophy here, "One university with eight front doors," may produce an architectural monstrosity but it is conducive to the development of off-campus delivery mechanisms. In addition, however, to the realities of financial concerns about fostering growth, we also took quite seriously our responsibilities to provide our unique products and services to all of the citizens of the state of Indiana. After all, the name of our school was and is Indiana University, and not the University of Bloomington.

The philosophy we developed included teaching courses on the Bloomington campus, teaching courses on all of the other campuses of the system, including the one in Indianapolis that, with 27,000 students, is almost as large, although other campuses have as few as 4,000 students and primarily undergraduate programs. We used regular faculty to teach in Bloomington, and we encouraged (and ultimately required) their teaching on other campuses through a process of release trade-off time (never overload, because that destroys the other aspects of academic value—including research). We also used adjunct faculty on both the Bloomington and on other campuses. These are usually library practitioners who, for a rather modest additional stipend, teach specific courses, rarely more than one per year. They do this because they want to help and because they enjoy teaching, not for the money. In general this works well, and indeed professional societies encourage library educators to use more adjuncts, perhaps because they do not trust us enough to teach "practical" things they believe we should teach. That, of course, opens up the whole Pandora's box of education versus training, about which I have written and spoken in other settings. I will summarize at this point only by saying that if we only train and not educate, we are not going to be much as a profession. Similarly, if academic librarians simply provide requested documents and do not concern themselves in the information process, then, no matter how well they do it, they will not have much of a professional identity, either. Supplying requested documents is a warehouse function.

In my experience the use of adjuncts has been highly successful, and student course evaluations indicate no discernible difference in their perception of quality of instruction. And yet, there are concerns, particularly with teaching off the main campus, that must be addressed. The first I have already mentioned. This is graduate education and not just training. Individuals who, no matter how well qualified, simply teach from the framework of what they do on a daily basis, the "how I run my library good" syndrome, are not acceptable. The syllabus for courses, particularly when the same course is taught by several people on several campuses, must be the same so that the educational outcome is the same. Teaching styles, of course, can and should differ. However, and particularly when students have taken a course that serves as a prerequisite to other courses, we must assure that students come equally prepared. At Indiana we do not have home campus full residency requirements. Almost all students spend at least one or two semesters, often in the summer, in Bloomington, although some are remarkably adept at avoiding that process. Because we send regular faculty members to them as well, the danger is minimized. Instead of residency requirements we control the process by a centralized decision over what courses we offer and do not offer. I insisted on centralized budgetary and administrative control over all non-Bloomington activities from the outset, in the realization that one of the expressions of the golden rule is that those with the gold make the rules. It had to be our program in terms of what courses to offer, and whom to assign to teach them. In essence, we simply rent space. With that as a framework, we were able to expand the program to two other locations that were not Indiana University campuses, but that operated in locations where there was no convenient Indiana University campus. One of these is the University of Evansville, a private university. The other is the Cincinnati Public Library. Why Cincinnati? Because there was no convenient and suitable location in southeastern Indiana, and Cincinnati is only 15 miles across the state line. We were not unmindful of the fact that this might bring us students from Ohio, and indeed northern Kentucky, as well as southeastern Indiana, and I will spare you the details of the lengthy negotiations with the Ohio Board of Regents. I will note only that our relationship between in-state and out-of-state fees (although we provide partial discount for out-of-state students) applies in Cincinnati as well. Ohioans in Cincinnati are out of state. The reason is simple. We expect that normally these students will enroll on two and perhaps more campuses. We want them to make this decision based on educational values, and not in the search for a tuition bargain.

Before I move to a description of our television courses, let me stress a point that I believe is crucial in all our determinations. The overriding concern is maintenance of quality. Distance education cannot be, and certainly need not be, an acceptable rationale for poorer quality.

That television system is a statewide operation, largely in the provision of equipment and other resources, that crosses not only campus boundaries (because all our campuses are funded separately by the state legislature despite central administration) but also institutional boundaries as well. We have not taught courses starting from any campus except Bloomington, and we have not to this point broadcast our courses to many sites outside our own university (such as Purdue University), but we could and probably will. My own experience here is limited to two courses I have taught over this arrangement, and the many others I have supervised in my role as dean, responsible for assuring that the quality of instruction is in no way diluted.

It is my observation that some courses are more suitable for this method of teaching than others. In particular courses that are largely lecture courses (and for example both mine and those of Dr. David Kaser are), are easier than if there is a laboratory segment (computer courses), or if there is constant review in the classroom. In these settings, but really for all courses, the provision of an on-site monitor in the classroom is essential. That individual can be a graduate student (such as a doctoral student or a junior professional, and, of course, in our field, doctoral students are already professionals). Classroom monitors are important for taking roll, for making sure that equipment works, for the distribution and collection of material, and perhaps most subtly to assure that the same kind of classroom environment and courtesy exist that would if the instructor were physically present. Students would not be reading a newspaper in my classroom, and I want to make sure they are not reading a newspaper in a distance education classroom. For their benefit, but also for the benefit of other students in the class.

In addition, we also employ a local coordinator on each campus, usually a part-time assignment for a librarian on the premises. This individual covers a myriad of duties—some routine, yet nevertheless all essential. This individual is concerned with course registrations that may be in Bloomington in absentia or may be local for the appropriateness of the classroom, for other physical facilities (we once found we had a classroom next to a band practice room and as they weren't going to move, it was essential that we could). Although we provide no-cost telephone contacts from all campuses to faculty advisors and the director of admissions, the local coordinator also serves as an advisor for the entire program, for students who sometimes don't come to Bloomington until well into their program if at all. We, of course, offer counseling on an equal basis to all students, but local students find it easier to take advantage of this opportunity. We could argue that for graduate students if a service is available that is enough, and then it becomes the student's responsibility to use it, but we try to take that extra step. In many cases the local coordinator knows the students and helps plan their curriculum program most directly, and this is particularly important to avoid the temptation, and it is a real temptation, to take a course just because it is conveniently available and because it counts toward the degree. Students will sometimes enter into unholy conspiracies, none of which will help them get the specific courses they're really out to get to meet their announced specialization. I have received petitions from a campus, asking for two elective courses—one on storytelling, the other on business literature. Both petitions have exactly the same 25 signatures, and, of course, that makes me suspicious. "I will take your course if you take mine." I recognize that this kind of "convenience" planning—taking courses because they fit a time slot—exists anywhere, but we try not to encourage and abet it.

This underlies once again the importance, as I see it, of running these educational programs as part of the overall school process, and not as dictated either by the local campus or by some centralized unit concerned with distance or off-campus education. What we do has a cost, and it is important that the process of employing monitors and coordinators not be shortchanged in the maximizing of "profits." This fact that we care about the total program and not performance in specific classes or on specific campuses has two immediate benefits. We truly do not care, as a school strategy, where the student takes the course. Financially it is all the same, and we can concentrate on what is best for the student. And we do not cancel classes once announced because of low enrollment. We understand that taking a particular course at a particular time is building a house of cards, and if you remove the assumed course that was the prerequisite for a future course, the entire plan collapses. We have taught courses with as few as four students, although it might, of course, teach us something about offering the course again. We, of course, have concerns about enrollment and cost, but those are for the program as a whole and not for individual courses. As an example, we look for an average of at least 12 students in each classroom, but we can accomplish this if a course in Richmond has eight students and a course in Fort Wayne has 16. In a decentralized setting the local authorities in Richmond would have canceled their class, and the authorities in Fort Wayne would have collected the money. More dangerously, Fort Wayne would have scheduled courses not based on need but based on projected enrollment only. How do I know? Because that is exactly what had happened before.

My insistence on total control over courses in my discipline was based on the stated threat that not only would we completely refuse to cooperate in such programs, but that our own quality control concerns would force us to refuse to accept these credit hours toward our degree programs. These would make the course largely worthless, and would in turn destroy their enrollment. In other words, it was our courses or none at all. Was that a bluff? No, it wasn't, but it was essential that I had first explained to my vice president and chief campus officer why he should support me: for the benefit of the educational process. There was another reason we succeeded, and this was really luck, but luck counts, too. Campus officials just don't get very excited about the potential benefits to them from library science courses, whether taught by adjuncts or over television. M.B.A. courses, by contrast, interest them greatly.

The point I want to stress is that while the expanded program in all of its formats was financially viable (our university budget office insisted on that), it was never intended as a money-making operation but as a break-even educational extension (and I insisted on that). Ultimately, because we had the expertise and the contacts with both instructors and students, it was our ball. Budget officers can sometimes bluster, but they can't teach anything.

In using television courses (and I know that Darlene Weingand at Wisconsin would disagree with my assessment that they work beautifully for some kinds of courses, with difficulty with some, and not at all for some), the most obvious advantage is the ability to use visual and graphic aids. Indeed, with proper planning such a course can be much more interesting than the rather normal practice of writing on blackboards and displaying overhead transparencies. This obviously requires that in particular at the displaying end, you work with a professional director and a professional staff, and that there is clear understanding of what is going to happen. We met each week three days before the class to discuss the class. We talked about guest speakers, camera angles, microphone requirements, and the visual displays we were going to use. For text material I found that if I gave them written copy they improved on it. That is their expertise, not mine. I was fortunate in having excellent and caring professional directors. Of course, if I hadn't had one, I would have complained, and I was pleased that one of these directors, in applying for a higher level job, used me for a reference.

The quality of TV reception is, of course, crucial, but that is not usually a problem. They have far more complex courses than ours—scientific experiments with visual impacts for one. Most of us just stand or sit there.

Two-way audio is, of course, essential, two-way video is probably not. However, the way two-way audio is provided is important. Having some central point in the classroom to which students can march to signal their desire to ask a question is simply too intimidating. Students have to be able to ask a question while they are in their seats, as in any classroom. In a recent visit to an IBM facility I saw an arrangement I really like. I recall the specific vendor, but I won't mention it because I am sure there are others. Depending on the size of the class there were one or more television screens. The microphones and signal buttons were arranged so that two students shared one piece of equipment located between them. We did not have this, and I was very conscious that some students in distant locations said nothing all semester long.

One last point in terms of negotiations with the TV director. Some directors prefer use of a small studio, with even local students situated in a separate classroom as though they were on another campus. I do not: perhaps I teach as an actor would perform. I want a live audience of students even as I have a distant audience. I want to see facial reactions, because I play off those. Most facilities have TV studios large enough to accommodate a class. They may find it inconvenient to set up that way, but it is certainly possible.

One final point of advice. Always make a tape of what you are sending. It may be only a backup in case of interrupted transmission (and that happens even in networks let alone instructional environments), but it may also have other uses. The cost is really minimal. It involves the cost of the tapes themselves, because making the tape usually just means hooking in a machine. If you like, you can erase the tapes once you are certain that transmission was uninterrupted, and use them again.

Use of this format requires more discipline from the instructor. It requires more formalized advance preparation and consultation with the director, and shipping material to be distributed in advance. Classes are likely to be much larger, when you add the students at all of the locations 80 is not unusual, and we have surpassed 100. All of this means that instructors who teach in this format have to be given some trade-offs. Not additional money, because this only detracts from their research responsibilities. Probably a reduced teaching load. In a total overall budget system it is easily possible. When you have 100 students in class, that income tuition allows you to spend money elsewhere, but only if the money is yours to begin with.

There must also be concern about support materials, particularly in the way of outside readings and references to be consulted. There is some flexibility here, but also some limitations. I would not offer a course on Literature of the Humanities at a small community college location; I probably would teach it at Notre Dame, and as dean I would ask the instructor to certify personally that the support materials were there. In libraries the use of reserves is easily accomplished through a cooperative reference desk, and that is why libraries are a lot better than empty stores. There are also some possible surprises. Children's literature courses are usually better supported in public libraries than in academic libraries, for reasons that must seem obvious. We also, in recognition of the fact that many of our part-time students have other responsibilities and show up for the class and only the class, make heavy use of distributed reading packets which we sell at cost. Fortunately, obtaining copyright clearance in the field of library science is not difficult.

For courses offered specifically on local campuses, we use a traveling reference collection moved from one campus to the next. Sometimes that is the base collection if the course is not offered that semester on the home campus, but usually it requires the purchase of duplicate materials. For TV courses it requires the purchase of lots of duplicate material, but think of all those enrollments! Because these are Bloomington courses and the University Library is responsible for supporting the instructional program, I have always held the library responsible for the cost of this process, although I am certainly willing to endorse and support its request for additional funds for this unusual purpose.

I should mention audiocassettes as teaching devices, if only to state that I don't care for them. Obviously they are not interactive, but if I am going to participate in a noninteractive process, I would prefer to read rather than listen. We read faster than others speak. Certainly, we could conceivably listen while we do something else, but then the question is of whether or not we concentrate. Let me just leave it, as an instructor, by stating that I am suspicious. To me, academic credit by home study or audiocassettes has severe potential drawbacks. Besides, that was an old technology, and not at all necessary any longer.

What does this experience as a teacher in library science suggest to me with regard to the provision of off-campus library services? If anything, it is that this process should be simpler. The technology is simple and in place. What may be missing is money, but I am a longtime adherent of the writing of Peter Drucker. It was Drucker who stated that in the question of offering a service that people truly want, cost becomes irrelevant. The issue is not cost. It is political justification.

I have spoken about this topic repeatedly in out-of-the-way places like Alaska and Wyoming, as well as to library groups indigenous to New Mexico. In all of these talks I insist that there is no practical, and certainly no insurmountable reason, to suggest that citizens of these locations, whether in public libraries or academic settings, should not be able to have the same kind of library access as residents or citizens of Boston or Cleveland, except for the ability to browse. Please forgive me for seeming simplistic, but I see no handicaps except for political barriers, and political barriers are eliminated whenever those who have erected them decide it is worth their while.

Bibliographic access has become literally instantaneous to any location that has electrical power or even a portable generator. It does not require a library at all, as the National Library of Medicine constantly reminds doctors. Document delivery does require some sort of centralized store from which to deliver, but the mechanisms are simple, ranging from the electronic to commercial delivery services like Purolator and even the good old Postal Service which also offers one-day delivery. Obviously for a price, but if you haven't heard me say that price is ultimately an irrelevancy you haven't been listening. The point is that document delivery from anywhere to anywhere within 48 hours is easy, within 24 hours or less possible. Where the physical library collections for document supply of already identified items will be is the non-issue of the next millennium and even the next decade, and if we refuse to deal with that reality somebody else will do it for us. We have come to depend on fax machines to such an extent that we can't remember how we did without them. E-mail is another example, although I find some excesses here in the use of e-mail for no real purpose whatsoever.

Technology, then, solves the bibliographic and document delivery problem as long as we are only dealing with specific requests for specific documents. Even here we have had options that an emphasis on tradition has perhaps caused us to ignore. Way back in 1975 I served as a consultant for the then planned Pahlavi National Library in Iran. That library never came to reality, for reasons you understand, although it could just as easily have been built by the next government, except for the suspicious approaches toward "Western" culture and information. In planning that library, the team of consultants recognized that interlibrary loan through the normal mail system—depending on roads, railroads, and airports—would not work in Iran. We designed a building with a heliport on the roof, with interlibrary loan service through helicopters. It was not a particularly startling thought, and the only thing I found startling is that many people considered it radically innovative. It would occur to me instantly that the best way to deliver interlibrary loan in Alaska, given the geography, would be by seaplane. Alaska has few roads and few airports, but many lakes. Fishermen certainly know the best way to get around in Alaska, why don't those concerned with moving documents?

One more example. Indiana is an institution in a group of midwestern universities called the Big 10, although now there are 11 of them. Indiana and Illinois, both major ARL institutions, are close enough to make an easy three-hour drive between the two routine. It has always occurred to me that the simplest way to handle interlibrary loan between the two libraries is not to mail or even fax requests and then mail requested books. It is to call the university travel office to find out what faculty members from our school are on their campus today. There are probably at least a dozen, who have room in their car for a little lone book, and would be glad to bring it back with them this afternoon if we just asked them. Why haven't we? Not as a favor to us, as a matter of academic courtesy to their colleagues. We could fax or phone the request, and then use the messenger.

For reference work, when users don't know specifically what they want, and this is the essence of our professional credit if it is anywhere, the issue is a little more complicated but not much more so. First of all, I note that in academia we tend to do very little reference work even for the people on our own campuses. There is a classic contradiction in value systems between education and information service—between an emphasis on self-help and on help, and we need to come to grips with that. We might want to ordain self-service in the information process for students because it is good for them, but there are limits to this. Don't try it with faculty or with administrators. One major university that sought to make faculty members self-sufficient by offering courses in online searching found very few faculty members in attendance. The faculty members had sent secretaries and graduate students. So much for the premise that faculty are just dying to do their own information work. Are you surprised? I'm not. My point is simply that if your programs to offer off-campus library services only go as far as document delivery, you are not doing the status of this profession any favors. You are not giving users what they really want, and if they haven't asked you it is primarily because they are sure you wouldn't do it anyway. Haven't you been telling them how swamped you are? Even more dangerous is the possibility that they haven't asked you for information interaction because they don't think you are smart enough.

The solution for library information work at a distance is, to me, the good old 800 number, available seven days a week, 24 hours a day. American Express has been doing it for a long time. If I can't sleep, I can always ask for a review of my account from somebody who is paid not to sleep. Think of what we could do with qualified librarians any time of the day or night, working with a local collection and with terminal access. They can answer your question directly, working with a local collection and with terminal access. They can answer your question directly or by getting back to you. They can send you material through a whole variety of delivery mechanisms—they can send you bibliographies, they can send you a whole combination of all of these. What is the problem, funding? Sure it costs money, but a nation that spends $50 billion on processed pet food annually can afford this. Besides, what are the alternatives? There are only two. Immense duplication of effort at exorbitant costs, or ignorance, planned and anticipated. Neither alternative is acceptable. And, indeed, this solution is so obvious that I can predict with confidence that somebody will do it. It just might not be us.

Our nation deserves not only an educational but also an informational system that is not restricted by arbitrary boundaries of geography. Such boundaries, in the present and evolving electronic era, are increasingly irrelevant. Ultimately people will get what they want and need, and if we don't do it somebody with an MIS background or a computer background will. That is bad for us, but also bad for the users.

The need is there. The opportunity is there. Our abilities are there. Do we have the courage and the conviction?

Meetings, Bloody Meetings

A recently published cartoon shows a vacationing couple reading a historical marker that proclaims, "It was on this spot that the leaders of the free world met and agreed to appoint a committee to study the situation." Cartoonists, who make their living assessing what their readers would find absurd and yet plausible, sense a perception that the committee process has run amuck. John Cleese of *Monty Python* fame has made a short film that bears the title of this column. That film is a favorite at library conferences. We laugh at the absurdity projected and then go home to participate in what may be equally absurd.

Librarians Find Meetings Fascinating

Our profession has a fascination with meetings, and if you have doubts, count the schedule in your next American Library Association conference program. Is it because our profession is so full of dynamic change that constant meetings to monitor it are necessary? Hardly. And yet support staffers have noted, with more detachment than acrimony, that they do all the work while the professionals attend meetings.

The comments I receive suggest that many of us resent these meetings, particularly if they are perceived as pointless and there is work piled up on our desks. However, these comments come to me in confidence because there is a perceived danger in attacking the concept and of being labeled uncooperative, not a team player, or opposed to the implementation of democratic principles. Such accusations would be devastating to career objectives, even as stupidity or laziness are very often forgivable.

The reader should not think that this column opposes the legitimate purpose of meetings. Indeed, proper matrix management—the establishment of temporary interdisciplinary work teams to deal with specific problems—has been shown to be

Reprinted, with changes, by permission of the author and *Library Journal* 117, no. 5 (March 15, 1992): 61-62. Copyright © 1992 by Reed Publishing, U.S.A.

highly effective in channeling the resources of an organization toward the analysis and proposed solution of a particular problem.

However, in that sentence also lies the constraint that many committees do not have. Project teams have a specific agenda. They have a specific life and target dates for completion. They are as small as possible because size becomes an inhibitor when it adds bulk but no insight. The question of what each individual uniquely and specifically brings to the process must be addressed in making committee appointments because committees are expensive.

In academic institutions, librarians may invest in the meeting process because that is what faculty do and we want to look like them. However, the comparison doesn't hold. Once faculty have met their classes, their time is their own, and attending meetings is a trade-off against the presumption of research and perhaps the greater likelihood of a round of golf.

In either case, the cost accrues to the individual. Librarians, by contrast, are forgiven none of their meeting time. The work still piles up, and it is either left undone with resulting frustration and burnout, or it is done at nights and on weekends with the same result. It was this unforgiving nature of the library's professional time assessment that led me, as a dean of a school that employed librarians as adjunct faculty members, to insist on paying them overload salaries for the extra time rather than "buy" their services from their library administrators. I understood quite clearly that there was no incentive for the instructors in such a process because their other work was never adjusted or forgiven.

Meetings Meet the Classics

The classic purpose of meetings is, according to the management literature, quite limited. It is for the examination and ranking of alternatives, and that is particularly important when the problem is interdisciplinary. The purpose of committees is not normally the making of decisions. That is a line management responsibility, acting on the basis of the recommendations received. Few managers would be willing to abdicate their ability to make decisions, and fewer still should, because they can and will be held responsible for all of the decisions made by subordinates, with or without their own participation.

It is a classic management principle that responsibility can be delegated but never abdicated. You get both credit and blame, and it would help if mayors, library boards, superintendents of schools, corporate managers, and university presidents understood that this basic management principle also applies to libraries. It is their excellent or their rotten library, and if there is no money for reference service or the book budget, they are as responsible for this as for crime in the streets.

Meetings can be used to seek advice, but here we know that discussion is much more facile in smaller groups and can become posturing politics with 20 or more in attendance. Nor are meetings necessary or useful for purely downward communication, if the decision has already been made and is not open to modification. The fascination with meetings is, of course, general and not unique to libraries.

Safety in Numbers?

Perhaps one reason is the assumption that committee action is safe because the greater number of individuals who share in what turns out to be a dumb decision, the less the likelihood that any of them will be punished. Unsuccessful baseball teams fire the manager because it is not possible to fire all of the players who can't hit or pitch. The safety of the committee process is also clearly seen by anyone dedicated to avoiding responsibility, and unfortunately the world is populated with individuals who want to be paid as managers but don't want to make decisions.

However, more important than my own speculations on the subject, Peter Drucker *is* no enthusiast for consensus decisions, either. In his recently published *Managing the Non-Profit Organization* (HarperCollins, 1990), Drucker writes:

> If you have consensus on an important matter, don't make the decision. Adjourn the meeting so that everybody has a little time to think. Important decisions are risky. Acclamation may simply mean that nobody has done their homework.

If there is a belief that consensus decisions reached in a committee are therefore good decisions, that assumption is at least suspect. It is also often postulated that committee deliberations are an exercise in democratic participation, and I suspect that may be the greatest attraction for our profession. However, the premise of democracy may be a delusion.

Committees can be ruthless suppressers of contrary, unusual, and dissenting viewpoints, and the pressure to agree to get along for the sake of the community can be brutal. If we recognize that most truly innovative ideas (some good and some bad, but that is the risk we must take) emerge from individuals willing to defy the conventional beliefs of their colleagues, and that it is precisely this uniqueness we must protect, then we begin to understand the dangers of a consensus process, a danger Drucker understands clearly.

However, there are even worse possibilities. When a manager has already decided what to do and uses committees simply as a cosmetic validation, then the committee members are trapped. They understand that their job is simply to agree, and it is these people—who find their time wasted and their minds manipulated—who are most angry. However, they are often also afraid to speak out, and the result is bottled-up anger and frustration.

There Is a Right Time for a Meeting

As a minimum, the scheduling of meetings should suit the purpose. Drucker reminds us that Monday morning, that most favorite time for meetings, is in fact the worst. We start with an assessment of what is already several days old. Drucker suggests that the practice of Monday morning meetings originated with Napoleon, but that was because Bonaparte liked to fight battles on Sundays in the expectation that enemy soldiers might get drunk Saturday night. Monday morning was for him, but not therefore for us, a good time to evaluate and assess.

Our best time, and probably that of any group of office workers, is Friday afternoon when we have some information about what happened during the week and when people might just be physically tired enough to prefer to sit down and talk. Meetings, we should also understand, stretch out until they reach a natural barrier. There are two: lunchtime and quitting time. A 9 A.M. meeting on Monday will last three hours because there is no point in starting anything else before lunch once two hours have routinely elapsed. By contrast, a 3:30 P.M. meeting on Friday will most certainly finish by 5 P.M. It will come at a time when there is something to discuss and when it might even keep some of the less conscientious from leaving early. However, even the most dedicated are ready to leave at 5 P.M., particularly when the carpool is waiting.

Individual Empowerment vs. Autocracy

I don't want to be misunderstood. There is a great and welcome new movement away from autocratic management toward individual (not committee) empowerment, an empowerment based most directly on expected contribution toward the organization's objectives. This empowerment ignores method and concentrates on results. Historically, managers have frequently stressed method over achievement (do it the way it is supposed to be done, or perhaps the way I have always done it). That is seen as counterproductive, but committee approaches, which stress pleasant and cooperative behavior, also emphasize style over substance.

I have never had much patience with what I see as a sham approach, and it will not surprise the reader that my management heroes include successful curmudgeons such as Winston Churchill and Hyman Rickover. However, and more to the point, the management emphasis of the 1990s stresses individual contribution to organizational objectives and does not award style points as is done in figure skating. That is why job titles such as coordinator and facilitator are the death traps of the coming decade.

Delegation of Duty

As with most management emphases, this is nothing new, only a rediscovered value. It has always had a name, generally lauded but rarely implemented. It is called delegation—allowing individuals their own style and freedom provided that organizational objectives are met. There is no inconsistency between this and the building of teams. Free to choose, individuals will usually form teams for greater effectiveness and achievement, but it is their own team and not management's. Management's job is the providing of clear directions and support through encouragement, requested advice, rewards, and necessary tools and resources.

It is at this juncture, and not because of management style, that librarians most often fail. If we lack objectives that are tied to resources and are achievable, then an emphasis on success through a focus on style as an end in itself is mischievous even as it is cheap.

It continues to be true, in libraries as elsewhere, that motivated, empowered, and supported individuals will succeed even in the face of an imperfect organizational or committee structure. No structure can bring success when people are disheartened, confused, and mistreated. The quality of a library, as of any other organization, is not in its holdings, its building, or its circulation; it is in the quality of its staff. Believe it, because until you do, you will never get outsiders to believe it.

The Reference Librarian as Information Intermediary: The Correct Approach Is the One That Today's Client Needs Today

As I observe reference service taught as a required course in accredited library education programs, I see a heavy dose of exposure to a variety of reference tools and sources framed in something of a vague concept that this is what we do as service professionals. Specialized and advanced reference courses tend to concentrate on more sources of material, usually separated into subject fields such as the sciences, social sciences, and humanities, and also into types of materials containing the reference work we seek, such as government publications, prints, photographs, and microforms. There appears to be little discussion about the various kinds of reference clients we might encounter, or the suggestion that different customers might have different levels of required information interaction. Indeed, the suggestion heard increasingly that we stop teaching courses oriented to types of libraries and concentrate on a generic whole, while perhaps desirable from some standpoints, would tend to obliterate those distinctions even further and substitute some sort of generic heading called "reference in any kind of library." However, there is little discussion about what constitutes adequate levels of reference service, only about the need to answer correctly in whatever framework is provided. The issue of adequacy of services is relegated to the discussion of library budgets rather than to professional considerations, and ultimately reference service results from decisions made by nonlibrarians who control our resources, but who have no basis for making such decisions except for a preference for spending as little as possible.

Reprinted, with changes, by permission of the author and *The Reference Librarian* 37 (1992): 23-35. Copyright © 1992 by The Haworth Press, Inc. All rights reserved.

We speak then of quality, but never within a framework of adequate resources or of approach, and rarely with a thought to determining what that should be.

It was not until my own career as a special librarian, and the opportunity for private tutorials from such intellectual giants in our profession as Mortimer Taube and Hans Peter Luhn, that I began to understand that whether we want to emphasize quality of subject analysis to make reference work simpler and largely a self-service process, or whether we prefer quick and dirty subject analysis and a concentration of sophisticated search strategies, is an option that requires serious discussion. It rarely receives consideration. Both strategies are heavily influenced by the availability of technology, although sophistication of search logic and the ability to search massive databases at a nominal cost are still more technologically sensitive than the process of subject analysis by a human being on a one-to-one basis. A case can be made for either alternative. In the first instance, we invest in an analysis process to save time at the search end where time pressures can be greater, although the existence of backlogs in subject analysis that suggest that subject headings will be perfect when and if they ever get done, also enters into the equation. An emphasis on sophisticated search strategies has the economic advantage of not "wasting" time and resources on items for which nobody will ever want to look, and there are studies that tell us that there are indeed such items.[1] Was the effort expended on subject analysis then wasted? The answer is often in the same framework as the response to a suggestion for weeding never-requested material. Somebody might want to see it tomorrow. However, the statistical probabilities from operations research are very clear, so that we do know that material not used in the first year is not likely to be used ever in the future either.[2]

The process of information intermediation, which I would argue pragmatically is the ultimate payoff in any reference interaction—did what we gave you help you?—runs into a number of barriers. Some of these originate with the patron, who brings varying levels of confidence in the ability of the reference librarian to understand let alone service the request. It has been long observed by reference librarians and teachers of reference that what we call the reference interview is necessitated by the recognition that the user frequently does not ask us what he or she wants to know. Librarians are asked what the user thinks we can understand, and usually this is at a generic level below that of the real request. They present us with simpler questions because they think we would not understand the real question. It is a phenomenon that can have formal names, but one of my students quite accurately calls it "dumbing down" the question, presumably to our assumed level of dumbness. Confidence in the reference process then obviously depends on the two individuals involved in the interaction, and that is a highly personal interaction even if the two have never met before. When librarians act as though all users are interchangeable (just ask whomever answers the phone or happens to be at the desk), we build bureaucratic barriers that may be almost impossible to overcome. In one of my consulting assignments, a corporate chemist served by a special library expressed enthusiasm about the reference abilities of his favorite librarian, whom he always consulted whenever he had a question. Puzzled, I pointed out to him that the woman was not a reference librarian, but rather a cataloger. His response, and I have since concluded the totally correct response, was "I don't care what her title is. She is my reference librarian." Edward Strable, then Head of the Information Center of the J. Walter Thompson advertising agency Chicago office, reported to my students that retired employees now living in Sun City, Arizona, and Sarasota, Florida, still called their favorite reference librarian at JWT in Chicago with reference questions that could undoubtedly be handled by the public libraries in their cities. I assume that now that he is also retired, Ed Strable does the same thing.

I can certainly attest that in my own university library there are reference librarians to whom I will entrust a question and others to whom I will not. It is a combination of trust built on prior experience and of perceived attitude. Do these individuals see my question as an opportunity or as an interruption from other duties? As long as an acceptable candidate is available for me within an acceptable time frame, I have no problem. A problem only arises when there is no reference librarian available within the necessary time frame to whom I can entrust my question.

I offered a management seminar recently at a large municipal public library, where a "problem" was presented to me. Telephone reference callers, or individuals walking into the library, were sometimes reluctant to deal with the person who happened to be on duty. Instead, they asked to speak with specific reference librarians, who were not on duty at the time. I was asked how such patrons could be persuaded to conform to library schedule; I suggested instead that this was not a problem but rather a compliment. It became a problem only if there were no reference librarians to whom the client was willing to speak. I asked the group how many of them were willing to be served simply by the next available beautician or barber, and whether they ever chose a longer check-out line at the grocery because they like or trust that particular clerk. I know that I do, and that does not even involve a professional interaction of significance. Managers might like to know the popular and unpopular reference librarians, and it might even suggest management actions for them, but that is another issue.

If the process of information intermediation requires the development of one-to-one trust, then why is it that only some special librarians seem to notice? Special librarians in the Indiana Chapter of the Special Libraries Association reported in an informal survey that their biggest problem concerned communication with users, and not budgets, staff, materials, or space. Communication problems, as we know, can defeat the reference process no matter how well intentioned the librarian. At least part of the reason for the problem is one I have already suggested. We subsume what is an intensely personal interaction in a maze of bureaucratic rules and procedures. It is totally absurd to set limits on how long a reference librarian may work on a question without considering the question. Some can be handled to the complete satisfaction of the need in one or two minutes, others can take two hours or two days. Is this wrong? Only if budgets drive programs rather than programs driving budgets, and that generates nonsense before we even start. The amount of "correct" reference service is a process that seeks its own level, but it should be noted in all fairness that good reference work leads to more reference work. However, can there be a better justification for budget increases? Or should we offer poor service in the certain knowledge that dissatisfied clients will not return, and therefore ease our budgetary pressures?

I would hope that no library administrator would consciously choose this strategy, although I suspect that many do indeed peg the level of service to budgets, rather than the other way around. The larger issue may concern some level of discomfort at performing reference work at all, because the premise of the library as a *service* institution is confused with the premise of the library as an *educational* institution. Indeed, the two are almost directly contradictory in the strategies they suggest. Which of these models should a given library adopt? It depends on the library. School libraries may be virtually all education with very little information intermediation service. Special libraries, and particularly corporate libraries, are almost completely at the other extreme. Public libraries must do both, certainly the first as part of a transferred responsibility they accept from the school system, unfortunately rarely with either funds or credit. However, adult patrons are not in the public library to be educated, unless they tell you specifically that is why they are there. They are usually there to be served when they approach the reference desk, and pointing them in the general direction of a stack section, a card catalog, or a terminal, is not reference work. The issue can be generalized. In supermarkets, when I tell a clerk that I have been unable to find a product supposedly on aisle five, I do not want to be reassured that this is where the product assuredly must be unless, of course, the store is out of stock. I expect the clerk to drop whatever he is doing and come look, and I will complain to management about the attitude of any clerk who offers less. Should I expect less from librarians, whose commitment to a service ethic is presumably of longer standing?

The really fascinating dichotomy is found in academic libraries. These certainly have students, and we are presumably only supposed to help them help themselves, but up to what point? Bibliographic instruction is the process designed to help eager young students to become self-sufficient for the rest of their lives, or at least until they graduate. However, I suspect that our enthusiasm for this goal may cloud any sort of realistic evaluation of how well the process works. I know that I do not care for how-to instruction in the abstract, the tactic employed in computer training. I prefer to be helped to solve specific and real problems as I encounter them, and if that instruction is useful I will be able to solve *that* problem myself the next time I encounter it. However, I will be back, because I will ask for the same kind of assistance the first time I encounter a different kind of problem or question, and I want to be helped quickly because that problem is now a roadblock for me. Are we so certain that this is not what students would prefer, and is there anything wrong with that preference? At a minimum, should bibliographic instruction not also include a component that alerts students to their rights and legitimate expectations in dealing with reference librarians, at this university and for the rest of their lives? Special librarians can attest to legions of corporate employees who expect no professional interaction because they were never offered any while they were students, and who do not even know that reference assistance is their right. They must be weaned to the reference interaction.

It is in dealing with faculty at the university level that the opportunity to provide reference service really breaks down, and it breaks down because of the assumption of three generally fallacious scenarios. The first is that all academic faculty are busily engaged in research. A number of articles by Ladd and Lipset in the *Chronicle of Higher Education* argue that only a small percentage of faculty at even major research universities are involved in original research.[3] Many others are simply milking for publication the research they undertook to obtain their doctorates. Confirmation of this judgment comes from data compiled over the years by the Institute for Scientific Information in Philadelphia for its citation indexes and the author address directory compiled from the articles covered in these and other publications, *Who Is Publishing in Science* (WIPIS). An astonishingly large number of individuals publish in one year but not in the next, and many of them publish once and never again.

In his own writing and research, the librarian and humanist scholar Charles Osburn dispels the myth that faculty are primarily basic researchers seeking raw material through which to sift, and that belief constitutes the second largely fallacious assumption.[4] Osburn notes that scientists long ago shifted their style of research to the patterns established by government contracts and grants. These involve not a search for knowledge but a validation of hypotheses established in obtaining the money. These are at best applied researchers, and they seek not so much raw data as proof in support of the conclusions already announced. The search for proof is a much narrower search. Osburn concludes that this pattern of information searching, always prevalent in industry, has now spilled, under the influence of similar conclusion-validating grants, from the physical sciences to the social sciences and even into the humanities. Entire disciplines of academic study have now sprung up for the simple purpose of developing proof for what the researchers stated long ago they knew. What this may suggest is that library practice in academia, which largely consists of shoveling large quantities of raw material at the faculty, may be serving a research style now increasingly rare.

The third fallacy is the assumption that faculty enjoy the process of searching through the literature for nuggets of information. Some undoubtedly do, but others abdicate and assign that process whenever they can to graduate assistants and even to others less qualified. It is this fallacy that primarily drives our insistence that end users ought to do their own database searching because deep inside they really want to, although it is, of course, possible that for some library administrators the argument simply serves as a convenient rationale for reducing exposed library costs by shifting them into other cost centers. Failing to consider what this does to *overall* institutional costs is irresponsible, but it is also considered financially prudent by managers who deserve little professional respect from any of us.

However, to the extent to which this is simply a case of honest self-deception we have plenty of help. Government agencies such as NASA and NTIS aim their programs at end user searching rather than at librarians, and we can understand the strategy when we realize, as government officials certainly do, that supplying information directly to engineers, scientists, economists, and business executives is more attractive to the

Congress as a funding justification than a program that supplies information to librarians. The National Library of Medicine, although its name suggests a library serving other libraries, has developed an ambitious strategy aimed at freezing librarians out of the information intermediation process entirely, by gearing its program development directly to physicians through initiatives entitled "Loansome Doc" and "Grateful Med." The role that this tactic reserves for librarians is the old warehousing and supply room role, for which NLM understands nobody gets professional credit, and that is why they would rather we do it. Never mind the overwhelming evidence that physicians do not, in general, like to undertake literature searches, and that they conduct them badly and expensively. We are not talking about quality here, we are talking about politics.

Database vendors, whose interests are quite naturally served not by fewer and better searches, but by more and sloppier ones, have even begun to amend their pricing strategies to lure end users. This is done by not charging directly for connect time (a process that rewards tightly controlled professional crafted searches), but by allowing new users to dabble at a relatively low cost.[5] Of course, once they are in the net the pricing ploys can change, as they have before.

The strategies of government agencies and commercial database vendors are reported without rancor, and even with some admiration for their understanding of both political and economic realities. Libraries are not seen either as powerful clients or as affluent ones. Better to bypass them as completely as possible as decision makers, as scholarly journal publishers have also learned to do.[6] What is less clear is why librarians would see merit for themselves in such a strategy, or for their users. As academic libraries have started training programs to teach faculty members how to do their own end user searches, they find that to a great extent faculty members do not attend the training sessions. Instead, they send their laboratory assistants, their graduate students, and sometimes even their secretaries. Corporate special librarians have known for some time that the process of information gathering and analysis is not a particularly sought-after activity, and is quickly shifted to clerks.

I have no doubt that librarians *could* play a major role in the information gathering and analysis process that shapes information intermediation. They fail to do so perhaps because the faculty, like users of the public library, do not trust them to understand the question. That lack of trust is heightened when they can not even differentiate the librarians from the student workers. However, they also sense that we are not particularly anxious to undertake reference work, in part because we claim to be understaffed and underfunded, and in part because it appears to them that there are other things we would rather be doing. Our clients will not fight about this with us. As demonstrated long ago by Calvin Mooers, they will adapt to and rationalize an inefficient information process rather than insist that the process adapt to their preferences, because that is simply too much trouble for them.[7]

I conclude that, despite our protestations, we generally do not like to do reference work, and that may go all of the way back to the premise that the primary role of libraries is education and not information, and that we do not want to do the work of "lazy" people for them.[8] That is a serious charge to make, but I submit there is evidence. "If you can find what we have in our collection and available on the shelf, then you may have it. If the material is charged out, or at the bindery, or simply missing, then that is your bad luck, and we will certainly not seek to obtain another copy of what we already own, just because we can't supply it today. In addition, if you are so presumptuous as to ask for something we have not purchased, we will charge you for the privilege of waiting while we obtain it for you. Of course, that process may take quite a bit of time." Is that our credo? There is something very backward in such a value system if we truly profess to concentrate on user information need rather than on bureaucratic convenience for ourselves. Perhaps we ought to adapt some version of the model governing Chinese medicine, under which patients pay their doctors when they are well, and stop paying them when they become ill, to give the physician an incentive for curing them. If we adopted this, there might be a fee for service but only if we provided it correctly and promptly, but there would be both a qualitative and time cross-over by which, after a while, we would have to pay the client a forfeit for our lack of performance. Some people might come to the library just to get rich.

If I suggest that our value systems do not esteem the value of reference service, it is because I see us adopting a value system that leads into almost directly contradictory directions. What we measure is not quality but quantity, as typified in academic libraries by holdings, and in public libraries by circulation. The most successful transaction is perceived to be the one that leads the user out the door with the greatest number of items; but I restate the obvious when I note that this is at best an educational and never an informational value system. Under the latter, less information, provided it is the correct information, is almost always preferred. I see this when I tell special library consultation clients that the upgraded and improved library will obtain and access more databases for their enlightenment. A look of panic comes over their faces, because they remember that they already have more materials from the library than they have hope of ever looking at, and all I seem to be promising them is more disaster. I quickly reassure them that the purpose of additional information access sources is not to provide more information but rather better information, and that it is not unlikely that the better a question is handled by the library the fewer the resources that need to be consulted by the client. Has any librarian ever attempted a management report that conveyed the *good* news that circulation had decreased, and that this clearly demonstrated that we were interacting with our users more effectively? I doubt it. The management structure, which makes circulation a part of reference, almost automatically suggests that more reference and more circulation are symbiotically related. I wrote more than a decade ago that proactive information service largely meant telling the client to stay out of the library and to concentrate on what he or she did well, while allowing us to concentrate on doing what we do well, to everybody's benefit.[9] Indeed, in an idealized information service the user does not have to ask at all, because we have anticipated the question. Selective dissemination of information services is the first cautious step in that direction.

All of the foregoing discussion still does not address the reality that there are many kinds of users, with many different information approaches, all equally valid. In a talk presented at a meeting of the International Federation for Documentation in Copenhagen, Herbert Brinberg suggested at least three kinds of users for library and information services.[10] The first group consists of traditional basic researchers, who ask for nothing more than large piles of raw materials that they will then sift, either because they enjoy the process, or because they trust nobody else to understand what they really need. In the communication shorthand of my industrial consulting, I refer to these people as classic German chemists, both because that is how these people were trained, and because every company has at least one. Brinberg's second group includes applied researchers, development people, marketing professionals, and engineers. These individuals are looking for specific answers to specific questions, and not for sources that *might* contain the answer. These people are heavily served by special librarians, and serving them correctly requires, as Grieg Aspnes has so eloquently put it, "assuming their stress and their burden onto your own shoulders."[11] For these users reference work means leaving the problem with the librarian, and either coming back for the answer, or having it sent. Academic librarians have problems with such a process, quite aside from the requirement for a large reference staff. What do these lazy people learn from such an experience? That, of course, is the old educational model. However, do not believe that there aren't users in academia who would not welcome such an interaction. They just do not find us very hospitable.

Brinberg's third group consists of executives and managers, who are looking neither for raw data nor specific answers, but rather for options. What are the choices, and what are the pros and cons of each? Don't tell me about things I can not do anyway! That represents a process of information intermediation, and the managers and executives who require this information are potentially our most powerful clients, most particularly in academia where the number of managers has proliferated. However, these are nonclients, because we tend not to serve them at all, and they do not even have a clue that we could or would help them. Is it any wonder that the academic value system treasures collections—the *library*—but not necessarily its professional staff—the *librarian*? Have we given academic administrators any reason to feel differently?

Parts of the Brinberg hypothesis are confirmed in an excellent recent Indiana University School of Library and Information Science doctoral dissertation by Thomas Pinelli.[12] He examines the use of NASA scientific and technical reports by engineers and scientists and finds patterns quite similar to those suggested by Brinberg. My own experience at NASA as Executive Director of its Scientific and Technical Information Facility in the 1960s confirms this as well. As part of our information program we constructed more than 600 selective dissemination of information (SDI) profiles for a variety of NASA administrators, scientists, engineers, and contractors. These profiles were drawn from the terms of the *NASA Thesaurus*, which was used for indexing all of our documents. We originally assumed that the users themselves were best qualified to draw up their own profiles, and thereby frame their own questions. We were wrong, as those who insist on the presumed quality of end user searching have been wrong since. These users certainly believed they knew what they wanted to know, but they had no ability to phrase their request either into search terminology or into Boolean search equations. Their questions led to poor and expensive searches, and it is this expense that database vendors now seek to "forgive" to lure end users into the process. We found at NASA that it was best for the users simply to talk to us or to write us a paragraph or two describing what they needed to keep abreast about. From this we constructed the search profiles. We also found that some users had a great deal of tolerance for document announcements that did not interest them as an acceptable price for making sure that they missed nothing. These are our basic researchers, and my "German chemists." Others did not care what they might miss but became enraged about even one notice they considered irrelevant and that wasted their time. We adapted to both preferences, without judging the requesters. There was a third group that stressed convenience over information to an even greater degree. These individuals specified that they wanted to be informed only about items written in English, regardless of the subject. Their rationale was simple. First, they already had more to read than they had time to read. Second, they did not want to be made to feel guilty about material that they would not be reading in any case. These characteristics have some similarity to those of individuals who do not want to be given any facts that contradict the conclusions they have already reached, and that group may include the greatest number of our clients, even in research universities.

None of this was true information intermediation, a process in which we would tell users not only what to read, but perhaps even more importantly what not to bother to read. That last concept was proposed many years ago by Alvin Weinberg of the Atomic Energy Commission.[13] Weinberg's suggestion, echoed by Garvin,[14] was for information analysis centers staffed by fellow scientists, or perhaps fellow economists, who would decide what others needed to bother to read. Weinberg's innovative idea has never taken hold, but it is significant for us to note that he did not trust librarians with this task. He did understand, as we need to understand, that most of our users are not looking for more information. They are looking for less, but better, information. Until and unless reference librarians are able to adapt to this, and until librarians can measure something other than quantities of transactions, much education of both librarians and users remains to be done if they are to work together optimally.

Ours is a service profession, and that means that we need to bring our unique skills and preparation—both managerial and technical—to a process of user information service. What that process of interaction turns out to be is the result of negotiation, and that negotiation is ultimately based not on our preconceptions, but on what users really need in order to get on with the rest of their lives. The need will vary depending on the problem and on the user, and I have suggested in earlier writings that users are not necessarily qualified to make that judgment, certainly not all by themselves.[15] What users need is not necessarily what they say they need, and certainly not always what they say they want. We should not blame them for that inaccuracy. Users bring with them preconceptions about the library, about us, about what we are capable of doing, and about what we are willing to do. I begin my interview process for clients of a corporate library, for which I am trying to determine the appropriate level of activity, by urging these individuals not to think about the library, and not to think about what might or might not be reasonable to ask of the library. I will tell them all that soon enough. What I want them to tell me is how, in an idealized environment of their own creation, they would like their information support services to function. It is hard to get this out of them. They feel foolish, they feel embarrassed, they feel selfish. But why? Is that not the question we should be asking them, in all information service settings? Have we beaten initiative and spunk out of them already, by our tales of overwork and the ethic of self-service, and have we subtly suggested that they are lucky to get anything at all?

One thing seems certain to me. Many of the functions now performed in all libraries, but particularly in academic libraries—functions such as document identification, document delivery, overdue notices, interlibrary loan, even cataloging—will become increasingly computerized and clerical. We have little professional future in these transactions. Our future is in the process of proactive reference work, of information intermediation, aimed not at validating a library policy but at the specific and unique needs of the person who just contacted us. And what that person needs may or may not simply be a book or even an article. However, whatever it is, that becomes our job.

Notes

1. Kent, A., et al. *Use of Library Materials: The University of Pittsburgh Study.* New York: M. Dekker, 1979.

2. Trueswell, R. W. "Some Behavioral Patterns of Library Users: The 80/20 Rule." *Wilson Library Bulletin* 44 (January 1969): 458-461.

3. Ladd, E. C., and S. M. Lipset. A series of articles written periodically for the *Chronicle of Higher Education*.

4. Osburn, C. B. *Academic Research and Library Resources: Changing Patterns in America.* Westport, CT: Greenwood Press, 1979.

5. Spigai, F. Observations in a chapter on information pricing prepared for publication in volume 26 of the *Annual Review of Information Science and Technology* (ARIST).

6. White, H. S. "Scholarly Publishers and Libraries: A Strained Marriage." *Scholarly Publishing* 19, no. 3 (April 1988): 125-129.

7. Mooers, C. "Mooers' Law, or Why Some Retrieval Systems Are Used and Others Are Not." *American Documentation* 11, no. 3 (July 1960): 204.

8. White, H. S. "The Role of Reference Service in the Mission of the Academic Library." In S. H. Lee, ed. *Reference Service: A Perspective.* Ann Arbor, MI: The Pierian Press, 1983, pp. 17-30.

9. _____. "Growing User Information Dependence and Its Impact on the Library Field." *ASLIB Proceedings* 31, no. 2 (February 1979): 74-87.

10. Brinberg, H. R. "The Contribution of Information to Economic Growth and Development." In V. Ammundsen, ed. *Proceedings of the 40th FID Congress, Copenhagen, 18-21 August, 1980.* The Hague: Federation Internationale de Documentation, 1982, pp. 23-36.

11. Aspnes, G. Remarks quoted in H. S. White. *Managing the Special Library: Strategies for Success Within the Larger Organization.* White Plains, NY: Knowledge Industry Publications, 1984, p. 8.

12. Pinelli, T. E. "The Relationship Between the Use of U.S. Government Technical Reports by U.S. Aerospace Engineers and Scientists and Selected Institutional and Sociometric Variables." Ph.D. Dissertation. Indiana University School of Library and Information Science, 1990.

13. U.S. President's Science Advisory Committee. *Science, Government, and Information.* Washington, DC: Government Printing Office, 1963. (The Weinberg Report).

14. Garvin, D. "The Information Analysis Center and the Library." *Special Libraries* 62 (January 1971): 17-23.

15. White, H. S. "The Use and Misuse of Library User Studies." *Library Journal* 110, no. 20 (December 1985): 70-71.

The Double-Edged Sword of Library Volunteerism

The role of volunteers in the structure of American institutions is a crucial and an honored one. Without volunteers, we would have no scouting or Little League programs; symphony orchestras and opera companies would be in even greater difficulty than they already are; and hospital patients might miss out on the books, magazines, mail, and flowers that delivery by volunteers provide. Like most readers of this column, I have worked as a volunteer—in my case, in scouting. There is no reason that public and school libraries should not also benefit from the additional support that volunteers can provide.

However, while the role of volunteers is crucial and deserves respect, it also requires a clear understanding of what volunteers do and, just as importantly, what they cannot do. My wife's role as a museum docent does not make her a curator, and in the absence of curators, museum galleries are sometimes closed. Volunteers do not need to trespass to be appreciated or feel important. It is no insult to them to be differentiated from the regular staff. Indeed, they usually wear distinctive uniforms and badges, not to be humiliated but to be honored.

Volunteers and Libraries

When I visit local public libraries I can tell who is doing what, but many patrons cannot. In academic libraries not only students but senior faculty may assume that anyone who works in a library, including the sophomores at the circulation desk, must be a librarian. Why are we so loathe to differentiate? Is it democracy, a sense of modesty, a lack of unique and professional pride? Our British librarian colleagues append their degrees to their signatures; we don't. We can see the reluctance to identify

Reprinted, with changes, by permission of the author and *Library Journal* 118, no. 7 (April 15, 1993): 66-67. Copyright © 1993 by Reed Publishing, U.S.A.

and credit ourselves in the objections to the rather modest Library Week slogan "Librarians Make It Happen." Some prefer the institutional identification in which libraries (with or without librarians) make it happen, whatever "it" is.

Why am I concerned about the prescribed role of volunteers? An article originally published in the *Los Angeles Times* ("Parents Filling Gaps in Money-Strapped Schools," June 6, 1992), and then reprinted in other newspapers, including my local one, notes that the Torrance, California, Unified School District does not have a single paid librarian on any of its 17 elementary campuses. Instead, the school libraries are run by more than 100 parent volunteers who raise money for books, rebind the collection, and staff the checkout desks.

The item goes on to quote Carol O'Brien, council president of the district's Parent-Teacher Association and former school board member: "The school district just doesn't have the money to staff elementary school libraries. Parents wanted their kids to have libraries, and they decided that the only way they were going to get them was by running them themselves." It is reasonable to assume that what has been reported in Torrance is happening throughout California, and the virus could easily spread.

With Friends Like These . . .

I have to try to remember that O'Brien is really a friend who believes in libraries, she just (and this is stated without malice) simply doesn't know what constitutes a library. However, I am certainly not ready to accept her assertion that the district doesn't have the money to staff elementary school libraries. I will grant that the district doesn't have enough money to do everything it would like to do, but the specific decision to eliminate librarians is based on a value system that assumes we are not as important as some of the other things in the budget. I don't know what all of these other things are, but I would be willing to attempt to analyze the district's budget priorities in order to find something else to cut.

It is easy to see why the decision to eliminate librarians was made so comfortably, if it can be argued that what remains—buying and mending books and staffing the checkout desk is what defines a library. If civic leaders don't know what defines a library, perhaps it is because we haven't told them clearly enough. Let me make an effort, and, of course, what follows could be adapted to any city.

> Parents of Torrance! There's more to library service than rebinding books and staffing the checkout desk. If libraries for your kids matter to you, work to put librarians back into the budget. Stop pretending to yourselves that you have libraries, because you don't. Your children won't have the tools to face a competitive marketplace. There appear to be only two possible solutions: Do something about a political process that strangles this crucial resource! Or move!

The reference to the mending of books as one of the most visible librarian activities really hurts, but where did the PTA get that idea?

Let me share another experience, without necessarily endorsing its extremism, although I do claim to understand it. I recall my service on an American Library Association (ALA) accreditation team for an urban library school in the mid-1970s. The city had just had a massive budget cut resulting in the layoff of librarians and the closing of branches. During my visit, the officers of the library school's student association met with a concerned citizen who suggested that library school students might provide a valuable public service—and also get some experience—by reopening the now closed branches.

They turned him down cold, saying: "We're not scabs. Hire librarians, or close the branches." The visitor was shocked at this reaction, and even I was surprised. These students were certainly atypical of the profession they were about to enter. Yet, all of the goodwill we have presumably generated by scrimping and saving, by doing backflips to be cooperative, and by not just permitting but often encouraging the use of volunteers to help hide the lack of regular staff have gotten us very little. Where we seem to differ from those who manage hospitals and museums is in our failure to delineate quite clearly what volunteers do, and what volunteers never do. Even in the worst budget crunch, no symphony league member plays second oboe.

No Substitutions

It is my fear, which I have articulated often, that the fascination with having something that can be called a library—under any conditions and with any staff, or even with no staff—may yet kill off our profession entirely. The argument that there is not enough money for all the things we would like to do will always be with us; indeed, that has always been true. The question, now as then, is what to do about it.

Substituting something *called* a library for an actual library is a bait-and-switch tactic that would be illegal in some fields and is certainly immoral in ours. The parents of Torrance are being cruelly misled because the solution is not as glibly simple as it has been presented. Their children do not have school libraries. What they have is a collection of books watched over by caring people. However, that doesn't make it a library any more than the availability of a cool compress for a feverish brow substitutes for a doctor. It is perhaps better than nothing but not at the price of confusion.

If our profession does not expose this tactic, and if every suggestion that only qualified librarians can uniquely accomplish certain specific tasks continues to provoke the anguished bleat that we should never promote ourselves so crassly, it is not difficult to predict what will happen next.

Under constant financial pressures that force choices, the services of professional librarians who are unwilling to define and defend themselves will get worse and worse and may ultimately disappear, to be replaced by the services of book guardians and book menders. If we don't spell out the difference between what the various kinds of people in libraries do, then certainly no one else will mention it. Making that distinction is not an act of arrogance or cruelty. All work, in any organization, is important. It should be done well, and it should be recognized and appreciated. However, without that distinction, the pressures to cut expenses will combine with the ability to pretend that there really is a library long after it is gone.

A Call for Self-Discipline

That is why the undefined and unregulated use of volunteers makes me nervous, even as I approve the general premise. Torrance is just a handy example of what even nice people can do to us. If this happens with our friends (at least the friends of libraries if not of librarians), then what can we expect from those who don't care about either? Do we have the self-discipline to define the appropriate role for all the people who participate in library activities, even in the face of never-ending pressures from budget-cutters and our desperate desire to save everything that now exists? Certainly school boards, city officials, and even parents will always take the easy and most painless approach. But what's in it for us and, ultimately, even for them?

I continue to stress that lack of money is the easy villain in this scenario, but it is not the issue. Insufficient funding is a permanent disease, and it varies only by degrees. Whether politicians provide funds, perhaps by cutting something else, or cut libraries in order to fund something else, or cut everything to protect the tax base, is a matter of assessing potential political consequences. If it is possible to stop funding libraries but still claim to have them, the decision is no longer painful; it is absurdly simple. We have to be the whistle-blowers, by stressing to would-be friends like Carol O'Brien that their "solutions" only make things worse.

There are, of course, other complexities in the use of volunteers, beyond the political issues. Volunteers are presumably cheap, but unless they are managed and directed, and unless they understand what they are supposed to do and what they are not supposed to do, they may cost a lot more than their nonsalaries. Volunteers may bring their own agendas, or they may be simply incompetent. One of my favorite lectures a number of years ago dealt with the question of how to fire a volunteer. That will have to wait for another column.

Scholarly Publication, Academic Libraries, and the Assumption That These Processes Are Really Under Management Control

It has long been assumed that the refereeing process used by scholarly journals served as an effective safeguard against the publication of work that is either inferior or repetitive of earlier publications. However, the tremendous increase in publication volume that cannot be reconciled with the number of scholars undertaking and reporting their research suggests that the process has developed cracks, if indeed it has not broken down completely. Pressures to publish everything "somewhere" not only protect the most significant journals but also channel the remaining articles into lesser journals, which are equally protected directly by the researchers forced to publish in them, even if they are reluctant to do so. This phenomenon also negates publishing on demand or electronic storage and retention as effective alternatives. Libraries are increasingly important to publishers because studies have shown that the nonlibrary purchasing base for scholarly journals continues to erode, while libraries are constantly pressured with regard to what they are supposed to buy. In addition, scholars often play the simultaneous and conflicting roles of author, reviewer, editor, reader, academic credit dispenser, and credit recipient. This paper suggests the need for new and more objective approaches to the "publication situation," rather than merely obeying the dictates of the marketplace and the "credit machine."

Reprinted, with changes, by permission of the author and *College and Research Libraries* 54, no. 4 (July 1993): 293-301.

The article makes no attempt at a complete survey of the literature on this topic, a literature with contributions from both librarians and publishers, and one that is growing rapidly. Much of this literature is narrowly self-justifying, and it has been addressed in this paper only as necessary to document its own assessments.

The Presumed Validity of Scholarly Peer Assessment of Publication Worthiness

Throughout recorded history, scholars, scientists, musicians, and artists have struggled for the freedom to set their own work agendas and to be judged by groups of their own peers rather than by outsiders. They have understood that evaluation either by a political body or by funding patrons might impose a value system of "political correctness," or one that simply rewards what interests and appeals to the patron and sponsor. Examples of this have ranged from the forced recanting of Galileo of what he knew to be true to more recent examples of politically acceptable music, with the determination made through the application of inexplicable and arbitrary standards we still do not understand.

The attitude of scholars has been consistently that they and only they should be the judges of what represents quality work, and that the decision should be made by the evaluation of peers in the scholar's own discipline. It is the scholarly argument that this judgment, and not the opinion of bureaucratic officials, should determine what is worthwhile and should be published.

Scholars, who insist on the premise that their own judgment of the work of colleagues is both fair and impartial, implement this process through the mechanism of peer review. This review occurs both in the determination of who should receive support and funding for carrying out his or her research, and in a refereeing process that controls publication in leading journals. From the start, it has been evident that this procedure, while perhaps preferable to any identified alternative, works at best uncertainly. Recently questions have arisen about how well it works at all.

The Elitism of the Process

It has been a long time since Derek de Solla Price first noted the existence of the invisible college, an informal network of scholars that bypasses both the rigor and the time constraints of the formal review and communication processes. The invisible college has both supporters and critics, and largely this depends on whether the individual making the judgment sees himself or herself as a member of the invisible college.[1] There can be little doubt that the process of informal and immediate communication, supported by electronic message systems, works well for those who are already recognized by their peers as legitimate scholars. It does not work nearly so well for the newcomers who have yet to achieve such status. In other words, it recognizes and credits *past* achievement in preference to the present work presumably being communicated and evaluated. It tends to be a historical rather than an up-to-date evaluative tool. And yet there are countless indications that suggest, for example in the areas of the physical and biological sciences (although a case could be made equally easily for poetry and music), that most of the breakthroughs later seen as significant are made by newcomers, and these contributions are not quickly recognized precisely because they come from individuals from whom such contributions were not expected. It is possible that celebrities in areas of scholarship and research are required to spend much of their time talking and writing about what they have already done, and therefore have little time to do anything new. That was the complaint of the developers of DNA. The invisible college, certainly prominent long before Price named it, works to some extent, but it works unfairly and inefficiently because it judges not the new specific contribution but the reputation that the individual currently holds. To place a contextual setting on an old joke: Where do Nobel Prize recipients publish? Anywhere they like!

The same sort of prejudging bias has been leveled, at least in the United States, against panels that award research funds. In principle, the process is supposed to focus on the proposed project, and not on the qualifications of the investigator that relate to previous work that may be irrelevant to this effort. However, panels are composed of human beings, and human beings frequently prefer to make safe rather than risky decisions. The opportunity for criticizing (with totally clear hindsight) the decision of an award jury, which did not use criteria that led to productive results, is always available. The criticism must be muted when it is noted that the past work of the applicant gave every indication of future success. Giving more money to former recipients is a safer decision. And that is why such panels look at citation statistics for earlier work by the same individual—sometimes claiming that past achievement predicts future success.

Why Researchers Must Publish

There is obviously a connection between funding support and the generation of the scholarly and research publications on which this paper focuses, but that connection is not as direct as one might assume. The purpose of publication is, after all, a twofold one. The first and the most immediately recognized purpose is the communication of findings, sometimes to an eager audience and sometimes to a disinterested one. The former is preferable, but even the latter is acceptable, because the other purpose of scholarly publication is the achievement of academic credit. Unfortunately, as will be discussed below, credit depends less on the quality and more on the quantity of activity in today's academic marketplace. Studies at the University of Pittsburgh indicated that much material that resides in research libraries is never read.[2] My own earlier studies indicated that for whole categories of disciplines, libraries were the only subscribers to certain journals. These studies suggest a situation in which scholarly publications are read by nobody and are of interest to nobody.[3] Does that negate their value? To society perhaps, but not necessarily to the author.

The premise of quality control in the evaluation of submissions to scholarly journals is based on the concept of double-blind refereeing—the author does not know who the reviewers are, and the reviewer does not know who the author is. The process might work for the author, but it works ineffectively for the reviewers. To a large extent the same preconceptions that affect the invisible college and the awarding of grants apply here as well. Many scholarly communities are small; specialties of members are well-known to all possible peer reviewers.

While there are still major interdisciplinary journals, the process of journal publication has become narrower and more specialized. Much of this trend developed with the entry of commercial publishers into the arena of publishing scholarly and research journals. Early studies indicated that scholarly journal publishing was a field dominated by the for-profit sector and by professional societies, with the second group largely emphasizing discipline-wide publications fitting the characteristics of the society membership.[4]

The Economics of Journal Publishing

The development of narrow, specialized journals owes its impetus to many sources, but the economic opportunities were grasped perhaps most directly by Robert Maxwell and his development of new journals for Pergamon Press. Maxwell clearly saw one obvious but rarely discussed difference between monograph and journal publishing. Monographic publication involves a great deal of cash flow investment and risk. Monographs must be contracted, edited, and printed, and a supply must be placed into the warehouse before the first copy can be sold. The publisher has invested in an expensive inventory, and then must play a highly dangerous game. Unsold copies, particularly concerning subjects for which information changes rapidly, have virtually no value. This fact discourages massive speculative print runs. However, it also eliminates the likelihood of huge profits, as even successful monographs rapidly go out of print. The publisher has then made what is probably a modest profit, but consequently faces a new and dangerous business decision of whether to reprint. If so, how many copies? Might this decision lead to the additional expense of yet another reprint? Or, might the publisher be burdened with an unsold and useless inventory? It might be better to look for an updated work instead, perhaps through a second or revised edition, or through another author. These are some of the difficult choices facing monograph publishers.

Journal publishers face far fewer risks. They receive payment for the entire subscription year (and sometimes for multiple years) before making any expenditures. Those funds, even if cautiously invested, produce interest income, in contrast to the interest expenses that monographic publishers face. Print runs are known well in advance, and the publisher has few responsibilities for maintaining back sets, particularly if these are available on microfilm. Unsuccessfully promoted titles can be aborted, sometimes before the first issue is printed, and it may not even be necessary to offer a refund. There is always the potential option of suggesting that the funds already contributed be diverted to other titles offered by the same publisher. This strategy was described in a presentation and subsequently in an article submitted to the scholarly publishing community itself. The members of the community expressed little dispute or disagreement with the conclusions presented.[5]

The mechanisms so carefully developed by Maxwell and others depended not on developing and publishing large-circulation, inclusive-topic journals, but rather on promoting highly focused publications. These journals are so specialized that they often have only one or two interested readers in any major university. Publishers can bring out these journals infrequently (quarterly, at the most) and they can charge high subscription rates to university libraries because the targeted reader considers these highly specialized journals to be more important than any other. Consequently it has become nearly impossible for university libraries to refuse to subscribe to key journals aimed at specific scholars and researchers whom the library serves.

The publication process described above thus created a whole series of invisible colleges, i.e., small groups of researchers working in a particular subdiscipline or even subsubdiscipline. Key members of each invisible college are identified and selected to be editors of journals or members of the editorial advisory board. These appointments engender a great deal of prestige but often very little work responsibility. New and junior researchers anxious to join this small and select group feel pressured to write articles for these journals in order to establish their professional credibility.

In this way, the anonymity of double-blind refereeing is weakened if not totally destroyed. The smaller and more specialized the field, the easier it becomes to recognize the researcher, if not through the work itself, then certainly through the references contained in the article. Moreover, while the entry of commercial publishers into the arena of scholarly journal publishing did not in and of itself decrease the quality of what was being published, it placed the emphasis primarily upon quantity. It is not necessary to adhere to a rigid page budget for the year if it is possible to use an increase in the number of pages as a rationale for an increase in subscription price. The authors, editors, and referees who determine the content of scholarly journals are not expected to buy the journals. That is left to libraries, and their funding is separate from either the salary or research budget of the scholar. Moreover, libraries have been, up to now, more likely to absorb the rising costs of subscriptions without protest.

Why the Process Works for Authors and Publishers

It is not my intent to suggest that authors and editors set about willfully to dilute the quality of research publications by increasing their quantity. It is possible that some unscrupulous publisher might be tempted to do this, but even that conjecture, if offered, could only be substantiated with difficulty. It is nevertheless clear that the publications resulting from the work of scholars have grown far more rapidly than the number of scholars themselves. People are writing more and more, but not necessarily because they have more to say.

Part of the explanation for the increase in publication has already been suggested. Neither authors, editors, nor referees have any financial responsibility for their decisions. While the content of scholarly journals is controlled by these groups, financial arrangements involve only the publisher and the organization that pays for the subscription—most frequently the library. Research shows that libraries have not found an effective way, in their institutional settings, to combat the pressures of increasing page counts and higher prices.[6] These two factors may be related, as indeed some publishers' statistics claim they are. However, for the bill-paying librarian this does not matter, since librarians have never asked for either new or larger journals.

Originally, the refereeing process was intended to weed out and destroy proposed articles that did not warrant publication, either because the material was repetitive or because it added nothing new. However, a recent study indicated that at least some publishers are willing to publish material even though they know it is not original.[7] They do it because of the pressure to fill their issues. However, they also do it to keep the article, particularly if written by a prominent or easily recognized author, from going to another journal, or perhaps contributing to the formation of a competing journal. Editors, therefore, feel some responsibility for including everything worth publishing in their discipline in their own journal because they don't want to encourage competition. As libraries increasingly face the prospect of canceling subscriptions (although budgeters tend to put off this decision as long as they possibly can by transferring funds from other internal priorities), the existence of a rival journal becomes of greater concern to the editor and publisher than the notion that some articles might not have warranted inclusion in the first place.

Why is all this happening? I suggest it is largely because the process of academic evaluation, as practiced primarily in universities through the promotion and tenure procedures, has moved gradually from emphasis on the quality of a scholar's publications to concern with the quantity of the work. This has happened because the sheer volume and specificity of dossiers overwhelms the ability of those from other disciplines to understand and evaluate the content. With the readiness of publishers to start new journals (statistics indicate that carefully planned journals—at least carefully planned in identifying their intended audience—rarely fail), the process of refereeing in the journal literature does not succeed in keeping articles from being published, only in shifting them from journal A to journal B, or perhaps even to journal C. Journal C then becomes a crucial journal for the scholar whose article will appear there, and it becomes politically essential that the library purchase it as a validation of the research. The pressure to purchase C becomes paradoxically greater than the pressure to purchase A, because A will be purchased in any case. It has already been shown that, to a far greater extent than those involved would like to admit, libraries base cancellation decisions less on careful evaluation of need, and more significantly on what they can get away with canceling.[8]

Possible Solutions and Changes

If there is a solution to this dilemma, it rests squarely with the academicians and scholars themselves, because it is ultimately they, and not librarians, who influence the actions of publishers. To a large extent librarians are seen only as purchasing agents with money, but with little say in what they are expected to buy. It is certainly also to the advantage of publishers, as for any vendor, to sell as much as possible at the highest possible price. Probably relatively few publishers act with such a cold single-minded approach to maximizing profits, but enough publishers do conduct business in such a way as to seriously damage the credibility of the larger publishing community.

The solution to this dilemma must come from the recognition by scholars themselves that the present system—dispensing credit based on the quantity of publications by a given author—ultimately does not benefit the academic community. Attempts to measure quality will always be controversial and disputatious, and there is no certainty that any new system will please more people or produce fairer results. As long as humans are doing the judging there will be charges of bias, and letting computers do the judging antiseptically is something we are not prepared to do. For many individuals, their entire career futures are at stake.

Yet, despite all of these caveats, it should be recognized that the present system emphasizing quantity of publication must change. It encourages irresponsible and needless publication, which deluges the reader with huge amounts of material. Any operations researcher can tell us that it is easier to find what we need in a small collection than in a large one, provided that there is confidence that the smaller collection contains what is needed. In other words, redundant information is not just trivial waste. It can get in the way of finding the important and useful. This is the first reason for the necessity to change the current system of scholarly publication.

The second reason for changing the system is that given the finite and even decreasing support of library funding, the present approach of unlimited and unmonitored growth will bankrupt the academic information process. If the current system does not do this, it will at least have drained off so many resources from other needs and other priorities in the academic enterprise that the results will be equally catastrophic.

Research scholars are emerging who understand this issue and who recognize that the solution does not lie in finding more money (at best a dubious prospect) but in developing a new system of evaluating and crediting quality. Publishers do not necessarily see these scholars as friendly to the interests of the publishing community, and some have sought to intimidate these scholars into silence by dragging them through costly and time-consuming legal processes. However, librarians certainly should see these scholars as allies, and offer them all the help and encouragement that we can.

Nevertheless, it would probably be unrealistic to expect that either faculty or academic administrators will address this problem until and unless they absolutely have to do so. Actions such as those undertaken by the Faculty Senate at Southern Methodist University (SMU), which threatened to punish those publishers "guilty" of the greatest price increases by canceling these subscriptions regardless of qualitative and other political considerations, are still very much the exception rather than the rule, and as long as that situation continues, neither publishers nor academicians will feel any pressure to respond to the problem. In a perverse way, the willingness and remarkable ability of academic librarians to somehow find the money with which to meet continuing double-digit publisher price increases virtually assures that nothing will be done. We were even paid what was intended as a compliment in a recent article by Timothy King, a publisher who congratulated librarians on their resourcefulness in finding the necessary money for publications.[9]

Strategies for Librarians

What strategies and alternatives does this situation suggest for academic librarians? The first is the recognition that they cannot solve the problem because they lack the power and leverage. Publishers will not be motivated to take action as long as they are supported by a faculty who exercise much authority over but take little responsibility for the issues in academic publishing. Some publishers even patiently explain to librarians that the reason for the large rise in the price of subscriptions is because of an increase in submitted articles, or of the weakness of the U.S. dollar. In a free-market economy, those are their problems and not ours. It appears certain that university administrators will make a concerted effort not when librarians demand it, but when faculty demand it. Economists predict that prices are not likely to rise substantially in the stores where we shop because customers have no money. Manufacturers and vendors know that, and therefore know that they cannot increase prices. Librarians do not have any money either, but that makes very little difference to vendors. If vendors perceive librarians as purchasing agents rather than as customers, they have little motivation to respond to librarians' financial limitations. Therefore, the well-meaning suggestion in the recent article by Bruce Kingma and Philip Eppard does not offer any solution.[10] Kingma and Eppard correctly describe the difference between individual and library subscription prices, but their suggestion that the economic solution is to increase the cost of faculty photocopying services for library journals neglects the reality we know so well, that when photocopying is made unattractive, "direct appropriation of material" or mutilation grows in proportion. These authors maintain that whatever emerges into the scholarly publication process was worth publishing, or at least that the process cannot be changed. I would rather not be that pessimistic.

What, then, is the academic librarians' most effective strategy? We must state loudly and clearly that this disaster of ever-increasing periodical prices is neither our fault nor our problem, and that we have no solution we can implement. The available options include increased funding of the periodical budget from already scarce university funds, an accelerated process of cancellations, or an academic power structure commitment to do something about an absurd pricing growth that has connection neither to inflation nor to the number of scholars presumed to have something to report in the literature. Academic administrators will do something about this problem if they become convinced it is important enough to warrant concerted action, just as they finally felt impelled to deal with the escalating cost, confusion, and embarrassment of their athletic programs. Dare we suggest to them that this might be just as important?

Using this sort of confrontational strategy is difficult and painful for librarians because our acceptance of the "moral imperative" (the premise that we must do everything with or without resources or it will all be our fault) appears to be an inbred value system that students already bring with them to library school without having to be taught.[11] Where they acquire this virus I am not sure. Perhaps they learn this commitment to self-sacrifice from their mentors in the libraries in which so many students already work on a part-time basis.

One thing, however, seems certain to me. The unchecked bloodletting of the periodicals budget has perhaps gained librarians some additional funds, even if not nearly enough. But it has also removed the initiative for doing many of the other things we should be doing (automation, resource sharing, preservation, increased reference and bibliographic work, staff upgrading, and continuing education) because all the money is already allocated before we get to any of these priorities. To increase the irony, academic administrators truly believe that they have been financially supportive of their libraries, when in fact they have only really been supportive of a pass-through financial game in the continuation of a process sadly in need of evaluation and refinement. We need to stress that periodicals funding is not our only priority, and at this point we can't even allow it to be our primary priority.

Some Final Thoughts

Articles such as this one are written at some risk of creating displeasure. The habit of executing the messenger who brings us bad tidings goes back a long way. There are academic library administrators who would prefer not to be reminded of how ineffective our strategies of the last twenty years have been. There may be other administrators who truly believe that progress is being made, and that there is light at the end of the tunnel. However, these optimists may confuse increased activity with progress. There has been an increasing number of meetings between publisher and librarian groups. Publishers may be inclined to talk as long as nothing changes while the talks go on. There has certainly been no modification in the price escalation of scholarly journals, and we can be certain there will be none as long as some publishers continue to suggest that this is our problem instead of theirs.

Meetings between librarians and groups of faculty members have also become more frequent, and some have been useful if only to explain the magnitude of the problem. However, while there have been some scattered reports of motions of concern expressed by various faculty bodies, and even vague threats of retribution, such scattered activities will not make an impression on the journal pricing process. What might make an impression would be a vote by the membership of an entire professional subject discipline to refuse to submit articles to particularly high-priced journals, or concrete action by a body of presidents representing major research institutions, such as the Ivy League or the Big Ten. There is no indication of such action on the horizon, and more talk provides a poor substitute.

There is also the hope that acceptance of concepts implementing what has been called the *virtual library* can offer some relief. Broadly based concepts of resource sharing are indeed very exciting, and it is important that they be pursued. However, they offer no relief for this particular problem unless institutions are prepared to divert funds from purchase of materials to a resource-sharing mechanism. Such action, if seriously contemplated, would probably require modification of present copyright legislation, particularly in light of recent narrow court interpretations of Section 107 of the U.S. Copyright Act of 1976. Such modification would not be impossible, but it is not likely to occur in the near future. Faculty and administrators presently understand the virtual library to be a means of sharing resources *after* librarians have already spent every last available dollar on purchase, and subsequently found that the resources are inadequate. Under such constraints virtual library concepts are still worthwhile, but they require much more additional spending. If the need for even more funding has been communicated to any university administrators, they appear to pay it little heed. And yet, somebody has to explain to them that libraries cannot continue to spend every last cent on material purchase and then *also* implement virtual libraries. Funds must be diverted from purchase, or new funds must be added. Faculty don't like the first option and university administrators don't like the second.

Librarians have been entangled in this web for the last twenty years, and extricating ourselves is a difficult task. The situation puts me in mind of advice from my college varsity tennis coach, many years ago. "Never change a winning game, but always change a losing game. You risk nothing when you do." How many sets do we have to lose before we reassess our strategies?

Notes

1. Price, Derek J. de Solla. *Little Science, Big Science.* New York: Columbia University Press, 1963.

2. Kent, Allen, et al. *Use of Library Materials: The University of Pittsburgh Study.* New York: Dekker, 1979.

3. Fry, Bernard M., and Herbert S. White. *Publishers and Libraries: A Study of Scholarly and Research Journals.* Lexington, MA: Heath, 1976.

4. White, Herbert S. "Publishers, Libraries, and Costs of Journal Subscriptions in Times of Funding Retrenchment." *Library Quarterly* 46 (October 1976): 359-77.

5. _____. "Scholarly Publishers and Libraries: A Strained Marriage." *Scholarly Publishing* 19, no. 3 (April 1988): 125-29.

6. _____. "Librarians, Journal Publishers and Scholarly Information: Whose Leaky Boat Is Sinking?" *LOGOS* 1, no. 4 (1990): 18-23.

7. Serebnick, Judith, and Stephen P. Harter. "Ethical Practices in Journal Publishing: A Study of Library and Information Science Periodicals." *Library Quarterly* 60 (April 1990): 91-119.

8. White, Herbert S. "Factors in the Decision by Individuals and Libraries to Place or Cancel Subscriptions to Scholarly and Research Journals." *Library Quarterly* 50 (July 1980): 287-309.

9. King, Timothy B. "Journal Publishers, Librarians, and Scholarly Information: Contemplating a Future Scenario." *LOGOS* 1, no. 4 (1990): 24-29.

10. Kingma, Bruce R., and Philip B. Eppard. "Journal Price Escalation and the Market for Information: The Librarians' Solution." *College & Research Libraries* 53, no. 6 (November 1992): 523-35.

11. White, Herbert S. "Playing Shell Games Without Any Peas." *Library Journal* 116, no. 12 (July 1991): 63-64.

Information Technology, Users, and Intermediaries in the 21st Century: Some Observations and Predictions

Operations research people tell us repeatedly that we tend to overestimate what will happen in the short term, such as the next one or two years, and that we underestimate what will occur in the next 10 years or longer. We overestimate our ability to make changes in the short term because we don't fully take into account the slow process of human communication, what we generally and sometimes with contempt call bureaucracy, and, of course, all societies and all countries have it, some more than others. We forget that committees take a long time to meet and to reach decisions, and then that the individuals who have to approve those recommendations also take their time. Sometimes they also appoint even more committees. To a large extent, and particularly in this field, we search not for a rapid majority vote, but rather for a consensus. Consensus decisions are not quickly reached.

We tend to underestimate what will occur in the long term because we can only predict change in the framework of what we already know to be possible. We cannot really estimate the changes that will occur in other fields and in other disciplines that impact ours, without even necessarily intending to. Let me give just two simple examples from our own field. Copyright laws worked effectively when copying meant literally that—sitting down with a pen and paper and copying Tolstoy's *War and Peace*. The development of dry electrostatic copying, the ability to download from computer files, the fact that the chairman of this conference and I communicated almost exclusively via fax machine—all of these innovations had an impact on the copyright

Paper presented to the 15th International Essen University Symposium. Essen, Germany, October 1992.

process, although the inventors certainly never gave it a thought. Copyright law had to adjust to what was now possible. That is the point about technology and its uses. If something is available and convenient, it will be used, whether it is presumably allowed to be used or not. Copyright laws had to be adjusted and are still being adjusted, to take into account not whether or not people should copy, but what to do about the fact that they will most certainly do so.

My second example concerns the whole issue of database searching from a terminal that might be located in a computer thousands of miles away. That wasn't really anticipated, either, certainly not by the library profession. The original premise of computer architecture was that one input/output device would be hooked to one central processing unit. That was found to be terribly inefficient, because CPUs work more rapidly than I/O devices. The approaches we have developed to permit online searching use an advantage that was there for us to use. Not only libraries, but also banks and airline reservation systems are the beneficiaries or, if you prefer, victims of this development. If someone in our field had predicted online searching when computers were still gigantic vacuum tube devices, such an individual would not have been believed. What will happen in the next year or two? Probably less than we think. What will happen by the year 2010? I don't know, but the changes will be gigantic and dramatic. The one thing we can safely predict is that there will be massive change, and that technology will play a heavy hand in the process. Because, as we meet here, hundreds of thousands of highly qualified specialists are working to bring us new enhancements, whether we want them or have asked for them or not. These are probably not designed primarily for us, but many of them will work for us, precisely because information files are large massive record files of which we ask relatively simple questions, at least compared to the adjustment of a space vehicle reentry trajectory. Those kinds of files in our libraries look very much like the files in accounting departments, in banks, in insurance agencies, and in warehouse and stockroom activities. Money will assuredly be spent to enhance the efficient use of these.

It is also difficult to measure the impact of technology because the availability of a technology brings its own needs and own uses. Before I worked at the NASA Scientific and Technical Information Agency—the U.S. space program's information system that I headed between 1964 and 1968—nobody did frequently cumulated indexes and bibliographies, because it was too difficult, too expensive, and too time consuming to do them. Once the ability became apparent, we decided that we had really needed them all along. Cost comparisons between manual and computerized systems therefore become meaningless. Computerization almost never saves us money, it ends up costing more. However, the question is how much more do we get, and is it important for us to have it? Cost-effective and cheap are not the same thing.

I am a pragmatic user, and neither an enthusiast nor a hater of computer applications in our institutions. The question is still, as it must always be, one of what it is we want to accomplish, and whether machines can help us to accomplish it. If we manage to produce something rapidly and efficiently but it is something nobody wants or needs, is that a benefit? Hardly. At the same time, I think it is important that we use the opportunity that developing technology brings us to destabilize our institutions, and to create an awareness of wants and needs, particularly wants and needs of which users had not even been aware.

That is the issue of marketing, and bureaucrats are not very good at it. It is the creation of the awareness of a need that people didn't even know they had. It means saying to people: "We don't do this now, but if we were to do it would it be useful to you?" That creates pressures on the budgetary process, but I happen to be an admiring reader of the writings of Peter Drucker. In the absence of money there is always money for something that is really worth doing. And: It is easier to get a lot of money than to get a little bit of money. That is because there is more excitement and reward in major changes than in small incremental modifications. It means that, for libraries, it might be easier to justify six more reference analysts with terminal and database access to do something for our clients that we have never done before, than it is to justify one more clerk because the backlog is so large. Nobody wants to approve a new clerk, because that cost is real and the justification is boring. For me perhaps the clearest example of a successful marketing destabilization approach is the one used by telephone systems on an international basis. Telephone companies once argued that people needed to have phones, one phone per household or office. Basically that was accomplished a long time ago, at least for the people who would buy phones at all. Having done this, I suppose they could have congratulated themselves and stopped. However, we now have color-coordinated decorator phones, multiple phones in every home, automobile phones, airplane seat phones, cellular phones, call forwarding, call interrupt, and many other features. We didn't even know we wanted or needed all those things until the phone marketeers showed us how valuable they would be to have. And this, of course, brings me to yet another Peter Drucker quote: "In the provision of a service or of a convenience that people really want, cost becomes irrelevant." It is easy to see that in stressing the freeness rather than the goodness of what we librarians do, we may have been stressing the wrong value.

The matter of creating a destabilized and unsatisfied clientele is particularly important to us, because the absence of information is easy to rationalize. At first glance, that statement may seem strange. After all, our whole world culture now accepts the premise that information is important, that knowledge is crucial, and that ignorance is not acceptable. Nobody, in government, industry, or academia, is likely to say "I don't know anything, but I don't care."

However, whether or not people really have information that they need is not as easily or exactly determined. In talking about this to my students, I stress to them that the impact of the deprivation of vitamin C is easy to demonstrate. We put two groups of rats into cages. One group gets a balanced diet, the other a diet without vitamin C. The second group becomes sick and dies. Point proven. However, how can we do this in the information field? Do we put our users into cages? Can we even assure that, if we don't give them information, they won't get it elsewhere without ever telling us? Perhaps the alternative information cost is greater, but that doesn't matter if they can miscode the cost to fool the accounting system. There is also the endless ability to rationalize. Calvin Mooers[1] told us more than 30 years ago that, in any information environment in which people know that there is more information than they have, but that it becomes too troublesome to get it, they will pretend that there is no information available at all. They aren't really aware of lying. Eventually they persuade themselves. I have seen the validation of Mooers' Law many times over. People with small and weak libraries who only get to see a half dozen journals in their field will insist stubbornly that this is all they need to see. What choice do they have? They can't admit that they don't know what they are talking about. I've never seen a meeting scheduled at 10 a.m. on a Monday morning canceled because the presenter admitted that he had been unable to get what he needed from the library. Whatever he got just fortunately always turned out to be enough. Indeed, librarians know that if they later find information that contradicts what has already been said, they provide that information at their peril. Those of us who work in universities know that unlike the popular perception, academic as well as industrial and government research is not usually a search for truth, whatever that might be. It is a search for proof for something we have already postulated to be true. In fact, it was on the basis of persuading people that the assumptions were probably correct that the research funds were granted in the first place. If they report, three years later, that they were wrong, but isn't everyone glad to know? they severely jeopardize their chance to obtain future funds.

The information process is therefore, with or without technology, very susceptible to self-deception and self-delusion. There is obviously risk for us in attempting to spotlight this, but I would argue that we should, in the most pleasant and reassuring manner possible. We should stress that it is indeed now possible to get more complete, more rapid, more accurate information. All it takes is money, and money is still the easiest thing to get, provided that people understand that terrible things will happen if it isn't provided. We have not stressed that issue very well. If properly used, technology in the field of information provides wonderful opportunities, precisely because it has the potential for being a great democratic equalizer. Because both bibliographic access and document delivery are now relatively simple—we are dealing in issues of minutes and hours instead of days and weeks—perhaps at most a day or two—there need no longer be a country, location, or individual deprived of needed information. The issue, we should certainly understand and tell others, is not ownership but access, and I urge my colleagues in university libraries in the United States to answer questions about the size of the library holdings by questioning the significance of the issue. They should stress that ownership has never assured access, and it is access that really matters. Trueswell told us[2], from his vantage point in operations research at MIT, that our chance of getting things today is only 50 percent even if the material is owned. Trueswell saw few options except in the rigorous application of the laws of Bradford in buying multiple copies of heavily used material and not buying material not likely to be used at all. That was a risky and traumatic recommendation at the time of Trueswell in dealing with users more fascinated with holdings than with access, but technology has eased the bite of that decision option. If we don't have it, we can still find it bibliographically and deliver it as well. We have done better with bibliographic access than with document delivery, but that is largely because we have refused to revise some of our rules and assumptions. As an example, I find that in many libraries material will not be borrowed if it is owned even if its own copy is not available. As though that mattered to the user. For him the request is a binary process. Either I get it or I don't. However, we insist on a full range of explanations that are really only unwelcome excuses. In addition, we may insist that when we do borrow something, the user must pay, although the user was totally innocent in our decision not to buy the item in the first place.

What I am arguing is that even as we look at technology as a series of service options, we have largely failed to modify our decision mechanisms to take into account the new options we now have. Is this because we are largely a conservative and cautious bunch, imprinted by our managers to worry more about money than about service? Perhaps, at least some of us are. However, to a larger extent our users are even more conservative than we are, in part this is because they are uninformed. We have not radicalized them to expect more, and as a result we find a great deal of goodwill for the library as a good institution. Indeed they think the library is good no matter how bad it really is, except that perhaps it might be nice if we added a few more journals in their discipline. Having the library assumed as a good thing run by nice people will probably protect our jobs, but it will not help us to make dramatic changes. As technology has brought options and opportunities, it should change options, and for this we must radicalize our users. Individuals I have interviewed in my consulting assignments accept the premise that sometimes the process of acquiring something from another library takes several weeks or months, and they are surprised at my suggestion that they simply state that such a delay is unacceptable. Could we do better? Of course we could. Using technology to its potential takes money, and money comes with an understanding that it is worth spending, or that important people want it spent. Without that understanding, the money doesn't come at all.

Even as we may fail, in part because of a lack of staff or a lack of money, to make users aware of new options and new potentials, other rivals of ours are doing it. Unfortunately, in this process they tend to bypass or ignore the library entirely, and to simply relegate our role to the warehousing function of supplying an item once the needed item has already been identified. This is the siren song of stand alone end user searching. There are many participants in this strategy. They include database vendors, and their preference for dealing with end users rather than with librarians is easily understood. End users are more prestigious, end users have more access to money and are more likely to spend it. They might do more searches, and if they do them sloppily so that they cost more, that's not bad for vendor income, either.

They include government agencies that try to build one-to-one linkages with the professionals in the disciplines they are chartered to serve, in my view largely because this brings more prestige and visibility. Almost 30 years ago when I worked in the space information program the suggestion that astronauts in their flight suits might want to do an online search just before entering the capsule was not discouraged, although it was really silly. The most obvious example in the United States today is the National Library of Medicine, which suggests through its Grateful Med program that searching medical information on the physician's own terminal is easy and can be fun. The message that you don't need a librarian or information specialist is not specifically sent, but it can be inferred, and is indeed inferred and implemented by administrators who close libraries and fire librarians, all the while professing a support for information service. Finally, they include some librarians, who may have a fascination with training users to do their own searching. I am not exactly sure why, except for the observation that the value system of the librarian as educator and the librarian as information intermediary lead us to contradictory emphases. In the one it is important that the user learns how to serve himself. In the other, it might be preferable that the user knows only whom to ask, without worrying about how this magician then goes about his work. I spent the first 25 years of my career as a special librarian. The motto of the Special Libraries Association, which has international chapters, is "Putting Knowledge to Work." In other words, knowledge is only significant if it is used. Perhaps this can be contrasted to an emphasis on putting knowledge on the shelf in the hope the people will find what they might consider useful.

I obviously have my own strong personal feelings about the issue, particularly in an evolving technological emphasis, of user self-sufficiency versus the use of surrogates, but will acknowledge that the question has no simple and direct answer. Whether or not end users can do better or cheaper searches is an issue that should be addressable through structured research, but it seems unlikely to me that self-service will result in greater cost-effectiveness for the end user, given the difference in salaries. We must be careful not to couch the issue in terms of a moral concern, that somehow end users *should* do their own searches because that is a more ethical approach. It differs to me very little from the question of whether or not automobile owners *should* repair their own cars.

Who are the end users, anyway? As it turns out, they are many and varied in number. Herbert Brinberg,[3] in a talk delivered at the FID Copenhagen meeting, differentiated among three types of information users in a formal information setting. There are the pure researchers and scholars, who seek only raw material from which they will devise their own evaluation and strategies. Charles Osburn,[4] a noted humanist and librarian, has postulated that in academia we treat all users as though they were pure and basic researchers and scholars, whether or not they really are. Brinberg suggests a second group of information users, whom he calls those primarily involved in practice and engineering. These people are looking for answers to their questions. Brinberg's third group are managers, who are not looking for sources of information or specific answers, but who are looking to learn what their plausible options are. Some present day librarians might serve Brinberg's second group, but I suspect that virtually none serve his third group. However, they exist everywhere, including universities.

What are the numbers of these basic and pure researchers whom, according to Osburn, we serve as though they represent everyone? In the United States, at least, there is evidence that there are very few of them. A 1990 survey of faculty by the Carnegie Foundation[5] showed that 28 percent had never published anything, and that another 28 percent had published nothing in the last five years. That is more than half. More than half had never published a book or a monograph, and only 6 percent of academic faculty members saw their primary role as research, as contrasted to teaching.

We can also be suspicious of suggestions that, simply because individuals now know how to use terminals, they enjoy the process of searching for information, if they could be doing something else. There are undoubtedly some who do, and there is no question that the terminal in your office is a useful device for a specific fact or document lookup. However, many senior researchers and particularly executives still consider anything with a keyboard as a clerical device. A long time ago, when I still worked for IBM, an internal survey which was obviously not publicized learned that the executives who had terminal access to all sorts of day-to-day financial and production data preferred to call their assistants to their office or on the phone to tell them to look up the information for them, and then provide either an oral report or a one-page summary. The reason the terminals still have printer attachments and that, despite Lancaster's projections[6] we now produce more paper than ever in the information process, is because people adapt systems to themselves and their convenience and preference, rather than adapt themselves to the system. It is something that the administrators of libraries could remember as they deal with systems analysts and systems manufacturers.

We have been told that the new round of computer systems are more user friendly than ever, and by that I suppose that they can allow the unsophisticated user to bypass a great deal of complex logic. However, when I last looked, computer terminals still tended to be rude. The response "invalid command" is not a pleasant greeting from an inanimate object, particularly when we are positive we have done nothing wrong, and most particularly when we consider ourselves to be more important than a machine. Telephone recordings, as we know, are just as rude as their price for what is seen as efficiency. The entire question of end user versus intermediate searching is, for me, a moot rhetorical point. We should allow the end user to interact with the system at his level of preference. This is not a moral issue. Users will probably opt for a mixture of self-service and intermediate service, with a heavy concentration on the latter for complex and time-consuming issues.

However, this will only happen if first we don't rig the economics so that end user searching appears to be cheaper even when it is not. Cheaper for the library is not necessarily cheaper. The issue is not who pays, but what does it cost for the entire organization. Unlike many of my colleagues, I like dealing with accountants and other financial managers, because they understand that point very clearly. They understand that money is money, no matter where it is hidden. Their agendas are simple and easy to understand, and they could be allied to ours. Second, the use of intermediaries depends on trust. Trust cannot be edicted, and it cannot be demanded. It is built one relationship at a time. A user does not interact with a library. He interacts with human beings who, if we are fortunate and have chosen well, are impressive professionals who work in the library. I find it hard to understand why some might think that users should willingly interact with whoever answers the phone or happens to be at the desk. We have favorite barbers and hair stylists, favorite supermarket clerks and bank tellers. Why not favorite information intermediaries?

I believe that, unless we restrict the process by either imposing some sort of morality standard that edicts self-service, or by practicing false economics, our future can be very bright indeed. I base that belief both on the recognized importance of information and on its growing size and complexity, and on the general societal preference for intermediaries. We know that in the more developed nations an overwhelming and still growing part of the work force is not in production of either goods or agricultural products, but in the service sector. Who are the people in the service sector? They are intermediaries. The world likes intermediaries because they make us feel important.

If we are to stress the options that information users have, it is important that they understand both those options and the full capabilities of the ever-changing information engine. I find that in my consulting work, particularly in the corporate sector, users do not know what the full range of information options are, and therefore they accept what they have because they don't know there is anything else. We must remember that many professionals have worked in one organization for 15 or 25 years, and many have never worked anywhere else. Deferred retirement benefits discourage people from changing jobs. If they know only one information system, how do they know whether it is as good as it could be? We must be careful in the way we structure user surveys, because these may yield not only ignorant but dangerous responses, dangerous in their naive acceptance. If you are going to undertake user surveys, at least make sure that you ask them about whether they would want things that are at least technologically feasible but that are not now being provided, usually because of a cost constraint. Would they be interested in any of these? As Drucker has noted, the emphasis in management communication must be on exception reporting, not on what we are doing well. We will report that in any case. People like to brag. The emphasis must be on what we are *not* doing, or not doing well, on why not, and on what could be done about it.

If we do all of these things, then the options that technology offers to those of us who work in the information professions will be rich and varied. It will require continued monitoring and assessment on our part, and it will require use of that much-maligned skill, vision. Bear in mind that the outflow from the technology mills will be endless, and that the people producing this will not necessarily understand what we do and why we might or might not need what they have developed. They will try to sell it to us in any case, as most salesmen would. We have to know what we need, and we have to know what we might find useful. That means that we must understand what we are not doing but wish we could do. We must not forget, in the pressure to deal with daily crises, that dreaming is part of management. We must remember that, particularly in academia, battles over territory are fought most ferociously because the stakes are so small. Territory, or turf, comes from being able to do something nobody else can do. They must come to you for help because you are the experts and they are unqualified. Doctors and lawyers— even automotive mechanics—understand this clearly. Do we?

If we remember all of these things; if we now look at technological options as opportunities rather than dangers, forgetting at least for the moment the problems and particularly the financial issues, then our future is potentially quite bright. Information will play an increasingly important role in all of the fabric of society. At least I am convinced that the role of information intermediaries, the ones who provide the linkages, will grow in size and importance. I am equally convinced, however, that if we don't do this, somebody else will. These people probably won't do it as well or as cost effectively, but since information intermediaries largely get to define their own territory and mission, users may not even know that.

If that happens, then our future would not be bright at all. Because the historic function that society identifies with the library profession still focuses on the acquisition of material in one centralized physical location; its careful and unique analysis; and the process of maintaining inventory control records over what is in and what is out; we must recognize that these are precisely the functions that will become either irrelevant or increasingly computer routines. Further improvements in bibliographic access and in document storage and delivery are a certainty, and that means that the entire premise of the library as a set physical location with doors and windows must not be allowed to define the information window on the world. Furthermore, the premise of digitized storage and rapid and cheap reprographic techniques will make the tedious process of circulation records and overdue notices irrelevant for all material except for that where format is more important than content, primarily rare books and manuscripts. For other material we are looking at a throwaway technology. I know about existing copyright laws, but copyright laws will adapt to the inevitable because they must. Hopefully the throwaway technology will feature biodegradation and recycling. I am also aware of the suggestion that we have a role as information advisors, something of a restatement and refinement of the librarian as teacher role. I have no problem with our being both intermediaries and advisors, but I am less certain of the guarantee of the second role. It is the equivalent of preventive medicine—of people going to doctors when they are well and not just when they are ill, to make sure that they stay well. That is desirable, but it doesn't happen very often. Nor do I think our role as advisors is assured if, as I suggested, people don't know what it is they don't know, and pretend they do know. Physical illness has clear symptoms, information illness often has none. I am not as prepared as some of my colleagues to assume that individuals will want to do their own information work just because perhaps they can. Of course they can if they must, but why do we have a stake in forcing them to? I have no more reason to suspect that people want to do their own information work than I think they want to fix their own cars when there is something else to do, something they think is more worthwhile or more enjoyable. From my observation few people want to do information work, and academic libraries have already found that sometimes faculty training for self-service turns out to be secretary or graduate student training. This helps nobody, but least of all us. If you want to teach faculty, then at least insist that they all come personally to be taught and advised.

Nor do I think our role as advisors is assured if, as I suggested, people don't know what they don't know, and pretend they do know. Physical illness has clear symptoms, information illness often has none. I do not see these issues as contradictory. I see them as providing us with additional options. They are exciting options, but we won't have them forever. We most certainly won't have them if we decide we don't want to do any of this work because we are already too busy, because our staffs are so small, and because we have no money. That is the surest strategy for never getting any.

Notes

1. Mooers, Calvin N. "Mooers' Law or, Why Some Retrieval Systems Are Used and Others Not." *American Documentation* 11 (July 1960): 204.

2. Trueswell, Richard. "Some Behavioral Patterns of Library Users: The 80/20 Rule." *Wilson Library Bulletin* 43 (January 1969): 458-61.

3. Brinberg, Herbert R. "The Contribution of Information to Economic Growth and Development." Proceedings of the 40th Congress of the International Federation for Documentation, August 18-21, 1980. pp. 23-36.

4. Osburn, Charles B. "Academic Research and Library Resources; Changing Patterns in America." Westport, CT: Greenwood Press, 1979.

5. Boyer, Ernest L. "Scholarship Reconsidered; Priorities of the Professoriate." Princeton, NJ: Carnegie Foundation for the Advancement of Teaching, 1990.

6. Lancaster, F. Wilfrid. "Libraries and Librarians in an Age of Electronics." Arlington, VA: Information Resources Press, 1982.

Bailing Out the
Pacific Ocean with a Teaspoon

This is the last of three consecutive White Papers dealing with distractions from librarians' professional purposes, distractions so great that we don't have time or energy to determine what they are. "Lead Me Not into Temptation to Do Good" (*Library Journal*, September 15, pp. 47-48) dealt with the distractions brought about by the desire to do "good," at least as we like to define it: as a synonym for moral, principled, and virtuous. That at least makes us feel good. "Our Goals and Our Programs: We're Better at Caring Than at Getting Others to Care" (*Library Journal*, October 15, pp. 38-39) discussed the gap between the generalities of goals and the specifics of objectives and our unwillingness to make our own managers deal with the responsibilities of management.

This column deals with the constant co-opting of librarians by the priorities of others. In olden days the Royal Navy found its "recruits" by kidnapping, or impressing, unwary tavern drinkers. History records, however, that those who were forcibly taken felt some resentment at the process. We librarians appear to feel none, and indeed sometimes we seem to volunteer to be kidnap victims.

The Government Process

At the keynote address to the 1975 Atlanta conference of the American Society for Information Science (ASIS), engineering graduate and then governor of Georgia, Jimmy Carter, confided that the federal government never solved any problems. It paid lip service to the need to find solutions for a while, and then shifted attention to other issues because both the bureaucratic and public attention span is short. That piece of honesty instantly attracted me to the governor, about whom rumors of presidential ambitions had begun to surface. Later, of course, upon being elected president, Carter could do nothing to change the process, assuming he wanted to. He became a captive of the government engine.

We have laughed at the phrase "I'm from the government. I'm here to help you." We laugh because we recognize that government agencies and programs have their own priorities, which include heady rhetoric about national crises but which never provide any solutions. If heady rhetoric is all you want, you should be satisfied. However, we know that the federal government both supports cancer research and the tobacco industry.

We should also understand that federal programs will not win the "war" on either crime or drugs. If those wars are going to be won, it will be because people care enough, either as a personal conviction or as a result of pressure from family and friends to stop using addictive drugs and holding up perfect strangers.

Defeating Illiteracy

We also have another war, one that is very dear to many librarian hearts—the war on adult illiteracy. Goal 5 of the National Education Goals states that by the year 2000 every adult American will be literate. Upon first hearing that goal I quickly switched from my initial euphoria to some real questions. How many adult illiterates are there? Why are they illiterate—because of a lack of caring or a lack of opportunity? Is the problem growing or receding on its own? Putting that in cataloging terms, is the backlog growing by itself, has it stabilized, are we simply trying to accelerate what is already a natural reduction?

It is now 1994: How are we doing? Are we halfway there, almost there, further behind than when we started? How will we know in 2000 whether we have succeeded? Are we planning to send government inspectors into every home to turn off the TV and administer reading tests? Of course, there are no answers to any of these questions, and the primary reason they may seem absurd is that the goal was absurd from the start. There were no programs and no objectives, and the tools provided had no relationship to the magnitude of the task. It would be like asking people to bail out the Pacific Ocean with teaspoons. This will upset some of my readers, because we librarians love this goal. We even honored Barbara Bush at an American Library Association conference—and this from people who couldn't stand her husband.

What's the Harm?

You might argue that fighting illiteracy, even if it never approaches the goal, will at least have done some good. So what if we only teach 10 percent of the adult illiterates, or 5 percent, or 1 percent? So what if the total number of illiterates is greater in 2000 than it was in 1990, as I surmise it will be? It is hard to quantify here, because we haven't devised a test for "passing" literacy. What is the harm?

The harm is in being shanghaied into this process without ever having been consulted. The harm is in the federal perception that this is librarians' greatest professional priority, perhaps our only professional priority. For individuals captivated by the process of "doing good"—even a tiny amount of good—that may be enough. It is not good enough for me.

I want a voice in determining the priorities both for my field's research and operational funding support, at whatever pitiful level we can negotiate. I want it because biologists, historians, sociologists, and certainly educators are afforded that courtesy.

Perhaps we can do some good in dealing with a part of adult illiteracy. However, not with our own federal money, because we have priorities of our own. Anyone want to hear about them? There is a real risk here, because if someone really wanted to listen, we would have to start talking on the floor of ALA Council meetings about American library issues rather than Middle East politics or the virtues and vices of Christopher Columbus.

Finding a Pig in a Pork Barrel

It is not my intent to be unkind to the staff of the Office of Library Programs of the Office of Educational Research and Improvement, U.S. Department of Education (DOE). Ray Fry is an old friend, and what I hope is our mutual professional respect goes back quite a way. However, it is almost inevitable in programs such as this that they turn into pork barrel exercises, designed to report to Congress how much money is being returned to local Congressional districts and to each state.

Accusing Library Service & Construction Act (LSCA) Title VI of being a pork barrel program is almost embarrassing. After all, it only cost the taxpayers $8,163,000 in FY92 (my calculator is not sophisticated enough to determine what tiny percentage of the national debt this represents). We probably spend at least that much every time we send a routine warning to the Bosnian Serbs or the North Koreans, and certainly LSCA Title VI does more good than that.

Nevertheless, it is a pork barrel program, and the proof comes from the program's document, "Library Literacy Program: Analysis of Funded Projects 1992." Thirty-eight of the 64 pages of the document are a list, arranged by state, of where the money went. We are told proudly that grants went to 46 states, the District of Columbia, and Puerto Rico. It becomes deliciously tempting to identify the four states that didn't get anything. Find them for yourself, but be assured that there isn't a major committee chair in the lot.

The Principle of Self-Determination

All right, why so much ado about very little? Because there is a principle at stake, and principles are important, even as some prefer to simply label all their personal opinions as principles. The principle is that librarianship, if it is to be seen as a profession, must have the right to determine its own priorities. Funding will certainly be low, and it will include a mix of operational and research funds.

However, we should back away from pork barrel programs—no matter how badly we think we need the money—because they're so easily subject to elimination by Congress. Pork barrel programs, even as they continue to be politically attractive, are nevertheless considered by many in Congress to be an inappropriate use of federal money; our programs are fragile enough to risk elimination, even if only to make a virtuous point. Funds for operational programs on a local level can be a part of massive block funding but should never be specifically selected in Washington. It is micromanagement without a single redeeming virtue.

In preparation for retirement (which will certainly not include silence), my wife and I have decided to make an annual contribution to the Indiana University Libraries in support of professional and career development. Not job training, because that is the responsibility of the employer. And not to buy a single book, because that, too, is the task of the funding body. If they won't pay for books, it is very important there be no books, or the whole point is lost. My professional priority is not with libraries, it is with librarians.

Seducing Librarians

We are easily seduced by "good" causes, we are casually pressed into service on behalf of someone else's priorities. We allow our own managers to interfere and posture without making them responsible and without making the point that when it comes to librarianship, we know more than they do.

As long as we are so easily distracted, indeed as long as we continue to distract ourselves, we will also continue to be easy marks for anyone who wants to use us in support of a particular cause. Unfortunately, they have no interest in supporting our causes. Our literature contains gushing praise for the appearance of Hillary Rodham Clinton at a library conference, and we didn't even notice that she didn't talk about libraries but simply used the platform to recruit our support for her version of healthcare legislation. We might have offered her a trade, by suggesting that in return for our support she persuade her husband to restore program budgets for libraries. However, we didn't. Perhaps librarians would consider such a suggestion rude, but it was political deals that passed NAFTA.

New Programs at Our Expense

It cannot escape our notice that no one has volunteered to pay higher taxes in support of our programs. If we are to achieve funding, it will be by persuading politicians to give money to us rather than to someone else. Therefore, healthcare, if it is to have an increased funding cost, will exact a library penalty. So will crime-stopping initiatives, drug interdiction, afford-able housing, and whatever policy emerges for Cuba, Haiti, Bosnia, and Rwanda. Social responsibility is a personal assessment and responsibility; I can make my own decisions without help from the ALA Council. I elected the Councilors to help support librarianship against all else.

However, the competition even becomes internal. When the National Library of Medicine provides free access to AIDS databases uniquely among all its databases and does so without budget increases, it obviously cuts other programs. Can we simply applaud the one action without asking what the other is? When the DOE decides that we should use library program money to fight adult illiteracy, it is instead of doing something else. Don't we even want to know, let alone help decide? Librarians need to develop our own priority agenda. We must then make certain that the politicians we elect understand that our agenda automatically becomes their agenda. We can negotiate funding levels but not priorities.

Library Research and Government Funding— A Less Than Ardent Romance

Federal funding for library research, although disguised in the 1960s and 1970s as science information research, nevertheless allowed both research libraries and library education programs to study the phenomena under which acquisitions and operational decisions could be made intelligently and cost effectively. This has now been almost completely eliminated, and it has been replaced by mathematical and sociological studies undertaken by individuals with neither a background nor interest in libraries, and by the funding of examinations that determine only how libraries might serve a larger national priority in which they play at best an incidental part.

It could logically be assumed that library research would be funded by the U.S. Department of Education. Not only do educators claim that librarians are a subset of their profession, but many librarians, particularly in universities and the school systems agree with that assessment. However, educators do not accord to librarians an equal status in their hierarchy. The fact that no research agenda developed by librarians for libraries exists among educational research priorities probably results primarily from the assumption, among professional educators, that there is really nothing for libraries to research. Educators often articulate the value system that libraries exist to respond to the specific requests of their educator clients. The best way to do this is to have the largest collection possible, selected under at least the close guidance of the educators themselves.

This value system lies behind the "quality" ordering of academic libraries by simply ranking the size of their holdings, and the publication of those rankings in tables that resemble the standings of baseball leagues. Librarians should certainly know better

Reprinted, with changes, by permission of the author and *Publishing Research Quarterly* 10, no. 4 (Winter 1994-1995): 30-37.

than to engage in such silly games. Improved techniques for bibliographic access and document delivery make the question of where a particular item happens to be at any particular moment at least secondary and perhaps even moot, and we know from the early work of Trueswell[1] that ownership is no guarantor of use. When ownership predominates the thinking of librarians, opportunities for access may even decline. Public librarians play into this same nonresearch numbers game when they stress that circulation is the most important indicator of their success, without bothering to find out *why* the material was borrowed, or *whether* it was even read, let alone understood or used. Those who think research is important are not impressed by such value systems.

There is also at least some evidence that many if not most librarians, preoccupied both with these value systems and with the "moral imperativist" fixation for protecting quality of perceived service despite budget cuts, have thrown their lot with a strategy of working harder rather than perhaps looking for ways to work smarter.[2] Further indications for this observation come from the lack of practitioner interest in research publications and conference research programs in their own field. Those who write for both a researcher and a practitioner audience understand that articles in research journals no matter how prestigious will never reach the second group. Research programs at meetings of the American Library Association (ALA) draw only a small audience with virtually no administrators or practitioners,[3] even when the topic promises to have immediate practitioner implications—for example a study of the diverse reading preferences of teenage boys and girls. The *Bowker Annual of Library and Book Trade Information* reports, in detail, the activities of professional societies and government agencies, but these concern operational programs. There is no section of this publication reserved for research. There has also been indication of a growing sense of irritation, if not animosity, by practitioners toward the fate of library education programs. Conference programs that ask "what is wrong with library education?" have been around for some time, and they are practitioner and not educator programs. In turn, educators have turned away increasingly from the desire to please and impress those who will hire their graduates to a desire to impress academicians and administrators in their own institutions, for both credit and survival. Two examples will suffice to note the growing schism between educators and practitioners, and that the schism appears to be growing.[4]

Whatever the causes and villains, the result has been a library profession that has accepted, at least tacitly, the lack of support for library research in the programs of the U.S. Department of Education. The most obvious examples can be found in the single-minded devotion to the Library Services and Construction Act (LSCA). This was initially devised to provide funding for rural libraries for which no adequate local funding could be expected, but the program was rapidly transferred into a classic "pork barrel" program to provide a little bit of funding for every Congressional district. Now that pass-along federal largesse programs are under attack by both political parties, at least in principle, the argument has shifted from the simple if heartfelt "there is a need that must be met" to the more acceptable 1990s argument that federal funding provides incentives for additional state and local activity. The evidence is at best scattered and may even suggest the contrary, that states and localities use federal activity as a convenient excuse for abdicating their own responsibilities, always under the excuse of an inability to pay. The problem could have been addressed by a stress on matching grants programs, but in general, librarians have preferred to accept the argument that the federal government must pay because states and localities are too poor, obviously ignoring the fact that local politicians could increase taxes even as they would rather not.

The difficulty for librarians here is that the argument that only the federal government can afford to pay is now so widespread that librarians find themselves in uncomfortable competition with housing for the poor and mass transit. Many library leaders do understand that as operational funding from the federal trough will continue to decline, new justifications will have to be found, and perhaps they will be. However, it can be argued from a historical perspective that the library profession's perceived role as mendicant, nor for its members but as intermediary for others, has earned it cheap praise but very little political leverage or professional respect.

An even more glaring example comes from the initial definition of the Higher Education Act (HEA), which at its inception in the 1960s provided a $5,000 "gift" for materials purchase to every academic library, from the smallest to the most affluent. There can be no clearer example of "pork" than this, and for a short time it worked. In defending the program, librarians came up with case studies that showed how small and weak libraries had indeed benefited, although that still ignored the question of why the larger body that had established this library now declined to fund it properly. There was not, nor could there be, an explanation of why major research libraries also deserved this money to supplement their own materials budgets, perhaps by purchasing one expensive foreign journal. HEA title II money as then defined slowly dwindled away and ultimately disappeared, but perhaps the championing of such priorities, while certainly not restricted to the library profession, does nothing to enhance professional credibility for prudent decision making and prioritizing. It may simply be that the profession, and particularly as represented by the ALA and its Washington office, represents such diverse constituencies with narrow support priorities that a rank ordering of good things is simply not possible.

That does not suggest that pork barrel programs have disappeared from the federal political process, but rather that they are increasingly perceived as an improper priority, and responsibility for ongoing operational funding has been increasingly shifted back to local political units, despite the cries of anguish that are certainly predictable. Such shifting of operational responsibilities is now the strategy of both Democratic and Republican administrations. Library programs are now routinely proposed for zero funding, although the Congress, perhaps more sensitive to these political realities, has continued to supply a small (but decreasing) amount of money. Library funding at the federal level, even operational funding, can certainly be considered trivial when it is measured in millions or even tens of millions. And yet, as Parkinson noted many years ago,[5] it is trivial funding that draws the greatest amount of scrutiny and protests of funding poverty. Library programs therefore suffer under the double curse of being small, and perhaps precisely because of this triviality, being under constant attack. Far larger programs, be they for savings and loan bailouts, drought and flood relief (perhaps simultaneously) or earthquake damage will always receive multibillion funds, and the point is not to challenge these expenditures but only to note that they are voted easily by individuals who argue that they have no money for libraries.

It can only be speculated that perhaps requests for research rather than operational support funds might have a better chance of success, because the federal government does accept, at least in principle, its responsibility for areas that are broader than local or state concerns. The federal government will continue to fund, at variable levels, medical and scientific research, and this has even provided some fallout for library research programs tied to these initiatives, either through the National Library of Medicine (NLM), or through the National Science Foundation (NSF) in programs that will be described later in this article. What library "research" funding may come from the Department of Education is inevitably part of a larger and more generic question, such as, "how library services might improve the quality of life for an isolated Native American community?" It is not suggested that such studies are not important, only that they are more appropriately funded by the agencies that deal with the larger questions. For librarians, the finding of such studies are too narrow and specific to have any generalizable applications. Similarly, when library "research" studies now investigate library effectiveness in programs for adult illiteracy, the thrust is not libraries but illiteracy, and the question in assessing library programs is not whether but only how. If librarians have never been consulted on the "whether" by the literacy experts who design these attempts to prove conclusions already reached, librarians can also be counted on, in the expectation of their reservoir of social consciousness, never to complain about how "their" research money is being assigned.

It is, of course, a well understood premise in all academic disciplines that the field establishes its own research priorities, and that it then negotiates and lobbies with the federal establishment for levels of funding of what *it* wants to do, but that level of credibility has not been established for the library profession. By contrast, all programs of the NSF, National Endowment for the Humanities (NEH), and National Endowment for the Arts (NEA) are at least initially driven by the profession's own value system, and that causes some of the political controversy that exists today. However, when NEH funnels money to libraries, it is often simply to provide some support for unemployed and starving humanities scholars. There is no library research agenda as defined by librarians in any of these agencies, and they do not populate bodies that make research policy.

An even more glaring example comes from the funding priorities of the Office of Library Programs of the Office of Educational Research and Improvement, U.S. Department of Education.[6] In its published analysis of 1992 funded projects under Title VI, Library Services and Construction Act, the agency states that it supplies approximately 250 grants to libraries in just about every state (pork barrel?), all oriented specifically to the support of adult literacy programs. This might indeed become at least a high emotional priority for public librarians were they asked to rank order this issue against funding for the LSCA, but librarians were never consulted. It was the educators who decided that funding from the Office of Library

Programs should go to this particular priority, and it can be safely assumed that research support was never considered as a possibly higher priority. Grants, according to the report, range from $5,302 to the maximum allowable amount of $35,000. What makes all of this so tragically comic for library priorities is the rationale, which is embedded in Goal 5 of the National Education Goals. These state that by the year 2000 every adult American will be literate. It is hard to believe that this was written with a straight face, even by government bureaucrats. We will be fortunate if, by the year 2000, adult literacy will not have declined even further. What are libraries to do when they are captives of such silly political sloganeering, with no criteria for measurement, and no chance for success?

Academic libraries and library education programs were at one time successful in receiving research funds from the NSF. This money was channeled to libraries and library schools not because of any interest in issues of librarianship or information science, but because NSF (then as now dominated in its priority setting by the agendas of biologists, chemists, and physicists) was concerned with the effectiveness of the science information (not to be confused with information science) process. Funds were made available to undertake studies to determine patterns of publication, distribution, and access, pricing strategies and their relationship to usage, and the connection between library and individual subscription rates for scholarly and research journals. During the 1960s and well into the '70s such funding and such studies were relatively plentiful, and the references to two such studies in which this writer was involved at Indiana University are only indicative of a much larger trend.[7] The research funded during this period included a wide variety of studies, ranging from the compilation of a bibliography of user studies and the development of library cost models to suggest options between owning and borrowing, which were carried out in universities, to contracts awarded to the private information sector (Documentation Incorporated, J. I. Thompson Company, Herner and Company) which studied such diverse topics as the characteristics of professional scientific journals, the federal government's system for distributing its unclassified research and development reports, and an assessment of the state-of-the-art of coordinate indexing. That this activity has now virtually disappeared can be attributed to a number of factors, independently and in combination. These factors are discussed in the following pages.

During the 1960s and into the early '70s funding for all types of research, but particularly academic research, was at its height. As the nation then entered both a shift in priorities and economic declines exacerbated by the oil embargo in the mid-1970s, competition for research funds would have become more ferocious, no matter what else happened. Perhaps in conjunction with this shift, by the mid-1970s the NSF programs that funded science information studies had become disenchanted with survey research, and much of this work had been survey research. It was the agency's observation that survey research often led to unclear conclusions and the desire to undertake more surveys. The development of models as a basis for prediction, and a greater reliance on theoretical studies, while perhaps less definitive in their conclusions, at least promised the appearance of some forward momentum without replowing old ground.

While NSF naturally assumed that the community of library practitioners would appreciate and politically support its efforts to provide tools for library decisions (even as these were primarily for acquisition alternatives or as a rationale for requesting more funding for materials purchase only), the agency was surprised and shocked to learn that librarians didn't seem to care. An evaluation contracted to the American Society for Information Science (ASIS) in 1974-75 in which this author participated, led to what was perceived as a gratuitously insulting response that librarians didn't really much care whether or not NSF activity promulgated its findings. No government agency can lightly accept such a snub, and that may explain why no public distribution of the report could be located by this writer.

In parallel with these other changes came the greater level of self-awareness by information scientists, particularly as this was articulated by groups within ASIS. Although no totally acceptable definition of information science had then been developed (or indeed has since been developed) by the society that chose this name in a change from the earlier American Documentation Institute (ADI), representatives of ASIS argued forcefully before NSF bodies that NSF's activities in this area, housed in an Office of Science Information Services (OSIS) belonged more properly in Information Science. In the absence of any contrary testimony (physical scientists felt comfortable that they could still assure NSF support for scientific communication even without library studies), NSF agreed to establish an office specifically devoted to information science. An interested and astute observer noted at the time that information scientists and librarians might have won the battle but that they had probably lost the war.[8] Funding for science information studies was no longer available to library researchers, and NSF, having established a program without a clear understanding of its role within the overall mission of the Foundation, spent the next decade in shifting this program from one directorate to another—social sciences, mathematics, and others. NSF decided at that time that it no longer saw as its priority the support of international participation in the International Federation of Documentation (IFD), many of whose national participants come from the areas of science information, such as the active Soviet participation under its Institute for Scientific and Technical Information (VINITI). What research funding there was now tended to go to mathematicians, logicians, sociologists, and other behavioral scientists who had never shown any interest in or allegiance to "information science," let alone librarianship.

Because information science has been shifted so frequently within the National Science Foundation, including stays amidst social sciences, mathematics, and computer science, it is difficult to identify any specific emphasis for research in this area. Primarily, the emphasis has shifted away from applied to pure or basic research, and the thrust has inevitably been colored by where the program happened to reside at the time. In general, it can be stated that these have been heavily weighted toward mathematical modeling, computer simulation, and sociological orientations.

The number of "old" science information researchers with the flexibility and willingness to adapt their own research agendas to these new priorities was small, and largely concentrated in only a handful of academic institutions. Berkeley, Illinois, Pittsburgh, Syracuse, and UCLA come most immediately to mind. However, it is not surprising that a number of other academic library programs have explored shifting their program emphases to these funding areas. This could be a positive development, but only if it is additive. Unfortunately, there is at least some evidence of a desire, perhaps more for political than conceptual reasons, to distance the school from all contact with the traditions of librarianship. It may be that an identification with "libraries" will be seen as irrelevant for both future research and the education of professionals, or simply as a tactic to, as surfers would put it, catch the wave.

What may be lost in this shift is difficult to assess. The profession of librarianship has always faced change. It has not always reacted as rapidly as desirable, but it has reacted over time in the development of networks, resource sharing consortiums, and in the application of technology, including the newly proposed information superhighway. If there is a moral in all of this it is perhaps that practitioner librarians have ultimately nobody to blame but themselves. A profession that turns its back on its own educational component in carrying out a research function, that insists that academic programs can only train or perhaps even that they can be supplanted by in-house training, that fails to demand research support within its own budget with the same level of insistence with which it clamors for operating support, will ultimately earn the perception that what it does is routine, clerical, and ultimately dispensable.

The sad point in this moral is that while there are certainly losers, there are no winners except perhaps for opportunists. Certainly a nation of educators and scholars who, while perhaps unconsciously, have always depended on strong and alert library programs of research, innovation, and testing will be the greatest losers of all. It will now be peddled slogans with catch words such as "virtual," without the slightest indication of what this means, what it requires in adaptation in scholar working habits, what it is worth, what it costs, and what the alternative approaches developed by research might have been.

Notes

1. Trueswell, Richard W. "Some Behavioral Patterns of Library Users: The 80/20 Rule." *Wilson Library Bulletin* 44 (January 1969): 458-61.

2. White, Herbert S. "The Perilous Allure of Moral Imperativism." *Library Journal* 117 (September 15, 1992): 44-45.

3. _____. "ALA Conference Raises Questions on the Purpose of Research." *American Libraries* 12 (October 1981): 568-69.

4. Berry, John N., III. "The Two Crises in Library Education." *Library Journal* 118 (September 1, 1993): 102; and White, Herbert S. "Your Half of the Boat Is Sinking." *Library Journal* 118 (October 15, 1993): 45-46.

5. Parkinson, C. Northcote. *Parkinson's Law, and Other Studies in Administration.* Boston: Houghton Mifflin, 1957.

6. Humes, Barbara, and Carol Cameron Lyons. *Library Literacy Program: Analysis of Funded Projects 1992.* Washington, D.C.: U.S. Department of Education, 1993.

7. White, Herbert S. "Publishers, Libraries and Costs of Journal Subscriptions in Times of Funding Retrenchment." *The Library Quarterly* 46 (October 1976): 359-77; and White, Herbert S. "Factors in the Decision by Individuals and Libraries to Place or Cancel Subscriptions to Scholarly and Research Journals." *The Library Quarterly* 50 (July 1980): 287-309.

8. Personal discussion with Lee Burchinal, head of the Office of Science Information Services, National Science Foundation.

Part

2

*Librarians, Their Self-Image,
and the Perceptions
That Define Their Preparation*

Introduction

To a great and unfortunate extent, librarians shape their own self-image and strategies to please others, and to validate the roles that others have already assigned for us. Our definition of a service profession does not involve, as it would in law and medicine, giving people what they need, because we are uniquely prepared to understand what that is. Instead, we adapt our service programs and our educational programs to what will please others, and we fail to consider the possibility that what these others tell us may not even be good for them, aside from the fact that it is obviously not good for us. Thus, the argument by some public library boards that the primary responsibility of the library is just to keep the doors open is never demolished as the nonsense it represents. If that were indeed the primary and ultimately the only purpose of the public library, we and they would be better served if the library were closed, because that would at least end the pretense. We show this same disinclination to claim a unique professional expertise when we allow university administrators to redefine the missions of the schools that educate our new professionals, or when we invite, every 10 years, hordes of individuals to propose library policy and priority in the White House Conferences for which we must first explain to them the terminology of the issues. Some of these individuals are friendly, others are not. However, that is not the point, because they are equally unqualified. Perhaps we need to adopt the language of Michigan State football coach Biggie Munn, who informed the alumni that he would appreciate their support but not their advice.

That we have not established or even claimed our own expertise as a unique qualification, which is something any self-respecting profession automatically and ferociously does, must be obvious to all readers who are librarians. Instead, we adopt slogans to give people "what they want," demurring from

155

any claim to assess what they might need. I cannot imagine "give them what they want" as the cornerstone of the nation's drug policy, but we not only accept such a relationship but eagerly embrace it.

For all of these reasons, no separate introduction for this section has been attempted. The reader may want to re-read the earlier introduction to establish a context for what follows.

Information Access and the Changing Library School Curriculum

The impact of changes in the information process on library education curriculum is difficult to assess and predict for a number of reasons. First, as we all know, the rate of implementation of change varies—not only country by country but within countries as well. In my state university in Indiana, we recognize our responsibility to prepare individuals whose first jobs will be in highly technological government and industrial information systems. We also prepare individuals who will be working in small public libraries in which very little has changed, and in which perhaps very little will change soon. In some ways the changes that the library profession already faces are substantial, almost traumatic. In other ways the role in which librarians interact not only with the mechanics of the profession but with its purpose is in great need of change. When some speak and write about the necessity of change in library education, they are usually concerned only with the former—the ability to address more complex databases, to search online, and to request items on interlibrary loan through networks rather than through the mail. If this is the focus of library education, I am afraid it misses much of the point.

The role of the educational process in preparing professionals for the present and for the future has always been a focus of discussion and controversy, and the recent revival of interest in this topic may be nothing more than a cyclical recurrence. As early as 1923, C. C. Williamson[1] suggested major changes in the preparation of American librarians from the practical skills development advocated by Melvil Dewey and others. Although Williamson's report to the Carnegie Corporation still mentioned training in its title, in fact he was suggesting a great deal more. He was proposing the development of a fundamental educational and professional preparation base. After World War II,

Paper presented at International Federation of Library Associations and Institutions (IFLA) Conference, Chicago, August 20, 1985.

most American universities with library education programs changed their focus from undergraduate to graduate preparation, and began to include in their curricula courses that dealt with concepts and principles. In the last decade, several library education programs in the United States and nearly all of those in Canada have changed to a longer degree program. Although the strategies vary, the clear intent is to overcome at least one perceived problem, that the one-year graduate degree superimposed on a subject bachelor's degree and even on a subject master's degree is not enough. Schools with longer programs vary widely in what they offer.

What *ought* to be taught has been and remains the subject of continuing controversy, and that controversy appears in the last few years to be accelerating. A variety of studies and opinion pieces have suggested that library education is not practical enough, and that what is taught is irrelevant to the needs of the "real" world.[2] On the other hand, some leaders in the practitioner community have argued that what is needed is less emphasis on credentials and more emphasis on talent. In a provocative article, Patricia Battin[3] has argued for the primacy of a first-rate mind, managerial abilities, and an intellectual commitment to research. All of these issues have been raised in Great Britain and have been analyzed by Blaise Cronin.[4]

This brief paper will not attempt to survey educational preparation changes in other nations. This author is not qualified to do this, and the length of this presentation would permit nothing more than a catalog listing. However, at the risk of appearing chauvinistic, this writer would suggest that these issues, as they represent the differentiation between intellectual preparation and pragmatic training, have received their sharpest level of discussion in the United States, Canada, and Great Britain. Moreover, what is decided here has influence far beyond our borders. Perhaps 15 percent of the graduate student body in library education and other fields at major universities in the United States consists of overseas students, primarily from Asia and Africa, and they in turn often become educational leaders in their own countries. What results from the present discussion about library education here will have far-reaching effects elsewhere as well.

Perhaps the very fact that librarians are discussing, and claiming the right to decide, what their curriculum should be, is in itself a major step forward, although it is one from which this author would take little consolation. After all, the Library of Congress and Harvard University are directed by individuals with no educational or philosophical preparation in librarianship, and who have up to now demonstrated no desire to acquire any such education after their appointment. However, for the most part, we do have the right to control our own credentialing process, and it is important that we neither waste nor trivialize that opportunity.

This writer has had little previous organizational experience with IFLA, and has not presented a paper to a conference since the 1972 meeting in Budapest. I am delighted to be invited back. However, the intervening years have seen for me a good deal of organizational experience in the Federation Internationale de Documentation (FID), which could certainly be called a sister organization. For FID, international information communication is largely in the hands of the scientific community, and it is the presumption that subject preparation and expertise take precedence over preparation in what librarians are supposed to do. The role of the future librarian becomes particularly significant as we view the shifting nature of information and its use. What do we really know with any degree of certainty about the future? We know that the total amount of information will continue to grow. That part is easy, it has never stopped growing. We also know that through computerized access, the availability of information to anyone with electrical outlets will also increase dramatically. Finally, we know that education in the communities we serve has become and will continue to become more specific, while the needs of students for information become more and more interdisciplinary. In other words, our clients will know more and more about less and less.

Does this suggest a changing role for the librarian? Of course it does. The passive model of librarians providing users with more information, on the premise that they are the only ones qualified to assess it, has never worked as well as we have all pretended it did. Most users do not really know their literature. Given its breadth and its diversity, there is no way they could. However, there is also no way for them to admit their ignorance. And so users are forced to pretend for a great variety of reasons that they know their literature, and, of course, what they don't know either is pretended not to exist or is assumed to be irrelevant. In a paper several years ago,[5] I suggested to a British audience that the need was for librarians to take on the responsibilities of information intermediaries—to concentrate not on providing our users with *more* information, but with *better* information. They already have more piled up on their desks than they know what to do with, and they are badly frightened at the suggestion that through "improved" access techniques, we might bring them still more. They want less but better information, but they don't know it is all right to make that request, and our value system certainly does not provide any hint of our willingness and preparation to assume this burden. The value system I am suggesting is somewhat foreign to the traditional ways in which we measure ourselves. It concentrates on techniques of access, as contrasted to measurements of holdings. Furthermore, it argues for a specificity in which an increase in circulation becomes at least potentially a negative indicator, because it suggests vagueness. Quantity and specificity are antagonistic value systems in this scenario.

Can librarians be prepared to work effectively in this setting? I would argue that they certainly *can*, but I am not certain that they *will*. In part this is because we confuse the very different concepts of education and training. In fact, these concepts have become one continuous word, "educationandtraining" in the same way that we have combined "libraryandinformationscience" as though they were the same thing.

Education and training are very different concepts, and generally education in a professional environment precedes training. It does in medicine, and it does in law, although the processes are not completely sequential. In one sense I find the very title of your section, "Library Schools and Other Training Aspects," disheartening. The implication is clear—library schools train, and, of course, others train as well. But who educates?

Do library schools train? Of course we do, and the often-heard arguments suggest that we don't train specifically enough. The articles referred to earlier and in the bibliography clearly indicate a preference that library schools prepare students better for today's jobs. As this writer has argued somewhat cynically,[6] the ideal state is one in which candidates can be hired at 9:00 A.M. and begin attacking the backlog at 9:30 A.M. This is an understandable reaction to the pressures of having too much to do with staffs too small to get it done. However, such training is preparation for today only, and this sort of value system suggests that planning for tomorrow takes a lower priority. It also suggests to others that our profession does not have a great deal of intellectual substance.

Education and training are very different things, and to some extent library schools must train, but never at the expense of education, because education (why we do what we do) must not only precede training (how we do it), but it is more important. Individuals who are educated can be trained and retrained as priorities shift and as the information spectrum shifts. Individuals who are only trained will strive mightily to shape the need to their system rather than shape the system to needs, and we know from looking at the library and information world that by and large they get away with it.

Education and training are not only distinct processes, but they are *both* continuing processes. One survey clearly indicates that both training by the employer and continuing education and training through a variety of mechanisms are perceived as desirable, but that there are no agreed upon mechanisms either for deciding what that education and training should consist of, or that it does happen. The library school degree is still largely a one-time preparation for a whole lifetime of work, regardless of what changes take place. That approach is not only training, it is poor training. It is certainly unprofessional, and may help explain the low esteem in which we are held.

Library schools operate in the present, and the more they are forced to prepare for "practical" skills, the narrower that time focus becomes. Good training facilities will in 1985 at least prepare their graduates for 1985 rather than 1970 positions (although as noted earlier there are 1970s positions still in existence in 1985). In any case, they will not be trained for the year 2000. No training program can do that. What we can do is provide an educational base on which later training can be applied, but that presupposes that training opportunities will not only be provided, but demanded. By and large I think that Patricia Battin and those who echo her thinking are correct. Broad skills and intellectual commitment are more important in the library educational process than specific tricks of the trade. Tricks can be learned later, and new tricks will be required by new technology. Moreover, as Daniel Bell[7] has suggested, we will be enjoying the luxury of a large coterie of service professionals with specialized skills. Librarians are service professionals, but there is no reason for us not to use the service capabilities of others, when these can help us or rid us of less important tasks. The preferred role for the library professional that I envisage is one of managing both the accelerated access to information systems that technology has made possible and will continue to enhance, and of making such an information flow fit the needs of users. It is for these reasons that broader skills and intellectual competency are more important than the training levels on which we seem to focus.

The phrase "user needs" also requires some definitions. We must not determine user needs only by asking users. A large number of surveys that profess to determine user needs do nothing more than measure user demands or preferences, based on the definition of a library system as they assume it must be. It should occur to us that if we provide more open-ended questions, we might receive answers that are both different and more inviting. The relationship between librarians and their users must be changed into one of mutual respect between cooperating professionals, who deal with problems and not with mechanisms. We can devise mechanisms ourselves. It is probably not we but today's students who will spearhead that change, if indeed it is to take place. There is no doubt in my mind that it should take place, because it is good for us and because it is good for the success of the information process.

How does all this affect what we should teach in library schools? Certainly there must be a mixture of education *and* training. Concentrating on only the former would be impractical, because librarianship is more than an intellectual exercise. Concentrating only on the latter, as some practitioners would have us do through curriculum validation of basic skill competencies, produces graduates who not only work as clerks, but even more importantly, who think like clerks. And this is something we cannot afford, and cannot allow to continue to happen.

What is needed in the continued development of curriculum is an ongoing dialog between practitioners and educators. Both have their priorities, and it is essential that the two groups come together in a compromise. The dialog must contain the complete spectrum of options for a lifetime professional commitment to both education and training, a commitment that must be demanded and supported by employers as well as professional bodies. It can't all be done in the single educational experience that the library degree represents, tempting as such an orderly suggestion might be.

It can't be done for what are primarily two reasons. First, the knowledge of our field grows and changes, and even the best of library schools can only teach what is known today. Second, the time for the initial pre-professional education process (you will note that I studiously avoid the word "training" as professionally degrading—I wish I could urge you to change the name of your section) must be related to the rewards that await the graduate. As we know, at least in those countries in which starting salaries are determined by the free application of economic market factors, those salaries are not high.

Studies such as the one by Nancy Van House[8] must give us pause if we think simply of adding to the curriculum. Van House has told us that we are already losing highly qualified students to better paying careers. The risk we must avoid is that if we increase the length and cost of the educational program to improve it, we might in the process worsen the quality of the student body. The pressures to teach any one additional course are not unreasonable, but these and the many other requests (or demands) from specific interest advocates are cumulative, and add to as much as a three- or four-year program.

Nobody has suggested what we should *stop* teaching, either because they consider it no longer significant for the profession, or because they are willing to take the responsibility as part of the job training. Simply telling me what you want me to add doesn't really help very much. Our school at Indiana already offers 55 courses of which five are required, and students then select seven others from among 50. That creates a serious fragmentation problem, particularly for students who are not sure how they want to specialize. I would be very reluctant to add to that fragmentation. We already offer eight dual master's programs and three specializations, and as career tracks they are almost irreversible.

The issues we face are not simple, and they defy simplistic approaches. On the other hand, if the solutions were easy and obvious, they would also be boring. I can assure you that the future of this profession and of its educational component will not be boring.

Notes

1. Williamson, Charles C. *Training for Library Service: A Report Prepared for the Carnegie Corporation of New York.* New York: D. B. Updike, 1923.

2. Clough, M. Evalyn, and Thomas J. Galvin. "Educating Special Librarians." *Special Libraries* 75 (January 1984): 1-8; Eshelman, William R. "The Erosion of Library Education." *Library Journal* 108 (July 1983): 1309-12; Koenig, Michael E. D. "Education for Special Librarianship." *Special Libraries* 74 (April 1983): 182-96; Marchant, Maurice P., and Nathan M. Smith, "The Research Library Director's View of Library Education." *College and Research Libraries* 43 (November 1982): 437-39; White, Herbert S., and Marion Paris, "Employer Preferences and the Library Education Curriculum." *Library Quarterly* 55 (January 1985): 1-33.

3. Battin, Patricia M. "Developing University and Research Library Professionals: A Director's Perspective." *American Libraries* 14 (January 1983): 22-25.

4. Cronin, Blaise. "The Education of Library-Information Professionals: A Conflict of Objectives?" *ASLIB Occasional Publication* No. 28, London, 1982.

5. White, Herbert S. "Growing User Information Dependence and Its Impact on the Library Field." *ASLIB Proceedings* 31, no. 2 (February 1979): 74-87.

6. _____. "Defining Basic Competencies." *American Libraries* 14 (September 1983): 519-25.

7. Bell, Daniel. *The Coming of Post-Industrial Society: A Venture in Social Forecasting.* New York: Basic Books, 1973.

8. Van House, Nancy. "The Return of the Investment in Library Education." Paper presented at the January 7, 1984, Meeting of the Association of Library and Information Science Education, Washington, D.C. *Library and Information Science Research* 7, no. 1 (January-March 1985): 31-52.

Evaluating Personnel

      The process of examining personnel evaluation in libraries must begin with an examination of the role that people play in the functioning of libraries. If that seems obvious to the reader, it is only because he or she has assumed that for everyone the needs of the library are not only paramount, but also so evident that we all agree on what the goals are, who should perform what services or tasks, and how they should be performed. Experienced managers know that this is anything but true. One of the characteristics that makes robotics so attractive as a concept to management is that robots are programmed to be totally predictable, and to perform exactly as planned. People don't function that way. They have value systems of their own, they have priorities of their own, and they reach different conclusions based on different perceptions of the same facts.

      In this environment, personnel evaluation can become either an irritating or an irrelevant process. A supervisory evaluation of whether or not an individual performs "satisfactorily" in a client environment assumes first of all an agreement on what that service relationship should be. The statement "we want to do what is best for the library" is, without some careful discussion, meaningless gibberish. Eight different individuals will have eight different value systems, most likely based on preconceptions and on the tendency of people to conclude what they find most comfortable to conclude. The determination that what is best for the library is therefore what is best for me is not difficult to make. In engineering that process is called retrofitting, first reaching a conclusion, then proving it to at least your own satisfaction, which is really the only satisfaction that seems necessary. In this environment, for the boss to unilaterally impose a personnel evaluation system (his or her own or as passed along by an administrative body) becomes simply an exercise in power. We let our subordinates know that we are bigger and

Background article prepared for a home study workshop on performance evaluation for the Stone Hills (Indiana) Area Library Services Authority (SHALSA), Bloomington, 1988.

163

stronger than they are, but they already know that, so personnel evaluation in this environment only causes anger and disenchantment. And this is exactly what does happen in many settings. Neither supervisors nor subordinates like performance evaluation as it currently works, and yet we know that subordinates want a fair method of feedback, and supervisors should want it as a management tool. Libraries in which individuals are working at cross-purposes, or in which the environment is one of anger, resentment, or betrayal, cannot succeed.

We know that people are the most crucial element in the success of libraries. This may come as a surprise to some management bodies or user groups who may think that collection is more important than staff, but we librarians know that this is not so. We know it in part because we recognize that users must be brought to a full understanding of the potential available to them. Otherwise they will simply accept what is offered and think it is good. It is particularly true as we end this century and technology opens up techniques for bibliographic resource sharing and document delivery, techniques with which our users are in large part unfamiliar. Finally, an emphasis on the people in libraries is as essential for us as it is for our users. Without that emphasis, and without a perception that people are important, and that good personnel are ultimately less costly than poor personnel, even if they are more highly paid, then the evaluation of the library only becomes an exercise in determining how cheaply we can run it, and that process has no bottom.

Who are the individuals who work for us in libraries? Obviously, some are professionals who made this field a career choice, but even for these individuals the selection of a particular library may be the result of outside factors, perhaps of geographic pressures. This means simply that while their loyalty and commitment are not unachievable, they are not necessarily automatic. With nonprofessional staff members, the range is even wider. Some are people who have always wanted to work in libraries, and their obvious commitment must be balanced against their very strong preconceptions about how a library should function, preconceptions not normally expected from subordinate staff. For other individuals, working in the library is nothing more than an accident either of geography or of timing.

It is important that we recognize that for many people (and perhaps the most healthy) working in the library is only a job, hopefully a job in which they can take pride and pleasure, but nevertheless just a job. They have other priorities and will attempt to balance all of these priorities. It is management's job to assist them in doing this.

If you are one of the very dedicated individuals who have accepted what Peter Drucker calls "the moral imperative"—placing your work above everything else in your life and being willing to make every sacrifice for it—then at least recognize that quite aside from whether or not this fanaticism makes you a good librarian (and that is questionable), you have no right to expect it from others. What *you* have the right to expect is that they will perform to the standards of the job description (as measured by performance evaluation). What *they* have the right to expect is fair treatment from you, and fair is a difficult term to define. At a minimum, it means equitable treatment as compared to the standards that apply to community salary and benefits. That is the way that subordinates evaluate their bosses, and evaluate them they do. Remember this the next time you read of a public library director making the grandstand announcement that a budget cut will be absorbed with minimum inconvenience to patrons through the expediency of giving smaller or no salary increases (presumably smaller than earned and otherwise warranted elsewhere in the community). How dare such an individual impose his or her value system as though it were that of everyone else? Performance evaluation must deal with such issues, because it concerns value given for value received, loyalty given for loyalty received. You have no right to expect dedication, most particularly from clerks. You do have the right to expect hard work, and they have the right to expect fair, proper, or at least consistent and explained treatment. If you do find that your subordinates are dedicated, then don't take advantage of that characteristic by treating it as a weakness.

It is essential that any discussion of performance evaluation begin with a discussion of the individuals whom we are evaluating, because the process cannot ignore that framework. Who are these people? What are their objectives? Why did they come to this job? In all likelihood no two employees will be alike, but most importantly, whatever their value system, it will not be yours. Some have come to get ahead and make money, although this is unlikely to happen in the library. It is more likely that this is the best they can do in meeting that objective in this time and place. When they can leave, they will, and they should. No hard feelings.

Other employees have a genuine interest in serving people, and the library field has counted on recruits from this sector for a long time. There are obvious advantages, but there are two dangers. One, that they may have preconceptions about the library and be reluctant to consider change, has already been mentioned. The other, which is a trap for managers, is that we will take advantage of them by treating this dedication as a weakness, either by giving them unreasonable workloads or by paying them less. When either of these things happen, we have taken library work out of the mainstream and relegated it to individuals who are, most charitably, "different" from the rest of us. When we do this, or when we allow others to do it, something is wrong. Workers in the tax office presumably give value for value received. Are library workers supposed to give more value, and receive less in return for their "dedication"? I think not, even if some of your staff members might be convinced you have the right to expect it of them, you still can't expect it of the others. The answer "because it is a library" as an explanation for injustice is no explanation at all, only a rationalization for incompetent or ineffective management.

It is important in approaching the issue of personnel evaluation that we understand first that it must be based on a realistic job; one that can be performed satisfactorily with a reasonable amount of effort, and one with a chance of success. When individuals are given jobs that cannot ever be completed; when the backlogs are so large that they cannot be eliminated without a change in work procedure, a reduction in input, or a modification in technique, and when none of these are permitted by an insensitive management; when the answer to an employee who can't get the job done with the resources provided is "do the best you can" as though that were an answer, then personnel evaluation is meaningless before it ever starts.

If we understand that no two people are alike, that they came to the library with different expectations and different values (and that, of course, is why some people like participative management and some people hate it), and that the boss must adjust *as far as the library's needs and priorities will allow* to the personal or professional needs of the subordinate, are there yet some things we can hold in common? Yes, there are. There are five points that, as studies have shown in depth, characterize the expectations of nearly every subordinate. They are reasonable and not at all confrontational points, and they include, as the reader will note, a significant amount of personnel evaluation. Subordinates want to be evaluated, and they understand that they need to be evaluated, in great part for their own protection. What turns them off are personnel evaluation systems without substance, without validity, and without impact. The five points, listed in sequence, are the following:

1. Let us both understand clearly what it is you expect of me. I must know what you think I can accomplish, and I need to understand why you believe I have the resources (material, money, time) to accomplish what you expect me to do. This is the *job description*. Without a job description that accurately and completely describes the position, and that both the supervisor and subordinate agree they understand (it is less important that the subordinate likes it than that he or she understands it), nothing else that follows, be it evaluation, salary increase, promotion, or dismissal, will make sense.

    Job descriptions have to be sufficiently accurate so that they will cover at least 80 percent of what really occurs during the average working week. There are always "other jobs as may be assigned," but when those become the majority we have no job description. It is then time either to write a new job description, or to think about why things are so chaotic that none of the job descriptions fit. Is it just possible that we have taken on a job without the resources with which to do it? If so, that is of course foolish for the supervisor to have done, but supervisors are allowed to be foolish. However, it is also unfair to the subordinates, and we are not allowed to be unfair. At least we are not if we expect moral justification as well.

2. Leave me alone! This is *delegation*, and it means quite simply that once individuals know what the job is and have been given the training and resources to do it, we should leave them alone. This means that we should judge them by results and not by methods. We tend not only to tell people what to accomplish but also how to do it. This is assignment, and is simply an exercise in authority. Most of us assign rather than delegate, under the guise of wanting to be helpful. However, subordinates consider that intrusive, and correctly so. It is over-management, and it is resented. It is also unnecessary. Your subordinates are not your clones, let them be themselves.

3. Help me if I ask for help! This is *mentoring*, or role modeling, or just plain support. It means that our subordinates understand that we want them to succeed and that we are not putting booby traps in their path in the expectation that they will fail. Helping people when they ask for help must be done in a non-pejorative manner. We want them to feel comfortable in asking us, because the alternative is guessing, and that can be disastrous. It is, of course, possible that the same subordinate may be driving us crazy asking the same question every day. That may either be a cry for attention and recognition, or nothing more than a manifestation of a real inability to perform the job. If this is the case, we may decide to fire the employee at the first opportunity, but until that day we want him to feel free to ask questions.

4. Tell me how I did! This is *performance evaluation*, and it may surprise readers to learn, after their own experiences, that subordinates not only want but desperately need to be told how they did. It should not be surprising, because after all their future plans and perhaps even their survival as employees depend on that evaluation. What they object to in the present practice is the perception of insincerity, meaninglessness, and manipulation in a process either structured to communicate nothing at all, or to rationalize decisions already reached.

5. Reward me based on my performance! This concept of *reward mechanisms* completes the cycle, because it places performance evaluation into an understandable framework. Talk is cheap: if you tell me I am an outstanding subordinate, prove that you mean it! Sometimes this is difficult, particularly when salary policies permit no distinction to be made between mediocre and outstanding employees. Where such distinctions are possible, they should be used, because it is not only foolish but unfair not to. Treating unequal performance equally is completely unfair. Moreover, it may anger your very best people.

Where salary increase distinctions are not possible because of overriding policies, the supervisor must look for other ways to indicate his or her pleasure (or the absence of the same). "Praise in public, criticize in private," is still sound advice. Superior performance must always be praised, and then other ways of showing appreciation must be found. These steps are essential, because if there is one group we cannot afford to alienate, it is our superior performers. If we do not in some way recognize their contribution, they will try to find a position where they do feel recognized, and what remains will be an automatic self-selection of inferior performers. If they cannot leave, they will resent being taken advantage of. They may poison the atmosphere with their resentment, and with valid reason.

Performance evaluation is a normal and natural part of a continuum, and that continuum must begin with the identification of what is being measured. Performance evaluation can succeed only if there is agreement between the supervisor and subordinate on the following: 1) what is the job? 2) can the job be done at all? 3) how do we *both* understand clearly and immediately whether the job was completed satisfactorily? This suggests putting measurement criteria on the task so that success or failure can be determined by both the supervisor and the subordinates. For some jobs, error rates and quantities of output are easier to determine than for others. Nevertheless, it is essential that there be understanding (agreement is still better) on what is being evaluated and what the criteria are, and that the results of that evaluation are communicated on a continuing feedback basis.

If those safeguards are in place, performance evaluation becomes a normal and natural process. It is also an ongoing process, and not to be saved for an annual or semiannual bloodletting. In reality, though, such bloodlettings rarely occur. Most supervisors are reluctant to criticize, and performance evaluations, rather than being specifically favorable or unfavorable, become bland exercises in mediocrity. Everybody becomes "above average" without ever defining what that means (we can't until we have specified the expectation as "average"), but we all understand that above average is really just average, or may even be below average, and in any case none of it really means anything at all.

If performance evaluation against real job descriptions both parties understand takes place on a continuing basis, then the only thing left to do in the "formal" performance review is to document what presumably both already know. If that session becomes confrontational or traumatic, then clearly effective communication has not taken place in the past, because there should be no surprises at this stage. The purpose of performance evaluation is not punishment, it is correction and improvement, and with a proper system of rewards, improvement is at least as important to the subordinate as it is to the supervisor, because it triggers rewards. If not, and if it also does not trigger punishments (rewards are always better) then why bother at all? Performance evaluation is a documented process, with both parties signing the form, and with the employee not only free but also encouraged to contribute comments and reactions. However, documentation of both praise and criticism should go on throughout the year, with the former being as public and the latter as private as possible.

If the annual (or semiannual) performance review is nothing more than a summing up of what we both already know, that part of the procedure should take perhaps no more than 10 or 15 minutes. During the rest of the meeting we should concentrate on the far more important issue, the future. It is really two futures, the library's and the employee's. Those two futures may converge quite nicely, or they may drift apart. If that's the case, that's all right, too. If we're going to part, let's part as friends, and make the process as smooth and painless as possible.

But if the employee plans to stay, the meeting should cover what the library expects in the foreseeable future, at least for the next year. Is the job going to remain about the same? Will there be more responsibility and more opportunity? If so, what are the mechanisms for providing the time, and what are the rewards? Are there new skills (database searching, for example) that the library wants the subordinate to learn? If so, then clearly it is the employer's responsibility to arrange for this learning process, provide the time, and pay for it. Are there skills it might be useful for the subordinate to learn, although there may be no immediate application or opportunity to use them, yet?

Responsibility here for what we generally call continuing education (what the job requires you to learn is not continuing education, it is part of the job) depends in large part on the support of the employing library. Conscientious employers handle the cost of job-related continuing education as part of their planned budgets, others at least make the time available to employees as paid administrative leave, even if they don't pay travel and tuition. In dealing with professionals you *can* do no less, in dealing with paraprofessionals you *should* do no less.

However, there is yet another dimension to the issue. The employee's career objectives may take him or her away from the library—into retirement, into family raising, into farming, or into an advanced degree in another field and an entirely different field. The specifics don't matter. What does matter is our understanding that our subordinates have needs and goals of their own, and deserve our support and encouragement. Never forget that people will always make decisions based on their personal needs and preferences. We can't stop them, and we shouldn't even try.

What we must do, in a continuing process we can call performance evaluation, is evaluate the needs of our subordinates against the needs of the organization we are responsible for managing, and look for ways to either make the two fit, or to agree that they don't fit. Ultimately that is all management really is. We give people doable jobs, we make sure they understand them, we leave them alone to do them, we help them if they ask us, we evaluate what they did, we seek correction and direction, we reward and punish, and we seek ways to balance our organizational needs against their personal needs and determine whether the balance that once existed (if indeed it did) still exists.

Specific personnel evaluation techniques are described fully in many writings easily available from any business school. Many of you are now subject to some sort of evaluation process or bureaucratic form developed by some larger agency of which you are a part. If it doesn't work, and yet you are required to use it, supplement it with something better. Techniques in vogue vary from checklists with ranges (from "does not meet expectations" to "greatly exceeds expectations"), relative rankings in which individuals are compared to their co-workers, critical incidents that document the unusual that did or did not happen, and many others. The potential pitfalls in all of these should be clear. If we are measuring performance against expectations, then both the supervisor and the subordinate must know, well in advance, what those expectations are, so that the process of evaluation does not become arbitrary and subjective. Telling someone they have done a "fine job" may be pleasing (unless the person recognizes that he is receiving lavish praise instead of a decent raise), but it is meaningless unless the employee can compare "fine job" against a standard of expectation, so that both know how it was exceeded.

Most performance evaluations currently do none of this. They are recognized widely as a pointless exercise in meaningless insincerity. The question is why we throw away our opportunities to help both our subordinates and our libraries, particularly when it is clear subordinates both welcome and need honest feedback, and that our jobs as managers demand it. It is probable that the concept of management by objectives, the only workable alternative to library managers trying to do everything in an environment in which expectations are considered separate from resources, also provides the only hope for the evaluation process. Treat the employee as an independent contractor—with tasks, resources, strategies, and checkpoints, and then use performance against these understood standards for evaluation. But make sure that these objectives are really germane, and that they describe what really happens. Irrelevance is still irrelevance, in any form.

Conclusions

Performance evaluation is not an end in itself. It is a means to an end, better performance by employees, and it must be judged on the basis of whether or not it accomplishes that end. It is now frequently an exercise in insincerity, in irrelevancy, and in feel-good trivia. This is useless to functioning of the library. As important, it is resented by the employee, who wants a fair and meaningful evaluation and reconciliation of individual and organizational needs.

Performance evaluation should address the following: What were the objectives of the library during the past year? Were they accomplished? (Bear in mind that objectives are specific targets. They are not goals.) Was there an adequate plan (including resources—people, money, materials, and time) for accomplishing these objectives? What were the subordinate employee's objectives? Were these accomplished? If not, why? In what way is the subordinate's job (his objectives as spelled out in his job description) important to the successful achievement of the library's objectives? What were the employee's own objectives for the past year? How do these mesh with the library's objectives? Were they accomplished or was satisfactory progress made? If not, why? What are the employee's plans, hopes, and aspirations for the coming year? How do these fit in with what the library wants and needs?

What are the library's objectives for the coming year? What is the plan for accomplishing them? What is the employee's role in this plan? Why is this role important? What does the employee need to do in order to meet the new objectives? What does the library need to do to allow the employee to do this, and will this happen? If not, then what are we really talking about?

All of these issues are an essential part of the employee evaluation process. The subordinate represents the library's most important resource. He or she must be treasured, supported, monitored, praised or criticized as appropriate, and rewarded or punished based on performance. However, this must always happen within fair and rational ground rules that are understood. For the employee, the organization is represented by the immediate supervisor. There may be other and higher-level supervisors, including nonlibrarians, but the basic line of communication is the direct supervisor, and it is the supervisor's job to work effectively with his or her own boss. There is nothing the subordinate can do about this, and there is no point in involving him or her in your problems, except in the positive sense of explaining what you are doing about issues and concerns. In a positive environment, the boss represents support, understanding, and fair treatment. In a negative environment it can be spinelessness, indifference, or manipulation. Much of the performance evaluation is simply communication: oral communication in talking about what we have written, are going to write, and what it all means.

Does your performance evaluation process meet these objectives and the needs of both the library and the employee? Probably not. Few performance evaluation processes do, most are simply a bureaucratic routine and a missed opportunity. If yours does not measure up, then fix it! Either revise the process if you can, or add to whatever it is that you now have to do as a matter of larger policy.

Additional Readings

DeProspo, Ernest R. "Personnel Evaluation as an Impetus to Growth." *Library Trends* 20 (July 1971): 60-70.

Hilton, R. C. "Performing Evaluation of Library Personnel." *Special Libraries* 69 (November 1978): 429-34.

Hodge, S. P. "Performance Appraisals: Developing a Sound Legal and Managerial System." *College and Research Libraries* 44 (July 1983): 235-44.

Ivancevich, J. M. "Different Goal Setting Treatments and Their Effects on Performance and Job Satisfaction." *Academic Management Journal* 20 (September 1977): 406-19.

Johnson, M. "Performance Appraisal of Librarians: A Survey." *College and Research Libraries* 33 (September 1972): 359-67.

Kikoski, J. F., and J. A. Litterer, "Effective Communication in the Performance Appraisal Interview." *Public Personnel Management* 12 (Spring 1983): 33-42.

Kroll, H. R. "Beyond Evaluation: Performance Appraisal as a Planning and Motivational Tool in Libraries." *Journal of Academic Librarianship* 9 (March 1983): 27-32.

Lewis, M. "Management by Objective: Review, Application and Relationship with Job Satisfaction and Performance." *Journal of Academic Librarianship* 5 (January 1980): 329-34.

Oh, Why
(and Oh, What) Do We Classify?

One of my most enjoyable courses in library school was that part of cataloging that dealt with classification, taught by the dean. I found it stimulating because it was one of the few aspects of the curriculum that then allowed for individual judgment and evaluation as opposed to memorization. I marveled at the large number of books that seemed to be multidisciplinary in nature, and I didn't find out until much later that it takes a career of teaching to accumulate such wonders as tomes that deal with the economic, social, and political development of the southwestern United States and northern Mexico during the period 1780 to 1875.

Many if perhaps not most books, I have since found, deal with rather more straightforward topics, such as introduction to organic chemistry, and can be classified as well as subject headed without being opened. Nevertheless, I recall arguing back then with my instructor when I classified a book on photography under physics, and he insisted it should have been either engineering or art (I don't remember which), that we were not dealing with an issue of right or wrong but with a matter of opinion and judgment, largely dependent on the emphasis of the collection and the needs of the users.

An Approach to Materials Arrangement

Classification is one approach to materials arrangement. There are obviously others, and the presumption is that we choose classification because it is best suited to the needs of our users. At least that seems to be the presumption, because I have seen no recent studies that compare its usefulness to alternatives. Asking users how they like it doesn't count. They have

Reprinted, with changes, by permission of the author and *Library Journal* 113, no. 11 (June 15, 1988): 42-43. Copyright © 1988 by Reed Publishing, U.S.A.

nothing to compare it to, and they usually respond that they like what we have told them to like. Interestingly, they rarely arrange the materials in their own offices by classification.

Shelf arrangement can be accomplished in a variety of ways, and it can be argued that as long as we have specific item look-up tools (card catalogs or terminals) that tell us the specific location, it doesn't really matter where we shelve a specific item. For this user, and I suspect others, the best way would be one that minimized the need for a secondary look-up, and allowed us to head straight for the shelf based on what we already know. Special libraries cater to this preference when they file technical reports by report number, because personal authors, titles, and even corporate sources of technical reports are rarely known or remembered at the time of search.

There are other ways we could arrange shelf material. We could most improve storage density if we filed by accession number to fill each shelf before starting the next one, in the total certainty that nothing else will have to be interfiled. Even "full" libraries have lots of empty space; it just happens to be in the wrong places. Unattractive as I suspect we all find this approach, I know of special libraries with space limitations so severe that they file in order of receipt.

The Long and the Tall of It

One operations research expert suggested that we not only file books by receipt, but take the process one step further by setting up separate accession systems based on height so that we could really space our shelves efficiently and not waste the space above a shorter book. We see a little of this in libraries for the arrangement of over-sized material, where size is so great that it even outweighs subject as a criterion for storage, or for the public library common shelving of "pocket books."

Furthermore, public libraries break ranks with their academic colleagues. They file fiction under the author and only nonfiction under classification, while academic libraries classify everything. I suspect this has a pragmatic basis, but I don't know what it is. On the occasions on which I read fiction I am usually more certain of the author's name than of nationality. Nor do I much care. I am sure others do, but is it enough to validate the arrangement?

Classification gives us neither the advantage of space density nor the advantage of minimizing intermediate look-up by allowing people to go straight to the shelf without stopping at the catalog. The presumed advantage for classification is that it puts like things together for ease of retrieval, and facilitates browsing. I say presumed because I'm not at all sure how well the process works.

How Atypical Am I?

In my own information searches, even on what I think is only one topic, the five things I end up looking for are usually shelved on at least two or three different floors of the library stacks. Obviously, the classifiers didn't have me in mind, and I wonder how atypical I am. It would be an interesting and relatively simple study to determine the extent to which the references extracted from the catalog in response to a question really do reside together.

I further use the term presumed because I see very little browsing taking place in research libraries. I see people working in the stacks, but with very specific lists and not with the casual approach that serendipity demands. Certainly never students, but also not faculty. What browsing I do see is only for segregated new material. There would in any case be little point in faculty browsing through the stacks, because they know well enough that the good stuff, or at least the new stuff, isn't there. It is in a faculty office, and the rules allow it to stay there until somebody else specifically requests it.

That recall is not prompted by browsing or even a curious interest. Individuals don't bother to trouble their colleagues unless they are certain they want something. If we believe in the importance of having like things together to facilitate browsing, then we should certainly enhance that process by insisting on having library material returned after a time reasonably long enough to permit it to be read.

Do people browse in research libraries? I doubt it, but even for those who disagree, the point is that we don't know, and yet we support an expensive and otherwise inconvenient organizational arrangement decision based on that premise. I can report from my consulting that many corporate special library users don't browse in the library because they perceive the library shelf collection as "self-selected junk." If they browse at all, it is in the offices of their colleagues.

The Pointlessness of Periodicals?

Nowhere does the process of classification seem more pointless to me than in the classification of periodicals. Public and special libraries file them by title, and so do departmental libraries in academia. However, American Research Libraries (ARL) statistics tell us that most research libraries classify periodicals in the main collection. For heaven's sake, why? Does anyone browse in 20-year-old bound volumes just for kicks on a slow day? How does one classify a periodical (we call them that, publishers and scholars call them journals) in any case except through gigantic approximations?

Every article is different, and, presumably, it is these we ought to classify. Ultimately, if we really want to facilitate browsing we should catalog and classify every article, and dismember every issue for shelving. The most convincing reason for classification of journals I have heard is one that affects our convenience and not that of our users. We don't have to shift when the title changes. However, I would suggest we wouldn't have to shift at all, because the look-up will come for an article under the old title.

How should I have classified that book on photography? Under physics, under technology, under art? I still can't answer the question any better than I did as a student, because I continue to insist now as then that it depends on the emphasis of the collection and where the users are likely to look. However, if we happen to have more than one copy it should make the decision easier. Classify them differently! At least we should if the intent is browsing. Putting two copies of the same book together appears counterproductive.

Establishing Territorial Boundaries

If we aren't going to do any of these things (and I suspect that I have not persuaded many to spring to immediate action), then the inconsistencies and uncertainties of what we now do suggests one possibility. We simply accept the classification numbers assigned by the Library of Congress, or of a range of designated "qualified" agencies who happened to do the book first, as the national classification number, and all use it without alteration in our own libraries. This would immediately permit the preparation of computerized national classed union catalogs, with local ownership as part of the accessible record from which orders can be generated. It would make interlibrary temporary acquisition much simpler. The proposal does create the possibility that, with the integration of locally cataloged unique material, two items might have the same call number. Would that really be so terrible? Wouldn't we be able to tell two items apart if they had different authors and different titles?

I suspect that the real reason for classification of everything including periodicals is far simpler and has nothing to do with easy access or with browsing. Classification, at least in research libraries, makes it easier to define territorial boundaries, and our user groups find that particularly important. Measuring the quality of a library by the size of its holdings is a game we taught them when it was to our advantage. Now it is no longer to our advantage because it interferes with cooperation in resource sharing and acquisition, but our users are still playing.

Moreover, they have refined the game into a process of Balkanization that infects all research libraries, by counting not the library holdings but their part of it, and that is most easily defined by classification. For most academicians (and I must include myself in that grouping and the generalization that follows), there is no such thing as *the* library, there is only *my* library and what it contains.

Humanists need the classification of journals to be able to claim them as part of their floor of the library building. Chemistry and library science professors with their own branch libraries don't need to classify the journals housed there because they already know they own them. With those issues of property determination out of the way, they can allow themselves to think about the easiest way to use material without first having to plot to move it to their floor of the library building, their corner of the stacks, their departmental quasi-libraries, or their own offices. That, of course, is their ultimate strategy: to establish their ownership imprimatur when all else fails. It helps explain why people are willing to walk across the campus to lunch at the faculty club, but insist that they can't cross the street, or even walk down two flights of stairs, to use a shared library.

Foundation Behind the Frills

I hope that the reader will not lose the serious point of this otherwise rather frilly column. When we catalog or classify we do so for a reason: to fulfill our responsibilities as information professionals to help users get what they need. We have devised, and continue to devise and modify, tools to permit this process to take place. These are judgments we must make, and not things we can abdicate to others, because we must never forget that users are not capable of distinguishing a good library from a bad one, only a big one from a little one. We have given them no other basis for comparison.

These are the larger issues we must bear in mind as we determine not only why and how we classify, but also why and how we do other things, and, ultimately, this issue, like so many others, becomes a question of acknowledged professional predominance and expertise, without which you have no status at all.

It affects, for example, the question of what we want from the next White House Conference, if it ever becomes "affordable" (and it is hard to keep a straight face with that one). Do we really need more advice from pressure groups, most of them with agendas that only provide us with contradictions? Or do we need a vehicle to persuade others that good libraries are worthwhile, that good librarians know how to run them, and that the rest of the population, at least when it comes to libraries, should at least momentarily stop talking and start listening?

Special Library Professionalism and Library Education

No issue so consistently captures and holds the attention of professionals as that of the educational preparation for work in their field. Inevitably each profession strikes out on its own and charts its own course. For the field of librarianship and information science, there are several widely recognized milestones. Before the turn of the century, there was the establishment of library training programs carried out in universities, as well as in libraries, by Melvil Dewey. The Williamson Report in 1923 set our sights on a higher level of preparation that involved education as well as training. The shift from undergraduate to graduate-level preparation took shape with the development of accreditation standards for graduate education and with the insistence by some libraries and groups of libraries on this level of educational achievement as prima facie evidence of the qualifications of job applicants. During the last 20 years, the profession has seen the rapid development of doctoral programs that have presumably changed the chief characteristic of library school educators from practitioners to researchers, a trend common in other educational disciplines as well. Some employers have been sorry to see this change and long for what they consider a more practical curriculum. Others have applauded it, but most have their own ideas which, dictated by their own operating environments, may fall somewhere in between.

We have seen in the last 10 years a renewed, possibly cyclical, interest in what students learn before taking their first jobs. There is an increasing insistence that educators teach what potential employers tell them to teach, but those voices are countered by the argument that library education in a university setting must adhere to value systems imposed by the academic community. Furthermore, studies in which I have participated clearly indicate not only that the expectations of practitioners are too narrow and oriented toward specific jobs in specific

Speech presented at the Special Libraries Association, Central Ohio Chapter, Dayton, November 9, 1988.

libraries, but also that such expectations accumulate into a curriculum of staggering dimensions, containing contradictions between one type of study and another. Efforts to implement these models inevitably lead to fragmentation into a number of different noninterchangeable preparation models. While we might at some point have to give up the idea of librarianship as a unified profession with a common core, we should certainly not do so rashly.

And yet the search for "solutions" continues headlong. It includes lists of skills developed in a variety of settings and belligerent letters from round tables, task forces, and other special-interest groups demanding to know why library schools aren't offering more courses in their own areas of interest. In one sense these demands remind the recipient of the nonnegotiable demands so popular with student groups in the 1960s. And yet negotiation and discussion are absolutely essential if we are to find workable and meaningful solutions.

Educators are also trapped—by the requirements of an academic value system and by the characteristics of their own small units (because, in addition to specialization in courses, employers want candidates available locally so there is no need to pay relocation expenses; students want the ability to attend classes part-time at a convenient location). Healthy and vigorous internal discussion can be a positive force in any profession, but when it spills to the outside it increases our vulnerability. Even if we could agree on educational preparation, we would continue to have difficulty enforcing our standards in the face of government agencies and private employers who do not understand what librarians are supposed to know and would rather not pay for that knowledge. Efforts by the federal Office of Personnel Management (OPM), various state agencies, and some library boards to seek relief from the "expense" (laughable as such a term may be) of hiring professional librarians can be expected to exploit any apparent divisiveness in our profession. For proof, we need only note the OPM suggestion of an inherent difference between so-called one-year and two-year graduate programs, a difference clearly invented for the OPM's own purposes and without the support of the educators who administer the programs.

The issue clearly involves an interaction between educators and employers. Because many employers are themselves graduates of the educational programs from which they recruit new hires, one can at least assume some mutuality of background and perhaps even some mutuality of overall interest. Almost all library educators are former library practitioners, because the process of moving through an educational program directly into a teaching post, which is so common in the humanities, is almost unheard of in the library field. Some are educators with recent and distinguished experience as practitioners, and part-time faculty members manage to keep a foot in each camp. Communication is not nearly as scarce as some would have us believe. Educators and practitioners belong to the same professional organizations and societies, and it is sometimes noted with irony that the process of evaluation and accreditation, presumably controlled by practitioner members of the American Library Association, has in fact been "infiltrated" or "subverted" by educators who turn out to have prominent leadership roles in practitioner societies.

Nevertheless, there are clear differences in value systems between a library and a university, and both must be recognized and accommodated. Recent studies show that when a library school closes, there may be a lack of understanding on the part of the academic community of how library education contributes academic rigor and prestige to the university. At least part of this may be because too much attention is paid to the preferences of library practitioners and not enough to those of the academic value system. In a recent theme talk at the January 1986 meeting of the Association for Library and Information Science Education (ALISE), Richard Budd suggested no less.

There has been no shortage of communication between library educators and those library practitioners who often employ new graduates; they are also the primary recruiters of new candidates for the profession; and they are the alumni of the schools they now tend to criticize so harshly. Of course, friction between educational institutions and the alumni who fondly remember how much better things were in the good old days is not restricted to any one particular discipline. As Cyril Houle has written so charmingly:

> The voice of the aggrieved alumnus is always found in the land and, no matter what the profession, the burden of complaint is the same. In the first five years after graduation, alumni say that they should have been taught more practical techniques. In the next five years, they say they should have been taught more basic theory. In the tenth to fifteenth year, they inform the faculty that they should have been taught more about administration or about their relations with their coworkers and subordinates. In the subsequent five years, they condemn the failure of their professors to put the profession in its larger historical, social, and economic contexts. After the twentieth year, they insist that they should have been given a broader orientation to all knowledge, scientific and humane. Sometime after that, they stop giving advice; the university has deteriorated so badly since they left that it is beyond hope.

We often hear that educators have lost touch with what is happening in real life, and the suggestion is made that they return to the experience of working in a library to update their teaching methodologies. This assumes that a great deal has changed in the workplace, changes of which educators are unaware, and it contradicts educators' perception that in fact very little has changed in libraries, and certainly much less than would be suggested by some innovative course descriptions. Are practitioners ahead of teachers, or are teachers ahead of practitioners in the advocacy of dynamic improvements and change? Undoubtedly there is some truth to both suggestions, depending on the one hand on the innovative currency of the library director, and on the other on that of the teacher.

In all of this discussion, at least two things seem clear. One is that practitioners appear to have little interest in conducting research. They do very little research and much of the research they do can be considered application development rather than scientific inquiry. They do not insist that their budgets include a research component, even in academic libraries where such a request would appear perfectly natural. The second point is that practitioners have very little interest in the kind of research that is performed in library schools, either by faculty members or by doctoral students. A recent Department of Education conference to identify a research agenda for the library profession heard no proposals from the practitioners who dominated the conference that could be considered to have a genuine research content, and it expressed no interest in examining the curriculum of library education programs. It may be that there is less of a perceived need to investigate library programs and more of a desire to force library educators to implement what they are told.

Whatever the quality of discourse between educators and practitioners and employers who are all librarians, there is no shortage of contact and communication. A far different condition exists when we deal with nonlibrarians who have the power to shape our professional requirements. In the federal sector, it was our own professional error that allowed a vacuum to develop into which the Office of Management and Budget (OMB) and the Office of Personnel Management (OPM) were able to step and define professional qualifications and professional criteria for us. Of course, we all face similar problems when we deal with school superintendents and principals, public library board members and city managers, and corporate personnel administrators who select and hire people who they then call librarians. The effort to reach an agreement among the various parts of this profession should have at least one powerful motivation—survival.

Are there then ways to determine, first, those general qualifications upon which all factions can agree, and then those specific skills and knowledge that may be required by individual branches of the profession? The differentiation between the attitudes of large and small libraries as employers rather than between types of libraries such as academic, public, and special, has not been addressed to any appreciable extent. Most studies have dealt with the attitudes of types of libraries; only the study by Marion Paris and me reported in the January 1985 *Library Quarterly* attempts to identify differences in approaches based on the size of the library.

That size of library, it appears, makes a significant difference in the attitude toward expected qualifications of new hires. Some of this comes from a perceived difference in the role of the library. Library educators are already familiar with the argument that research libraries have requirements that differ from those of other academic libraries. Recently library educators have begun to hear from junior college and community college librarians, who also argue that their missions and needs are unique and that they require students with unique characteristics and educational preparation.

Contributors to the book I edited on library education agree that large academic and public libraries should be prepared to mount training programs for new graduates, designed not only to teach particular skills but also to acclimate new employees to the specific needs of that particular library and its user community. By contrast, it was noted that in smaller academic, public, and school libraries the resources and people for such training may be limited or nonexistent. Elin Christianson talked of on-the-job training in special libraries as a sink-or-swim process.

This obviously raises a difficult and immediate issue for library education. If large academic and public libraries can agree with regard to what elements of job training can be left out of the master's curriculum because employers will take responsibility for it, then obviously the emphasis on general and theoretical education can be strengthened. But if training is now to be de-emphasized, how will new hires be trained for libraries where there are no training facilities? It is a difficult issue, and it demands at least a clear and forceful statement on the part of professional associations, that the new hire is only an apprentice and not a fully qualified librarian and that training (as well as education) must continue. There will no doubt be difficulty in establishing, let alone enforcing, such a continuing learning process, particularly in an environment in which employers don't necessarily assume that a library degree, let alone a graduate library degree or an accredited graduate library degree, is required at all and in which professional associations have made no real attempts to mandate such a requirement.

There are complexities even with the educational mechanisms for the profession. There are relatively few graduates with unaccredited library science master's degrees, because such an unaccredited degree entails the same cost and effort as an accredited degree without offering the opportunity for employment in the academic and public libraries that require certification. Most individuals now stuck with such degrees either had no geographic choice or had never been told what limitations they would encounter. Undergraduate degrees are different. Not only have such degrees existed all along, but graduates of such programs have found employment, particularly in school and small public libraries. Whether this is because these students are more specifically prepared for the needs of smaller libraries or because they can be hired more cheaply is obviously open to question. The difference between a library science graduate with a bachelor's degree and one with a master's degree is frequently in the eyes of the beholder, and undergraduate degree holders argue with vehemence that they are as fully professional.

Ultimately, it is the employers who must establish a distinction if indeed one is to be established. Although it is dangerous to oversimplify the case, it can be argued that undergraduate library degree holders may be better *trained* because in four years of schooling they have a greater opportunity to take more specific courses, but they are presumably less well *educated* in the liberal arts background assumed to be desirable for professional librarians. They would certainly appear to lack the management and computer preparation now demanded by many employers, and they have probably had few if any courses that discuss *why* we do what we do and what the alternatives might be, although in my view the present accreditation process does not really assure this even for accredited programs. There is also some apparent contradiction between an emphasis on library education at the undergraduate level and the increased emphasis in academic and special libraries on subject degrees, particularly graduate subject degrees. People with undergraduate library degrees may find it difficult to enter a graduate program, because graduate library education programs look at candidates with undergraduate library degrees with little enthusiasm. Some refuse to admit them at all or only on condition that they remedy their liberal arts deficiencies. The undergraduate library degree would also appear to offer little if any preparation for graduate work in any other area.

Library schools that grant both bachelor's and master's degrees in library science are relatively rare, and they are rarer still among schools with accredited M.L.S. programs. Certainly where the two degrees coexist in the same institution, the school faces the responsibility of explaining how the programs differ, particularly when undergraduate and graduate degree candidates are enrolled in the same courses. But this problem does not appear to be of major proportions, because students rarely move from an undergraduate to a graduate library degree. Most often holders of undergraduate degrees have their eyes on jobs that do not require graduate degrees, either from choice or necessity. One thing appears certain. The profession is going to have to establish and enforce criteria about what jobs require a graduate degree, what can be done with an undergraduate degree, and what can be done with some other kind of degree or no degree at all. It seems clear that employers who are not librarians will not make that distinction for us, particularly in view of the statement often repeated by me that users cannot be trusted to differentiate between a good library and a poor one, only between big or little ones and cheaper and more expensive ones.

Another thing also appears certain. If practitioners expect an upgrading in the educational programs that produce graduate-level employees, then they must also move to protect the investment that these individuals have made. That protection includes assurance that the jobs for which they have specifically prepared are indeed reserved for them, and that less-prepared applicants cannot have them. It is to some extent because we have tolerated and even encouraged this confusion in nomenclature by allowing our volunteer helpers to call themselves librarians that we now encounter turf problems.

Other issues remain, and these can be perplexing. A number of individuals stress the importance of subject degrees, sometimes advanced subject degrees, and that emphasis appears particularly important in large academic and some special library settings. However, it is not clear what the sequence of these educational experiences ought to be. In my experience, it is not uncommon for individuals who already have some career experience in subject fields, following education at the bachelor's, master's, and even doctoral level, to become attracted to library education programs. Having seen many librarians who later sought law degrees for work in law libraries, we also see occasional candidates with law degrees who now desire a library education. At the same time, it is less likely that M.B.A. graduates will flock to our library education programs, and here the present sequence of first library and then business is likely to remain. A number of schools have developed dual master's programs to allow students to pursue two advanced degrees simultaneously, with some advantage in scheduling and cost. Indiana is in the vanguard of these programs with nine such packages. While not hugely popular, such dual-degree programs attract a steady stream of applicants.

The question of subject preparation inevitably brings us back to undergraduate preparation. To earn a graduate subject degree, one must first have an undergraduate subject-specific degree. Most library educators would agree with the widely held view that a good broad-based liberal arts education is the best preparation for librarianship. If the student's undergraduate degree is in the humanities, the social sciences, or some of the physical sciences, the liberal education background is there. However, if the degree is in engineering, we must recognize that the pressures of the engineering curriculum still tend to shortchange the liberal arts.

The limits on what can be accomplished in one year of graduate library and information science education may also tempt us to push some of the coursework back into an undergraduate curriculum. Again, however, we do this at a price. Demanding specific undergraduate library science courses taken as part of some other bachelor's degree inevitably displaces other courses. What those courses might be and how useful they might prove to be for the librarian is, of course, problematical. An undergraduate program in library science is not a liberal arts educational process. Library science courses, in particular at the undergraduate but even some at the graduate level, are often more involved with issues of vocational preparation.

For many reasons the suggestion that we add to the end through continuing education rather than to the beginning of the graduate educational process is the cleaner and simpler approach. Attractive as that suggestion is, we are still left with the uncertainty about guaranteeing its implementation. Can we leave this process to chance and to the recognition by both professionals and employers that such ongoing education is a good thing? At this time, only medical librarians have taken any concrete steps toward assured implementation, and even they have backed away from enforcement mechanisms with teeth in them. We now find that continuing education is being mandated for teachers and not just physicians, but that imposed requirement has not as yet spilled over into school librarianship, public librarianship, or special librarianship. It is not unreasonable to expect that such a demand would be opposed not only by employers reluctant to spend the money, but also by some of the librarians who would have to take the courses or attend the workshops and seminars.

Both library schools and their graduates face the insistence by some libraries that candidates have prior professional experience. Carried to an extreme, such a requirement would be absurd, because if everyone demanded prior experience there would be no place to obtain it. Some of the positions advertised require prior experience for the individual expected to cope with the job description, and that raises further questions, particularly in larger libraries, where it should be possible to differentiate quite clearly between junior and senior positions and the work performed in them. Other libraries prefer experienced candidates because they would rather pay higher salaries than take the time to train junior professionals. Finally, still others are not prepared to pay more but are willing to take advantage of a job market that may permit them to bring in experienced candidates without paying for that experience. This approach is found, at least to some extent, in special and large academic libraries.

Library schools could obviously concentrate on principles and concepts if specific skills adaptation became a recognized responsibility of the first employer, acting either independently or on behalf of the profession.

Such arrangements are not unusual in professional education and training. Graduate chemists and accountants enter into positions in which their lack of initial productivity is accepted and expected, and the receipt of either an M.D. or a J.D. degree signifies only the beginning of a lengthy and laborious training program to achieve professional status.

In library education, the receipt of a master's degree (and sometimes much less) implies instant preparation to do whatever needs to be done, and that public perception is highly injurious to our professional image. Serious logistical problems immediately suggest themselves, particularly in institutions in which the individual being hired is the sole professional librarian, and also in those even more common institutions in which the candidate is eagerly awaited because the organization is already under-staffed and the backlog is crushing. However, mechanisms can be devised for internships or other forms of learning experiences *if* the employer is prepared to accept both the cost and inconvenience of this process as a professional commitment. Even for small libraries, networks and consortia could provide further education and training.

The question of who is going to take responsibility for recruiting individuals into our profession remains unsolved. Library education programs are accused of not recruiting the "right kind" of candidates, and that charge may or may not have some validity. In a larger sense, however, library schools don't really have the opportunity to recruit, only to accept or reject. Recruiting is done by the profession, and by the image it projects. We must also bear in mind the concerns expressed by Nancy Van House, a faculty member at the University of California at Berkeley. There is an inevitable relationship between the candidates we are able to attract and retain, and the salaries we are prepared to offer them upon graduation. Ultimately, we must realize that if we want bright and energetic students, other disciplines want them, too.

In conclusion, a number of issues suggest themselves as topics for further professional discussion, and these questions must be dealt with seriously before we try to tackle solutions and implementation mechanisms:

1. Can we specify a common professional level of educational preparation or intellectual awareness that everyone who is called a librarian should be able to demonstrate? I am not talking about specific skills or even competencies. The ability to remember Anglo-American filing rules or to dial up databases does not make a person a professional. Can we insure and protect this process against outsiders and interlopers who want the credit without doing the intellectual work of preparing properly? Is it perhaps already too late to save the term *librarian*, and should we abandon it to the volunteers and student assistants who have already laid claim to it?

2. Can we develop distinct specialization tracks that meet the needs of specialized constituencies as separate from and in addition to the requirements for basic professional competencies? And what will we decide to call the individual who demonstrates these

specialized competencies? Do we develop these skills as part of the basic degree after paying some attention to a common core, and can we make all of these specializations fit into a single manageable program? Do we expect all specializations to be offered at all schools, or certain specializations at certain schools? If it is to be the latter, how do we establish national search pools so that only the individuals with the proper specializations and not just the nearest available candidates will be considered for available jobs? In other words, as with the basic degree, how do we protect the intellectual investment of the candidates? If courses in special librarianship and business databases are essential for work in an investment firm library, will all such libraries consider only those candidates who have obtained the specialized qualifications? Under such conditions, virtually all searches become national searches. How will small public libraries, which rarely pay either interview or relocation expenses, searching for children's librarians feel about a nationwide search? What about corporations that advertise in the local Sunday paper and hire the first candidate on Monday morning who appears reasonable?

The imposition of specialization tracks within the degree program would cause further problems. Many students don't know about the options available to them in the profession, and it seems unreasonable to demand that they choose at some point in their first semester. Some students who end up as special librarians had never heard of special libraries when they came to Indiana. Other students, of course, are constrained by geographic factors, and this is particularly true for the increasing body of older students returning to school and the workforce after spending time as full-time homemakers. Many of these students would prefer to keep their options as open as possible, and removing that opportunity is not something we should do lightly. Ideally, specialization would take place only after the completion of a generalized degree, and that is certainly possible if internships become more broadly accepted. But at least at present, this concept conflicts directly with the demand of employers that newly hired graduates be immediately productive and useful.

3. Inevitably we will have to differentiate between pre-professional experience (practice work with or without academic credit), degree education, job training, continuing education, continuing training, and internships. How can we make these differentiations more consistent? How can we make them more attractive to students, who invest their time and career potential? How can we sell the recognition of professional responsibility to nonlibrarian employers such as corporate personnel managers, school principals, and public library boards?

4. Finally, what sort of people do we *really* want to join us in this profession? There are clear contradictions between the general public

perception of librarians—introverted book lovers that guidance counselors are happy to send to us; the so-called, people-oriented people we now believe we really prefer and need; and subject specialists to work in particular disciplines. That last concentration appears particularly important to special librarians, but even the Library of Congress makes it clear in its advertisements that in the recruitment of an Arabic cataloger, a knowledge of Arabic is more crucial than a knowledge of cataloging. Furthermore, the insistence on subject concentration can be interpreted narrowly or broadly. Will a geology library insist on a degree in geology or petrochemistry? Or will it consider a macrobiology major because such an individual is at least familiar with the process of scientific inquiry and with methods of communication common to scientific disciplines? Is it possible that such a library might accept a nonscientist who has had the necessary library school courses to understand a scientific communication? At present there are barriers to such an appointment, and those barriers stem largely from the biases not of librarians but of scientific users, who prefer to be served by individuals whose academic preparation resembles their own, and with whom they feel more comfortable.

We have a great deal to talk about and decide before we begin the prescriptive process of examining and approving specific curricula or developing checklists against which to measure specific candidates. Fortunately, as noted earlier, in this field in particular, educators and practitioners closely share a heritage and a professional identification. The process of communication does not face insurmountable barriers, only the need to rid ourselves of self-righteous preconceptions.

School Librarians and the Rest of Us

There is probably no branch of librarianship with which I am less familiar than school librarianship. As an administrator in a university that takes the education of school librarians as a serious charge, it is precisely because I recognize my own shortcomings in this and other parts of the library profession (I don't know anything about rare books, either) that I try to surround myself with colleagues who know the areas I don't know.

And yet, even with this increasing fragmentation of our profession into distinct and often noncommunicating specializations, the reality has grown that despite the variety of settings and clienteles, librarianship possesses a commonality that transcends where we work and whom we serve. Moreover, unless we preserve that commonality across institutional boundaries, we become nomads who are considered junior accessories to whatever the other professionals with whom we work happen to do.

That is as true for school librarians in their relationship with teachers as for academic librarians in their relationship with faculty and corporate librarians in their relationship to other organizational professionals. We may be teachers or professors or organization men and women, but we must be much more than that or we are very little, or at least little of significance.

Holding Our Turf

Turf is that which is uniquely yours, and which nobody else can claim. The turf we must control is the library, through our unique knowledge of what the library can do and should do, and through our development of programs and strategies to make the library (or media center or technical information center or resource materials center) an effective tool for helping to establish and to meet the parent organization's mission.

Reprinted, with changes, by permission of the author and *Library Journal* 114, no. 5 (March 15, 1989): 54-55. Copyright © 1989 by Reed Publishing, U.S.A.

Simply doing what the users (teachers, administrators, or students) tell you they want done does not accomplish this. On the contrary, it is bad for our professional status, and, more importantly, it is bad for the organizations we serve. The ignorance of our users with regard to the potential we represent is excusable. What is inexcusable is their failure to acknowledge that they don't know. What would be unforgivable would be our shedding our responsibility to point out their ignorance and our expertise.

The determination that school librarians must be school teachers was made a long time ago, and it was not made by librarians. It was made by teachers, who have established a stranglehold political control over the entire institution, including its library. The situation is not unique. Corporate users of scientific and technical libraries frequently insist that the librarians who serve them match them in educational qualifications with degrees in physics or chemistry.

Whether this is simply because of a preference for collegial comfort or because of a specialized need they truly recognize is difficult to generalize. As often as not, it is probably a little of both. Academic librarians spend a great deal of time and effort attempting to emulate teaching faculty members, because they believe that this will impress them. Unfortunately, it does not. Academic librarians are only considered second-rate professors. More significantly, what they uniquely can contribute as librarians may not be recognized at all. The pattern and problem can be seen to be generic.

First and Foremost, a Librarian

One thing that is clear is that librarians, regardless of what else their employers require them to be, must be first of all librarians. In that sense the minimum level of education for librarians is not dilutable. We all do the same things, we just do them in different settings, and with different emphases and different added responsibilities.

There is certainly room for argument about what constitutes an acceptable level of library education, whether present standards of the American Library Association accreditation are too high or too low, or even whether or not ours is a profession even requiring education at the graduate level. Whatever that level of appropriate education turns out to be, it is the correct level for all of us.

I am certainly not unaware of the reality that it is precisely in the education (or training) of school librarians that we permit the substitutions and shortcuts that we have by and large foreclosed in academic, public, and even corporate settings. Why is this? Is it because school librarians don't need to know as much as other librarians, because their libraries don't serve as significant a need or as complex a requirement?

If anything, the reverse is true. If it is important that school librarians must be teachers as well as librarians, then they are teachers of teachers as well as of students, because they must know what teachers know and more. It is the "more" we must emphasize for true professional status.

The Lowest Opinion of Librarians

There is perhaps no professional community with a collectively lower opinion of the importance of librarians than that of education (medicine perhaps runs a close second, but doctors tend to discount all other fields). This is not because educators are inherently evil or power crazy. Heaven knows they have enough troubles of their own. It is rather because, unlike some other professionals who don't know what libraries and librarians can do and are willing to admit that ignorance, teachers think that they do know. Unfortunately, they are wrong.

If librarians in the school system, just as librarians in the university and in the corporation, are to achieve acceptance as professionals in their own right, it will be because as full librarians and as teachers, they are unique. It will not be as pale replicas of some other profession. California librarians need not be reminded that in times of stress there is a tendency toward paranoia.

As the impact of Proposition 13 gripped the state, classroom teachers defended their own precarious hold by badmouthing everyone in the educational system who wasn't a "real" teacher like themselves. It could happen again or elsewhere, unless school librarians make the point that they are full-fledged members of two professions, with no substitutions or shortcuts.

It is an important political argument, because we will not be treated as equals if we are perceived "only" as teachers who don't "really" teach. How many school librarians become principals, with authority over other teachers? However, beyond the political implications, the insistence on full, undiluted librarianship as well as teacher qualification makes sense, because only fully prepared librarians can serve their clienteles anywhere without shortchanging something or somebody.

The ALA Controversy

I am, of course, aware of the recent ALA controversy concerning the desire of the American Association of School Librarians to participate in the National Council for Accreditation of Teacher Education process of legitimizing library education programs that do not meet ALA standards for accreditation. The issue is fraught with emotion, and understandably so. It brings out intensely personal reactions.

Whatever our level of educational preparation for the positions we now hold, we must insist that those qualifications are adequate or we brand ourselves as illegitimate. Not only are we unwilling to do this to ourselves, such generalizations are also unfair. There are always exceptional examples of individuals who are self-learners and who beat the system, as there are individuals with graduate degrees from prestigious library schools who appear to have learned nothing, or at least remembered nothing.

We deal with generalizations and we deal with averages, and yet those averages mean something. Students not exposed to the diversity of a more complex curriculum, to faculty with genuine research as well as teaching credentials, or to other students with different backgrounds and value systems lose something in the process.

How the Indiana Dean Views It

A colleague who works closely with school librarians and media specialists tells me that, at least on the average, these individuals are less prepared for concepts of resource sharing and computer networking, at the very time these initiatives become essential for school librarians. Perhaps it may be because nobody taught them.

As the dean of one of the largest and most highly rated accredited graduate library education programs, I would be a hypocrite if I did not truly feel that ours is the better way to educate librarians—any professional librarian and, most certainly, school librarians. As I look at the AASL/NCATE initiative so emotionally pushed through the ALA Council meetings in San Francisco and New Orleans, I have mixed feelings. I can certainly understand the demand for recognized legitimacy from a large group of ALA members. Beyond that, I see both dangers and potential. If AASL participation in NCATE accreditation only acquiesces in what educators assume to be proper standards for the preparation of school librarians, then we will have done nothing more than legitimize their ignorance. Changing the wording so that it mentions only media specialists and not school librarians fools nobody.

However, if opening the NCATE process to AASL allows for the introduction of new vistas and standards in explaining to NCATE accreditors what good libraries really are all about, then I see a potential for great promise. There is no logical end to this growing and learning process, short of a set of requirements. These include both what educators consider uniquely important in the preparation of school librarians, and the full accreditation requirements specified by the ALA Committee on Accreditation for all librarians.

That committee determined a long time ago, while I was a member, that specialization could not be a substitute for generalized library educational values common to the entire profession. It supplemented it, and that decision was wise. I know that there are constant attempts to dilute those requirements, but it is important that they fail because they would undermine the legitimacy of the entire process.

We know that the graduates of programs who argue that they do not plan to prepare academic and special librarians and should therefore not be held to that standard end up in such libraries. Graduates go where the jobs are, and nobody can really blame them. School librarians can and do become public librarians or special librarians. The determination of what it takes to be a librarian, *any* librarian, must ultimately become the bottom line for all of us.

If school librarians must be teachers and technical librarians must also be chemists, then so be it. But they must all be fully qualified librarians, meeting whatever standards are deemed appropriate in a professional accreditation process controlled by librarians, and not by either the American

Chemical Society or NCATE. These bodies can appropriately evaluate chemists and teachers, and some of us are chemists or teachers. However, we are also librarians, and that is something they can't evaluate.

Saddest of all is to see fellow educators step forward to great applause stating their disinterest in having school librarians earn their accredited degrees, but those gestures may be less than gracious acts of statesmanship. There are library schools that consider the education of school librarians, or perhaps of children's librarians, a distraction from the game plan designed to bring the school status and prestige.

At Indiana we also have our strategies, but we see the issue differently. We are negotiating with the School of Education for the implementation of a dual master's degree in library and information science and in instructional systems technology. We believe that this will be a superb way to prepare school librarians. However, it has a cost for the students and they must also be able to see that it has a value perceived by employers. If librarians don't protect the importance of their own education, certainly nobody else will.

The Tyranny of the "Team"

As I was growing up and entering the work force, I saw discrimination become more subtle and softer, but again just as effective and devastating. The signs "No Hispanics Need Apply" (or Jews, blacks, Irish, etc.) came down, and were replaced by a different logic, with the same end result. We don't discriminate, but we don't hire individuals who wouldn't "fit in." Besides, they wouldn't be "happy" here.

As I began teaching management I still found vestiges of this perhaps even unconscious brand of bigotry in personnel textbooks. If you have a young group of female bank tellers, was the advice, hire only additional young female tellers. Older women, or men, wouldn't fit the social group. They might cause friction, they wouldn't be welcome at postwork social gatherings, and they would adversely affect the morale of the team.

It might even have been good advice from a purely mechanistic standpoint, but it was immoral, it was unfair, and it was beside the point. "Look," the manager is supposed to say. "You are hired to do a job, your co-worker is hired to do a job. I expect you to do it competently. If you get along with one another, so much the better. However, even if you don't get along, I expect you to interact civilly and professionally with one another. I will be watching, and I will fire the first one who starts playing games."

Good Management and Courage

I even had the opportunity to put my evolving theories to work in one management post in which it was necessary to assign two competent professionals who literally hated each other to work on a cooperative project. I would have preferred to avoid it, but there was no alternative. I called them both into my office, stated that I knew they disliked each other and didn't really care whether or not they ever had lunch or coffee breaks together. However, I expected them to work together professionally and courteously, and I would be monitoring them closely. Moreover, I would evaluate their performance as a unit of two. Drastic, certainly. But necessary, at least in my judgment, and, of course, it was my judgment to make.

Good management, I constantly stress in my writings and seminars to anyone who will read or listen, requires many attributes, but the most important of these is courage. Sometimes that means protecting individuals who may be a little different (it may be racial or religious, or it may even be that they work harder or smarter) from a group consensus that can become a lynch mob.

One of my favorite management histories concerns the Southern company that finally, after much foot dragging, decided to fully integrate its plant. It announced that, effective immediately, blacks would be eligible for all positions, and would be sharing the workplace, the cafeteria, the locker room, and the restroom.

The company went on to say that it understood that this might prove difficult or stressful for individuals brought up under a different social system, and that some might even find it unacceptable. If there were such individuals, the company would, with complete understanding and perhaps even sympathy and compassion, accept their resignations.

Was there risk of mass resignations? Perhaps, but probably not really. Was there a single one? No. The point is an important one that managers must sometimes make with recalcitrant employees, for a wide range of issues that can even encompass library automation. We are a free society and you are not a slave. If you feel truly offended by what I have done after we have fully discussed it, you can certainly quit.

Saving the Wild Duck

Thomas Watson Jr., during my days at IBM, spoke and wrote eloquently to the staff to urge protection for what he called the "wild ducks," the individuals who might be different from the group norm. I am not sure whether this was from a sense of fairness or the realization that while these "wild ducks" are sometimes trouble they are also sometimes brilliant innovators well ahead of the group, perhaps without the social graces to persuade others, but nevertheless important to the success of the organization.

I am not sure, but it doesn't really matter. It certainly didn't work all the time, but it worked some of the time and IBM benefited; this most bureaucratic of organizations found room for individualistic initiative and innovation, and supported it.

I had thought that much of this emphasis on conformity (we could use mediocrity and unimaginativeness as synonyms) was behind us until my career start as a teacher in 1975 put me in touch with how many libraries and librarians still hire and select their new recruits. I thought that, perhaps like Tom Watson, they might be seeking bright, brash, abrasive, courageous, and individualistic wild ducks.

After all, a range of writers from Peter Drucker to Gifford Pinchot have been telling us for a decade that the concept of the team effort as the basis of measurement, so popular in the 1960s and 1970s, was dead in industry. It was replaced by a concentration on individual contribution to performance and profitability. The key words are personal responsibility and personal accountability, and those are not team judgments.

This is intrapreneuring (entrepreneuring within the library), and it relies not on consensus seeking but on consensus building, which is ultimately a process of persuasion using tools as positive as consultative management and as negative as manipulation. Even our historic view of manipulation can depend on the results achieved. Nobody can deny that Melvil Dewey was a master manipulator who rarely sought consensus but fought for his own viewpoint.

Do Incompetents Stay Forever?

There is room for consensus decisions and team evaluation, but not nearly as much as might be supposed. Both cataloging and reference are individual and highly personal activities; so is literature searching. If you as a manager don't reward the best employees and punish the worst ones, you are not only unfair but also a fool. And make no mistake. Some are better than others; they will perhaps leave unless you reward or at least single out what they have accomplished.

Obversely, the incompetents will stay forever. There is room for team activity, most particularly in the gathering of information, in the outlining of alternatives, and in the communication of overall objectives, plans, and strategies. However, even in the area of automation in which communication is perhaps most essential, Susan Baerg Epstein has warned us that one individual must be in charge.

We work hard to explain and persuade, but when that process has been completed and perhaps only one malcontent remains, that person can be invited to either shut up or quit. When consensus seeking is misused, it results in decisions that are safe but also unimaginative and overstructured, as we seek to accommodate every viewpoint instead of just outvoting some of them. We have national systems that fit the description.

Casting Aside the Capricious

It is not difficult for library school teachers to identify the best, the brightest, the most innovative, the most curious, and, perhaps at the same time, the most capricious. Readers will understand my particular affection for these students. It is also not difficult for a large number of employers to identify them so that they can avoid hiring them, presumably because they might disrupt the "team."

Will our profession ever develop the librarian equivalent of Thomas Edison? It might be just as well if we don't. He or she would have a lot of trouble making it past the search committee. Generalizations are inevitably unfair, but much of our tactic in running libraries is to be inoffensive: to each other, to corporate and municipal officials, to academic faculty members and administrators, and to school teachers and principals.

We succeed admirably in this endeavor, far more than lawyers, doctors, truck drivers, and even school teachers, who can be obnoxious but always in what they see as a righteous cause. But what does this insistence on safe and bland mediocrity get us except still more trivialization?

How Did We Manage?

In *Library Journal*'s April 15, 1988, How Do You Manage? column (pp. 57-59), A. J. Anderson describes the plight of an excellent acquisitions librarian who announces to the director that he plans to resign because his colleagues make him feel unwelcome. My immediate reaction was to be unimpressed with a director of a small library who in five months had not noticed.

However, the case becomes more interesting. When confronted by the director, one of the "team colleagues" readily admits that the perception is accurate. They don't want him around. They will never accept him. Although their dislike cannot be put into specifics, they find him "slimy." The accuser in this case study, named Christina, goes on to explain. "We're dealing with emotions here, not reason. Surely how people feel about a co-worker are grounds for keeping or letting them go. Must it always be whether they're good workers or not?"

The director who hadn't noticed the problem, perhaps rather typically has no response except to curtail the conversation. At least one analyst suggested that the director work with the poor victim to see how he could be made more acceptable to the lynch mob. I have a much shorter and more direct answer for Christina. It is to tell her that the librarian will be judged by his performance, particularly as there is no evidence that he has done anything specific to offend except perhaps be different.

> However, now that I am finally aware of this situation I will be watching carefully to see that you and your co-workers are in no way disruptive, uncooperative, or uncivil. If I find that you are, it is you who will be in trouble. If you find what I have just said unacceptable you are, of course, free to resign, and you can also tell that to your friends. If ultimately necessary, I will keep only him and replace all of you. Bear in mind that this is a library, not a club. In a library you don't get to vote on your co-workers. Now I would suggest that you concentrate on your own tasks, and not make unsubstantiated comments about others.

Is such direct and confrontational action to protect an innocent wild duck necessary? Yes, it is. Is it risky, with the possibility that somebody might quit? Not really. They may grumble at first, but who ever suggested that management was a popularity contest? They adjust rather quickly, as the segregationist white workers did. Just check with our manufacturing company in the South.

Making the Group Look Bad

If I modified the objection to this co-worker from his being "slimy" to being "too old" or "not white like the rest of us," it would be instantly apparent that such a value system would be unacceptable. That is because we now have laws to protect individuals from discrimination on the basis of race, color, creed, sex, or age. We accept the fairness of these laws. We even have laws to protect individuals who have served prison terms against having this held against them later. However, we don't have laws to protect individuals whom their co-workers consider odd, unusual, lacking in their own outside interests, or uncongenial. Or perhaps they are disliked because they work harder than the others and "make the group look bad."

It is discouraging to hear from some of our best graduates who are geographically limited to perhaps one location and one employer that their supervisors have warned them to temper their enthusiasm and not accomplish more than the group norm. I get such letters every few months, and it is difficult to respond to them. If they were geographically flexible I could find them a supervisor who would treasure their attitude, but why shouldn't all supervisors treasure it?

Or perhaps the management advice is just to stop being so "slimy," a condemnation for which no rational explanation is offered or considered necessary. The scenarios that cause irrelevant and unfair evaluation are really all the same. For some there is legal protection; for others there is even the smug safety of mob consensus. And that is why we need managers with the courage and will to do what is fair and not necessarily what is popular. We need such managers because not enough laws can be written to protect every minority group. We need them to protect the "wild ducks." We need them to protect the "slimy."

The "Quiet Revolution":
A Profession at the Crossroads

Special librarianship is at a crossroads. In one direction lies the importance implied in the word "information" and in the universal understanding that information may represent the most important resource in any organization. The other direction may not lead to extinction but certainly to trivialization, because much of what others will gladly leave us is clerical and routinely computerized. The revolution we face is "quiet" because nobody is scheming to kill us off. However, we could commit suicide.

Teaching special librarianship to largely inexperienced students for 12 years, and offering countless continuing education seminars to special library practitioners for almost as long, has allowed me to develop and strengthen my convictions, and probably also my biases. I believe that special librarianship cannot be defined by type of library, but rather by the value system that is brought to the information interaction we have with our clients. Special librarianship, I am quite certain, is a state of mind and an attitude, and it is most directly defined by that marvelous motto that has served us so well for more than 60 years: "Putting Knowledge to Work." Putting it to work is not a passive process; it does not consist of developing huge collections without measuring or caring whether or not they are used, or caring whether or not the information being searched for can be found, a practice too prevalent in many academic libraries in which ownership and not availability is all that counts. Special librarianship is a process of giving users what they need, and what they need is not necessarily what they want or what they ask for.

Reprinted, with changes, by permission of the author and *Special Libraries* 80, no. 1 (Winter 1989): 24-30. Copyright © 1989 by Special Libraries Association.

Because of our emphasis on information service, special librarians are not likely to fall into the "type of materials" trap that bedevils other libraries. We know that World War II spawned the technical report as a mechanism for rapid communication, and it soon moved from sci-tech to the business community. For many special libraries, it is these reports, and certainly not books, that form the lifeblood of the collection. For others, it might be engineering drawings, patents, laboratory notebooks, or newspaper clippings. The rest of the profession has yet to make this adjustment. It catalogs books in great detail on a descriptive, but not subject, basis; it depends on professional societies to analyze periodicals; and it files everything else in cabinets with only perfunctory control. Our willingness to forego an emphasis on type of material for an emphasis on information need stands special librarians in good stead, because it avoids quite neatly the question of what belongs in libraries. We are best primed, if we see and seize this opportunity, to become the supermarket for organizational one-stop information shipping.

One of the tremendous advantages that special librarians have over their colleagues in public, school, and, particularly, academic libraries is that they have more freedom to do what they feel needs to be done. They are, of course, constrained by budgets and headcount ceilings, but these are minor constraints if they can demonstrate that what they want to do makes sense in the overall organization, provides better information for decisions, and saves money.

Nevertheless, there are pitfalls and traps we must recognize and deal with. For the remainder of this paper, I will try to identify these, and outline what we must do about them.

The Special Library "Versus" the Information Center

To a considerable extent, this has become, or should by now have become, the great non-issue of the 1980s. The initial development of information centers, and most particularly technical information centers, was based on the premise that libraries only operated in the passive environment of ordering material as requested, circulating it on demand, and borrowing it where necessary. Information centers, staffed by subject specialists, would interact with the information needs of the client, and then refer the specific document request to the library. Information centers and special libraries cannot coexist in the same organization without trivializing the library into a supply room or purchasing department. For several years my facetious, and yet serious, response to questions about the difference between managers of special libraries and managers of technical information centers has been "about $5,000 a year in starting salary."

The Special Library and the Information Analysis Center

This also must be listed, although it should no longer be an issue. The implementation of information analysis centers (IAC) was first urged by Alvin Weinberg, who argued that scientific and technical information analysis was one of the greatest responsibilities of senior scientists.[1] IACs, as envisaged by Weinberg, analyzed documents, determined those with and without value, made recommendations to ultimate users, and prepared briefings and digests that dealt with content analysis and evaluation. The idea may have been good, but it never came to fruition. A few such centers were started (Weinberg's recommendations, then as now, must be taken seriously), but they foundered and disappeared when the suggestion of cost recovery began to be raised. Moreover, Weinberg's belief that the best and the brightest of the cadre of technical and scientific professionals should concentrate on information work never took hold. These individuals perceive, and continue to perceive (probably correctly), that their rapid path to advancement lies not there but in the laboratory, in marketing, or in administration. The reverse phenomenon occurred, and individuals with technical, but without library, backgrounds who have gravitated to our arena of work must be looked at with suspicion.

The Special Librarian and the Computer Center Manager

Increasingly, corporate organizations have placed the library under the management control of the group that selects, manages, maintains, and programs computer hardware. The decision to place special libraries into this organization probably follows most directly from the fact that nobody really knows where libraries do fit. They can be placed in Research and Development, but librarians are not laboratory scientists. They can be placed into an Administrative Services group, but they have little in common with the supervisors of cafeterias, mail services, and duplication centers. The truth is, of course, that libraries don't really fit well into any larger group any more than the corporate legal staff does. However, of all the possible reporting relationships for the special library, reporting to the computer services organization is perhaps the worst. Years on the board of directors of the American Federation of Information Processing Societies have convinced me that there is almost an unavoidable conflict between those who promulgate computers and their use as inherent and obvious good things, and those whose search for solutions to information problems inevitably brings them to a consideration of technology. Special librarians do, indeed, need computer professionals, but they need them as service experts contracted to implement needed protocols, to acquire the hardware and software appropriate to what the special librarian wants to do, and to fix what is broken.

The Special Librarian and the M.B.A.-Trained Management Information Specialist People

Special librarians rarely report to these individuals, in large part because they rarely care to be weighted down by operational management responsibilities, perhaps least of all by librarians. The difficulty here is that these individuals, well versed in writing concept papers, making impact presentations, and presenting three-color graphics, don't know how to run information systems that deliver information in a form in which people can use it. The greatest danger, then, is two-fold. The first is that because they are pretending to run the information system, there really won't be any at all. The other is that the special librarian will end up doing all of their work, while they get the credit.

The Special Librarian and the Organizational Philosophy Toward Decentralization

The tendency toward decentralization of organizational decision making into so-called profit centers is both the result of an attempt to bring responsibility to the lowest possible organizational level and to implement the "small is beautiful" philosophy so prevalent in the last decade. In principle, and probably in practice, the premise makes sense for a lot of operations. After all, individuals at the most operational level should know best of all what they need and what they are willing to pay for. This does not work for special libraries, precisely because users can't really tell a good library from a bad one unless they've previously had access to a really good one. They can, of course, tell a cheap library from an expensive one, at least in terms of immediate and visible cost. However, special librarians know that cheap libraries can lead to very expensive problems. Decentralization of decision making and library service tends to lead to very unequal levels of library service within the same parent organization. Information ignorance that may seem acceptable (more likely unknown) to the local management develops, but the subordinates, whose development is thus stunted, frequently end up working for someone else, who then becomes the victim of the first manager's avarice. Decentralization of library service also leads to overlap and duplication, gaps, and confusion. Library service points do need to be decentralized and brought close to the work area of the specific patrons, although telephones, terminals, and electronic messaging can go a long way toward overcoming this problem. The development of special library policy for the organization and its management, however, needs to be a centralized process to ensure consistency and effectiveness. There is precedent in maintaining centralized services in an otherwise decentralized environment. It occurs most frequently, and quite correctly, in the approach to legal departments. Corporations can't afford inconsistent and contradictory legal advice, and the level of legal service is taken out of the hands of local managers. The same scenario should apply to special libraries, but we haven't made it as obvious.

The Special Library and the Overhead Budget Process

Special libraries are overhead organizations. It is probably better to recognize rather than hide this fact, because attempts to find ways to allocate library costs to direct groups, by asking them to buy needed library services, usually lead to expensive record keeping and to the perception of libraries as nickel-and-dime operations concerned primarily with detail. There are many parts of corporate organizations for which the premise of a centrally budgeted overhead operation is accepted and recognized. These include accounting, personnel, and, of course, the chief executive officer and his staff. Their costs are allocated to user groups but not negotiated with user groups. The only difference is that they protect themselves better than we do.

The Special Library and User Expectations

Many professional users come from academic institutions to posts in which they will be served by special librarians. As students, they were prepared to expect little except harassment by rules. Through experience in numerous special library posts and consulting assignments, it has been my observation that the users of special libraries, like the users of other libraries, accept what is offered to them and consider it adequate, even good. They accept our limitations of service in part because they like us and don't want to make trouble for us,[2] and in part because they have at least two alternatives to getting things from the library—getting it themselves or pretending they didn't need it in the first place.[3]

The development of adequate user expectations requires that we create, quite consciously and despite the probable reluctance of our own managers, an imbalance between what we can give people and what we tell them they ought to have. Creating that imbalance is marketing, and one very simple definition involves convincing individuals that they need what they do not now have. For special librarians this is not a self-serving process, because our users frequently do not know what they could have until we tell them. Special librarians and, for that matter, managers in any other field, who never offer a service until they know how they are going to budget for it during the following year, are not likely to offer many new services.

The Special Library and the Failure to Control Organizational Information Cost or Turf

In other writings, I have commented on the failure of librarians to control their "turf," and probably nowhere does that issue become more crucial to success and survival than in corporate libraries.[4] It is the uniqueness of a skill or capability, or the unique authority to perform a certain function, that provides us with our primary source of authority. We already know from many management writings that most authority is not acquired through the legitimate process of formal assignment. It is seized as necessary to complete whatever it is we have to do. Purchasing agents understand issues of turf very well. After all, anyone can purchase. One finds a vendor, arranges a deal, and pays the invoice. The turf of the purchasing department comes from the fact that the rest of us aren't allowed to do what it does.

What is the special library's turf, and its exclusively? Here we run into two potential problems. The first is that we have no automatic exclusive hold on the information-gathering process. Others can do it, as long as they have money and higher-level management lets them. They can acquire books and journals; they can contract for online searching and document delivery. This leads to the second problem. They usually *do* have more money than the library does, because it is the formal library budget and not the dozens of pseudo-library budgets that receive scrutiny. Some special librarians even hasten this dilution of their own authority by urging user groups to spend their own money for library materials in the absence of adequate library funding, and, of course, library funds are always inadequate. The role for the special librarian here must be to claim and insist on his or her exclusivity, as purchasing agents have always done.

It is easy to demonstrate that such centralization is economically efficient, both because we can inevitably do information work better, faster, and cheaper and because centralization of information costs provides far better organizational monitoring and mechanisms. The application of turf here is really quite simple. Either we get to do it or nobody gets to do it. If there really is no money, then make the others stop. Direct/indirect differentiations are irrelevant in the framework of corporate profitability. Money is money, no matter how spent.

Special Libraries and Organizational Propaganda

Management pressures for greater economy never end. In part, this is because there really may be financial problems, but primarily it is because corporate executives don't know what to spend in support of subsidiary activities, and because they know that assertive and ambitious managers will acquire more resources if there is ever any letup. Pressures to save money usually couched in hysterical terms are incessant, and individuals must learn to sift the reality from the verbiage.

Special librarians appear particularly vulnerable to the suggestion that they be "good soldiers" and absorb into their units misfits whom the personnel department would rather not fire, but for whom no other willing supervisor can be found. This phenomenon has become so common that special libraries can become known as a personnel dumping ground. Personnel administrators do this quite dispassionately, in part because they (along with others) don't understand the importance of high-quality staff in the library, and in part because librarians appear to be tractable victims. Special librarians also become easy targets for the suggestion that they somehow do more with less or at least as much with less, despite the warning by Hedberg a decade ago that such absorption only serves as a self-indictment for having squandered money in the past.[5] Management has the right to change budgets and, specifically, to decrease them. However, budget changes lead to a reformulating of programs and plans, which must, in turn, be approved by the very management that cut the budget. Declines in service, therefore, become their decision and their responsibility.

Special Libraries and the Need to Justify

Tons of management literature tell us that higher-level management requires exception reporting. That is, it is assumed that subordinates will claim credit for everything that went well, but they are likely to hide their problems from their bosses, and it is precisely that information that managers most need. Special libraries tend to be measured not by what they do, but by how much they spend. Because they spend very little, but are usually suspected of spending too much, any management discussion limited to the budget is a disaster from the outset.

Special librarians, in their formal and informal communication devices, need to do exception reporting. They need to communicate what went wrong or, more likely, what didn't happen when it should have. Some special libraries do attempt to do this, in documents that describe the size of backlogs and lists of unpurchased materials. However, such justifications that focus inwardly on the library and its value system are doomed from the start. The parent organization is not in the business of having a strong library, but it may want a strong library if it can be demonstrated that other things of more direct consequence will happen if there is a good library, or won't happen if there is a poor one. Library shortcomings need to be expressed in terms of impact on users and, most specifically, the key user groups whose success is so crucial that nobody will risk shortchanging the library if, as a result, he or she might be blamed for a larger failure.

The Special Library and the Clerical Trap

We have all known for some time that all libraries are clerical traps; that is the work needed to keep the library functioning and the work most closely perceived by our patrons is clerical in nature (ordering, filing, photocopying, circulation, overdue notices). The professional work (literature searches, information dissemination, advanced reference) is not necessarily expected of libraries; although, when provided, it is always welcome. The clerical trap is sprung on us when there are not enough clerks, and, of course, there are never enough clerks. In corporate situations, where hiring freezes and headcount ceilings are a way of life, this problem is considerably worse than in academic libraries, which have an endless supply of cheap student labor. In companies, by contrast, clerks are expensive, and clerks in overhead organizations bear the double burden of being considered expensive and not visibly contributory to overall organizational goals. Special library managers are not likely to change this mindset, but they must be careful to make their plans and programs fit the resources provided, particularly in the clerical area. Otherwise, all the professionals become clerks, and this is perhaps strangely acceptable to our management, because its own history tends to consider librarianship as a series of clerical routines. It is a necessarily strong special librarian who insists that clerical functions be staffed or left undone, and this must be justified not in terms of personal pique or pride but of organizational effectiveness and economy. It makes no economic sense for professionals to do clerical work, and accountants can understand this. Precisely because clerical staffing in corporations is in such short supply, the clerical tasks available to libraries without competitive challenge are almost limitless. The clerical trap for special libraries is that professionals perform clerical *instead* of professional work. That cannot be tolerated, precisely because it is wasteful for the parent organization.

Special Libraries and the "Morality" of User Self-Service

It has already been noted that libraries, as they are visualized by users who have run the university gauntlet, are educational adjuncts designed to promote user self-sufficiency. Some of these individuals become corporate officials, for whom the issue of self-sufficiency becomes a self-evident moral good. The issue never arises with regard to clerical tasks, which are willingly shunted to the library, but it comes to view most frequently in discussions of such activities as online literature searching, because, with decentralized terminal access, ultimate users *can* do their own literature searching. The question is whether or not they should. Here the special library's stake is crucial, and it is bewildering and depressing to find special librarians who seek to rid themselves of the task of bibliographic searching because "they are too busy." Can users do this better and at a lower cost? Generally not, although there are exceptions. There is no moral issue here. Users who want to do their own online searches should certainly be taught to do them. However, most will quickly tire of the novelty, and, if they find they can delegate this process to a special librarian who will do it quickly, effectively, and without economic hassle, they will.

The real crime comes when libraries vigorously espouse end user searching, not as some perceived increase in service quality or effectiveness, but rather because this becomes the most "convenient" way to accommodate a cut in library budget or in library staffing. When this happens, the organization does not save money; it spends more money, but forces the cost underground. Such a scenario might be acceptable to the librarian's immediate supervisor, but it cannot be acceptable to top management if top management can be made to see what shell games are being played. It then becomes the librarian's clear responsibility, as the organization's cognizant information professional, to make sure that top management does know, even if this involves some risk.

Conclusion

Despite all of these dangers and pitfalls, the future for special librarians is bright if we seize our opportunities. This is because information needs are great and growing, and they are recognized as growing and deserving of financial investment. Our risk is that others may take this work away from us, and relegate us to the clerical tasks. We can always continue to count circulation and interlibrary loan statistics if that will satisfy us. If we lose this battle, though, it will be strictly a political loss, and not based on evidence, because there is no question in my mind that we are best prepared and best qualified, and that we can handle professional information needs in the special library's parent organizations more cost-effectively than anyone else.

To do this, we must remain incessantly professional. Professionals, according to some definitions, are individuals who control the interaction between themselves and their clients. Doctors, of course, do this, and so do lawyers. For special librarians, this means that we frequently give our patrons what they want, but it is more important that we give them what they need, and it is most important that we understand and make them understand that at times they don't know what they need, and that there is nothing wrong with that admission.

Special librarians can, and must, lead the way into this new professional area of interaction, as they led their librarian colleagues into the integration of non-traditional materials, automation, selective dissemination of information, and the recognition that, in delivering materials to patrons, speed is more important than cost. Special libraries are better equipped to ward off trivialization—the greatest of all enemies. Our users are not fascinated by what we do, and are willing to judge us by results rather than by methods. The next step is to make them care more about what we do than how we do it, and that can be accomplished. Being cheap will not save a special library. Only being valuable enough will. Good libraries are not necessarily cheap, because cheapness is the ultimate irrelevancy in a billion-dollar corporation. But they are effective, and they are worth what they cost. We do indeed put knowledge to work, because no organization can afford to have knowledge ignored or wasted.

Notes

1. U.S. President's Science Advisory Committee. *Science, Government and Information: The Responsibilities of the Technical Community and the Government in the Transfer of Information.* (The Weinberg Report.) Washington, D.C.: U.S. Government Printing Office, January 10, 1963.

2. White, Herbert S. "The Use and Misuse of Library User Studies." *Library Journal* 110, no. 20 (December 1985): 70-71.

3. Mooers, Calvin N. "Mooers' Law: Or, Why Some Retrieval Systems Are Used and Others Are Not." *American Documentation* 11, no. 3 (July 1960): 204.

4. White, Herbert S. "Library Turf." *Library Journal* 110, no. 7 (April 15, 1985): 54-55.

5. Hedberg, Bo, et al. "Camping on See-Saws. Prescriptions for a Self-Designing Organization." *Administrative Sciences Quarterly* 21, no. 1 (1976): 41-65.

Librarian Burnout

An old joke goes something like, "He's the most unhappy person I know. He has ulcers, and yet he's always been a failure." Similarly, a friend who operated in a truly pressurized decision environment once confided to me: "No, I don't get ulcers. I give ulcers to others." The point of all of this is to stress something society assumes. Ulcers, and with them job burnout, result from positions of high authority, and may be the price one pays for power, prestige, and wonderful salaries.

Executives are supposed to be prone to burnout, and IBM is so cognizant of this that it considers 55 the maximum age for executive effectiveness. On the other hand, gardeners, shepherds, and file clerks are not supposed to suffer from work stress. And, of course, not librarians. The general public believes that we lead gentle and bucolic lives in which we have a great deal of free time to read at leisure. They may not envy our low prestige and our low salaries, but they do envy what they see as our languid lifestyle.

We, of course, know better; it is one of the indictments of this profession that in addition to our failure to do much about our stature and our salaries, we haven't even communicated the truth about our job pressures to the outside world. We do talk about it in our own groups and in increasingly frequent professional articles. We have thus, as a profession, managed to reverse Dr. Pangloss and create the worst of all possible worlds. We are poorly paid, certainly not well enough paid to endure stress. We are perceived by those who pay us poorly as having no stress. Something is very wrong here.

Reprinted, with changes, by permission of the author and *Library Journal* 115, no. 5 (March 15, 1990): 64-65. Copyright © 1990 by Reed Publishing, U.S.A.

What Causes Burnout?

Burnout does not come simply from working hard, when that work is toward achievable ends that carry successful conclusion, credit, reward, and celebration. Hard workers do not get burnout, and they sleep well at night. Burnout comes from frustration; from insoluble dilemmas; from the recognition that the backlogs cannot be eradicated no matter how hard we try; that we can never succeed and never get credit; that irascible users will never understand and never be satisfied; and that certain managers will neither understand nor care while they blithely cut budgets in the confident expectation that nothing bad for them will result.

Why do we have jobs like that? Why are we unable to comprehend and to communicate the most basic management relationships involving authority and responsibility? The ceding of authority to us by our managers does not really concern us as much, although it is an inconsistent process at best. In some instances our managers are very willing to let us expand our authority; they will even lend us the shovels with which to dig our own graves.

For other issues that really matter to them (and they may be less important in the larger framework), we may get little or no authority at all. That causes confusion and inconsistency, but at least individuals who retain authority for themselves to make decisions get whatever credit or blame accrues from their actions. Authority ceding is a constantly negotiated process; your simple bottom-line argument is that you must have enough authority to do what you are expected to do, or you have every right to refuse the responsibility.

The Issue of Responsibility

It is the issue of responsibility that really concerns us here. Responsibility, any basic management text will tell you, can be delegated, and should be delegated as widely as possible. However, responsibility cannot be abdicated, and the more it is given away the more it remains with the giver. It is this simple management truth that we frequently fail to enforce.

Your bosses, be they corporate officials, university presidents, or public library board members, are responsible for everything for which their subordinates are responsible. This means that in good times they get at least as much credit as you get, in bad times they get at least as much blame. Sometimes more, if it can be demonstrated that it was their blindness, stupidity, or cowardice that caused an otherwise successful library and its staff to fail. And make no mistake, your managers can see to it that you fail, no matter how good you are.

They have no particular reason to want you to fail. However, they can inadvertently cause you to fail if they don't understand that objectives, plans, and strategies are tied to resources. This is something they probably do understand in the abstract, they just don't know it applies to libraries. However, everybody understands the value of saving money, and in the absence of contravening pressures, managers cut budgets.

There is always credit to be had for this, and it is certainly worth a try if it is perceived to be without risk. The action is usually covered by a variety of platitudes. They include:

1. We're sorry, we just don't have the money;

2. We're confident that you can find a way to absorb it;

3. We'll all have to work harder (meaning you, not necessarily they in their use of the royal "we").

Sometimes librarians add their own fourth platitude, and we have to do this because even they don't have the nerve. We may argue that service to clients must be protected in spite of everything else, even if this means cutting staff or granting smaller or no raises. Why? And why just by us? Why can't police get smaller raises so that library services can be protected? Or why, if ultimately necessary, can't taxes be raised? Somebody has that authority, and sometimes it is exercised for reasons less significant than providing library service.

Measuring by Money, Not Programs

We suffer burnout when we have allowed ourselves to be saddled with undoable jobs. It is that hopeless frustration that eats away at our minds and saps our wills. Peter Drucker has described the symptoms. We are measured by money rather than by programs, and that assures nonsense before we even begin, because it should be programs that drive budgets. When budgets drive programs, it is at least essential that we identify not only what will be implemented but also what will not. And, most importantly, why not.

Drucker also notes that our agendas are set for us by outsiders who have different and contradictory agendas. In the academic world so clearly described by Anne Woodsworth ("Getting Off the Library Merry-Go-Round," *Library Journal*, May 1, 1989, pp. 35-38), faculty members have no responsibilities with regard to the library. They can demand whatever they claim to need in the name of academic freedom and let somebody else worry about the cost.

Presidents of universities, by contrast, have lots of responsibilities, and ultimately they are responsible for what happens in the library every bit as much as the librarian. Woodsworth notes that library directors often no longer report directly to the president, but through an intermediary. However, that should not matter, because everyone above the level of the library is responsible. Responsibility can be delegated, but it cannot be abdicated.

Opting for Excellent Libraries

Our bosses can opt for excellent libraries. We can tell them what that requires, and then make sure that they get all the credit they deserve. Alternatively, they can opt for terrible libraries, or, of course, something in between. This is easy for them to do; the natural tendency is to cut budgets as part of the guessing game in which subordinates try to anticipate the cut by overbudgeting in the first place. We don't play that game very well, but they don't know that. If they did know they might not care as long as they know they will never be blamed.

Managers (and people) can accomplish a lot more by working politically smarter than by working physically harder. You cannot offset lack of support with more frenzied activity. If your bosses have programmed you for failure you will certainly fail. A second point concerns the ultimate doomsday scenario in which you finally conclude that, for whatever reasons but usually for only presumed economy, "they" will not let you do what needs to be done, although platitudes are plentifully provided.

If that occurs, I have a two-pronged suggestion. Change jobs if you can, and find one in which you have more of a chance for professional success. However, that may not be possible because of geographic limitations, salary, or vested benefits. In that case, shift your priorities away from the job to protect your sanity. Do what you can in a reasonable time frame and effort, and then concentrate on some more rewarding and gratifying outside activity, such as reading, long walks, golf, contract bridge, or taking those courses you never had time to take. Does that betray your clients? Don't forget that they are your bosses' clients just as much as yours. Are you expected to care more than they do, when they get paid more and have more prestige and power?

It all sounds simple, but we don't do it. After years of observing this phenomenon, I think I know why. The first reason is that we tend to be direct and honest, and sometimes expecting the same in return makes you trusting and gullible. When others tell us that they have no funds, and urge us to do more with less, absorb, and "cooperate," they repeat ancient bromides that probably go back to the pharaohs. These statements cannot be challenged or refuted. They are simply to be ignored as the nonsense they are. After all, if a mere absence of funds could spur us to work harder, then we have been goofing off all along. Who besides us swallows this drivel?

Our Own "Moral Imperative"

The reason we do undoubtedly goes back to Drucker's third description of service professionals. We accept the "moral imperative," the belief that with or without funds, with or without staffs, with or without resources, we must do everything that needs to be done or it will be our fault. And once "they" understand that, they have you trapped. In advising us on how to manage our managers, what he considers our most important task, Drucker makes several points. The first is that we establish a relationship of trust, and if we do not think we have it, ask why not and what it would take to establish it.

Secondly, Drucker reminds us again that it is the job of managers to make decisions and then to take responsibility for them. In order to make decisions, our bosses can demand information from us in a variety of formats and mechanisms, but decision-making is their job and decide they must. Finally, Drucker stresses that the essence of management communication is exception reporting, spelling out what did not happen and what is not going to happen. There are two possible reasons: given our priorities, it is not important enough, unless they want to provide extra funds; or, although we do think it is important, the needed resources have not been provided.

Burnout for librarians seems to me both foolish and unnecessary. It results from the absence of a work contract, generally known as management by objectives, the simple understanding of what will and more importantly what will not happen given a particular scenario of resources and time schedules.

If we don't establish this relationship then we endure stress, pressure, and ultimately burnout simply to cover up for others. These others, in the most delicious of ironies, don't even know what we are sacrificing to protect them. It is past time to put a stop to this nonsense. Work hard, work well, work effectively. Work until quitting time. Then go home and enjoy the rest of your life. If that leaves an unsolved problem, tell your boss on the way out the door or write the boss a note.

Let the people with the proportionately higher salaries do the higher proportion of the worrying. I wouldn't recommend burnout as worthwhile to anyone, but certainly in no case without significant financial rewards. Let's get Donald Trump to set a value for it. However, if the media are to be believed, he both makes money and has a good time. Instead of asking him, let's watch to see how he does it.

The Accredited Library Education Program as Preparation for Professional Library Work

Herbert S. White and Sarah L. Mort

Responses to a survey of 346 1980 graduates of 13 accredited library school programs indicate that geographic convenience is the primary factor in selecting a library education program and that this consideration is more important than perceptions of quality or the availability of specialized courses in anticipation of certain careers. The responses also demonstrate that expectations about both type of library and job specialization shift from when students enter into the degree program through graduation and the first job to positions nine years later. Implications for students, employers, library educators, and the accreditation process are discussed.

Introduction

The adequacy of the master's degree as preparation for professional library work has been the subject of considerable discussion, much dispute, and some research for at least as long as library education programs have been receiving or being denied the formal imprimatur of accreditation by the American Library Association (ALA), acting as the authorized agent for the Council on Postsecondary Accreditation (COPA). Discussion has centered largely on the adequacy of the degree program as preparation for the first professional position, and this in turn has sparked discussion of the significance of education, training, continuing education, and the continuing training process.

Reprinted, with changes, by permission of the author and *The Library Quarterly* 60, no. 3 (July 1990): 187–215. Copyright © 1990 by the University of Chicago. All rights reserved.

211

Professional societies in the library and information science field have argued largely for an increase in specific courses made available to students as they prepare for work in what the profession sees as increasingly specialized settings. A recent review process involved participation from a broad range of professional societies and led to a multivolume report prepared for the ALA Committee on Accreditation (COA). COA has now decided on a multiyear effort to review and revise the present "Standards for Accreditation," a document that has served without amendment (although with a growing body of interpretive guidelines) since 1972. The timing of the study reported here, if it provides information of value to the accreditation review effort, appears appropriate.

This rather narrowly focused investigation will not attempt to retrace the voluminous literature dealing with the preparation by library education programs for the first professional degree, the expectations of educators and practitioners in this process, or the strengths or possible shortcomings of the present accreditation procedures. The purpose of this study is more specific. It is designed to ascertain to what extent students select library education programs because of their presumed quality and to what extent they consider all accredited programs to be equivalent and therefore choose on the basis of geographic convenience or cost. A companion question, not addressed in this study, would be to determine to what extent employers use similar criteria in evaluating candidates for hire. Observation suggests that only major academic libraries consistently hire first professionals from a national pool. Others hire from a local pool, sometimes after a search that may include nothing more than a notice to the nearest library school, an ad in the local Sunday newspaper, or even just word of mouth.

This study also seeks to determine to what extent there is mobility between specializations in the library profession. To what extent do individuals who entered an academic program assuming they would become academic librarians, and who perhaps then took courses in preparation for academic librarianship, then become academic librarians? Even more significant, what were they doing nine years after graduation? Still working in academic libraries? In other libraries for which they had not anticipated working? These questions are particularly important when we recognize that, despite a great effort and a great deal of publicity, continuing education is still a rare experience for many professional librarians. Even the most optimistic statistics prepared by professional societies clearly indicate that, on the average, professional librarians participate in no or perhaps just one continuing education experience over the course of several years of posteducational work. For many and perhaps most librarians, what they learn as part of their library degree may be all that they are going to learn in any sort of classroom setting. What are the implications of this in the design of common core curricula for library education programs and on the insistence on such a core or on diversity of program contents by the Committee on Accreditation?

Here, as in several other areas, some of the hypotheses that framed the study are based on observation. Students come to our school and undoubtedly other schools without a full understanding of the kinds of options available to them. They may be familiar with small college libraries, major university libraries, public libraries, or school libraries. In all likelihood they have little familiarity with all of these and are even less likely to know about special libraries in the corporate or governmental sector or about the newly emerging information-for-a-fee industry. Their knowledge and experience with the use of computers as information processing and information seeking tools varies widely. In a one-year library education program (and most accredited programs are still 36 credit hours or less), much of the academic year has passed before the student is fully aware of the various options.

Having been prepared for specializations other than those that the student might ultimately prefer either upon graduation or after the elapse of a certain amount of time, the graduate may indeed find that the absence of certain courses of preparation may not be an insurmountable barrier after all. This would also be true if employers of librarians look at geographic proximity and economic advantages (local candidates do not require relocation) as more important than specific academic preparation. At many presently accredited programs some specializations may not be offered at all, and if geography and cost predominates, the student might sublimate his or her preference even when such had been developed. Does a student who wants to be a special librarian nevertheless choose a geographically convenient program that offers no appropriate specialization?

There are indications beyond personal observation for the suggestion that librarians do not consider themselves fixed in one type of library. In the King Research, Inc., study,[1] the researchers found that 37 percent of the librarians changed jobs in the year 1981 and that, of these, 27 percent (or 10 percent of all those surveyed) moved to another type of library. If this is the pattern in just one year, what are the implications for a career that may span 40 years?

In a 1984 survey undertaken by the ALA Office for Library Personnel Resources,[2] 24 percent of the respondents indicated a desire to move to a different type of library or organization in the next three to five years. Although that figure does not differentiate between library and "organization" (perhaps an entirely different field) the presumption of desired mobility for at least a significant portion of the library profession can be established.

The ALA report was followed by an article by Michael Koenig and Herbert Safford[3] that argued that there was considerable stratification in the library field and that it was difficult to transfer experience from one type of library to another. The authors particularly noted that this was the case in large academic libraries. However, academic institutions have hiring and promotion value systems that transcend their libraries, and the observation concerning immobility for academic institutions might not hold equally for other types of libraries. An emphasis on minority hiring might override specific academic library preparation. In any case, even these authors acknowledged that individual librarians frequently would like the opportunity to change areas of specialization and that such transfers should be facilitated.

Purpose

This study was developed to examine the extent to which assumed areas of specialization in one type of library or library activity or another affected the selection of an accredited library education program in preference to another; the extent to which such perceptions might change during the span of the educational experience and affect the selection of courses taken from the available curriculum; the relationship of these preferences to the first professional job taken; and the mobility in career tracks involving a directional change over a period of nine years since graduation.

Hypotheses

The following hypotheses were established. First, we expected that our survey would show that reasons of geography and of cost (sometimes related in public universities because of in-state tuition rates) would outweigh perceived higher quality, the availability of specialized courses, or other factors in the selection by students of a particular library school.

If this hypothesis proved to be valid, then it would place a tremendous responsibility for quality control on the accreditation process, because that process often simply becomes a binary exercise. Programs are accredited or they are not, and if they are, then students and, as already noted, employers may consider them sufficiently equivalent to make other factors secondary. For example, an earlier survey[4] found that while employers might look with favor on the idea of longer (two-year) graduate library education programs, they do not pay higher salaries to graduates of two-year programs.

Second, we believed that we would find a considerable amount of change between the kind of library job assumed when entering school (and therefore the basis for selecting available elective courses), the job taken after graduation, and the job held nine years later. We felt that anything over 20 percent after nine years should be considered significant because of the implications for the development of core curricula.

Third and finally, we anticipated finding little difference in response patterns between the graduates of highly perceived and less highly perceived, between public and private, and between state and more specialized institutions. The extent to which this hypothesis and the first one proved to be valid would suggest significant implications for the accreditation process itself as well as for the development of curriculum for each school. It would suggest that a mere acceptance of the present accreditation curriculum standard, "[to] provide for the study of principles and procedures common to all types of libraries and library services," with the program then free to claim a specific concentration on certain specializations and the abdication of others, would be inadequate for the needs of the profession being served. If indeed, as we hypothesized, graduates of accredited programs move among various types of libraries either at once or within a time frame of nine years or less, then it would suggest that the standard needs to be revised so that each program, to be accredited, must offer a curriculum adequate to prepare students for a first professional position in any type of library; that is a very different requirement. Moreover, if it is true that students switch emphases as they change their minds, then it is not enough that these courses simply be available as part of the curriculum. They would then have to be embedded in the core curriculum required of all students before graduation. The implication of this hypothesis, if validated, would be that all accredited library education programs prepare academic librarians, school librarians, public librarians, business librarians, medical librarians, and rural librarians, regardless of what the programs would prefer to claim or avoid claiming.

If, in addition, these characteristics hold regardless of the size, location, or perceived quality of the program, then this places on the Committee on Accreditation the additional monitoring required to see that all accredited programs have a sufficient strength in regular faculty, who will also be available for counseling to advise students about opportunities in any kind of library setting and to teach all students about these settings, and who will have sufficient resources and equipment to provide students with learning opportunities for the settings they might well encounter. This in turn suggests minimum characteristics in all of these areas, characteristics that might not be rigidly defined quantitatively as the minimum requirements for faculty, students, research, collection, and equipment that both COA and COPA find so uncomfortable, but might come close in stating expectations that would, realistically, only be achieved by certain minima. All of this could be necessary if it appears that the binary process of accreditation or nonaccreditation provides the only quality control mechanism used by students (and perhaps employers). If prospective students (and employers) view all programs as equal, then the worst program becomes the standard. All library schools do basically the same things. Some do more, but they are all assumed by both students and employers to prepare any first degree graduate candidate to work in any kind of library. If the library schools do not and if COA does not insist that they should, then there is a gap between student and employer expectations and the reality of accredited education.

Sample

Twelve accredited library education programs in the United States were initially selected for the survey. They were chosen to represent a diversity among library education programs as follows:

A. Two programs housed in public universities that had been consistently ranked high in perception studies of the quality of library education were selected. These studies have been done for some time by a variety of investigators, and while specific rankings change over time, the cluster of what are perceived to be perhaps 15 high-quality programs does not significantly change. We wanted to determine whether or not responses solicited from graduates of such highly perceived graduate education programs housed in public institutions would differ from those of graduates of library education programs with other characteristics as noted below. We also wanted to investigate the extent to which such a ranking might affect the ability to get a desired first job or later job mobility. The list used was the most recent published library perception study.[5]

B. Two programs housed in private universities also consistently ranked highly in perception studies.

C. Four programs housed in public state universities that, while they do not appear among the "top 15" in perception studies, nevertheless represent the only accredited library education programs in their states. These then are public universities that have the full responsibility (to whatever extent they choose to accept it) for all accredited library education in their states. We chose four because they are such a large part of the spectrum of accredited programs.

D. Two programs housed in public universities that serve a narrow geographic territory, a narrower professed educational specialization, or both. They are in states in which in-state students have more than one option for the library education program.

E. Two programs housed in private universities that were established at least initially to serve a narrower constituency, whether or not in fact they still do.

It was our intention to mail questionnaires to 30 1980 graduates of each program, for an ideal mailing of 360. Nine of the eventual 13 schools in the sample did have 30 or more 1980 graduates for whom they were able to provide addresses, and three schools had fewer than 30. One school was unable to supply reasonably current addresses for enough of their 1980 graduates, so a 13th school with similar characteristics was added to bring the response rate in each of the categories to reasonably equivalent proportions.

Method

The method chosen was a questionnaire administered by mail, with cover letter and return envelope, sent to a sample of 1980 graduates of accredited library school programs. The questionnaire was pretested with a group of 1980 graduates of our own institution, which was not one of the programs included in the survey, and modifications were made based on their responses. The respondents and the participating schools were promised anonymity.

Study Findings

Survey Response Rates

A total of 372 questionnaires were mailed with stamped return envelopes to graduates whose names and addresses were provided by the 13 participating schools, with two of the schools doing the mailing directly. Twenty-six questionnaires were returned by the post office as undeliverable.

(Seventeen of these were from schools in group D.) Of the remaining 346 questionnaires, 218 usable responses were received, for a return percentage of 63 percent. There was considerable variation in response rates between groups, with a descending return rate from group A to E, a pattern that was entirely unexpected and that can lead to conjecture but not to any substantiated conclusions. It would seem clear, because all 346 questionnaires were presumably properly delivered, that the recipients in certain groups simply cared more about issues of library education and this survey than others. The rates of response within groups are listed in table 1.

Table 1.

Sample and Return Rates

Type of Library Education Program	Number of Graduates in Sample	Number of Surveys Returned	% Return
Group A (highly perceived program, public university)	60	45	75.0
Group B (highly perceived program, private university)	59	41	69.5
Group C (only accredited program in state, public university)	107	65	60.7
Group D (narrow constituency, public university)	72	42	58.3
Group E (narrow constituency, private university)	48	25	52.1
Total	346	218	63.0

Selection of Library School

Respondents were asked to select, in rank number order, the reasons that prompted them to select this particular school. The options provided were: availability of specialized courses, geographical convenience, perceived high quality, lower cost, and other. Those selecting this last category were asked to explain, but the responses here were too infrequent and too scattered to warrant tabulation. In counting the responses, three points were given for a first choice, two points for a second choice, one point for a third choice. Some respondents failed to list as many as three ranked options, and a number did not bother to list more than one. Table 2 (page 218) shows the responses to this question.

Geographic convenience was by far the most significant reason for selecting a school. This option garnered 505 points. The second choice, but trailing substantially with 235 points, was the perceived high quality of the school. Third, with 136 points, was the availability of specialized courses of particular interest to the prospective student. Fourth, with 119 points, was lower cost; it seems probable that this factor's low ranking is due to the fact that, with geographic proximity the most significant factor, cost becomes relatively unimportant in selecting the school because most prospective students really see no choice. Finally, the "other" category garnered only 79 points, and too varied a series of responses to warrant listing.

Table 2.
Ranking of Reasons for Selecting a Particular School

			Total of All Groups				
	Rank	Weighted Points	A	B	C	D	E
Geographic convenience	1	505	1	1	1	1	1
Perceived high quality	2	235	2	2	5	3	2
Specialized courses	3	136	3	3	3	4	4
Lower cost	4	119	4	5	2	2	5
Other	5	79	4	4	4	5	3

When this ranking by the respondents as a whole is compared to the preferences of each response group, some differences emerge, although each of the five groups listed geographic convenience as the most important factor by a wide margin. Groups A and B, the public and private schools ranked highly in perception studies, ranked second for high quality as did group E. High quality ranked third for group D, and last for group C, the statewide public university programs. Specialized course availability was rated third by groups A, B, and C and fourth by groups D and E. Lower cost was the second choice for groups C and D, the fourth choice for group A, and, not surprisingly, the last choice (receiving no mentions) for the two groups of private universities, B and E.

Type of Library Expectation at Enrollment

Table 3 shows the type of library expectation upon enrollment. For the total sample, the distribution among types of libraries was relatively close. Academic librarianship was initially preferred by 25.8 percent (55) of the respondents, and public librarianship was second with 22.5 percent (48). Special librarianship was third with 20.2 percent and school librarianship fourth at 16.4 percent. Twenty-five respondents (11.7 percent) answered that they did not know at the time of enrollment what kind of library they would like to work in, and 3.3 percent indicated other and scattered career options. Academic librarianship was also the first choice in each of the three groups of public institutions (A, C, and D), with public librarianship either second or tied for second. School librarianship fared no worse than a tie for third, while special librarianship ranked as high as tied for third, but primarily fourth. However, in both categories of private institutions (B and E), special librarianship ranked first as the expected type of library option, with academic librarianship dropping to third, in one case behind public librarianship, in one behind "did not know." There is no simple explanation for this clear differentiation, when it is recognized that even these individuals still chose their school primarily on the basis of geographic convenience. It may be that private university library schools promote special librarianship more heavily to their prospective students, that these schools are located in areas in which special libraries are more prevalent, or perhaps even that prospective special librarians are more affluent and likely to attend a private university. The subject invites further study.

Table 3.

Type of Library Expectation at Time of Enrollment

| | Rank by Total (N = 213) | | Rank by Type of Library School | | | | |
			A (N = 44)	B (N = 39)	C (N = 64)	D (N = 41)	E (N = 25)
Academic	55	25.8%	1	1	3T	1	1	3T
Public	48	22.5%	2	2	3T	2T	2	2
Special	43	20.2%	3	4T	1	4	3T	1
School	35	16.4%	4	3	5	2T	3T	3T
Did not know	25	11.7%	5	4T	2	5	3T	5
Other	7	3.3%	6	6	6	6	6	6
Total	213	99.9%						

Note.—T indicates a tie.

Changes from Enrollment to Graduation

In the relatively short time (as little as one year) between enrollment in library school and graduation 23.4 percent (44 out of the 188 who did have a preference) of the respondents who had expressed a preference at the time of enrollment had changed their minds (see table 4, page 220). For both academic and public libraries, the gains and losses almost canceled each other out, although 20.4 percent of the now prospective academic and 28.3 percent of the now prospective public librarians had not initially chosen to work in this area. The most significant change comes in the expectations of those planning to become special and school librarians. Those intending to become special librarians increased from 20.2 percent to 24.9 percent and passed public librarianship for second rank. Furthermore, 32.1 percent of these new prospective special librarians had not planned to become special librarians. In contrast, school librarianship as a career preference declined from 16.4 percent to 13.6 percent and picked up only one new convert along the way. An explanation for these shifts suggests itself in the realization that many new library science students do not know about special libraries at the time of enrollment, while just about all are familiar with school libraries from personal experience. The shift would then represent nothing more than a growing awareness of career options. However, the analysis of the response data suggests a more complex pattern. While a considerable number of students were attracted to special librarianship, 16.3 percent of those who had originally thought they would like to become special librarians had changed their minds. On the other hand, the migration affecting school libraries as a career option is almost exclusively one way.

Table 4.

Change in Expectation from Enrollment to Graduation

					Expectation at Graduation			
	Expectation at Time of Enrollment		Stayed the Same		Change			
Type of Library	No.	%	No.	%	From (No.)	To (No.)	New (No.)	Total (%)
Academic	55	25.8	43	78.2	12	11	54	25.4
Public	48	22.5	33	68.6	15	13	46	21.6
Special	43	20.2	36	83.7	7	17	53	24.9
School	35	16.4	28	80.0	7	1	29	13.6
Did not know or no preference	25	11.7	7	28.0	18	13	20	9.4
Other	7	3.3	4	57.1	3	7	11	5.2
Total	213	99.9	151	70.8	62	62	213	100.1

It was expected that the percentage that did not know or had no preference at the time of enrollment would decline, but it did not decline as sharply as anticipated, dropping from 11.7 percent to 9.4 percent. Furthermore, the majority of these are individuals who thought at the time of enrollment that they did know in what type of library they wanted to work. Apparently, during the time of enrollment some students reach a conclusion, while a significant number abandon the conclusion they came with. The percentage of individuals who clung to other career settings as librarians remained small, but grew from 3.3 percent to 5.2 percent. Furthermore, as with the previously described group, these are not necessarily the same people. The majority of the "others" at graduation had not planned this when they enrolled.

These findings have significant implications for curriculum planning on the part of the student and curriculum advising on the part of the faculty, depending on when the change of heart takes place, and on the extent to which these changes in career preference would be considered important by the employer for the performance of the first professional job. It certainly makes the insistence by any library school that students choose an educational track at the time of enrollment a suspect strategy, and if the school insists that the student remain in a track once selected that tactic could be seen as disastrous.

An analysis of the responses by specific groups divulges no significant patterns of differentiation. Students at private university library schools (groups B and E) were more likely to change their minds than students at public universities (48.7 percent and 32.0 percent, respectively). Beyond this the results are marginal. Students in group A indicated a decrease in commitment to public and school librarianship and an increase in the desire to be special librarians. Group B showed a decline in academic and an increase in special, group C a drop in school libraries and increase in academic libraries, and group D showed an increase in potential public and special librarians offset by a decline in the uncertain. By contrast, group E had an increase in uncertainty, and a decrease in those planning to be public librarians.

Although these shifts within distinct response groups are difficult to chart, one conclusion remains clear. A great many students change their minds even in the short time between enrollment and graduation with regard to the kind of library in which they want to work.

Change from Enrollment to First Job

Although some might assume that students invariably work in the kinds of libraries in which they would like to work after graduation, we know both from observation and from this study that this is not the case. The pressures of finding a job (sometimes any job) and geographic limitations obviously affect the student. Employers are also frequently limited by geographic and financial limitations to select from a pool that may be less than ideal, and, of course, it then becomes ironic later when these employers complain that their new hires were not properly prepared for the jobs for which they were selected.

Of the 209 respondents who answered this question, only 44.5 percent were, upon graduation, working in the settings they had expected when they enrolled in library school, although, of course, some had not known what type of library they expected. On the whole, there were declines from the number of expected academic and school librarians and increases in the number that chose professional library jobs in other settings. The net change in expected public and special librarians was significant, although these individuals were not necessarily the ones who had thought they would be public and special librarians. Three new categories of responses emerged: those individuals who moved into other professions, those who accepted nonprofessional positions in libraries, and those who opted for continued education, as shown in table 5 (page 222).

The implications for curriculum planning by both the school and the student are significant. It would be unrealistic to expect anyone to "plan" for those who were required to take nonprofessional jobs, who went to another profession, or who chose to continue their education. However, to use academic library work as an example, only 27 of the 55 students who on enrollment expected to become academic librarians did so in their first job. At the same time, 17 of the 44 who did become academic librarians had not originally planned to do so.

Table 5.

Type of Library Position from Enrollment to First Job (N = 209)

Type of Library or Position in First Job	Expected at Enrollment	Not Expected at Enrollment	Total	
			No.	%
Academic	27	17	44	21.1
Public	22	25	47	22.5
Special	19	20	39	18.7
School	22	6	28	13.4
Other type of library post	3	13	16	7.7
Another profession	...	13	13	6.2
Library nonprofessional post	...	18	18	8.6
Continued education	...	4	4	1.9
Total	93	116	209	100.1

Analyzing the same information for each of the five response groups provides no major significant deviations. Group D provides the highest level of correlation between the setting expected on enrollment and the setting achieved in the first job (51.3 percent). Group B provides the lowest (32.5 percent). The other three groups fall into the mid-forty percentages, as does the survey population as a whole. Students in the two highly perceived groups (A and B) showed the greatest shift from enrollment to the first job. We do not know whether this is because they became aware of more options, because they were offered more opportunities to choose, or because of some other factor.

Graduation to First Job

Responses to this question test a variety of factors, including the openness and flexibility of the job market as it affects both graduates and employers. Obviously, if either or both are constrained by geographic or financial limitations, a national search for graduates with professional master's degrees may not occur. The question also tests the willingness of a graduate to take a job outside his or her own expressed preference. Finally, it tests the willingness of employers to hire individuals who presumably made no particular effort to prepare themselves academically to work in the employers' kind of library. Of the 209 respondents who addressed this question, 113 (54.1 percent) took positions in the kind of professional library settings in which they anticipated they would work after graduation (see table 6). Though this is a majority of the responses, it is nevertheless surprisingly low when we recognize the immediacy between graduation and the first job. This suggests what can be called either an openness or a casualness in the job search, in matching qualifications and expectations to positions. Graduates can certainly not be blamed for accepting positions that are offered, but there is some question as to why the positions were offered to them by employers, and what those employers were looking for. This is particularly true for the 60 respondents (28.7 percent) who did accept professional positions, but in settings other than they had expected. The final 36 respondents (17.2 percent) did not enter professional library positions. They took what they classify as other professional positions, nonprofessional positions in libraries, or continued their education. How much of this was planned by the graduate and how much simply a reaction to the job market is something this survey did not seek to determine.

Table 6.
Type of Library Position from Graduation to First Job (N = 209)

Type of Library or Position in First Job	Expected at Enrollment	Not Expected at Enrollment	Total No.	%
Academic	36	8	44	21.1
Public	27	20	47	22.5
Special	26	13	39	18.7
School	21	7	28	13.4
Other type of library post	3	13	16	7.7
Another profession	. . .	13	13	6.2
Library nonprofessional post	. . .	18	18	8.6
Continued education	. . .	4	4	1.9
Total	113	96	209	100.1

While the correlations here are better than in the comparison between enrollment expectation and first position, particularly for academic and school libraries, there are still significant discrepancies. For example, only 57.4 percent of those who became public librarians thought on graduation that they would be public librarians, or at least wanted to be public librarians. For special librarians the figure is 66.7 percent. This raises questions about the rigidity of the hiring process in these areas in particular, and this could be a subject of further inquiry. One further piece of analysis is of interest. If it is assumed that the 18 individuals who assumed library nonprofessional positions did so reluctantly (certainly none had planned to do so), it is important to know what these individuals had thought and expected they would be. Five had thought that they would be public librarians, four had planned on special librarianship, and three on academic librarianship. The others gave scattered responses. Of those who entered another profession, four had planned to be special librarians, and three each academic and public librarians. The other three gave scattered responses.

Analysis of these data for each group showed deviations, but none that suggest any significant patterns. The two groups of private institutions had both the greatest and smallest levels of correlation between expectations at graduation and job achieved; group E at 60.0 percent was contrasted to group B at 47.5 percent. For all groups, the number of graduates who ended up in positions different from those expected on graduation is significant.

Change from First Position to Current Position

Although the data permit tracking changes at all stages, from the start of academic program and graduation to the position being filled nine years after graduation, we decided to publish only the movement between the first and current position. Every career change, from enrollment expectation to graduation expectation to first job to the job held after nine years, increases the probability that the initial education received in library school might need to be augmented.

For the survey group as a whole, 68 of the 218 individuals in the survey population chose not to answer this question, most of them because their present activity is not in the professional library field. Of the 39 who commented on their lack of response, 13 are now at home raising children, while eight have taken what they describe as more lucrative positions, largely in computer-related fields. One individual left the field with some regret but commented that genteel poverty was nevertheless still poverty. Seven individuals have retired, a response that might be surprising until it is recalled that a significant number of students earn their library degree after many years of working in libraries. Four individuals were now teachers, and an equal number were practicing or studying law. Two respondents, initially special librarians, reported that they had moved into corporate positions above and beyond the level of librarianship.

For the 150 who responded, 91 (60.7 percent) were still in the same type of organization into which they had entered in their first job on graduation. An additional 39 (26.0 percent) had changed from one type of library setting to another. Finally, 20 of the 150 respondents (13.3 percent) had taken professional library posts after having held either nonprofessional posts in libraries or professional posts in other organizations after graduation. One piece of good news is that only one individual reported still being in a nonprofessional position nine years after graduation.

The fact that 26 percent had changed from one type of library to another over a period of nine years suggests that such changes are not impossible but are nevertheless difficult. Certainly they appear more difficult than a career change at the very outset, before experience is acquired. We think it probable not only that professional experience in one kind of library does not always transfer into credit toward a higher-level position in another kind of library, but also that some hiring officers might look askance at individuals seeking to make a change (although this last comment represents conjecture). The population of professionals in this sample, as represented by the 150 respondents all employed as professionals in libraries, is now distributed as shown in table 7.

For this group, at least, academic libraries represent the largest percentage, followed by special libraries, public libraries, and school libraries. It is interesting to compare this ranking of expectations expressed at the time of enrollment in library school as shown in table 3 (see page 219). Academic library work then led, followed by public libraries, special libraries, and school libraries. Although public and special libraries have changed rank order, the differences in totals are not particularly dramatic. What is significant is the fact that while the totals may not have changed very much, the individuals who make up those totals have.

Table 7.
Changes in Type of Library Positions Nine Years After Graduation (N = 150)

| | | | Total | |
Type of Library	In Same Type as at Graduation	In Different Type Nine Years Later	No.	%
Academic	30	15	45	30.0
Public	22	13	35	23.3
School	14	12	26	17.3
Special	22	17	39	26.0
Other	3	2	5	3.3
Total	91	59	150	99.9

Type of Work Specialization Expected Compared to First Job

We also sought information about type of work specialization. As with type of library, students are encouraged to take courses leading to preparation for a specialization, and employers have reported in a number of surveys that they consider such preparation during the library degree program to be important. In this survey, respondents were given the option of several choices: bibliography, reference, technical services, work with children, work with special populations, and other (with the request that they specify). They were also given the option of indicating that they did not know.

A comparison between specialization expected and the first job achieved was intended to give us some measure both of the preparation provided in the library degree program and the special preparation expected or insisted on by the employer. The survey population as a whole provided 182 usable responses which are shown in table 8 (page 226). Only three individuals planned, on enrollment in library school, to work primarily as bibliographers, but 77 expected to be reference librarians. The number who anticipated work in technical services was a low 21, while 40 thought they would work with children and four with special population groups. Eighteen mentioned a variety of other and scattered library assignments, and 19 stated that they were not sure or did not know. Among the nonrespondents may have been individuals whom we know from other parts of the survey to have accepted nonprofessional positions or nonlibrary posts, and who may not have known how to answer.

Table 8.

Expectation of Work Specialization at Enrollment ($N = 182$)

Specialization	Number	% of Total
Bibliography	3	1.6
Reference	77	42.3
Technical services	21	11.5
Work with children	40	22.0
Work with special population	4	2.2
Other	18	9.9
Not sure/did not know	19	10.4
Total	182	99.9

In their first job only 87 (47.8 percent) achieved the kind of assignment they had expected on enrollment and for which they may have at least partially prepared (table 9). There was a sharp decline in reference librarians, although these remained the largest group. There was an increase in technical service work; this contradicts the suggestion made in several articles that library educators discourage prospective catalogers from pursuing this specialization. Quite the opposite appears to be true. While few individuals originally seem to want to be catalogers, upon graduation more individuals accept such assignments, either because they are encouraged in this direction by faculty members or simply because jobs are available. The most surprising statistic was the growth in the number reporting "other," and this reflects a shortcoming in the questionnaire. Nowhere did we list administration as an assignment option, and it was clear both from the explanations of "other" and from the job titles provided in response to question 11 that not only did a significant number of respondents consider themselves primarily administrators nine years after graduation, but also that a surprisingly large number became primarily administrators (at least by their own evaluation) immediately in their first jobs. This then raises questions for library educators. Many of us teach courses in management or library organization as part of the curriculum, but few if any specifically focus on preparing their students to be administrators.

In examining these same results for each of the response groups, we find a number of interesting patterns, although the response levels are not large enough to claim significant implications. The greatest mobility from a planned specialization to an achieved specialization is for groups A and B, where only 39.0 percent and 41.4 percent, respectively, took first jobs in the anticipated areas of work. The greatest migration is to the "other" category, primarily including administrative positions, and it may be that graduates of schools highly perceived by employers are also considered more attractive candidates for immediate management positions. For groups C, D, and E, the retention in specialization levels remained above 50 percent, at 50.9 percent, 59.5 percent, and 55.6 percent, respectively. Movement was primarily from reference to other kinds of assignments.

Consistently throughout these responses the very large number of those who initially planned reference work assignment decreased between enrollment and the first job, although reference work still remained the single most popular assignment. We could not determine to what extent this represented a change of heart and to what extent a lack of job opportunities, but it is also true that the largest pool of those entering administration immediately on graduation comes from those who had been planning to be reference librarians. Although employers may claim that there is a shortage of individuals accepting technical services positions upon graduation, this is not because would-be catalogers change their minds or have their minds changed for them. In fact, the number of recruits grows. The problem for technical services recruiters is in students' perceptions of specializations before they enter library school.

Table 9.
Specialization in First Professional Position (N = 182)

Specialization	Planned Initially	Not Planned Initially	Total	
			No.	%
Bibliography	0	1	1	.5
Reference	37	17	54	29.7
Technical services	14	23	37	20.3
Work with children	27	10	37	20.3
Work with special populations	1	7	8	4.4
Other	8	37	45	24.7
Total	87	95	182	99.9

Change in Specialization from First to Current Position (Nine Years Later)

As in the question that sought to determine the movement from one type of library to another over nine years of a career, this question attempted to measure the mobility among assignment specializations. Here the data were obtained from current job titles as listed by the respondents, so that it could be determined which jobs were primarily administrative. Nine years later the migration into administration as a specialization is considerably clearer.

As in the identification of current position by type of library, many individuals failed to answer the question because most of them are not presently active as library professionals. Only 121 of the 218 individuals in the survey population provided responses to this question. Of that number, 27 (50.5 percent) were in the same type of work specialization as when they entered the profession as graduates. It can be seen that 19 of the remaining 49 entered administration, leaving only 30 (24.8 percent) who over a nine-year span moved from one professional specialization into another (see table 10). Although this issue has not been addressed as fully in the literature, it may be that changing specializations may be even more difficult than changing types of libraries once the initial job is accepted, despite all of the arguments that catalogers and reference librarians should be interchangeable. The selection by students of the first kind of job is at least as important as that of the first kind of library. Career track opportunities that lead to administrative assignments nine years later appear particularly open to reference librarians and, to a lesser extent, to technical services librarians. Such a progression is far less frequent in responses of individuals who chose to work with children. For each response group, stability in work specialization ranged in the upper 50 and 60 percents for each group, thereby matching the sample as a whole, with the exception of group A, where it dipped to 48.4 percent. For this group, in addition to the general drift toward administrative assignments, there was also an increase in individuals drawn to reference work from a variety of other areas including work with children.

Table 10.
Type of Work Assignments Nine Years After Graduation (N = 121)

			Total After Nine Years	
Type of Work	First Job	Transfers into This Specialty	No.	%
Bibliography	0	0	0	0
Reference	32	11	43	35.5
Technical services	14	4	18	14.9
Work with children	19	7	26	21.5
Work with special populations	2	0	2	1.7
Other, including administration	5	27*	32	26.4
Total	72	49	121	100.0

Includes 19 specifically identified as administrators.

Importance of Elective Courses

We included questions concerning the availability and importance of elective courses with some hesitation. Nine years after graduation many individuals do not even remember what courses they took, let alone what course offerings they did not take, or what courses they now see as having been lacking in the curriculum. Nevertheless, we wanted to explore if there was a significant difference in the perception between the graduates of highly perceived schools (which are also in general larger and offer more elective courses) and the other schools.

We asked first whether or not the respondents had consciously selected certain courses to prepare for their intended specialization, either in a type of library or in a type of work assignment. In evaluating responses to this question we already knew, as the readers of this paper already know, that individuals change their minds during the pursuit of the degree, and change their minds (or have their minds changed for them) in the acquisition of the first job and of jobs held nine years later. We expected almost unanimous expression that indeed elective courses toward the intended end had been taken. Nevertheless, for the response population as a whole, only 79.9 percent of the 213 individuals who answered the question stated that they had done so. More than 20 percent paid no attention to the availability of elective courses toward their specialization. Some of these individuals, undoubtedly, did not know what they wanted to be. Others might have been constrained by work and home schedules that particularly caused part-time students to take courses when and as they were conveniently available.

Some differences emerged when this analysis was applied to the five groups. Response levels were uniformly excellent, ranging from a high of 88.4 percent in group A to a low of 67.5 percent in group D. Since the investigators know what schools make up each sample and what courses are offered in its catalogs, we can report that there is some correlation between the offering of more elective courses and the selection of those courses to meet the student's plan, but not nearly as much as might be assumed. Convenience of scheduling, as tied to geographic convenience, still appears to be a major factor, and students may indeed consider the binary result of achieving versus not achieving an accredited degree as more important than what is specifically learned in that degree; there is some indication that the actions of employers in making their selections validate that assumption. That is particularly the case when we analyze the next question. Respondents were asked whether the electives they had taken were perceived by them as very important, somewhat important, slightly important, or unimportant in their being hired. Displayed in table 11 are the response percentages for the 186 individuals who answered this question for the response groups.

Table 11.
Importance of Electives in the Hiring Process (N = 186)

	Percentage of Responses					
		Groups				
	Entire Sample	A	B	C	D	E
Very important	25.3	26.8	26.5	24.6	15.2	38.1
Somewhat important	17.2	17.1	23.5	15.8	21.2	4.8
Slightly important	10.2	14.6	2.9	9.8	12.1	14.3
Unimportant	47.3	41.5	47.1	50.9	51.5	42.9
Total	100.0	100.0	100.0	100.1	100.0	100.1

"Unimportant" is in all response groups, the most frequently chosen answer, and combined with "slightly important" makes for all groups except B a clear majority, and for that group exactly half. We find this result both startling and disturbing. Since professional groups have expressed strong concerns about the adequacy of educational preparation for specific jobs, it is surprising to learn how little they as employers appear to care about the specific preparation of the applicants they hire, although, as already noted, both geographic and financial constraints may intrude on the options of the employer as well as those of the student.

It is, of course, possible that time has blurred the recollections of the respondents. However, it must be remembered that many public librarians, most special librarians, and just about all school librarians are hired by nonlibrarians who may understand what certification or accreditation means, but who may not know what courses were taken, what courses were offered, and what courses should have been taken.

Second Guessing about the Curriculum

Three questions—asking respondents to comment with the benefit of hindsight about the curriculum offered while they were students—are reported without detailed analysis and without breaking out the specific group responses, although these are available. As many observers have noted, it is difficult for individuals to remain objective about their alma mater, and there is the tendency either to romanticize the experience or to blame the school for all of the ills that may have befallen the graduates later. That observation is not restricted in the least to library education.

When asked to comment about whether there were courses then offered that the students wished they had taken, 45.4 percent of the 207 individuals who answered this question replied in the affirmative and an almost exactly equal percentage, 44.9, answered in the negative. Perhaps the 4.8 percent who were not sure and the equal percentage that did not remember gave the most realistic responses, given the blurring of memories over nine years. When asked whether there were courses they had taken that they had not found remotely useful, 31.9 percent replied in the affirmative, while 51.7 percent found everything they had taken at least of some use. The remaining respondents included 16.4 percent who were not sure or did not remember.

Of greater interest to us were the responses to the question as to whether there were courses that the respondents wish had been available when they were in school. Although no school can teach what is not known or available, some academic programs adapt curriculum more rapidly than others. We were therefore interested not only in the response to this question by the entire group but also in whether there were significant differences by type of library school. For the survey group as a whole, of the 207 individuals who answered this question, 52.2 percent said there were such courses, 27.1 percent said that there were not, and 20.8 percent either were not sure or did not remember.

For group A the positive response level was 48.9 percent; for group B, 47.4 percent; for group C, 64.5 percent; for group D, 51.3 percent; and for group E, 34.8 percent. There are some differences here, but patterns are difficult to determine. The two groups of private universities scored lowest, suggesting that their graduates indicated the least concern about courses they might have missed, and the two groups of highly perceived library education programs also scored lower than the survey population as a whole. However, the responses here, like those to earlier questions, point out that it is difficult for graduates to evaluate the quality of their educational experience nine years later.

As a follow-up to this last question, respondents were asked to indicate what they had done about the gap they had just identified, and they were given four options: on-the-job training, formal continuing education, self-teaching, or need largely not met. The responses were not mutually exclusive, and respondents could check more than one source. In the instructions it was specified that only individuals who had answered affirmatively to the previous question should respond here, but others did and these responses were included as well in table 12 (page 232).

A total of 79 individuals reported further learning through on-the-job training, 35 through formal continuing education, and 63 through self-teaching, a phrase that is recognized as vague and elusive by most researchers.

One must be careful not to overexaggerate these findings. This was not a survey of continuing education or other learning mechanisms, and it is possible that there are other ways in which further learning could have been acquired. Nevertheless, having reported that there were things they had not learned in library school, nine years later these respondents report at best imperfect mechanisms for closing the gap. Even on-the-job training, the most frequently mentioned alternative, fails to draw even a 50 percent response rate from any of the groups. Formal continuing education, the most specific and therefore the easiest to evaluate in terms of content, consistently scores last, and except for group A does not involve even one respondent in five over a period of nine years.

Evaluation of Hypotheses

The first hypothesis stated that geography and cost would far outweigh perceived quality, the availability of specialized courses, and other factors in the selection of a library school. The importance of geographic convenience as the most significant decision factor was clearly determined. Lower cost, which ranked second for two of the response groups (C and D) nevertheless ranked only fourth for the respondents as a whole, and the individuals who chose the private institutions (B and E) clearly did so despite their high cost. It may be that the convenience of geography (which, of course, also has cost implications) may simply obliterate other factors, most particularly cost. An individual forced to attend library school on a commuting or part-time basis attends the school within reach or none at all, and cost is irrelevant.

We expected a considerable amount of change (above 20 percent) between type of library and type of work specialization assumed when entering library school, upon graduation, and nine years after graduation. This hypothesis was also validated. The changes in expected type of library and type of assignment well surpassed 20 percent, and in some instances approached 50 percent.

Table 12.
Sources of Additional Skills and Knowledge

	Group A (N = 48)		Group B (N = 29)		Group C (N = 61)		Group D (N = 35)		Group E (N = 16)		Entire Sample (N = 189)	
	No.	%	No.	%	No.	%	No.	%	No.	%	No.	%
On-the-job training	20	41.7	18	62.1	23	37.7	11	31.4	7	43.7	79	41.8
Self-teaching	14	29.2	6	20.7	24	39.3	14	40.0	5	31.3	63	33.3
Formal continued education	13	27.1	5	17.2	8	13.1	6	17.1	3	18.7	35	18.5
Needs still not met	1	2.1	0	0	6	9.8	4	11.4	1	6.3	12	6.3

We established the hypothesis that there would be little difference in the responses among the graduates of the various types of programs, highly perceived public (A) and private (B) programs, state universities offering the only library education in the state (C), and more specialized public (D) and private (E) institutions. To some extent this difference was really predetermined by the fact that individuals choose their institution not for reasons of quality or curriculum but simply because it is there. Having attended that school they have no basis for comparing it to any standard, and it appears from this and other studies that employers are equally oblivious to whatever distinctions between programs may exist. Accreditation is, and is perceived to be, a binary process. Programs are accredited or they are not, and that is just about all that seems to matter. If there is a difference between kinds of programs it may be in the sense of loyalty and responsibility to both school and profession that perhaps some schools stress more than others, if the differentiation in response rates to this survey is to be taken as an indication of such an attitude.

Commentary

The findings of this study can be considered to have implications for four groups: students, employers/practitioners, library education programs, and the ALA Committee on Accreditation.

Students

There is little advice this survey can offer students or prospective students, and indeed little that they would seek. If they wish to become librarians and determine that this requires an accredited library degree, they will most often attend the library education program that they can conveniently reach. If they are constrained by geography or job or family pressures, they will argue for part-time enrollment, extension courses, even correspondence courses. If they cannot find a program that meets these special needs, they will insist that their failure to obtain a library degree should not be held against them in the job search. If they attend library school they will select courses most likely to fit what they think they would like to become at any point during their time in school, but geography and scheduling concerns may be overriding. What is taught in the evenings? Since they select their library school on the basis of geographic convenience, they must depend on others (the school itself, the parent university, the Committee on Accreditation, the employer/practitioner community) to protect the quality of their educational experience. They do not necessarily think about that quality, they assume it. While they would like to obtain the best education possible, ultimately they do what they must to get the degree. There is little indication of students taking more courses than those required for graduation, and given the expense one cannot blame them. They are concerned about receiving an accredited degree or meeting certification requirements to the extent to which a failure to do this will keep them from getting the job they want. "The job they want" may be clear to them from the outset, or it may emerge simply as an opportunity they had not anticipated. They prepare themselves as well as they can, but when in doubt they apply anyway as indeed they should. Quality control in the hiring process is the employer's responsibility. The school may be able to certify that the student met the requirements for graduation, but only the employer can determine whether this person is qualified for the particular job.

Employers/Practitioners

If, as this survey suggests, students apply for positions for which they may not have been specifically prepared through course specialization, employers have only two practical choices. They can insist at the time of hiring on an adequate level of specific preparation, and they can eliminate candidates who do not meet that expectation. Implementing such control will be difficult, in part because of the financial constraints (usually the better people opt for the higher-paying jobs, and finding the right person might require a national search and both interview and relocation expenses), and in part because for many library positions, particularly in small public, special, and school library settings, the hiring is done by nonlibrarians who may have only a perfunctory or no understanding of what library education entails. To the extent to which these individuals, and even librarians who are limited by geographic and financial constraints, simply accept the premise that graduates who have achieved the degree from an approved program or who have met certification requirements are good enough, they place a great deal of reliance on the quality control exercised in the educational process.

The second possibility for the employer is that the "fine tuning" of new recruits to their institutions and their job assignments must come later: through on-the-job training or continuing education. Training the new employee is not cost-free, and mechanisms for either having the employer pay or rewarding the candidate for paying tend to be lacking. There is perhaps some irony in the survey finding that students have little difficulty in entering a job specialization even after having prepared for an entirely different one. Employers seem to show a great deal more concern in qualifications for later positions; this is suggested by studies that indicate that mobility from one kind of library or one kind of specialization is difficult in later years.

Selecting new professionals as casually as they appear to be selected, at least in terms of specific and specialized preparation, and then complaining later that the new hires do not possess the detailed knowledge that was not demanded in the first place is unfair. We would suggest that there probably are qualified candidates, but they must be searched for nationally, and the better ones have to be competed for. That tends to be true in any profession. Furthermore, the questions of what is properly education for the first professional position—the responsibility of the school—and what are training and continuing education—the primary responsibility of the employer—are still left to be defined.

Library Education Programs

Library education programs need to recognize that, regardless of their intent, they prepare their students for just about any kind of library work in just about any kind of setting. This will continue to happen as long as both students and employers are as casual about meeting specific qualifications for first jobs as they appear to be. All accredited library programs, it appears clear, prepare academic, public, special, and school librarians, whether they would like to claim this honor or not. This suggests that all accredited library education must possess both the faculty and the resources to prepare their graduates for at least initial professional work in any kind of setting. This also suggests a reexamination of the core curriculum, and probably its strengthening. If it is determined that a certain level of computer technology is required for anyone who is going to be a professional librarian, then those schools that offer courses in computer technology only on an elective basis are going to have to reevaluate their programs in order to fulfill their responsibility to prepare their graduates adequately for the real world.

The same sort of argument can be made with regard to exposure to principles of collection development and intellectual freedom, government publications, and many more. Finally, and to use only two illustrative examples, arguments by library schools that their lack of advanced computer facilities is not important because their graduates will not work in such settings, or that their failure to introduce students to issues of public librarianship is equally irrelevant because they are not educating public librarians, are at least inadvertently, untruthful. All schools prepare all kinds of librarians, including those who will be expected to work closely with technology and those who will work with children and senior citizens in public libraries.

The ALA Committee on Accreditation

The responsibilities of the ALA Committee on Accreditation follow from the above, because COA does not prescribe, but only monitors. However, the responsibilities of the accreditation process are heavy indeed, particularly as there is little evidence from this study of discernment by students and, from other surveys, by employers that accreditation is anything but a binary process. As students will attend the most convenient program if it is accredited (as long as accreditation is important), and as long as at least many employers hire from the nearby "approved" pool, COA must understand that the lowest quality accredited programs do not just meet the standards, they represent the standard, because anything beyond that level may not even be recognized and appreciated by either students or employers. If that occurs, it is only a question of time before university administrators will be unwilling to pay for "excess" quality. As a chain is only as strong as its weakest link, accredited library education is only as strong as, and not one bit stronger than, the weakest accredited program. The review of accreditation standards is therefore timely. Much has undoubtedly changed since 1972; and it may be that other things have not so much changed as only just been recognized. As one simple and most obvious recommendation to the accreditation standard review process, it does not seem enough to demand that accreditable programs prepare students in the concepts common to all parts of the profession. Accreditable programs must prepare *all* of their graduates for initial work assignments in any kind of professional setting for which an accredited library degree is relevant. That is because the graduates will apply for such jobs and employers will hire them. This survey, whatever else it demonstrates, demonstrates this clearly.

In a number of pronouncements, COA has made it clear that it sees its role primarily as assisting in maintaining the quality of library education and not as serving as a watchdog and gatekeeper. It is a laudatory principle; we wish it were practicable. Unfortunately, it is not, because if COA does not serve as the impersonal and perhaps even ruthless monitor to protect the quality of library education, certainly nobody else will. Students will not do so—their purpose is getting a job. Employers could, but seemingly do not do so. We must not forget that much of the hiring of librarians is done by nonlibrarians who do not necessarily know what an accredited library degree represents, but assume that the professional accreditation process knows and will protect them. Library schools, much as some would like to, will not do it either. As others have noted,[6] library education programs adhere to a variety of value systems, institutional both in broad qualitative terms and in financially responsible terms. Accreditation is the only reward recognized generically by universities, and because it is a binary process there are no ranges here. The withholding of accreditation, or that threat, provides the university with another essentially binary option. The administrators can improve the program, or they can close it, and improvement demanded should be significant enough not to trivialize the process. Either of these selected options is ultimately acceptable to the profession. We undoubtedly prefer the first, but even the second is preferable to any third, in allowing the accreditation of poor programs because that is all the institution is willing or claims to be able to support.

Notes

1. King Research, Inc. *Library Human Resources: A Study of Supply and Demand: A Report Prepared for the National Center for Educational Statistics and the Office of Libraries and Learning Technologies.* Chicago: American Library Association, 1983.

2. American Library Association, Office of Library Personnel Resources. *Career Perspectives of American Librarians.* Chicago: American Library Association, 1984.

3. Koenig, Michael E. D., and Herbert D. Safford. "Myths, Misconceptions and Management." *Library Journal* 109 (October 15, 1984): 1897-1902.

4. White, Herbert S., and Marion Paris. "Employer Preferences and the Library Education Curriculum." *Library Quarterly* 55 (January 1985): 1-33.

5. White, Herbert S. "Perceptions by Educators and Administrators of the Ranking of Library School Programs: An Update and Analysis." *Library Quarterly* 57 (July 1987): 252-68.

6. Rayward, W. Boyd. "Conflict, Interdependence, Mediocrity: Librarians and Library Educators." *Library Journal* 108 (July 1983): 1313-17.

A Requiem for the
Mother School of Us All

I did not attend the Columbia University School of Library Service, but it did not take me long to learn of the enormous historic debt we owe to the pioneers at that institution, starting with Dewey and Williamson, and of the tremendous esteem in which the school was held.

On my first day as an intern at the Library of Congress, the greeting included special congratulations to those of us selected for the program "despite the handicap of not having attended Columbia." When I heard this I thought that Lucille Morsch was joking, but, of course, she wasn't.

Fifteen years later, as a vice president at Documentation, Incorporated in Bethesda, Maryland, I watched Mortimer Taube rush to the airport every Friday afternoon, in fair weather or foul, to catch the plane for New York to teach his 4 p.m. Columbia seminar class. There were nearer library schools at which he could have taught and they would have been happy to have him. He understood that it wouldn't be the same.

By the 1980s, things had changed. Perceived excellence in library education had broadened, and in particular had begun to shift to public universities. However, Columbia was still viable and proud. By the latter 1980s it was making a strong comeback from the low periods that all academic programs sometimes encounter.

Reprinted, with changes, by permission of the author and *Library Journal* 115, no. 12 (July 1990): 63-65. Copyright © 1990 by Reed Publishing, U.S.A.

In the Final "Analysis"

In perception rankings, Columbia never left the top echelon, a group that shifts in numerical ranking but never seems to change in composition very much. At its worst, Columbia was still a very good library school. And now it is gone, together with Chicago and Case Western Reserve, and part of us is gone along with it.

I have read the report of the special committee that "evaluated" the program, as well as the analysis by the provost. They were careful to spell out alternatives without formally making a recommendation. I have lived long enough in both the corporate and academic sectors to recognize that the difference is primarily in the style in which throats are cut, and not in either the intent or in the deed. The report reads like Greek tragedy; we can rail at the blindness and unfairness but we understand the inevitability of the outcome.

There are things in the report to make us angry. One of the factors that endangered the SLS was the "cost" of moving the school to new quarters to make room for renovation of the Butler Library. While the committee noted that incurring this cost might be possible, it also wondered if there were not perhaps other unmet priorities at the university that should be considered. Are there ever not unmet priorities? Suggesting the question is like pouring blood in front of sharks.

Let's be honest. If Columbia is considering renovating the Butler Library as opposed to other options—including the building of a new library—then moving the School of Library Service, as an equal co-occupant of the building, is one of the costs to be factored into the renovation option. No one unit in academia "owns" a building. We don't have landlords and tenants.

Omitting Professional Schools

The committee noted that "research" institutions like Columbia may not really have room in their mission for "professional schools"; I'm not sure what that makes Illinois, Michigan, and UC-Berkeley.

However, the committee realized where that might lead them with regard to Harvard Law, and immediately clarified that it did not mean "learned professions" such as law and medicine.

The learned profession of law? Law school faculties cannot even agree on whether it is the role of judges to uphold the law and the role of legislatures to repair rotten ones, or whether judges are there to see that justice is done, with or without legal precedent.

It is a crucial issue, but there seems to be room for only one point of view per law school, at least for junior faculty risking the tenure process. And senior law professors fight like alley cats at Senate confirmation hearings, sometimes providing more entertaining action than tag-team wrestling. What I suspect the committee meant to say instead of learned professions is rich and powerful alumni.

However, railing at an academic committee process that goes through elaborate rituals to document carefully what has already been decided is only an exercise in killing the messenger. The Columbia SLS probably was doomed by the realization that none of the institutions Columbia considers as peers (chiefly the other Ivies) had library education programs. That was, of course, always true, but at one time it was a source of unique pride. Now it is a source of worry.

Library Education/Public Institutions

The Columbia evaluation report suggests that graduate library education may become the exclusive province of public institutions, which must presumably absorb this burden as a service to taxpayers who demand properly educated librarians.

As a general trend the observation is accurate, although there are fine library education programs in private institutions, usually because the library school has been able to demonstrate that it brings prestige to the parent body that the institution might not otherwise so easily claim.

However, we also know it would be simplistic and inaccurate to assume that all public university library education programs are therefore safe and secure. Public universities are just as capable of applying the double criteria of income and prestige used in the evaluation of academic programs. It happened at Minnesota, the only accredited program in the state, and before that it had happened at Oregon. We will always have some difficulty with income, but the crucial concern is prestige.

The responsibility for what happened at Columbia is not that of a planned library renovation or of a review committee. Those are only the triggering mechanisms. The responsibility is ours. If we want quality library education we must demand it, insure that it happens by policing the process, and make our employers pay for its products.

Quality costs more. In particular, it costs more because it values education and research as the twin pillars on which a profession stakes its turf. Training, the teaching of specific skills, follows after education, and is provided or funded by the employer.

Wedgeworth the Hero

One genuine hero emerges from all of this sadness, and it is Robert Wedgeworth, the dean of the SLS. Already identified by Alice Gertzog as one of the recognized leaders of our profession (see her article, "Library Leaders: Who and Why?," *Library Journal* 115, July 1990, pp. 45-51), Wedgeworth adds only distinction to this reputation by his actions.

His response to the suggestion by the Columbia president that, even if the SLS were closed, the university would hope to retain as distinguished an educator as Dean Wedgeworth is worth quoting. In the April 25, 1990, issue of the *Chronicle of Higher Education*, Wedgeworth said, "I find it hard to believe that someone could value me and not also value my profession."

Wedgeworth's forcefulness and eloquence make the total silence of the librarians at Columbia particularly noticeable. Aside from issues of courage and integrity, it is a foolish silence. Can Columbia University librarians really believe that the closing of their library school for a claimed lack of professional rigor does not touch them? Or do they think that fascination for library collections and library buildings still automatically transfers, after the statements made, to their own status? The SLS survival fight was their fight.

Whose Responsibility Is It Anyway?

The real responsibility for what happened at Columbia, however, belongs to all of us in the profession. We drive nails into our own coffins every time a letter appears from individuals who insist that, despite the lack of any educational preparation, they consider themselves fine librarians.

Confidence is always admirable, even when it becomes foolish. But how could they possibly know when they don't even know what it is they don't know? Why do we dignify such letters by taking them seriously? Who are the "other" librarians we keep being lectured about (Editorial, *Library Journal*, July 1989, p. 4)? Where are the equivalent other doctors?

We are perhaps unique in trashing our own profession on a regular basis. Even an automobile mechanic, no matter how well he considers himself qualified, must go to school and earn a certificate to become Mr. Goodwrench®. By contrast, anybody can claim to be a librarian and everybody claims to be an expert on libraries. And we worry that they might be right and that we shouldn't offend them.

The bottom line is that the faculty committee that looked at the option of closing the Columbia SLS was not competent to make that judgment, certainly not without the library educator and library researcher advice and evaluation they so carefully avoided.

The Demand for Intellectual Rigor

There are library graduate programs in institutions that do not value or demand education or research from either faculty or students. Those library schools can probably continue to stay out of trouble, at least for the present, if they are in institutions that do not demand intellectual rigor from this discipline or any other.

It is therefore the stronger library schools in major universities that are in greatest danger. The accreditation process adapts to this, because while it argues for faculty research, it is willing to judge this within the overall institutional context. Library schools in less demanding parent institutions are much safer, because less is expected of them.

The Ramifications

The Columbia SLS closing has received wide publicity. It creates immediate problems for library schools in those institutions that compare themselves to Columbia, and they are not all in private universities. Their presidents begin to think about the alternatives that the Columbia action suggests, ranging from an outright closing to some form of downgrading or merger. If Columbia can close the most historic library education program of all, anything is possible.

We will have high-quality library education programs (and we really know which they are despite all the egalitarian arguments to the contrary) only to the extent to which we insist on having them, or at least to the extent to which we credit them for making the extra effort.

The process that we are allowing to develop endangers not the weakest of the library schools but the strongest. We have had ample opportunity to observe this phenomenon at a variety of institutions. Add Columbia to that list.

How often do we have to see this happen before we understand what it means and what the profession has to do about it? Columbia is not the end of the line.

The Conflict Between Professional and Organizational Loyalty

There has been a good deal written lately about the responsibilities of professionals, particularly when the value system of the organization that employs them clashes with these concerns. We had a highly visible example of this conflict of value systems in the tragic explosion of the space shuttle *Challenger*, with the death of seven astronauts, including teacher Christa McAuliffe.

The National Aeronautics and Space Administration (NASA) insists on referring to this as a tragic accident, but we have learned that it was really a calculated risk that went awry. The engineers at Morton Thiokol recommended against a launch in cold weather. That was the professional view. The management view at NASA and at upper-management levels at Morton Thiokol was that it was essential for this launch to take place without further postponement—to impress a dubious administration and Congress—and that nothing could go wrong. The engineers were thought to be ultra careful and unreasonable, as engineers are often thought to be.

Self-Sacrifice to Self-Hypnosis

Nobody would suggest that anyone willfully decided to sacrifice individuals for a schedule. It was rather a process of self-hypnosis that I have seen many times, such as when proposal writers are absolutely certain that their proposal is best, and the writers of the other 15 competing proposals are just as certain.

Reprinted, with changes, by permission of the author and *Library Journal* 116, no. 9 (May 15, 1991): 59-60. Copyright © 1991 by Reed Publishing, U.S.A.

Ultimately this rationalized process persuades us that we were really correct all along, only unlucky, and adherence to this belief becomes a test of loyalty. This allows NASA to insist that what took place was not a bad management decision but only an unfortunate "act of God," and loyalty demands that the engineers who told Congress what really happened had to be punished, because organizational loyalty was most important.

How Professionals Face the Problem

Professionals face this conflict from time to time and they react in various ways. They can go along; they can protest and then acquiesce; they can protest and ultimately resign; or they can protest and ultimately subvert. Some would applaud such an act, but others might feel that it raises other ethical questions.

It is interesting to note how some organizations try to have the best of all worlds. Dow, which acquired an unsavory reputation with some for its production of Agent Orange during the Vietnam War, is aiming its institutional advertising at altruistic young men and women who want to provide a better world. The U.S. Army, with its "Be All You Can Be" campaign, makes the same attempt. The approaches may even work with the general public, but I find them just a little hypocritical.

Dow recruits employees whose ultimate task is to earn profits for the stockholders of Dow, and the Army trains young people so that, if called upon by their nation, they will fight and kill. I am not necessarily comfortable with either premise, but obviously advertising consultants think that a lot of people are. It recalls the old joke: Join the Army but don't get into any fights!

Accepting the Employer's Values

When we take a job we are expected to accept the employer's value system, and I urge students to examine carefully what that is. Some organizations stress their approaches rather heavy-handedly through songs and sweatshirts, others may be so subtle that newly hired professionals may not even realize into what they have just bought.

Libraries usually fall into this second group. For many individuals there may not even be a conflict, and some employers sincerely believe that letting the employee do the best possible job professionally is also what is ultimately best for the employer. These organizations give their employees a great deal of freedom and flexibility to insist on doing what is professionally proper. For librarians in the bureaucracies called libraries, a conflict is likely. This is because, while we are prepared and inculcated to provide good libraries, the nonlibrarians who hired us can't define good except as cheap, or big, or even good enough.

Who Says What Is Good Enough?

Good enough or as good as we can afford is always the outlet of the rationalizer, but how are individuals unqualified to judge going to determine what that is? Should NASA administrators ever be allowed to overrule Morton Thiokol engineers on issues of technical judgment, and should mayors be permitted to overrule librarians on what constitutes an adequate library?

In an article entitled "Professional and Business Ethics: Bridging the Gap" in the November 1989 issue of *Management Review*, Professor Joseph Raelin attempts to differentiate between what he calls "cosmopolitans" and "locals," and argues that the tendency to be either cosmopolitan (identifying with the views of your professional colleagues rather than your local work orientation) or a local is developed quite early in one's career. Raelin identifies socioeconomic background, schooling, and personally held values as contributing to the ultimate orientation and suggests that we may even choose professions because they will allow us to be either cosmopolitans or locals.

Cosmopolitan or Local?

As I think about the application of these criteria to professions with which I am familiar, some clear differentiations emerge. Social workers appear to me to be classic examples of cosmopolitans, even to the extent of identifying with the problems that caused them to be hired rather than with the managers who hired them. As a result, case workers no longer deal with "cases" but with "clients," and the attitude toward the employer who pays their salaries is frequently embittered and confrontational.

Military personnel are the classic example of locals, and loyalty to the team, the unit, the organization, and one's buddies is stressed. Managers are expected to be locals, and indeed the very term bureaucratic, in its most negative meaning, suggests an individual who values organizational rules above even common sense.

The Two Faces of Librarians

Librarians appear to exhibit a split personality on this issue. On the national scene, we are very much cosmopolitan, arguing passionately for the establishment of principles and service qualities at the federal level. This is expressed in activities of the American Library Association Washington Office, in letter-writing and petition campaigns, and in both the rhetoric and motions of ALA Council meetings.

Back home, where the real battles are probably going to be fought if they are fought at all, we tend very much to be locals. As I track the records of my own school's graduates—even the most cosmopolitan ones as students—I find this transformation occurs almost without exception; it may simply be that they slide into a value system that is already there and deeply rooted. They accept the local scene as they find it.

Whether we are academic, public, school, or special librarians, we become members of the team, and even when we know the results for our users are unsatisfactory, we abandon at the local level our nationally staked ethical positions.

Thus, public library annual reports never acknowledge that there might be anything wrong, and school librarians accept without much visible protest the premise that they will now have three instead of two libraries to run, and never mind what happened to the idea of one librarian per school library.

We even make excuses for our management, insisting that this level is the best their budgets can afford. I have already noted in an earlier column ("Librarian Burnout," reprinted in this book on pages 206-210) that we will even sacrifice our bodies and minds to protect the penny-pinching of others. This inconsistency—of clamoring loudly for federal document dissemination without also protesting the backlogs and staffing shortages that mean that nobody can find what we fought so hard to get—is barely recognized.

The Librarian as Victim

I am not sure why we do this, although there are certainly theories. Some would suggest that the profession automatically attracts willing victims who expect little except self-sacrifice for the greater good. It may be more likely that some individuals ascribe to an extension of the "it is better to light a candle than curse the darkness" concept: anything is better than nothing.

That may be satisfying up to a point, although I might prefer to agitate for a power plant. The premise of half a loaf being better than none, and that even crumbs are preferable to an empty table, is expressed by those who argue that any library on any terms and at any quality is better than no library at all.

I am not so certain, perhaps because I have always been a cosmopolitan, but more likely because I am convinced that we can do better on the local scene if we can persuade outsiders to support us, because the money is there and has always been there. It will be fascinating to continue to watch how this cosmopolitan/local dichotomy, for our profession, in which we undertake professional criticism of federal government library policy but not our local library board, will play itself out in comparison to what happens in other professions.

Other Professionals Making Noises

Teachers and nurses, who at one time shared the characteristic of being cosmopolitan at the national level and very local back home, are beginning to make ugly noises about inadequacies for which their home-based bosses must take responsibility, and this fits in quite nicely with the management concept that states that responsibility can never be abdicated.

Ultimately, the *Challenger* launch decision was somebody's wrong decision at NASA headquarters, even as the agency tries to protect its own managers. Inadequacies in library service are the responsibility and the fault of an entire management chain above us.

However, nobody will ever be aware of the problems if we don't stress the inadequacies, because they won't even know there are inadequacies, or at worst they will blame factors outside their control. Whatever we as a profession decide to do, it is important that we recognize that the present strategies do not work.

There are apologist librarians who have no patience with that assertion, either, and argue that we should stop complaining and try harder to make a good impression. Nonsense! We make such a wonderful impression now that the world thinks we are capable of doing everything with nothing.

What we need to understand is that all the people who pat us on the back also trivialize us. Our present failure to take a consistent cosmopolitan stand hurts us, and we see the damage in our status, our low salaries, and the trashing of our educational programs.

However, there is room in this argument for the altruistic as well as the narrowly selfish, because our failure to speak and fight at the local level, which is the primary place where fighting really matters, also hurts the clients we are dedicated to serve. They may not even know that, but we do. When as loyal locals, we forgive the low funding of our libraries not as a conscious decision but as the result of a lack of money, we can eventually explain it all as simply an "act of God."

Professional Ethics in
Library and Information Science

Discussions of ethics have been with us for hundreds, indeed thousands of years, and have recently received considerable new attention in our own profession. In an article in the May 1987 issue of the *Journal of the American Society for Information Science*, my late friend and colleague Manfred Kochen offered a useful analysis of ethics. He attempted to track the development of ethics, a domain that many people have claimed as their own, but with regard to which there remains a great deal of confusion.

In his article, Kochen notes that ethics deal with principles for judging right and wrong. That sounds self-evident enough, but what is right? Right as defined by who? Machiavelli had no difficulty with the issue, because to him, might made right. Eighteenth century theologians postulated that ethical behavior was behavior in accordance with the will of God, but to recognize the difficulty with that definition, we need only remember that most religious persecution, including the Inquisition and the death warrant on author Salman Rushdie, was and is ostensibly in the name of God. Burning accused heretics at the stake was justified quite neatly on the premise that God would not let an innocent person burn. Because they all did burn (human beings were then as now flammable), they were also clearly guilty of heresy, or whatever they were charged with. William James helped us along by noting that it was the duty of man to know the will of God and keep it. Easily said. John Stuart Mill postulated that right is that which produces human happiness, while Immanuel Kant equated right with reason.

We know, of course, today what difficulties we have in work settings with the word "reasonable." "Be reasonable" is an often heard admonition, and, of course, that means that I already am and you are not. We are about to enter the same arena with the word "fair." As a teacher of management I point out that the

Speech presented at a meeting of the Wayne State University Library Science Alumni Association, Detroit, Michigan, March 27, 1993.

search for compromise as a reasonable solution runs contrary to the general belief that we are reasonable because we are right, and you are unreasonable because you are wrong. Therefore, it is you who should compromise, giving a new meaning to the term. To confuse things further, we are also urged to stand by our principles, and never compromise them away. Nietzsche was a great pragmatist when he argued that "right" was that which produced the next stage of evolution, what Nietzsche called the Übermensch, or superman. That makes ethics easy to define for yourself, because right becomes whatever you want it to be, from conclusions you have already reached, and we need only note what Hitler was able to do with an extension of Nietzsche's philosophies.

However, this is not a talk on the historical development of ethics. I only want to note that the confusion and difficulty continues to this day. When newsman Bill Moyers conducts an in-depth interview with modern-day ethicist Michael Josephson in the July/August 1989 issue of the *New Age Journal* (I must confess some nervousness about people who call themselves ethicists as a full-time occupation; like full-time book censors or full-time Detroit Tigers fans, they can cause no end of difficulty), many pages of eloquent exposition in conversation with one of the brightest interviewers of our day still only leaves me with the impression that Josephson is dealing with interpretations of the Golden Rule: "Do unto others as you would have them do unto you." It is certainly a useful and valid statement, but it does not really help us very much except in a limited sense. Do not murder, do not steal. Fine. But, as a librarian—do not give information to individuals who would do with it what you would not do with it? That doesn't fit nearly as well. And that spotlights the problem. Ethical concerns for professionals are not the easy and obvious issues. Librarians oppose censorship, and as I will state in a minute, the Library Bill of Rights and the Codes of Ethics adopted by various American Library Association bodies really state the obvious and solve no problems for us. Our professional conflicts, and those of any professional, fall on more complicated ground. What are our responsibilities to our employer, be it a corporation, a university, or a public government? Can these responsibilities be in conflict with those we owe our library users? Of course they can. What if the inadequacy of funding or staffing provided by our funding agencies means that we are providing inadequate service to our users? What do we do then? Lead marches on City Hall?

It is a fascinating characteristic of our professional literature that we worry a great deal about whether or not government documents should be released to the public through the depository library system, and we worry not one whit whether or not anybody can find them in our massive cataloging backlog, assuming we catalog government documents at all. What is our professional ethical concern in a cataloging backlog? Or in a failure to have adequate reference services available? Or in the recognition that while we have bought a copy of the book, you can't have it because it is charged out, and having bought it we have discharged our ethical responsibility and won't borrow another copy of what we own because that is against library policy? It gets a little more complicated than our cherished freedom to buy whatever we like, doesn't it?

The conflicts between responsibility to the profession and to the employer have been discussed in many fields. In general it has been noted that humanists (such as history or philosophy professors) see their primary responsibility as being to their profession, and their employer and his value system play only an incidental role. By contrast, scientists and engineers are seen to owe their greater allegiances to their employer, and they do what the employer asks them to do. Thus, when I came to Oak Ridge, Tennessee, in 1953, I found many individuals who had worked long and hard on the development of the atomic bomb in the early 1940s. They found out only after Hiroshima and Nagasaki that they had been working on a destructive bomb. They might have done it anyway, but that's not the point. It is an interesting sidelight of ethical history to know that some of the refugee scientists from Germany who did know were perfectly willing to drop the bomb on Germany, but after the Germans had already surrendered in the spring of 1945, were reluctant to drop it on the Japanese, whom they saw as a lesser enemy not as deserving of impersonal annihilation. Other individuals, of course, fought the Japanese with far more enthusiasm than they could muster for fighting the Germans, because, after all, the Japanese were not white like the rest of us, and, therefore, somehow less human. That is, of course, blatant racism, and totally unacceptable even as practiced today, but quite acceptable in 1942 if we remember the totally illegal (as well as unnecessary) Nisei internment. What is the role of ethics if we bend it to personal and convenient value systems? If it is wrong to block the entrance to an abortion clinic, is it okay to block the entrance to a nuclear power plant?

It is interesting to me to note how the Dow Chemical Company, right here in Michigan, is attempting to straddle the issues of public image when it comes to ethics. Dow was one of the developers of Agent Orange as used in Vietnam in response to the government's perceived need for a defoliant. It is clear that Dow is now sensitive to implications it had no particular reasons to anticipate, and certainly any chemical contractor could have produced this product whose chemical formula was known. However, Dow is now recruiting young people who want to find "chemical solutions to societal problems." Pardon my cynicism. Dow's primary objective, now as then, is to its stockholders, who expect it to make a profit, and the president of Dow certainly knows this. The young Dow chemist will learn it. Bankrupt ethical organizations aren't much good to anybody, and the difficulty is in maintaining a balance. Sometimes it isn't easy. Exxon is now roundly condemned for allowing the Alaska oil spill to take place, but as we understand it, that oil spill was probably caused by an Exxon employee who was a long-time substance abuser (in this case, alcohol), and some of the people who now condemn Exxon are the same ones who would have objected if Exxon had implemented a tough program of mandatory or random drug testing, and fired the offenders. A jury has now exonerated him in large part, by saying it was an accident. Was it not an accident for Exxon? Neither the public nor the courts see it that way.

As private citizens we have responsibilities, presumably to do our best to prevent injustice, evil, racial hatred, nuclear holocaust, and environmental blight, and we are free to develop our personal interpretations. What do we do when our personal standards get in the way of our assigned professional duties as subordinate employees, and just perhaps even in the way of our professional ethics? It is, as with the Exxon case, always easy to judge with 20-20 hindsight. German scientists should have refused to develop the poison gases used in Auschwitz and the other death camps. Werner von Braun was a "bad" German when he helped develop the V-2 bomb used to bomb London. Later, of course, he became a "good" German, and finally the quality of Germans became irrelevant, and the Russians were "bad."

The situation changes rapidly. Retrospective judgments, in any case, are always applied by winners to losers. Thus, we had the Andersonville Trial because Andersonville was a Confederate prison, while what happened in the Union prison at Elmira, New York, was irrelevant because the North won the war. Those who have seen the play "The Andersonville Trial" will recall the idealistic young prosecutor, who is ultimately brought into line by the military judges who understand the trial is not a search for justice or ethics, but has been convened to find Captain Wirtz guilty, so that he can be hung. There are those who are rhapsodic about the Nuremberg trials, but I have my difficulties. Countries are still using poison gas and tactics of starvation on their own citizens, and the world does not even seem to notice. Indeed, representatives of these countries participate in U.N. symposia that extol human rights and blame other countries that may be less guilty than they.

In any case, professionals have their ethical codes, and they can get in the way. Thus the Hippocratic Oath, which all doctors take, would require a Jewish surgeon to have attempted to save the life of Adolph Hitler. Lawyers are supposed to do their best to defend their client, and if possible get him freed on a technicality. So that he can commit more crimes? Yes, if that is the outcome. The lawyer is not considered ethically responsible. It is interesting that the general public requires, through TV, more comfortable solutions. When Perry Mason shows that his client is innocent, as he always does, he also quite conveniently finds the guilty party. I am waiting, I am sure in vain, for one episode in which Hamilton Burger says—"but if your client didn't commit the murder, who did?"—and Mason replies—"that's not my problem."

I was interested last year to hear of a graduation speech on ethical conduct delivered at the Wharton School by an investment banker, Felix Rohatyn, who clearly has a social conscience as well as a knack for making money. Rohatyn, noting the emphasis in American business on making money through junk bonds, leveraged buyouts, greenmail, and golden parachutes, urged these new graduates at Wharton to go out and not simply manipulate blips on a computer screen, but to build the country. We can cheer, as Rohatyn's audience of future financiers did, but we won't know until much later what impact his talk had. I think it is probably significant that Rohatyn said what he did, because he thought that the Wharton professors hadn't said it, and later interviews with the audience of graduates indicate that his assumption was correct. What the professors had been teaching is what the financial community had wanted them to teach, and by extension, that includes leveraged buyouts and junk bonds.

What do we teach in library schools, and what does the profession want us to teach? Yehoshua Bar-Hillel, in a talk presented at a conference in Aberystwyth, Wales, in the early 1970s, stated quite simply that the jobs of librarians and information specialists was to help their patrons find whatever information they needed, and what those people did with that information was not our concern. It is certainly a simple ethic if we can adopt it, and it has similarities to what doctors and lawyers are supposed to believe. However, if we adopt Bar-Hillel's thesis we leave ourselves open to a great deal of second-guessing. I suspect that we also contradict the mood of many of the individuals who come to library school because they want to make the world better. Rohatyn would not have had to make his speech at a library school graduation. Our students are not really in this for the money, and given our salaries, that is fortunate.

The big ethical issue for librarians, in their professional literature and in their educational emphasis, has been on access to information. It is, of course, an important issue, and it concentrates on themes with which we are all familiar. We champion unfettered access, and take strong stands against government policies that attempt to withhold information, either through restrictions on distribution, or by attempting to limit distribution through pseudo-security classifications such as "unclassified but sensitive" (certainly an oxymoron), or by charging for government information. We also oppose government attempts to limit access, and have been effective and articulate fighters against F.B.I. surveillance.

Our most significant and visible impact is in the fight against censorship, and the banning of books, although banning usually applies only to removal after purchase. We have fought strongly against attempts to remove such material as the works of Judy Blume or Kurt Vonnegut on the grounds of unsuitability, or *The Diary of Anne Frank* because it is "depressing" (a charming term—yes, genocide is depressing to think about). We also fight, some equally vehemently and some less so, against censorship from the "good" side, individuals who consider *Huckleberry Finn* or *Little Black Sambo* racist (although Sambo was an Asian Indian boy), or works such as *The Taming of the Shrew* as sexist. This is always a difficulty with classics. Shakespeare would not have considered *The Merchant of Venice* blatantly anti-Semitic, it was just the normal thought of the time. All of the better English people were as anti-Semitic, and none of them (including Shakespeare) knew any Jews because they had all been expelled. In any case, we librarians fight these issues with a will, sometimes even to the extent of finding ourselves allied with child pornographers.

Below the surface there are other issues, not as readily addressed. It has already been noted that censorship in libraries consists primarily of removing material already purchased. The decision not to buy something in the first place is more easily defended, as long as we claim this is not censorship but just the implementation of value judgments, because we obviously can't buy everything. If there are librarian biases in this process, it is a thicket into which lawyers would have difficulty following us unless we were foolish enough to put some of these things in writing.

Do librarians discriminate in their own decisions? Perhaps not blatantly, but it is human nature to consider the things we agree with as more important than the things we disagree with. In other words, librarians are human beings. Perhaps strangely, because we have very little latitude in other areas, librarians have a great deal of latitude when deciding what to buy and what not to buy. Students are urged in library school courses to purchase "quality" books, but how is that judgment to be made?

A *Library Quarterly* study by Indiana University professor Judith Serebnick notes that librarians buy books that are reviewed in preference to books that are not reviewed. Not necessarily books that are reviewed favorably, just books that are reviewed. Critics who argue that libraries fail to purchase material published by alternative presses may have a point, although they may be stressing the wrong emphasis. They argue that libraries must acquire such alternative publications dealing with alternative lifestyles as a public service, while others would take the Baltimore County Public Library view that libraries should buy books that users want to read. That is an important issue of distinction, and it does get discussion in some major library education courses. However, the reason librarians fail to purchase alternative books would appear from the Serebnick study to be interesting. They are not acquired, not as either an ethical or reader-oriented value judgment, but because finding and selecting them is too much trouble. Does the library have a role in promoting a "right" point of view through selection policies on such issues as nuclear disarmament, freedom of choice for abortion, or the Equal Rights Amendment? We have the opportunity to do this if we want, because to a large extent our initial decisions are largely unfettered. They are only second-guessed.

Bar-Hillel would argue clearly that such value judgments are not a part of our business, and the Library Bill of Rights and various Codes of Ethics statements would sort of agree. Certainly they would argue that we should not consciously withhold information because of its content, but if we fail to buy it as a qualitative decision, that can be defended. So when ultraconservatives complain that the library does not have material representing their views (even as alternative press advocates complain), librarians respond that ultraconservative literature is lacking because most of it is badly written and the arguments are shoddily presented. It is a dangerous argument, because it is totally subjective, but we discuss this very little.

Far more open are the social activists who argue that libraries cannot be neutral in the battle between right and wrong. The difficulty is, of course, in the definition of right and wrong. Sometimes this discussion takes subtle turns. I have raised in my own writings the questions of whether librarians, who clearly have the obligation of helping destitute tenants research ways to avoid eviction, also have an equal obligation to help landlords looking for ways to evict, so that they can tear down the building and erect a shopping mall or high-priced condominium. A few individuals answer "of course," a second group find it a "contrived question," which is always a safe response for a question you don't want to answer. A third group argues that tenants need libraries, but that landlords have other outlets. All three arguments can be found among library school faculties, and like faculty anywhere, they do as much inculcating as teaching.

It is the group of social activists who see a pro-active role for the library in helping the poor (presumably against the oppressive rich), who raise issues not covered in the rather bland Bill of Rights and Codes of Ethics, that address only issues on which we all agree. Thus, Fay Blake has argued that libraries discriminate de facto against poor people, because poor people don't need bibliographies. It is an intriguing argument, because oppressors don't need bibliographies either, and because librarians don't compile that many bibliographies because of all the clerical work we have to do. Michael Harris has argued for some time that the public library is a capitalist contrivance to keep poor people in their place, and that Andrew Carnegie knew exactly what he was funding and why he was funding it.

These are extreme positions, but a recent president of ALA opined that the public library of the future undoubtedly had a greater role of serving poor people, because the affluent would have other access to information. It is for many an attractive argument, but it can lead us into ethical difficulties. Libraries have taken on increasing responsibility for helping the illiterate. It is in one sense a curious reversal of the classic library role, quite aside from its moral values, and I have warned about being tempted by self-defined moral values. Libraries by their very nature serve people who know how to read, and it is the schools that have by and large failed abysmally in preparing our customers. If we now assume this responsibility, *and do so without additional funding*, then we are deciding to take priority and money away from other clients. How do we make that decision?

Even more curious, at least to me, is the issue of latchkey children. This is a social problem that has nothing to do with libraries at all, unless the children are drawn to the library as a library rather than just as a place with a roof and fewer muggers. But if they come to read, then nothing stopped them before and nothing has changed, assuming that now as then those who come seeking knowledge are well behaved. If that is not why they came or why they were sent, then why the library? Why not the mayor's office? Is it because important things are assumed to happen there and not at the library? I have already noted that different professions approach the dichotomy between the responsibilities to their profession and the responsibilities to their employer quite differently. Librarians, in my observation, like social workers, find a third responsibility, in a devotion to their "clients" (it has been a long time since social workers called them "cases").

Librarians, it seems to me, nevertheless also harbor considerable responsibility to their employers, and I will explain. They carry out some of their responsibilities to their clients, but inconsistently, choosing some over others. They carry little, if any, responsibility to their profession, and that too warrants an explanation. Librarians are men and women who are extremely loyal to the organization. As a special librarian, I find that example most obvious in watching my colleagues who at conferences concentrate not on social involvement, but on learning things to make them more effective employees. The Special Libraries Association faced, at one point in its history, the possibility of a ruling from the I.R.S. that it was not a professional association at all, but rather a business league, because its primary business and indeed its bylaws stressed improving service to the employer. I also see this acculturation clearly and immediately as former students who are now special librarians come back to lecture. They are clearly representing the organization, the quality of its products, and the uniqueness of its services.

Public librarians show this organizational loyalty in a different way, most directly in their unwillingness to complain openly about the inadequacies of support, and in their willingness to rationalize that whatever library they are allowed to run is a good library, through a process sometimes called community analysis, which is really only a retrofitting of needs to match resources. If any of you doubt this, read any public library's annual report. The essence of management communication, exception reporting, the clearest indication of what is not happening and not working, is not to be found. We let our bosses off easy.

Responsibility to our clients is unevenly carried out. While we protect their right to access, that access is limited to what we can get for free, or what we can get within our budgets. As I have noted, we insist that the federal government supply us with documents, but whether or not individuals can find what they need because of cataloging backlogs or because of a shortage of reference librarians is not seen as the same kind of moral issue. And yet, if you can't get information does it really matter why not? If we charge for interlibrary loan service or online searching, does that not impose a barrier to the use of information every bit as formidable as censorship? The response of some libraries—free or not at all—does not provide a solution if the result is not at all. Our battle on behalf of our clients as a moral imperative is therefore half-hearted, or at least inconsistent. If we have huge cataloging backlogs or too few reference librarians, is this not just as effective as censorship, particularly for those who have no alternatives? When we don't blow the whistle on our funding bodies are we accessories to censorship?

We treat our ethical responsibilities toward our staff equally haphazardly. We agree that their salaries are low, and that it is unfair for public library employees to work evenings and weekends at regular pay while other city employees are routinely compensated at premium rates. We complain and we commiserate, but that is all.

However, perhaps our greatest professional ethical shortcoming is in the way we treat ourselves. We fail to protect the profession by letting others who are unqualified into it, either because of administrative pressures by university presidents or presidents of the United States, or because of the rationalizations that we must use unqualified staff because we don't have the money to hire qualified staff. Doctors would never do this. In the absence of a physician, what physicians are supposed to do doesn't get done, and so money is found for more physicians. The result is not worse medicine, it is better medicine. Our result is worse libraries, and nobody else even knows it!

I think the role of library education is *not* to provide answers to these questions, because they have no right or wrong answers, but rather to make students aware of the complexity of problems and options, and to make them understand the potential conflicts between their professional responsibilities and what they may see as their societal responsibilities. Can they differ? Certainly they can. What do we do then? I might know what I would do, but I have no right to instill my value system under the pretense of teaching. Not at the graduate level, certainly. We are teachers, and not either trainers or indoctrinators.

I therefore make a heavy use of case studies, as I can find them and as I can write them to illustrate issues. Students almost immediately head for solutions rather than analysis, and it takes me half a semester to wean especially the most articulate and self-assured away from solutions and toward analysis. Dilemmas involving people usually have two or more alternatives and viewpoints, and ultimately we must choose, sometimes when there are several excellent alternatives, sometimes when there are none. It is important that we understand before we solve, and perhaps this is where Josephson's Golden Rule approach needs to be modified: "Understand the other person, so that you can do unto them as they would have you do unto them." How you would have them do unto you may not be relevant. It may be important to understand what *they* want, and not just what you would want were you they. Do unto them as they would have you do unto them. But in practice that causes problems, as any manager can tell you.

My role in the classroom in attempting to awaken this analytical approach to ethical considerations is to challenge and question everything students say to make them defend it. I play devil's advocate with their approaches to make sure that they have considered every possible idea that they emotionally reject in their other dispassionate role as a professional. Of course, I also have personal feelings, and there are those who would consider me quite opinionated. However, as an educator, I understand that this does not matter. As an educator my role is to prepare students to be able to deal with the ethical decisions they will have to make later.

In a larger context, I am certain the analytical approach is what education for professional ethics requires. It is a preparation for life in a complex and pressure-filled world, in which the pressures will be particularly to conform, to compromise, to get along, and to avoid rocking the boat. Perhaps doctors and lawyers understand these pitfalls better than we do, at least they spend more time talking about them. And yet, the newspapers are full of stories about doctors and lawyers who violate this trust. Are librarians therefore more trustworthy? Or is it simply that our violations of professional ethics are not considered important enough by outsiders to be noticed? It is one of the paradoxical temptations in our field that, despite the fact that we have little power and low salaries, in this area we can get away with a great deal.

It seems to me that education on professional ethics is really only an education in decision analysis, and an education in self-discipline. It is precisely because in a one-year program this gets in the way of teaching a long list of reference sources and AACR-II interpretations that employers would prefer us to teach, that I fear we will continue to do it half-heartedly, concentrating on the easy stuff—on bashing book burners—and end up congratulating ourselves for our high moral and ethical standards without knowing what we mean when we say it. Issues of professional ethics require the painful balancing of contradictory values. Stopping drunk driving is desirable, but if random breathalyzer tests are not desirable, then how do we get from A to B? Society is full of such contradictory pressures, and so, of course, are libraries.

Let me close with just a couple of further examples of the ethical dilemmas we face in this profession, and I stress again that I offer no solutions. If solutions were simple, there would be no problems.

I have already mentioned that we care deeply, as indeed we should, about attempts to keep things from being put into our libraries. We seem to care less about whether or not material can be found in the library once it is there. Is a cataloging backlog and a lack of reference librarians a form of censorship? Have any of us made that accusation against the people who cut our budgets, or do we pretend, as we always seem to in public library annual reports, that everything is really pretty good?

Let me get myself into a lot of trouble. ALA, the National Football League, and just about everybody else, decided to punish the citizens of Arizona for their failure to declare Martin Luther King, Jr.'s birthday a state holiday. King was a great and eloquent leader, and what he had to tell us should be remembered and celebrated. I might think that keeping the schools open and discussing his work might be preferable to a celebration of going to the mall. I lived in Washington, D.C., for many years. The way that city celebrates the birth of the father of our country is with crazy sales, such as a television set for 99 cents, for which people line up at midnight. Is that a fitting memorial? However, that's not the ethical issue. Don't the people of Arizona have the right, if they so choose, *not* to declare this a legal holiday without interference from the citizens of Michigan, just as the citizens of Michigan can celebrate anyone they want, including, although probably not likely, the president of General Motors.

Let me suggest just three additional ethical conflicts between concerns, with adherents on both sides insisting they are right. We have a direct conflict, certainly in my university, between our concern about hurtful speech, which bigots use to offend individuals and groups, and the doctrine of freedom of speech that permits such hateful expression, much as we dislike it. This is why the ACLU still occasionally, but not nearly as often as it once did, fights for the right of Nazis to march in Skokie, Illinois.

At ALA conferences we have almost annual battles between the Intellectual Freedom Committee, which urges that information be given to anyone who asks for it, and the International Relations Committee, which strongly supported a ban on sending materials to South Africa. I owe you my own viewpoint on this. I really don't know why people in Cuba, in Iraq, and in South Africa want reprints of my articles, but I always send them, and am delighted to do so. I think the best way to fight apartheid is not by banning information from the Western world, but by flooding the country with it. But even if I didn't believe that, I would still send my reprint. Why? Because I have a copy and the person who asked doesn't. Why he or she wants it doesn't matter, although in this case it is hard to invent an earth-shattering reason. Librarians are always enthusiastic about the potential of the information provided by the Census Bureau. As an individual randomly selected to fill out the long form, I found the questionnaire nosy and intrusive. Why is it anyone's business when I purchased my refrigerator, or when I think I might buy a new car?

Librarians classically face not only that conflict between freedom of information and the right of privacy—and we usually deal with that correctly, as we did by telling the F.B.I. to fly a kite when it inquired about borrowers with foreign-sounding names. Foreign sounding? Irish like Reagan? Or German like Eisenhower? As opposed to American like Sitting Bull and Crazy Horse? But why do we keep circulation records around at all once the material has been returned? We can tabulate and summarize and then get rid of the details. Anything that exists is potentially accessed. We were once told nobody would know our Social Security number.

I think that fundamentally we must return to the principles enunciated by Bar-Hillel. We owe everybody our best efforts to provide them as much information as we can give them. What they do with that information is none of our business—whether they use it altruistically or to make a profit or to evict a tenant is still none of our business while we're on the job. We can't start charging for our services in public libraries, because that discriminates on the basis of an ability to pay, and in a public setting that is intolerable. However, making the statement "free and not fee" is not an answer if not fee turns out to be not at all. If we don't want to charge for our services, and I agree that we shouldn't, then we must make sure that those services are properly funded, including what I mentioned before—eliminating the cataloging backlog, and having enough reference librarians.

Lack of money is no excuse. It is a truism that even in the absence of money there is money. The city of Chicago, always broke, found the money to pump out the floodwaters under the city, and if a disaster struck Detroit or Michigan, and I obviously hope it doesn't, money will be found. As Peter Drucker has put it so simply—in the provision of a product or service that people want or need badly enough—cost becomes irrelevant.

Ethical issues are difficult enough not to allow the principle to be subverted by money. I know that sounds glib, but it just points out how great our challenge is, and how great the self-discipline demanded of us. We all have strong personal feelings about many issues, librarians no less than anyone else. The challenge for us is to discipline ourselves to rise above personal feelings in our professional work, and to leave the rest for our free time. I ask my management students to make the strongest case they can for the position in opposition to what they personally believe. I can assure you it is very difficult, but I also think that this training in seeing viewpoints other than our own is essential if we are going to grasp the meaning of ethics, an area in which we librarians have been cast in a crucial role—the role of protecting the library rights of everyone, including even those who would envy us ours.

John Swan, one of our profession's great leaders for the cause of intellectual freedom, makes this point well in writing about what he calls the right to lie—as it must be granted at ALA exhibits to those who want to mount a display arguing that the Holocaust is a myth and that it never happened. As an individual who is a refugee from German-occupied Austria and who lost grandparents, aunts, uncles, and cousins in the extermination ovens, I can tell you that agreeing with John Swan is incredibly painful for me—but he is correct because he deals with the principle. "Do the right thing" is perhaps the most dangerous statement I know, dangerous in its simplicity. "Doing the right thing" triggered the Spanish Inquisition.

The Library Implications of
Individual and Team Empowerment

The development of new management theories sometimes reminds me of seeing the wave performed in a large football stadium. Begun by a few committed individuals, the process rapidly gains support and soon sweeps its way around the arena. Because there is no logical stopping point in a circular stadium, the wave eventually dies out from sheer boredom.

After a while, and particularly if the game is one-sided, someone will start a new wave. During all of this, librarians are sitting in the upper, end-zone seats. The first few passes of the wave go by before they even notice, but eventually they try to participate because it is important to belong to the group.

Management Nuggets

New management concepts, from Taylor and Weber through McGregor and Herzberg past Pinchot and Peters to an unknown future, usually contain something digestible, like ballpark peanuts. Also, like the same peanuts, they leave a lot of garbage to be cleaned up. All management concepts are by necessity generalizations, because individuals differ and nothing works for everyone. The experienced manager adapts policies to people rather than people to policies.

All of the theories mean well, but some of the euphoria they generate is, at best, simplistic. The promise that we would all benefit economically if we made people happy in the workplace turned out to be only half true. Unhappy people don't work productively, but happy people aren't necessarily productive, unless they have some idea about the why, the what, and the how of their jobs. The phrase "Well, do the best you can" is still just about the ugliest management cop-out there is.

Reprinted, with changes, by permission of the author and *Library Journal* 118, no. 11 (June 15, 1993): 47-48. Copyright © 1993 by Reed Publishing, U.S.A.

Embracing New Management Creeds

I have noted in earlier columns ("Participative Management Is the Answer, But What Was the Question?" *Library Journal*, August 1985, pp. 62-63 and "Meetings, Bloody Meetings," (reprinted in this book on pages 99-103) that librarians embrace new management creeds at least in part because they are assured it is the right thing to do, and because it feels good and seems democratic.

Any tool can be used properly or improperly. A wrench can be a useful implement, or it can be a murder weapon. Heat-seeking radar can be used to find a lost child or to pinpoint a target. Committees also have a range of proper uses and misuses.

In any case, some of the waves for which we are still standing and sitting ended some time ago. It may even be that the other spectators have left the stadium. In the 1980s, the premises of participative management and of the direct committee process, championed 10 years earlier, were largely abandoned in the management literature just as we began to discover them for libraries. They were replaced by an emphasis on the building of teams, based on the nervous observation of Japanese successes and the perception that the Japanese worked in teams.

For some of the libraries that saw this as an opportunity to jazz up their nomenclature, the real point was lost. The reason for Japanese team building was the belief that it made the accomplishment of work more effective.

As I saw the process being implemented in libraries and stressed in the interview process, the building of teams became an end in itself rather than a means to an end. We stressed collegiality in preference to accomplishments. The performance evaluation phrase "gets along well with others" doesn't mean very much unless it continues "in the timely and effective completion of assigned responsibilities." Somehow, that second part is often left out.

Individual Accountability

In any case, while the fascination with team building that developed in the 1980s is still with us, it has been overtaken by the new management wave of the 1990s, the creation of individual (and not collective) accountability and responsibility. We see a sweeping trend in the elimination of intermediate managers and most particularly the disappearance of hordes of the facilitators, coordinators, and enablers we stockpiled in the 1970s.

The operative phrase is becoming "What exactly do you personally do, and how does it contribute to the organization's objectives?" For librarians, who really do a great deal in support of education, information, and knowledge and at a very low cost, it should be a welcome question; we ought to be able to answer it very well. Of course, first we need to brush up on what the parent organization's objectives are.

Recent management literature suggests that these two current themes can be brought into union through the development of *self-directed* teams. These are the voluntary and noncoerced association of individuals into teams, because individuals see that through the formation of teams they can more easily accomplish their own job assignments. This means either that teams will form and dissolve as appropriate (the historic role of task forces), or that the team members will at least be free to oust from their midst those who do not contribute as well as the other members think they should.

The Dangers of Group Empowerment

There is danger in the empowerment of groups. It can legitimize such thinking as, "We are not biased against nonwhites, or Jews, or homosexuals, or older people, or men—we just don't think they would fit well into the spirit of our group."

Supervisors responsible for hiring are also sometimes guilty of this rationalization. Whether or not they mean well does not change the fact that such thinking is totally unacceptable in the hiring process. If the person does not "fit the group," perhaps the group needs to adjust. There is also the hope that if teams are properly charged, motivated, empowered, and regarded, they will be selfish enough both to tolerate an obnoxious member who has talent and oust a pleasant nincompoop. We still tend to fail to deal with nincompoops as long as they are at least pleasant.

The process of team responsibility and team empowerment (and without empowerment, responsibility becomes gibberish) will appeal more to some individuals than to others. It should appeal most to those who make the biggest contributions, and, ultimately, they are the ones who matter most. It is also important that worker teams be given the tools and resources to do their jobs, and that the jobs can be accomplished within the time and resources provided.

In other words, if programs don't drive budgets (as all management theory tells us they should), then at least budget limitations should define programs. In many libraries the slashed budget and the programs we struggle to maintain no longer have any relationship to each other. When the money is gone, we blame ourselves for our failure to provide the services, forgetting who refused to provide the funds.

Self-Directed Work Teams

We have reason to believe that empowered and motivated self-directed teams of workers will be much tougher on nonperformers than classic management has been. When such approaches were first attempted in Germany and Scandinavia, there was fear that workers would see this as an opportunity to get by with less.

The fear proved unwarranted as fellow workers, who have always known better than the bosses who was contributing and who was goofing off, began to see such foot-dragging as a danger to their own recognition and rewards. They were applying subtle and sometimes not so subtle pressure on their co-workers to shape up while the old "professional" managers might have been too busy writing memoranda and attending meetings to notice.

The concept of self-directed work teams can then be at odds with the premise of classical trade unionism, which presumes an inherent conflict between management and labor, even if sometimes settled smoothly and amicably. There have already been legal challenges to the implementation of work teams, and these are wending their way slowly through the court system.

However, I suspect that the concept of team self-direction and empowerment will prevail, at least for the 1990s, particularly if it results in a promise of organizational success and therefore greater job security.

As we should have learned from Abraham Maslow's hierarchy of needs, having food and shelter (and this classically means having a job) becomes a very central focus of attention. Laid-off workers don't really worry about all of the committee meetings they are missing; they are concerned about their paychecks.

We Will Need Fewer Managers

What does this suggest for the traditional role of managers? Most immediately, it means that we will need far fewer managers—we already see this happening in the industrial sector. Such changes come more slowly in libraries, where we first attack student and clerical staff and, ultimately, professional staff. Department heads may remain even when there is no longer a department.

However, inevitably, change will come to us as well. Self-directed teams define an entirely new role for managers; it is a less complex, even if more important, one. Since it is the team that will determine how it will accomplish the agreed-upon objectives, volumes of detailed procedural documentation can be scrapped. We will judge by results and not by methods, something we should have known all along from the management literature.

If the present major role of managers to pry and snoop ends, what will the fewer remaining managers do? They will set the overall goals and objectives and fight to obtain the resources with which their subordinates can accomplish them. A director returning from a budget meeting may be met with the direct question: "Did you get the money this time, or did you fail again?"

Perhaps the most important role of management will be in the creation of an environment in which teams can succeed. That means proper hiring, the provision of education and training on a never-ending basis, and the development of mechanisms for evaluation and reward that are easily understood and perceived as fair.

The Hope for Change

There is at least some hope that these changes will evolve in the American workplace as we move toward the new millennium. When librarians will stop doing the old wave and start doing the new one is a little more difficult to predict. It depends in large part on the ability of these managers to get their own managers to understand that the library is not simply a "good thing," but that acceptable and appropriate levels of service must be established, quantified, funded, and then measured and evaluated.

Without that crucial intermediate action from their own managers, even the best self-directed library work teams will not be able to succeed, any more than a carpenter or mason can work without tools. In the final analysis, once there is agreement on what needs to happen and that it can happen, the primary responsibility for the new cadre of managers becomes two-fold: provide the tools needed by the team and then get out of the way.

Is There a Correlation Between Library Education Programs and Athletic Success?

There are probably no two topics that appear less likely connected than the existence of a graduate library education program in a university and the success of that school's athletic teams. First, library and information science is not noted for its athletic vigor (although the annual American Library Association [ALA] conference does feature a five-mile run), and second, our academic programs operate at the graduate level while varsity athletes are undergraduates. Also, there is little evidence of former football or volleyball captains enrolling in library education programs. The connection surprised me as much as it may surprise the reader.

Basketball and football are the main producers of revenue, and excellence here is therefore particularly important to the university presidents and state legislators, who should be impressed with these findings. It will be your job to send all of them copies of this column. Let's look at basketball first. The 1993 college basketball play-offs started with 64 teams. Of these, 15 were from schools with accredited library education programs.

That's an amazing statistic by itself, when you consider that there are only slightly more than three times that many library education programs in the United States, and that some of these don't compete athletically in Division I. However, those 15 schools also went on to win 28 of the 63 games played, while losing only 14. The reason there were only 14 losses is that the championship school has a library education program. So does the runner-up. Indeed, the Final Four included three schools with accredited library education programs.

Reprinted, with changes, by permission of the author and *Library Journal* 118, no. 13 (August 1993): 75-76. Copyright © 1993 by Reed Publishing, U.S.A.

Library Schools and Gridirons

What about football? Our current national champion, as many reference librarians know, is the University of Alabama. Some people were surprised at Alabama's easy win over Miami in the Sugar Bowl for the national title, but they shouldn't have been. Miami, without a library education program, never really had a chance. As might be expected, there are 20 universities in the combination of what are called the Big Ten and the Pac Ten, the two conferences whose champions play in the Rose Bowl. (Actually, this fall, there will be 21.)

Nine of the universities in these two conferences have accredited library education programs, but in the last 10 years, 14 of the Rose Bowl participants have had such programs. The figure would really be an astonishing 18 if we also included the four appearances of the University of Southern California (USC). USC once had an accredited library education program, and it may not be coincidental that its football fortunes declined at the same time the last freshman athletes recruited when there was a library school began to graduate. USC hasn't been in the Rose Bowl for quite a while, and it may never return unless and until university administrators reactivate its library school.

As Clear as a Glass Backboard

What causes the connection that is so clear from these statistics? I don't know, but I am familiar enough with the history of science to recall that many of our greatest discoveries, including the breakthrough work of Marie Curie, came from accidental findings for which explanations were only found later. Such correlation for us will require a great deal of research, and it may be decades before we find out why accredited library education leads to athletic success. While that research is taking place, academic administrators would be totally irresponsible if they endangered their athletic programs by closing their library education programs. The cost is so trivial, and the risk is so great!

The Ball Stops Here

That concludes the part of this column that you are supposed to photocopy and send to university presidents, trustees, governors, and state legislators. The rest is for my librarian readers, and it is *not* to be forwarded under any circumstances. Do I believe a single word of what I have just written? Of course not, although I have seen "research" studies, in our field and others, for which the hypotheses were no more credible.

My point in suggesting this tactic is that it may hold more promise than our current approach in what is often a futile and always a defensive strategy. It has been a long time since we persuaded anyone to start a new accreditable library program, although perhaps this column can serve to frighten the potentates at USC. After all, the building is still there. All that is required is the removal of the squatters.

We have all read the excellent writings of Marion Paris that analyze the political competitions that take place in academia, where some, although certainly not all, library school administrators compete so ineffectively. However, her more significant observation may be that graduate library education is in trouble because it is so poorly championed and protected by its own professional community.

It is not surprising then that academic administrators will fail to consider an educational program important if the profession it feeds does not consider it crucial. Pogo Possum noted that we had met the enemy and found that it was really "us" (in Pogo's own words). It is my observation that we do not bleed from any massive injury, because nobody really hates us that much. We bleed from a thousand self-inflicted cuts, and unless we can stem the flow, we may well bleed to death as a profession.

No Support from Our Association

Most of what is only a very partial list of examples is well known to you. ALA, through its board, has refused to support a public library that tried to protect access for all of its patrons as it was threatened by the behavior of one patron (*Kreimer* v. *Morristown*). However, at least some ALA groups seemed more interested in protecting him, suggesting a fascination with trees and an indifference to forests.

ALA also left unprotected, more than a decade ago, an academic library that tried to insist on implementing the requirement of ALA's own accredited degree. According to the good judgment of one judge (not all judges can be counted on for such good judgment), an insistence on an educational degree in a field in which 80 percent of the people who hold that degree are female was not an attack on women and their rights (the Merwine case). On the contrary, it is the process of casually waiving or trivializing that requirement that demeans the status of women as professionals. It sometimes seems to me that, except in the glorious struggle in the arena of intellectual freedom and censorship, ALA will rally to the support of just about any librarian, but only as long as that librarian isn't an American.

Salaries for Book Budgets

We have seen the publicity given to the tactic, primarily out of media bewilderment at such strange behavior, of public librarians who give up part of their already pitiful salaries so that they can buy more books because others have cut their budgets. That theme has now been given an additional twist in one of those same libraries in the decision to get rid of professional librarians in order to save the money for the materials budget and for the clerks to charge out all of those new books. The argument is that library users prefer libraries that have current and new material. Of course, we all do. If it comes to that, who would oppose a free neighborhood Waldenbooks?

However, we should realize that the individuals for whom the library is nothing more than an outlet for such trivial convenience will never support us against other priorities during a budget crunch. Education is seen as important; information is important. Recreational reading is not only a lower priority in the public mind, but it is also seen as intellectually insignificant by the academic community that judges our graduate library schools. The search for support on that basis contradicts what those who make a living out of predicting human behavior know. TV programmers give us reruns without fear because they know we feel comfortable with certain characters and situations even when we have seen them before—perhaps especially when we have seen them before. We look forward to the annual showings of *The Wizard of Oz* and *It's a Wonderful Life*. Readers who read for pleasure do so because they enjoy reading, and what they read is secondary. They even discover fresh nuances in the rereading. Perhaps libraries should push *Gulliver's Travels* with the point that there is more to it than we caught the first time. Dumping librarians for circulation clerks and best-sellers resembles the firing of doctors because a hospital needs to repave the parking lot.

WHCLIS as Photo Op

One can only wonder at White House Conference on Library and Information Services (WHCLIS) recommendations that number more than 100 but never mention the role of librarians in implementing any of them. How can we take pleasure at such cruel trivialization and even call such conferences successful?

We seem content at photo opportunities with whomever happens to be president and the warm and friendly greeting we always receive for our annual conferences and National Library Week. Yet we choose to ignore that those statements contain nothing of substance. We celebrate this year the tenth anniversary of *A Nation at Risk*, although librarians have nothing to celebrate in an educational review and planning document that never mentions us. That exclusion continues.

The Clinton-Gore administration announced in February its comprehensive new initiative for technological stimulus and investment. The plan deals with technology, government information policy, networks, and the National Research and Education Network (NREN). It makes mention of grant funding to purchase computers and network connections, and some of those crumbs might even fall off the table so that libraries might snatch up a few.

However, the plan barely acknowledges libraries and never mentions librarians, whose role in the successful implementation of this effort ought to be crucial because we bring knowledge no one else has. No librarians served on the planning task force. It seems ignorance about us has thus passed safely from one administration to the next.

A Lack of Professional Definition

Displeasure with the current National Library Week theme has already been commented upon ("Look at All Those Beautiful Birds Overhead!" *Library Journal*, February 15, 1993, pp. 143-144). We don't need to agitate for the support of something called a library because everyone loves libraries so much that they will insist on having them. What is lacking is a professional definition. It is only fair that an alternative theme be proposed, without a shred of hope that we could adopt anything so practical: "In the dictionary, as in the shaping of information organizations, we must define librarian before we can discuss the meaning of the word library." We can see what kinds of school "libraries" are now being palmed off on parents who don't know the difference ("The Double-Edged Sword of Library Volunteerism" (reprinted in this book on pages 115-118).

If we don't protect our profession and its educational component from the thousands of cuts we allow to be inflicted upon us, and inflict on ourselves, we can easily bleed to death. In the absence of any other strategies, relating library education to athletic success may turn out to be our best, and perhaps our only, strategy. That is, unless somebody can come up with a theory that relates library education to the stock market or the budget deficit.

Why Do "They"
Close Library Schools?

If it is indeed a curse to live during interesting times, library educators certainly qualify for that dubious honor. Hardly a month goes by without news of another library education program in danger, and what appears in the press is only the tip of the iceberg. Most library educators, challenged to defend their viability and importance, would rather not talk about it publicly at this early stage lest the news discourage prospective students and make things even worse.

Much of the news is certainly depressing. Over the last decade we have seen the closure of some of our most prestigious and historically important education programs. Occasionally, there is good news: when schools wriggle free from the executioner's block. However, even in the glow of success we must realize that we haven't really won anything, only kept from losing something else. It has been a long time since any university started a new library school.

What has happened in higher education itself is well documented. Academia is now shrinking for a whole range of reasons. We understand all of this, but why are library education programs in such particular difficulty? It is not necessary to comment in detail on the well-received writings of Marion Paris ("Why Library Schools Fail," *Library Journal*, October 1, 1990, pp. 38-42). Graduate education without an undergraduate base is inevitably expensive. Library educators are perceived by their academic colleagues as functioning in isolation and without any noticeable research vigor to bring distinction to the university.

Reprinted, with changes, by permission of the author and *Library Journal* 117, no. 19 (November 15, 1992): 51-52. Copyright © 1992 by Reed Publishing, U.S.A.

Everyone tends to like librarians, but not to see them as wealthy alumni. Nor are people really sure about what it is that librarians do that requires graduate education and research, and we stubbornly refuse to tell them. Outsiders see very little connection between our work and the so-called information disciplines, which make them think of computer scientists and M.B.A.s. These are generalizations, but I suspect that as public perceptions they are not inaccurate.

Irrational School Closings

Bad news about library schools makes librarians angry, however, and someone has to be blamed. Who is doing this to us, and why? Are we upset because we see the closing of academic programs in our discipline, particularly in schools we consider to be of strong reputation, as an insult to our professional standing? I would certainly hope so, because it is.

However, I see very little beyond annoyance at the inconvenience caused when a library school within commuting distance is closed, and here our expectations may be unrealistic. A statewide report once seriously suggested that Indiana needed at least four library education programs. It is perhaps a paradox that even as we rail against the closing of library education programs we probably still have too many, at least when we recognize how small and fragile many of them are. It is not that library schools are being closed that bothers me. It is that schools are being closed without any particular overall rationale and without the qualitative input from the profession that is affected.

What bothers me most of all is the loss of convenience. I have already noted that the 1991 White House Conference on Library and Information Services (WHCLIS II) argued that there needed to be more access to library education, but said nothing about a concern for quality. I don't disagree with the importance of meeting students' needs, particularly as more students attend part-time. During my term as dean at Indiana University, the school offered its courses on eight other campuses.

The program was financially viable or the university wouldn't have let us do it. Still, the primary concern was that it also had to be academically acceptable, and in that win-win situation, we ended up strengthening faculty size, support dollars, and school reputation. For the students, convenience was the most important consideration, because they could always worry about quality after they had received the degree, if then.

I can understand such a primary concern that focuses on convenience while ignoring quality standards, but the library educators who live in the academic pressure cooker cannot accept it and cannot let it dictate their agenda. "Save the school" is important, but it is at least as important as having a school that is good enough to save. Who can make that distinction? Not those who measure quality in commuter miles.

Pleas of Poverty and Red Herrings

It is sad although not surprising that librarian anger at being so trivialized by university closure decisions turns to a search for scapegoats. That is why a certain *Library Journal* editorial ("Can This Library School Be Saved?" May 15, 1992, p. 6) is so unfortunate, particularly when it attacks the American Library Association's (ALA) Committee on Accreditation (COA), which cannot defend itself.

Northern Illinois University's (NIU) decision to close its library school rather than retain some level of required quality does not surprise me. The school has been poorly funded and supported even during the good years. Nor do I challenge the right of university administrators to make this decision, even as I would have preferred that they had done the little that would have kept the school's program acceptable. I know and certainly they know that this financial issue is far too trivial to affect the overall budget of such a large university. The plea of poverty is a red herring.

The tactic chosen by NIU administrators of attempting to bargain with COA for a cheaper price is sad and unworthy and embarrasses only the university. It is equally sad to see a *Library Journal* editorial that suggests that COA has some responsibility for perhaps diluting its standards, or at least delaying their implementation until newer and, by every indication, tougher standards go into effect.

COA and Enforcing the Rules

COA has no responsibility for saving library schools, any more than basketball referees are responsible because a team can't make its foul shots. The job of COA is to develop, administer, and enforce the rules without which we have chaos. If necessary, COA blows the whistle.

I served as chair of a site visit team at a large university in which the vice president for administration attempted to explain to us the financial exigencies that had caused them to gut an already fragile program. The campus official was told that his explanation was eloquent but irrelevant.

The decision of whether or not to have a library education program and at what level to fund it was strictly theirs, nor did we question their option of either strengthening this program at the expense of something else, or of weakening the program to save money for other purposes. Our sole responsibility was to tell them whether that was good enough to retain accreditation.

It is pleasant to report that the university decided that accredited library education was worth the extra effort, but that is not the point. Even closing the program would have been preferable to making it worse. It has long been my management observation that library education is in trouble not because it is so expensive, but because it is so cheap and so tiny and invisible on any particular campus. However, most importantly, it is in trouble because the internal evaluators can't see the educational rigor of the discipline itself.

Who Is Responsible?

Who, then, are the "they" who close library schools? It is not COA. The university administrators who use their computerized projections to identify library science, along with nursing and home economics, for closure are handy candidates. Is there a bias against the largely female professions in this process? Probably, but for us the issue is larger than that. Administrators are using decision models, and we should understand what these are. Paranoia may be a comforting refuge, but the truth is that no one is really out to get us. We don't have enemies, because we aren't important enough to have them.

Sleeping with the Enemy

Who is the "they" then most responsible for the demise of library schools? In Act I of *Julius Caesar*, Cassius notes, "The fault, dear Brutus, is not in our stars, but in ourselves." More than 300 years later, Pogo Possum told us the same thing in "We have met the enemy, and it is us." The *they* then becomes *we* in the signals we send: our unwillingness to establish a unique agenda for ourselves outside the myriad social agendas that can make us baby-sitters and lenders of construction tools and that saturate our professional conferences; our reluctance to redefine our role in terms of an Information Age that everyone thinks they understand except that their understanding doesn't include us; and, most of all, our unwillingness to specify what it is that a library degree provides as a unique qualification that cannot be bargained away with a claim of no funds. Any professional should understand that the premise of a closed library is preferable to that of a bad open library, particularly if no one notices it is bad. Closing it first is the only hope of ever making it better.

Dumping the Albatross

There is a real danger that is even greater than the possibility that more library schools will be closed. It is that library educational administrators, perceiving what they see as an albatross around their necks, will take steps to eliminate their visible identification with the library profession. If that happens, we will have library schools that downplay that responsibility, and then the profession through COA will lose all control over curricular and faculty evaluation because accreditation by ALA will not matter. Will this improve the quality of the educational process? According to whose criteria?

Is my concern farfetched? In the 1970s and early 1980s, many library schools added the phrase information science or information studies to form a double-barreled name. I don't think this diluted the emphasis on the quality of graduates, or on where most of them ended up working.

Two of our most highly regarded education programs (Drexel in Philadelphia and Syracuse in New York State) have seen it as politic to remove the word "library" from their school name, although many or most of their graduates still get jobs in libraries. The recent decision at the University of California at Berkeley to join that list makes only three, but can anyone doubt that it is likely to grow, or that these schools will also include many of our top institutions?

Quality over Commute

There is no "they" in this process, unless the culprit is in the blindness of colleagues from whom we seek to distance ourselves. Perhaps, instead of worrying about whether or not there is a library degree within a one-hour commute, we need to worry about whether that graduate degree can be protected to be worth having in the first place.

That, in turn, raises issues of educational rigor and of starting professional salaries. Ultimately, and most directly, we must discuss the importance of librarians before we can talk about the importance of the institutions that they shape and manage. Can we tell the internal academic evaluators what it is that only graduates of our programs are qualified and permitted to do? Can we tell them why this process requires not only educational rigor but also a highly regarded constant emphasis on research and evaluation?

Doctors, lawyers, and mechanics who display their diplomas as Mister Goodwrench® answered that question for themselves a long time ago. Isn't it odd that we never display our diplomas?

The Perilous Allure
of Moral Imperativism

Peter Drucker, who has promised to concentrate all of his future emphasis on the not-for-profit and service sectors, describes the fascination that service professionals may have with the moral imperative.

Somehow, with or without funds, with or without staff, time, or other resources, these individuals tend to feel that they must do whatever needs to be done for the good of the organization in which they are employed. If they don't, then whatever fails to happen will be their fault. And, as Drucker notes, once those responsible for supplying the resources to moral imperativists understand that, they have them in the trap.

There is no need to give such people any money. Bosses may not be certain as to how they became so lucky, but moral imperativists blame themselves and not their bosses. It is far more practical to concentrate on placating individuals more likely to blame those in charge, and that is exactly what hard-pressed officials do.

I deal with moral imperativists constantly in my seminars and lectures. I am forced to stress to medical librarians who see the inadequacy of needed information service to doctors and researchers that they should do all they can within the framework provided. However, the much greater burden for adequacy of medical information rests with the hospital administrator, who has the responsibility, the authority, and the power. Medical librarians should make certain that both physicians and administrators (and indeed, if possible, patients) understand clearly what needed services are *not* being provided, although they could and should be. Then I advise them to go home and relax from a hard day's work.

Reprinted, with changes, by permission of the author and *Library Journal* 117, no. 15 (September 15, 1992): 44-45. Copyright © 1992 by Reed Publishing, U.S.A.

It Isn't Our Fault

A similar question arises when public and academic reference librarians ask me how they can provide adequate reference service when there are so few of them, and when they are limited by administrative orders in the time they are allowed to devote to any patron—a time constraint they consider both arbitrary and unreasonable.

I tell these reference librarians to recognize that this obviously means that they *can't* provide adequate reference service and that they should stop feeling guilty. They should make sure, however, that the patrons understand clearly that the librarian is both anxious and able to provide better service and that such better service would be possible if the resources were available. In other words, I urge them to delegate responsibility upward, where management theory tells us it inevitably belongs.

Trading Salaries for Books

It is a constant struggle, with some victories and at least as many setbacks. However, there have been recent examples of moral imperativism that reach such heights (or depths) that I am moved to write this column about what is really a very old issue. There have been reports in the media about the staffs of two public libraries (by the time this appears, there may be more) who have voluntarily ceded their earned salary increases so that the library can augment its depleted materials budget. It may be that these individuals bask in the warm glow of their noble self-sacrifice. If so, please allow me to pour some cold water on the embers. I am not impressed. Indeed, I am appalled.

The gesture is at best symbolic. From the numbers provided in the articles, it is clear that this contribution offsets only a small part of the edicted budget cut. It is reminiscent of the spoof of old British colonial army movies: "We need a volunteer for a heroic, fatal, and futile gesture." Public library budgets are being cut, and it may be more comfortable to think that this is happening because of a shortage of municipal funds.

This is probably true, although funds can also be raised by those in authority. However, the budget cuts would occur in any case. Studies for the National Science Foundation show clearly that library funding, when measured in inflation-adjusted dollars, has been going steadily down for the last 20 years. That is a long time to be losing, and some of those years were, for the rest of the world, pretty good ones. Things being really bad now provides a greater level of credibility for budget cutting, but library budgets are cut in good times as well as in bad. They are cut because nobody in politics wants to favor spending more money, but largely because library budgets are safer and easier to cut than those of less tractable programs.

If and when municipal budgets improve, there is no reason to assume that library budget increases are first, second, or for that matter anywhere on the priority list. Cuts once implemented are only reversed when they have to be reversed. With the help of moral imperativists in the library, that need never happen. In other words, the individuals who contribute their salaries to help offset the materials budget deficit are not helping the future library budget. They are only insuring permanent damage.

Trivial Pursuits

The salary trade-off—which focuses on the library as a collection of things rather than as a staff of professionals—only serves to trivialize the role of professional librarians even further. The present slogan "Librarians Make It Happen" causes some of the moral imperativists who write letters to professional journals to be uncomfortable because they prefer self-effacement. It is immodest to suggest that they make anything happen in the library. They just happen to be lucky enough to be standing around when something does occur. However, if we prefer "libraries make it happen," we could take the credit back one step further, to construction firms and architects who made the thing that now makes it all happen possible in the first place.

These would-be martyrs should understand that in their willingness to sacrifice themselves for the "it," they also trivialize the library, even if inadvertently. Politicians now argue that libraries, like parks, are nice things to have but that there are, unfortunately, more important (or at least more loudly clamoring) priorities. This action simply proves them right.

Buying more new books may create a much more pleasant work environment, as some of our self-sacrificing friends point out, but that alone becomes impossible to defend as a truly important priority. Information is important, literacy is important, but old books can be read with as much pleasure as new books. Soldiers who served in foxholes recall the great interest that could be generated by the label on a tin can when there was nothing else to read. Having copies of the latest books featured on TV talk shows may be "pleasant," but it is hardly vital, and such a library is then perceived as nice but hardly crucial.

There are still other books in the library if the object is reading, and the new ones can be obtained from Waldenbooks by anyone who really wants them that desperately. What is crucial, and what is irreplaceable, is the bridge to learning, to literacy, and to information for growth and survival. What is crucial is the professional librarian, and librarians, in any library, are a higher priority than the materials. I can make this case, but it becomes difficult when some of us trash ourselves.

Not in the Profession's Best Interests

Even if they don't want or need the money or are guided by what I would consider a misguided sense of altruism, are these individuals aware of what they are doing to the rest of us? To our aspirations for a professional career that is not inconsistent with appropriate status and salary? The students I teach in library school have a great sense of dedication, but no one has yet asked them to take a vow of poverty. Are some moral imperativists, convinced in the ugly selfishness of their "rightness," prepared to take such a vow on behalf of students, colleagues, and for all professionals in the future, just because it makes them more personally comfortable?

Abdicating Managerial Responsibility

My final point is a management observation and is aimed at the administrators who even allowed such a vote to renounce raises to take place. Such a vote places a tremendous pressure on everyone to conform. Those who would prefer to keep their earned raises cannot win. They are stampeded into agreeing for the sake of the community in which they work; they are forced to accept a majority decision, or at best, if they still get the money, are branded as selfish by their own colleagues.

Permitting such a vote in the first place is a total abdication of the responsibility of any manager. You don't receive your salary increase because you want it; you don't get a larger raise because you would like more money or a smaller one because you would prefer less. Nor can you refuse a salary increase at all, because that increase comes to you, not as the result of an expressed preference, but because you have earned it and deserve it.

Of course, once you get the money you are free to give it away, as you always have been, but you are not free not to receive it. You can then give your money to the library book budget if you wish. However, before you contribute any of your salary in this manner, you might want to ask for a similar contribution from the salary of the city manager, prorated to his or her higher income. You can also give your money to other charitable causes, whether or not they are library related. There is certainly no shortage of candidates. Or you might want to split the increase between contributions, increased grocery prices, and the down payment on a Caribbean cruise.

Misguided Altruism

I have written before about the potential conflict between responsibility to one's profession and to one's employer—a responsibility that real professions are supposed to take very seriously ("The Conflict Between Professional and Organizational Loyalty," reprinted in this book on pages 242-246). The sad irony in the actions of public librarians willing to sacrifice themselves for the purchase of books is that, by leading others above them in responsibility down this easy path, they are contributing to the weakness of the very libraries and library services they are trying to bolster.

We can be certain that these public library budget cuts, once enacted, will never be willingly restored. We can also be certain that we will never have proper support from public officials for libraries until they understand that poor funding produces bad libraries (not just pretty good libraries) and the disasters that must result from their actions are their fault and their responsibility. When adequate library service has been destroyed and we tell no one, how will they know?

Which is more important, library materials or librarian salaries? Obviously both are essential. Still, even if some of us might want to argue in favor of one priority or another, for specific settings, we can never advance that set of options to the administrators above us. These people *will* choose, and their choices are based only on their own sense of survival.

Rank ordering certainly has its place, but only in a framework of resulting alternatives that we must describe. When salary cuts to buy more books have no other price that is visible to those above us in organizational hierarchies, the choice becomes absurdly easy for them—and not just in public libraries. Or do any of us think that our salaries are already too high? If, on the other hand, our salaries are far too low, do we have the self-confidence to assert that fixing this problem is the first priority, and until we do, no other problems concerning library service can be properly addressed? Moral imperativists might call that selfish. I call it sane.

The Freedom to Write a Research Paper Without Being Mugged

In the winter 1990 issue of the *Journal of Education for Library and Information Science* (*JELIS*), the official journal of the Association for Library and Information Science Education (ALISE), University of California at Los Angeles faculty members Donald Case and John Richardson reported the results of a study funded in part from a competitive ALISE research grant. The findings were initially presented at the January 1989 ALISE conference and drew no particular reaction. However, the article a year later unleashed what passes for, at least for our field, a torrent of letters to the editor.

The ability of this article to stir such emotion in a field that barely acknowledges its own literature in citations, and from individuals who are dedicated to protecting the right to publish and read all sorts of sleazy things in our libraries, is more interesting to me than the article itself. Unfortunately, since all of this correspondence has taken place in the pages of *JELIS*, a journal read primarily by library educators, this will all be news to many of the readers of *Library Journal*. It is important that you know.

Library Science Students Who Drop Out

The study examined the enrollment patterns, success rates as measured through graduation, and drop-out statistics of UCLA library science students between the years 1972 and 1987. Such studies have been done before, and they are usually institution-specific. They are popular in part because the necessary background information is easily at hand, but that reason would not apply to Case and Richardson, who already have substantial research credentials.

The primary hope in such studies is that they will allow us to gain information we can use in the admissions process. We already know that undergraduate grade performance, which most schools still use as the primary indicator, works imperfectly at best. Some students who have achieved high grades as undergraduates do badly in library school. Others for whom acceptance to the program was granted with reservations or on probation end up in Beta Phi Mu, our national honor society.

The issue also interests me personally because I was one of those low predictors whose grades in library school were more than a full point above my undergraduate average. If I still don't know why, I can hardly expect anyone else to understand what happened to me.

Generalizations Caused Concern

Library schools consider it important to try to know. We want students to succeed once they have been admitted, even though protecting the integrity of the program means that some won't. If they fail to achieve the degree they sought, the faculty will have spent a considerable amount of time to little effect, but the student will have spent a good deal more, and his or her loss is greater. Unlike some disciplines that look at failure rates almost gleefully as a validation of their rigor, we are not so insecure.

Even with this as a background, I glanced at the Case-Richardson study only cursorily. Although as an administrator for many years the ability to predict success in students is at least as important to me as to most other faculty members, I doubted that the specific findings at UCLA would be very generalizable, because earlier studies weren't. It is the letters that have followed publication of the article that have now caused me to reread it.

The researchers concluded from their data that three groups of students had higher-than-average drop-out rates. These were minority members, foreign students, and male students. It is a grouping that is perhaps surprising only for the last category. Certainly other disciplines such as law have also reported a higher incidence of drop-out rates for minority students.

Conjectures as to explanations are always potentially controversial because they represent not facts but an expression of opinion, and individuals are free to disagree. Nevertheless, if properly labeled, conjecture is part of the system of free expression that allows people to express in print what they think. This has always been crucial for librarians. Or is it more acceptable for some topics than for others?

Comments on Minorities Particularly

Case and Richardson put their analysis in the context of the recognized desire to increase and retain minority students. I am not sure that one should assume from this that foreign and male students are irrelevant and can shift for themselves, but certainly the reactions to the article have also concentrated on only one of the three categories identified by the researchers.

The authors hypothesized (and perhaps some wish they hadn't dared) that an explanation of what they saw as three distinct minority group failures to complete a program in a student population that is largely white and female could result from a sense of isolation. Since this has been mentioned as a potential source for minority student discontent in many other academic studies, it is hardly startling.

The researchers also opined that minority graduate students in library education programs have other opportunities for professional careers. This statement has drawn the particular ire of one of the *JELIS* letter writers, but, of course, it is true. Minority students who have made it through a significant undergraduate program with the equivalent of qualifying for the Dean's List (our general 3.0 average requirement) are in high demand, and our competition here comes particularly from law and business schools, which can promise higher starting salaries.

The problem of attracting high academic achievers into our programs does exist, and it is particularly prevalent for minority students. Perhaps Case and Richardson should have stressed that point more clearly than they did to please some readers, but they were certainly not required to do so by the rules of reporting research. The greater and societywide problem, that of getting more minority group members through high school into undergraduate programs and through undergraduate programs so that we can have a crack at them, was outside the scope of the study and is probably largely outside our ability to influence as graduate educators, although certainly not as library practitioners.

Lack of Minority Commitment?

Probably the greatest gaffe committed by the authors was the speculation that perhaps a failure to complete the program was from a lack of dedication and commitment. I strongly disagree with this. I particularly dislike negative generalizations, but I really object to all generalizations about race or religion. There is a precious individuality in all of us.

However, making decisions for individuals based on generalizations from group data is certainly in vogue, and those who approve of the process when the statistics please them can't really complain when other statistics suggest something they do not like. In any case, I would expect those who are outraged to be equally upset about the study implications for foreign and for male students.

Only one of the letters triggered by the article attempted a serious analysis of its methodology. That letter, by three faculty members at Louisiana State University, concludes that the authors "may have made a simple and understandable error in statistical analysis." This is their only criticism, and it is hardly front-page news. By contrast, another letter, while acknowledging the right of the authors to publish their research and opinions, charges that the article is "seriously flawed at best," without bothering to explain in what methodological way, or the letter writer's own qualifications for making such a sweeping assessment.

The UCLA Dissociation Letter

The most significant communication, however, and perhaps the one that triggered all of the others, came in the Fall 1990 issue of *JELIS* and was signed by 11 faculty colleagues at UCLA, a number of them very prestigious researchers. These individuals were certainly qualified to critique the methodology and statistical techniques employed, but they didn't bother to do this.

Instead, in a communication of less than 150 words, they sought to dissociate themselves from the article (although they had never been mentioned in it), to reaffirm not just their own but also the school's commitment to a representative educational community (thereby presumably suggesting that the authors had attacked such a commitment, although there is nothing to suggest this in the article, either), and finally, and most surprising to me, to express dismay because "several statements in the article may be interpreted as racist. [We are] faculty members and administrators who believe that even the appearance of racism is unacceptable. . . ."

In one sweeping generalization, these 11 colleagues have created a scenario that is untenable for any researcher or writer, because it holds that person responsible for what somebody else *may* do with this research, or for the appearance it *might* create in the eyes of myriad and unidentifiable beholders. Surely the signers of this letter, all personally known to me as respected colleagues and friends, should understand that such an argument is totally unacceptable if the research process is to survive. They must also realize that such a letter, signed by a majority of one's faculty colleagues, is the academic equivalent of burning at the stake. Why this anguished outburst of disassociation when the authors had never tried to associate them?

As librarians, we are not only familiar with, but particularly responsible for collection, promulgation, and protected access for diverse opinions. Almost instinctively, all of the critics agree to this principle, but then proceed to something much worse. I recall a similar instance of almost equal but different emotion when researchers at the University of Pittsburgh reported that some materials at the Hillman Library were hardly, if ever, used.

That study was defended and criticized for its methodology, and that is fair enough. However, it was also attacked, by librarians as well as faculty "colleagues" at Pittsburgh (in this case not in the library science program at least), for daring to undertake any sort of study that measured at all whether or not material was used in a research collection. Somehow, the study became an affront to academic freedom.

As the protectors of the rights of unfashionable and unpopular literature, we have, it seems to me, a particular responsibility for protecting and even cherishing the diversity of our own. We throw a lot of stones on behalf of principles of freedom of expression, and I am glad we do. They need to be thrown. However, we had better make sure that we don't do this while living in a glass house.

Bibliographic Instruction
and the Library School Curriculum

In this opinion piece, the skills and attributes of an effective bibliographic instruction librarian, as cited in a study by Shonrock and Mulder, provide material for reflection. The degree to which these skills and attributes should and can be taught as a part of library education is also considered.

I was asked to react to a study conducted by Diana Shonrock and Craig Mulder, in which members of the Bibliographic Instruction Section (BIS) of the Association of College and Research Libraries (ACRL) sought to identify the most important skills required for effective bibliographic instruction and how these should be obtained.[1] It is not my intent to summarize the findings of this study except insofar as they affect my own reactions to them. Unfortunately, to the best of my knowledge, the study has not yet been published, and I can only refer interested readers to the authors, at Iowa State and Johns Hopkins University, respectively, for copies of the paper. It is also not my intent to criticize either the authors or the paper in any way. It was, to my observation, an effectively performed study. One does not criticize the messenger for the message being delivered. If I have a criticism, it is of what the respondents reported to the investigators, and what this means both for library education and the status of the profession.

Through a series of winnowing processes, Shonrock and Mulder were able to identify 25 proficiencies that the respondents, themselves bibliographic-instruction (BI) librarians, felt that successful BI librarians had to possess. Theses proficiencies were then broken down into broad categories. They included: the ability to write goals and objectives (1 proficiency); instructional ability (2 proficiencies); planning ability (4 proficiencies); administrative

Reprinted, with changes, by permission of the author and *Journal of Education for Library and Information Science* 32, no. 3/4 (Fall-Winter 1991): 194-202.

ability (1 proficiency); the ability to train and evaluate others (2 proficiencies); the ability to promote and market (3 proficiencies); and the ability to evaluate programs (1 proficiency). It can be readily seen that this represents a broad and sweeping list of capabilities, and this brief encapsulation cannot do justice to the thorough and competent data analysis performed. For this, the reader must consult the original manuscript. I can only comment on the issues selected and on their implication for library education.

My first observation is that some of these sought-after attributes do not in any way describe librarianship as a discipline, but only identify personality traits that the respondents found important for BI librarians. That is natural enough, but I am not sure to what extent such a list can be fairly thrown at library educators for implementation. Some candidates for library school are articulate and self-confident, some are more diffident, shy, or "bookish." To reject otherwise-qualified applicants to our programs because they did not meet preconceived personality traits would not only be unfair but illegal. It seems certain that some library school graduates will end up possessing greater communications skills (the area most often cited in the survey) than others. They may well have brought with them to the library education program greater or lesser articulation or teaching skills, quite probably from other academic programs. The solution for employers in seeking to emphasize these skills seems simple. Employers should concentrate in their search on the kinds of people they are looking for. If they encounter candidates who do not meet these criteria, they should not hire them. Of course, this assumes that, when employers hire individuals, they know which ones will be assigned duties as bibliographic instruction librarians. On that assumption, more later.

What of the actual and preferred source of the needed knowledge? Survey respondents were asked to differentiate for each of these proficiencies where they had been acquired, and the primary emphasis of responses focused on formal education, on-the-job training, and continuing education. Other education in a formal setting, the use of mentors and models, self-teaching, and a response suggesting that the proficiency had not been obtained or that the respondent was not certain, were also offered as questionnaire options. Having indicated where they acquired this proficiency, respondents were also asked where they felt they should have acquired it. For only two specific proficiencies (the structure of information and search strategies) did a majority report that library education was the primary source of knowledge. By contrast, 11½ proficiencies (there was one tie vote) were learned primarily on the job, six were primarily self-taught, and five and a half involved skills acquired through other formal education programs, which could have preceded or followed library education.

By contrast, the respondents identified 13 proficiencies for which a majority felt that the skill *should have been* acquired in the library education program. These include the ability to design goals, the ability to develop lesson plans, skill in instructional methods, the ability to market (or sell) bibliographic instruction as a good thing to faculty and students, and the ability to tie relevance to student assignments. For seven proficiencies, a majority of the respondents felt that learning on the job was the most appropriate setting, and for five, the preferred area was through other formal education programs. However, for every one of the 25 identified proficiencies, a greater percentage (usually a much greater percentage), felt that the skill should have been acquired in library education, compared to those who reported that this had happened. There is at least some support for acquiring everything while studying for the library degree.

I have not commented on responses listing either continuing education or the role of mentors and models. Neither acquired a single first-place vote in either the category of acquired proficiencies or preferred source of acquisition. In the reported acquisition of these skills, continuing education never ranked even as high as second, and it drew responses from a flat 0 percent (none of the respondents learned this proficiency through continuing education) to what has to pass for a "high" of 9 percent. The role of mentors and models as a source of skill acquisition fared equally poorly, ranging from 1 percent to 8 percent. The 8 percent was for the ability to promote bibliographic instruction within the institution, a category that I would have assumed the role of senior colleagues would have been far more helpful. Indeed, in commenting on where proficiencies should be acquired, this skill area drew 22 percent of the vote. In general, ratings were consistently higher here in virtually all categories but still not very high, and this could be interpreted as a hope (even if a forlorn hope) that senior colleagues ought to do more as mentors but that they would not. Exactly the same relationship of responses occurred for continuing education. "Hoped for" learning in continuing education is higher but still not very high. The highest is 9 percent, and it is expressed as a wish for more marketing preparation. Marketing is an area in which there is a great deal of continuing education available, in both library-specific and general programs.

What does all this mean? Most obviously, it repeats the fairly standard pattern exhibited by virtually all those who respond to practitioner surveys of blaming library schools for just about everything that they wish they knew how to do at this point. However, in the repetition of responses from a whole range of practitioner groups, the complaint is not about a lack of education but about a lack of training to prepare for a specific job. We already know the jeopardy this creates for library schools in major research institutions, which specifically do not want to be seen as training programs. They want to be seen as educational and research institutions and argue that such an insistence does not just benefit them but also the profession at large. Training, it is argued, primarily follows education and occurs after the candidate is hired from some of the very sources that draw so little support in the survey of bibliographic instruction librarians, a survey that appears quite typical. The difficulty of understanding, let alone following, practitioner preferences is, of course, an old one, and the charming quote from Cyril Houle is as appropriate today as when originally written.

> The voice of the aggrieved alumnus is always loud in the land and, no matter what the profession, the burden of complaint is the same. In the first five years after graduation, alumni say that they should have been taught more practical techniques. In the next five years, they say they should have been taught more basic theory. In the tenth to fifteenth years, they inform the faculty that they should have been taught more about administration or about their relations

with their coworkers and subordinates. In the subsequent five years, they condemn the failure of their professors to put the profession in its larger historical, social, and economic contexts. After the twentieth year, they insist they should have been given a broader orientation to all knowledge, scientific and humane. Sometime after that, they stop giving advice; the university has deteriorated so badly since they left that it is beyond hope.[2]

What is still lacking, without a glimmer of solution, is any discussion of the relative role of education and training, and of the responsibility of the school and of the employer, or indeed of the professional. A resignation to a perceived reality that nothing much will happen after they are hired is shown in response to questions concerning continuing education and mentoring. Their hopes and dreams here are very modest, in any expectation that somebody will help them—either by in-house teaching and guidance or by a formal education process provided through the funds and release time of the employer.

And so these bibliographic instructors, like all of the other job specializations that send us their surveys and ask us what we plan to do about it, want us to provide more training at the front end. However, even if we were to agree that such a larger emphasis, in this and in many other areas, should be offered, how should we do it? Because the topic interests me greatly, I have reported the findings of two surveys in coauthored papers. Both are published in *The Library Quarterly*, and that immediately spotlights the dilemma. We published in *LQ* because it is a prestigious publication for academic research credit. However, *LQ* is read primarily by educators and researchers, and so is the journal in which this present article appears. With rare exceptions, practitioners read neither, nor do they attend conference presentations except for those that promise to "fix" immediate problems. I am particularly conscious of this dichotomy because I write, quite separately and distinctly, and with different styles, for both audiences. The practitioners and bibliographic instruction librarians I am discussing in this article probably will not read it.

The first study reported major differences in what various kinds of libraries, both by type and size, considered an appropriate core curriculum of required courses.[3] We can perhaps agree on as many as three courses in such areas as reference materials and collection-development philosophy, but we usually have these courses in the required core. There is a very narrowly specialized preference for what other required courses should emphasize, tied directly to what happens in that particular library. This leads us back to the demand that we prepare not for a profession but for a first job. However, how do we do this, even assuming we are willing, and at what risk of diluting our institutional collegial regard? The second survey determined what graduates of library schools were doing 10 years after graduation, and what sort of jobs they had taken immediately after graduation.[4] The survey determined, for the alumni of 13 schools of all types and sizes that 50 percent and higher had accepted jobs other than those for which they had planned to prepare themselves as they entered school. The primary emphasis in accepting a job, and this certainly did not surprise me, was that a job was offered in an acceptable location and at an acceptable salary. The responses from these graduates [10] years later to the question of how their preparation in elective courses had prepared them for an entirely different specialization was that the employer did not really care what elective courses they had taken. The employer's emphasis (with exception only in some academic hiring involving tenure tracks) was similar to that of the student, and not surprisingly those priorities, at least for those who get hired, match well. The employer cares about expected salary, about geographic ease of location (few nonacademic employers pay for relocation, and many do not even pay interview expenses), but most importantly they care about the impression created in the interview. What sort of impression do we seek in candidates? Students know, or at least quickly learn, that it varies with the library and with the interviewer. Some prefer bright, assertive, and articulate individualists. Some shun such people with vehemence and search for an easy accommodation to existing styles and whatever experience the candidate can already bring to the job.

This, then, focuses sharply on the dilemma educators face. We might, somehow, incorporate the proficiencies desired by bibliographic-instruction librarians into our curriculum. I do not know if it would take one course, several courses, or the revision of the whole bunch of courses to offer this specific level of training. Obviously, were we to do this, what do we do to match the expectation of other groups? Special librarians and prospective special librarians are probably not enthusiastic about training in bibliographic instruction. They tend to prefer more preparation in online searching. The pressures grow constantly, and they range from the broadly societal (diversity and multicultural preparation) to the very specific. It has been suggested that any single course in academic librarianship (no matter how well taught) can never suffice to explain the complexities of research libraries. Others argue that the course also does not adequately prepare those who will work in community college libraries with part-time and evening students.

Concentrating for the moment on the expectations of bibliographic-instruction librarians—assuming that we teach this, how and where do we teach it? Continuing education, we are informed, is not really a viable option, and the reality that we espouse continuing education far more than we do it is something I have already reported.[5] The mandate from the ACRL BIS is that we do this during the one ride on the merry-go-round, because this is the only try at the brass ring. However, that still does not answer the question. Do we put these courses into the required curriculum, and insist that all students qualify for BI competence? In this case, what should we *stop* teaching instead? Nobody has yet been willing to tell us. Alternatively, if we make these elective courses, we immediately find two further problems. Additional elective course options for a static student population increase cost but not revenue. In addition, we have no assurance that these courses, if offered as electives, will be taken by the students who end up becoming bibliographic-instruction librarians. Certainly taking the course anyway can be argued to do no harm, unless it keeps the student from taking a course about the lack of which another employer will complain later. At present we have no assurance that the hiring of prospective bibliographic-instruction librarians will be predicated on the completion of the appropriate BI courses. Indeed, is this even possible, when many individuals become BI librarians after having initially been hired to do something else?

Without any bias toward the authors and their work, as they were asked to undertake it, it seems to me that perhaps we need fewer surveys of the kind reported by Shonrock and Mulder, competently done (indeed more competently than most) as this survey is. Perhaps a more viable approach comes to us from a less obvious source like comedienne Joan Rivers: "Can we talk?" Of course, even that is not easy. Who will represent whom in such discussions? Can we fashion an agenda that does not automatically become an irritant? Perhaps the Committee on Accreditation, which under the leadership of Robert Hayes did a masterful job of holding broadly based, and yet nonacerbic, meetings to discuss the purpose of accreditation, is most strategically positioned to tackle this issue. The most obvious questions to be addressed and resolved are those of the relationship between education and training, between education and continuing education, and between job pressures and professional responsibilities. The problem is not made any easier when we recognize that professionals in different kinds of libraries and in different work specializations have different urgencies and priorities but that library schools still turn out a generic product called "librarian" and identified as such by hiring officials, even if fancier words are used that really mean the same thing.

I could end my comments at this point, but I am nevertheless tempted to take them a step further. Practitioners feel no compunctions about critiquing how library schools prepare their new hires. Is it then equally appropriate for library educators to be concerned about what happens to our graduates after they leave? If indeed we prepared them only for the jobs that presently exist, that would be classic training. Education involves thinking and evaluation, and that may bring us to questioning and challenging what may be happening simply as a matter of routine practice. Is this acceptable as well? I will assume that it is.

Raising questions about bibliographic instruction is a risky endeavor. Like adult illiteracy programs, this is an activity whose virtue is assumed, and it therefore brooks no challenge. In the area of library programs that deal with adult illiteracy, I am struck by the fact that we have no data on success rates, no information on recidivism for those taught to read, and little information on who these adult nonreaders are. The Cuban physician who speaks no English but fluent Spanish is quite a different case from the inner-city dweller who ostensibly attended school for at least 10 years but still cannot read and who has no books at home. Why do nonreaders now want to read, and indeed is the initiative ours or theirs? What are they likely to read once they know how? Job training manuals, grocery labels, *Anna Karenina*? ALA president Richard Doughterty's catchy slogan "Kids Who Read Succeed" has a preamble that most of us also recognize: "Kids Who Are Read to Will Read." Can we compensate for this gap if we refuse to acknowledge it?

With regard to bibliographic instruction, aimed primarily at undergraduate college students, I would like to raise a fundamental issue. Is the point to make these individuals self-sufficient, so that they can function on their own without further professional assistance? If so, one test of success would be the fact that we never see these students again. Or is it rather (and this is certainly my preference) that we expose these students to the mysteries, challenges, and most of all opportunities of the information process? These consist, inevitably, of a mixture of self-help and of professional help, and for a service profession that judgment is largely left to the client. In other words, do we teach students not just what they can do on their own, but also what a professionally staffed information process can do for them? Under such an interpretation, I would expect that bibliographic library instruction also includes a major segment on what reference librarians do for clients including students and on what every student has the right to expect in terms of professional assistance. It is an old observation that, for everything learned, we become aware of a hundred things we do not know. The only individuals who consider themselves fully knowledgeable are the ones who know virtually nothing but are blissfully unaware of what they do not know. Is it then our purpose to increase our work load by unleashing information-inquisitive monsters who will henceforth torment us incessantly to help them find all the things of which students now become aware but which not all students can find for themselves (as indeed Ph.D. researchers need our reference help to find things)? Are we simply offering bibliographic instruction, at least in part, as an investment in the avoidance of having to deal with students during the rest of their academic stay? Is it only my observation, as a special librarian, that very little reference activity of depth and substance takes place in academic libraries except behind the scenes, and certainly not at the reference desk, which is the only contact point of which students are aware? I understand that there are not enough reference librarians, but surely we also know that any potential for increasing the number results not from avoiding work but from inviting it. Simply summarized, do we teach bibliographic instruction as an end in itself, or simply as a beginning that opens the eyes of the student to the professional interactions possible in libraries?

My second concern, again equally personal, involves our method of instruction. We teach bibliographic instruction in what I would call the hypothetical model, and, of course, much other instruction follows the same form. If and when you need to do this again, remember how it is done! Take notes and remember! It is also the way academic computing departments try to teach all of us. Here is how to build an index from the exercise book, so that if you need to build one later on you will know how! It does not work for me, and I suspect it does not work for a great many others. The exercise teaches me how to build this particular and, for me, extraneous index as a hypothetical game. When it comes time for me to build my own unique index six months later, I still need and expect individualized one-to-one instruction for what I am about to do. Fortunately I can demand and get it, and if I am well taught, I can now compile this one index or even a sufficiently similar index the next time. However, as I gain familiarity with the computing tools available to me, my demand for continuing one-to-one instruction never lets up. In other words, instruction in the context I prefer (and that others may prefer) does not turn students loose, it bonds you to them for life.

Have we any reason to suspect that the learning model for undergraduate students is any different? I know that I have now studied several languages in a classroom setting, and I learned none of them, except for such useful phrases as knowing that the pen of my aunt was on the table of my uncle. What languages I know I have learned by talking to individuals who were willing to talk to me and to correct me, and I suspect that much bibliographic instruction may be equally extraneous or at least not retained because it is hypothetical, unreal knowledge. I suspect. I do not know. I do know that if the reason for teaching it as we do is simply because this approach is all that our resources allow, that becomes a terrible and defeatist reason. Do bibliographic-instruction librarians know how well their present approaches work? Or do they, like so many other librarians in so many settings, simply throw their bodies into the breach in the hope that they will at least make some difference? There is a good deal of potential cooperative research here for librarians and library educators and doctoral students. However, we need also be aware of the possibility that such findings are not the kind of things that some people want to know.

Notes

1. Shonrock, D., and C. Mulder. "Bibliographic Instruction Librarians: Acquiring the Proficiencies Critical to Their Work" Chicago: ALA, January 1991. Submitted for publication in *College & Research Libraries*.

2. Houle, C. O. "The Role of Continuing Education in Current Professional Development." *ALA Bulletin* 61 (March 1967): 263.

3. White, H. S., and M. Paris. "Employer Preferences and the Library Education Curriculum." *The Library Quarterly* 55 (January 1985): 1-33.

4. White, H. S., and S. L. Mort. "The Accredited Library Education Program as Preparation for Professional Library Work." *The Library Quarterly* 60 (July 1990): 187-215.

5. White, H. S. "Continuing Education—Myth and Reality." *Indiana Libraries* 4 (1984): 138-45.

Your Half of the Boat Is Sinking

That was the title of a cartoon that Bernard Fry and I included with our 1976 study for the National Science Foundation on the economic relationship between academic libraries and scholarly publishers, in which a publisher and a librarian, both sitting in a boat about to be swamped, pointed accusing fingers at each other.

That 17-year-old cartoon is obsolete. Commercial publishers left long ago in their diesel-powered yacht, perhaps wondering why librarians didn't have the political wisdom to insist that academic faculty and university administrators at least join them in their soggy craft.

It is only human nature—when things go as horribly wrong as they have for our profession for the last 20 years—to blame someone else. The ability to rationalize and to retrofit are alive and well in the human mind. However, the difficulties that confront libraries and library schools are simply two examples of the same problem.

White's Disclaimer

Therefore, when John Berry states in his editorial "The Two Crises in Library Education" (*Library Journal*, September 1, 1993, p. 102) that they are really totally distinct problems, I must posit my disclaimer. It is not the first time, and probably not the last time, that I find myself in total disagreement with Berry, and perhaps my ability to state this in *Library Journal* says something good about the publication.

By trying to separate what is happening to library education from what is happening to practicing librarians, Berry is tragically wrong. I tried to make this point much earlier when I noted that the Columbia University decision to close its library

Reprinted, with changes, by permission of the author and *Library Journal* 118, no. 17 (October 15, 1993): 45-46. Copyright © 1993 by Reed Publishing, U.S.A.

school because our field lacked "intellectual rigor" should be clearly seen by every professional librarian at Columbia as the cavalier personal insult it was ("A Requiem for the Mother School of Us All," reprinted in this book on pages 237-241).

What the public thinks of library education affects what it thinks of librarians, and what the public perceives librarians to be doing affects their perception of why this discipline requires professional education at the university level and, indeed, at the graduate level.

We are in large part to blame for our low perception, by allowing nonlibrarians to administer our library education programs and our libraries and by focusing our energies on the quantity of what we produce (circulation and holdings) rather than on its unique quality. Higher circulation, if that were all that really mattered, can be produced by just about anyone, with enough giveaway specials. It can even be made self-service.

Berry's editorial makes some points with which I agree. Library education programs have increasingly looked at technology in education as an end in itself, rather than as a means to an end that has expanded in both importance and complexity but that has never really changed as we try to bring our customers closer to the information and documents they need.

Technology as a Means, Not an End

In the assessment of technology we must understand what is germane and what is irrelevant to our own purposes. We must decide whether to acquire the specific hardware or software skills, or whether at the very least to know how to hire and manage subordinates who do have the skills.

In my management experience in technology-sensitive organizations, the latter course has been preferred. Programmers and systems analysts are easy enough to hire; the difficulty may be in telling them what we want. Nor have I ever seen any conflict between the importance of academic research and academic teaching. The two should feed on each other.

A colleague from another discipline put it quite nicely when he noted that research is sinning and teaching is confessing. Without confession, sins lead us to perdition; without sin, confession becomes incredibly boring. Teaching can be likened to acting on a stage; one has to project, and one has to be interesting. One also has to know what the play is about, as well as one's lines.

I have no patience with the premise that quality education cannot be delivered to branch and regional campuses, or even through technology, although teaching that way is inevitably harder on the teacher, and concerns about quality must always take precedence over concerns for cost and convenience. With that caveat in mind, during my own deanship at Indiana we offered our program at nine locations, and that process strengthened the academic program as a unified whole. It even strengthened quality at the home campus, and, of course, it met a responsibility of the public university to bring education to its citizens.

Berry and I Disagree

However, I begin to disagree with Berry's editorial when it accuses educators of failing to support library practice. It is here that perhaps we need to differentiate once again between education and training, a differentiation that can become blurred in our field precisely as we scramble around to overcome the financial damage done to our institutions by cutting corners.

It is understood in any profession that as new junior subordinates are hired, productivity temporarily decreases, even though eventually it will go up. Productivity goes down because not only are new hires unproductive (they are educated but not trained), but senior staff have to drop their own work to train them. Every organization with which I have dealt as a professional or as a consultant has understood this.

If people outside our field, or, even worse, if people inside our field think that new librarians can tackle a backlog as rapidly as a newly hired counter attendant can dispense hamburgers, then perhaps this says something about how others see us and perhaps more importantly how we see ourselves. Yes, I know we don't have enough money. That's hardly news. However, if we sacrifice our standards for this expediency, there will never be an end.

Education and Training

The blurring between education and training in our field (sometimes pronounced educationandtraining) is a constant source of communication difficulty between academia and practitioners. I left practice to become an educator. I could have joined the circus to become a trainer. Inevitably, I must teach some of my students the "how," but fundamentally I try to prepare them to deal with the question of "why," and certainly in our field the equally important "why not" (because in our field we try to do too much with too little to keep everyone just a little bit happy).

I prefer to teach my students to look at broader options; their supervisors can then teach them the how as it applies to their specific library. I understand that this takes time, but I also understand, as any management textbook would tell us, that time spent with subordinates is the most productive time we can spend. What could we possibly have to do that is more effective for the organization in which we work?

I am not at all sure what we are supposed to do about what Berry calls the "so-called nonprofessionals"; I don't understand what he means by "so-called." Any profession knows who its professionals are and who they are not. That doesn't mean that they are trivial or important, just that they have different preparation requirements.

Don't Educate Where You Train

It is training that probably should take place in the library; if you also educate your own professionals, you easily can develop an inbreeding process that perpetuates all of the present dumb policies. "Training" professionals in libraries, as the editorial urges, revives an old disaster simply because it is so old we have forgotten that its only virtue was self-righteous comfort. It negates everything we have learned from C. C. Williamson and the Chicago Library School. What we can give nonprofessionals (not so-called nonprofessionals) is a level of training that fits the job and that can be provided through the employer, through the plentiful job-training institutes, and even through community colleges.

The primary reason these programs don't work very well to produce what we once called paraprofessionals is that we don't pay the graduates enough to make the process worthwhile. When we pay our support staffs as well as other municipal agencies and the local private sector pay them, and when we treat the requirement for work in the evening and on weekends as these needs are generally remunerated, the problem of training and motivating our clerical staff will disappear, particularly once the library budget funds training. Training has never been anything more than a question of resources. Lack of money is at the root of many of our evils, but perhaps we have become so adept at pretending to ourselves that this doesn't matter that we think it shouldn't matter to our support staff, either, and that someone should train them as an exercise in charity.

There is only one tactic for obtaining the money we need, and it consists of rewarding or punishing those who decide. They can't "afford" libraries? A nation that spends $65 billion on video games annually? Money is certainly the issue in the mirage that there is a shortage of continuing education opportunities.

There is no shortage of teachers, lecturers, and courses, and some could be shared through the regular curriculum, particularly as new technology courses are developed. Others are offered through seminars, workshops, and guest speakers. I consider myself something of an expert on this subject, participating in what can be called continuing education activities at least 20 times a year. So do many of my colleagues, and so would many others, both inside and outside of academia.

Rodger's Point Is Well Taken

The problem with continuing education is the unwillingness to pay for it, but Urban Libraries Council Executive Director Joey Rodger makes the point much more concisely than I could ("ULC Study Finds Libs. Invest Little in Staff Development," News, *Library Journal*, September 1, 1993, p. 112). "The issue is that most public libraries cannot get enough training money through their host governments. It's a matter of 'keep the branches open, don't train the staff,' " stated Rodger. Or, I would add, don't continuously educate them, either.

However, Rodger states that the libraries are not to blame, and here I would disagree. I would blame library directors in particular for permitting such a value system, especially from trustees who as doctors and lawyers certainly understand the importance of education and training—for themselves at least. If the primary responsibility is simply to keep the doors open, does education really matter? For that matter, does training? Do we?

It is important that we keep the many parts clearly in focus and that we understand what the role of educators is and should be, but also what it is not. As I deliver continuing education to special library practitioners, I am sometimes asked why we educators don't simply teach what the practitioners want us to teach. My answer is always: "What makes you think I want to turn out clones of you? My whole effort is to try to turn out librarians who are going to be better than you." That might sound arrogant, but any educator who doesn't believe that shouldn't even bother to attempt to teach.

Whether we like it or not, library education and library practice share one very leaky and nearly awash rowboat, and we are both judged under one standard. One hopes that no one suggests that the way to get the water out of the boat is to drill more holes in the bottom.

Library and Library School Management: Strangers in Our Midst

Regular readers of this column know that I am almost obsessed by issues of turf, something that street gangs and the residents of the former Yugoslavia understand. One of the accepted definitions of any profession is that it brings a level of unchallenged expertise to meetings with those with whom it interacts.

It is difficult to identify what is granted to librarians as our professional expertise, and this may be a large part of our problem. We can begin with the White House Conference on Library and Information Services (WHCLIS), in which we spend long hours explaining to delegates what the problems and nuances are, so that they can then make decisions for us.

In universities, the faculty committee on the library may overstep the bounds of an advisory committee (at least in principle all of us should welcome advice, although that would extend to librarian advice on the structure of the German Department) and begin to act as a management committee. That becomes a total travesty of any accountability/responsibility relationship.

After these complaints, some of my friends might be surprised that I welcome advice from all corners, but I do. However, there are two caveats. One is the clear understanding that advice is exactly that: it can be accepted or rejected. Two, I am far more willing to accept advice from individuals who are willing to accept it from me.

Reciprocal Advice-Giving

My continuing observation has been that librarians, and library educators, are not only frequently offered gratuitous advice on how to do their jobs, but that often we solicit such advice in conference programs. That does not trouble me. What does trouble me is that the courtesy is never returned. We invite these people to speak at our meetings; some do so politely and others, arrogantly.

However, I have never been asked to suggest more appropriate value systems and decisions at meetings of doctors, engineers, accountants, and the myriad academic disciplines found in the university. I suspect that you haven't, either. Doctors regularly speak at meetings of the Medical Library Association, but how many librarians are asked to speak at meetings of the American Medical Association? Am I being too touchy? Or are there basic problems in how we are perceived as colleagues in these actions, problems that inevitably spill over into other areas of interaction?

If I am touchy it may be because I have seen too much. In the interest of hiring in the university to attract academic couples, it has sometimes been suggested to me that perhaps the rules can be bent a little to hire the librarian spouse of a prospective star historian or physicist. The reverse has never happened to me, i.e., that perhaps the rules can be bent to hire the historian or physicist spouse of a prospective star librarian. If any of my readers know of such an academic instance, please let me know.

Cronyism in Library Positions

We all know of the appointment of nonlibrarians to major administrative posts in academic and government research libraries. Sometimes the profession shows some annoyance, sometimes we are genteel enough to pretend not to notice, but in any case we never do anything.

It has been suggested that the appointment of a political crony to head a public library system may even be a good idea, because it promises a higher level of financial support. Those who make the argument automatically assume librarians are by nature poor politicians and fund raisers. Some are, and some are not, but that is true in any field. The suggestion that it is specifically true only in librarianship seems to be simply an example of self-hatred.

The concept of hiring people from other disciplines to bring fresh insights into any field might have some merit for experimentation, but only if consistently carried out. It was once suggested that the next dean of my university library might not have to be a librarian. I congratulated the writer on his courageous vision and informed him of my interest in being considered for the next open academic deanship. I would consider any field but particularly business or law, where I saw a lot of academic problems I thought I could fix. In this case, the opportunity for me never arose, perhaps because all of the library dean finalists turned out to be librarians. It is really not that impossible to find them.

Nonlibrarian Candidates on the Scene

In more recent developments, deans are appointed to head the programs in which we prepare our own future professionals (almost inevitably in a program that straddles potential questions by including both library and information in the school name) who are not librarians. Their only experience in library operations may be from the user end of the reference desk. Perhaps my chances of becoming a business or law dean still glimmer.

It would be a mistake to dismiss these candidates casually. Schools that prepare librarians and information specialists (it is difficult to differentiate because all good librarians are information specialists, and there are some who call themselves information specialists who aren't even bad librarians) find it increasingly difficult to develop a brief curriculum that deals with the needs of the present and the needs of the future and that prepares graduates to work in small rural public libraries as well as the for-profit information sector, and as specialists in children's storytelling as well as in organic chemistry databases.

Balancing Education and Preparation

Yet according to studies, our graduates often change career emphasis, and our preparation must acknowledge this. I am not so insular as to think that no one else can contribute to the education of our junior professionals. Of course they can, and that contribution to the specializations into which our students are now delving can be crucial to both balanced education and job preparation. There is nothing new in any of this. Law schools have been employing sociologists, political scientists, and economists as part of their faculties for a long time. It is a fair question to ask a political scientist who applies for a law school faculty post why he or she wants to make this change in career emphasis, because a change it not only is, but indeed must be.

This is a question we should certainly also ask of the economists, psychologists, computational linguists, and operations researchers who apply for faculty vacancies in library programs. The right answer can make them very welcome. What do you think you can contribute to the expansion and growth of our discipline? What do you know about it? How do you propose to learn what you do not know? How do you expect to interact with students in basic classes, who inevitably bring a wide range of backgrounds, interests, and experiences to the classroom? Are you prepared to modify your own research and writing to make contributions that will be relevant for us? Are you planning to write for our journals at least in part and to speak at our conferences? Will you try to learn our vernacular, so that you can interact with other faculty?

Collaborating with Librarians

When the appointment under consideration is for the head of the program as dean or director, the questions of necessity must become even sharper. Assuming that you believe that there are things we can learn from you, what do you think you can and need to learn about us to be able to hold this position? What is the symbiotic relationship between your background and the more traditional background of the school you are seeking to head? Or do you see yourself as a savior here to rescue us from our ineptitude and blindness?

Such questions are not unreasonable. If the candidate has already demonstrated experience in working collaboratively with librarians, then the answers may be easier to accept. However, if there is suspicion that there is neither respect nor devotion, but simply a perceived opportunity to seize the dowry represented in a deanship or directorship, then we should demand more evidence of sincerity and commitment. Students and their future employers are entitled to educational leaders who respect their values and traditions, even as they perhaps seek to broaden and expand them.

One of the perceptions of some of these strangers is that they ought to dump the word library from the school title. They see it as no longer politically correct in the academic value system, even as the institution continues to have large buildings called libraries staffed by individuals who are expected to obtain accredited graduate degrees. It would be irresponsible for us to trust anyone who talks about the future without understanding our past. We do have a glorious history, and we have been around a lot longer than those who now propose to "save" us. We certainly have problems, but decapitation is not an ideal surgical solution.

During the Spanish Civil War, four columns of General Franco's army marched on Madrid, aided by a fifth column inside the city. Quite aside from the number of columns marching to attack our profession, we don't need another inside our own gates.

Librarians and Information Specialists on the Information Superhighway

No reader needs to be persuaded about the growth in information. That growth is demonstrated, and amply documented, in the quantities of information generated through research, analysis, and expository pronouncements, but perhaps even more significantly through the ability, with the aid of technology, to disseminate that information far and wide. Nor do I need to persuade anyone that society has become increasingly aware of the importance of information. Ignorance has never been an acceptable rationale, and it is now widely believed that information power for making decisions holds the key to success for governments, industries, and universities.

It is also true that individuals, as they emerge from our school systems, are far more comfortable in using computers. In a relatively short 20 years, my own university's academic programs have moved from the assumption that arriving students knew little if anything about computers, to the realization that most students not only feel comfortable using them not only for direct computing applications, but also as writing machines. At this point 75 percent of the assignments turned in by my students are done on computer, although none have to be.

However, the fact that individuals are no longer computer-phobic does not necessarily mean sitting at a terminal represents their greatest aspiration. For most of my students, and for former students who are now professionals, the computer terminal is a tool to be used when it is appropriate to do so. The emotional fear and hatred has disappeared, but it has not been replaced by a value system that sees sitting at a terminal as a virtue in and of itself. I believe that this pragmatic approach is completely appropriate. Technology is, and must always be, our servant, never our

Reprinted, with changes, by permission of the author and *Information, Communication, and Library Science* (Taipei) 1, no. 1 (Fall 1994).

master. Occasionally, technologists wonder why a certain application, the elegance and power of which is certainly impressive, is not used to the extent that it appears to them that it ought to be used. The answer is very simple. The information-searching process is emotional at least as much as rational, and independence from technology allows us to be able to justify our own decisions to our own satisfaction, even if not that of others.

I use computers, but I also continue to use typewriters, and I use the latter almost exclusively for creating papers such as this one. Why? Because the great virtue in writing on the computer is the ability to move paragraphs and phrases around, to rewrite and edit online. I don't write that way. I write front to back, and I change very little. Given that, I find a typewriter keyboard much more forgiving of the heavy-handed way in which I hammer keys. In other words, for me, for certain applications, the typewriter is easier, faster, and more comfortable. That doesn't make me a Luddite, it simply makes me selfish. I do what works best for me. I think it is important that all of us in the information field remember that our clients will always do what they think is best for them, regardless of what the so-called experts say.

I find that thought comforting, and I remember hearing a talk by Norbert Wiener, the father of cybernetics. Wiener was asked, perhaps by someone who had just seen the film *2001—A Space Odyssey*, in which a computer kills an astronaut, whether or not we had to fear computers controlling our lives. Wiener was reassuring. He doubted that this would or could happen. However, if he ever feared that possibility, he would simply pull the plug out of the wall socket. I note this because I served for six years as a member of the Board of the American Federation of Information Processing Societies (AFIPS). AFIPS included representatives from the computer professionals— the Association of Computing Machinery (ACM), the Institute of Electrical and Electronic Engineers Computer Society (IEEE-CS), and the Data Processing Management Association (DPMA). It also contained representatives from a whole range of user societies—educators, historians, biologists, political scientists, and, of course, librarians. The key debates, always argued pleasantly and courteously, centered on whether machines should adapt to people, or people to the machine.

I also recall virtually my first day as Executive Director of the NASA Scientific and Technical Information Facility, when I found editors trying to work with computer-generated data that seemed to me to be very inconveniently arranged. I was assured that this was indeed the case, but that the material had to be arranged in that way. The programmer had told them so. I called in the chief programmer, who reported to me (and there is a lesson in this about who should be boss), and told him that I had no interest in discussing programming intricacies, but I was certain that the information could be reformatted for the convenience of the people who had to use it. It might take effort, and it might even introduce some computer inefficiency, but it was certainly worth it in terms of overall cost and effort.

These are old war stories, and I know that we have come a long way in developing what are now called "user-friendly" systems. Then why don't I always find them so friendly? "Invalid instruction" is a rude response when made by a human being, it is an even more rude response when made by an inanimate object. If that computer doesn't become more polite, I may just do what Wiener suggested.

Unfortunately, I sense a growing hypnotic preference for buzz phrases, and certainly "information superhighway" is a buzz phrase. Just exactly what does it mean? And what does "virtual library" mean? As I speak to various librarian groups in the United States and Canada, I give them a list of terms that should always be included in management communications. They are valuable because they sound so expert, and yet are so meaningless. Let me just share a part of that list here. The terms include: balanced, compatible, functional, integrated, optimal, responsive, synchronous, systematized, total, user-friendly, virtual, forward-looking, cost-effective, flexible, mobile, needs-oriented, broader mission, payoff, quality assurance, value-driven, and vision.

If we can ever dehypnotize ourselves from all of the verbiage suggesting that we are about to be launched into some sort of new and utopian age, perhaps we can recall why it is that individuals want information, assuming that they do want it. They want it so that they can do something else with it. That means, quite clearly, that they want what they think they need, and they don't want what gets in the way of understanding and using it. Operations research people have known for some time that the ideal information collection is the one that contains everything that the individual wants, and nothing else. Large libraries are harder to use than small libraries, and their only possible virtue is in the assumption that, by being larger, they also contain more of the things we want to use. Librarians have seen this phenomenon many times when users take material out of the library to keep in their own offices. They do this because a library in their own office that anticipates most of their questions is the perfect size, and the material is always available. As we have worked with selective dissemination of information, SDI user reactions have also told us this. Some users don't mind the irrelevant along with the good stuff. Certainly newspaper readers have developed a great deal of tolerance for information that does not interest them. Other clients become very angry when we tell them anything that does not interest them. Different people have different reactions, but in general researchers have a greater tolerance than executives and decision makers. Can we design generic systems for the simultaneous satisfaction of all of these people? Any reference librarian knows better than that.

However, there is also a great danger in the concept of the information superhighway as it is being designed for us. There will be lots of information on our terminals, and it will get there very rapidly. However, the decision of what is transmitted is being left to the disseminator, and his reasons for generating something may not be the same as mine for receiving it. In fact, they are almost certain to be different. The great attraction of the invisible college, for those who are members, is that the information being transmitted is small in amount and important in content, because the quality control mechanism is the exclusive membership in the invisible college. These are people who also think as we do, and we trust them. If they betray that trust, we simply evict them from the club.

The problem of trying to protect ourselves against too much information goes back, in my own personal recollection, more than 30 years, and if getting too much information was a problem then it is certainly a problem now. In the early 1960s, my IBM colleague Hans Peter Luhn proposed a way to allow scientists and other researchers to bypass the slow and strangling management approval process and communicate their ideas, research findings, and questions directly by computer to their colleagues in the far-flung international IBM empire. This was, of course, before online access, but the concept of electronic messaging was certainly workable. Management liked the idea, approved it, and it was implemented. Technically, it worked beautifully. However, it failed, and it failed because of people. It quickly became apparent to those with really good new ideas that they should not put semi-developed concepts into the network. At best they were deluged by questions and visitors who kept them from their work. At worst, their ideas were stolen. On the other hand, many people with absolutely nothing valuable to report proceeded to report that nothing on a regular basis, sometimes daily. Posting messages became an exercise in self-promotion. Can we be sure that everything now dumped into our computer systems has passed some sort of value judgment? Who will impose that test? The originator? Management writers such as Tom Peters understand the problem. Peters has written "A flood of information may be the enemy of intelligence." Are we communicating intelligence, or at least information for a purpose, or are we communicating a flood of information that we measure in quantity rather than quality?

I know from my own consulting assignments that library and information systems users are desperately afraid of drowning in information, even as they are afraid that they might miss something. As I tell my clients that we plan to add more databases for access on their own terminals, I can see terror in their eyes. They are not using what we give them now, because they have things to do besides just access information. Their boss wants them to create something.

Should any of this really surprise us? Surely those of us who distribute material with routing lists know that some people simply cross their names off the list and pass it on. I know I do it all the time with material I get from administrative offices or my school's library. Many librarians I know are still fascinated with the opportunity to provide our users with more information. Placing value on quantity over quality began with the reporting of increased circulation as a virtue rather than as an admission that we didn't know exactly what to give users, so we gave them more just to make sure. The reporting of the size of a library in terms of holdings, without any analysis of how needs are being met, is part of that same trend. I know that many of our bosses measure us by circulation and holdings statistics, but that is only because we have never given them anything better with which to measure our contribution.

Users, of course, treat a library or information system far differently. For them, there is no library as such, there is only THEIR library. If it contains what they want, that is good; if it doesn't contain what they want, but instead has 2,000,000 other items, that is hardly a substitute. Nor is it a consolation to be told that the library owns an item but that you can't have it, for any of a number of reasons, none of which matter to the user. The process is binary. Either the material is available, or it is not.

Information users long ago learned to protect themselves, and to make the system work for them. They do this by pretending that they have read the material, or by pretending that they don't need to see it. What they want is not more information, but to be able to glean more useful information from what is available. And they certainly don't want to spend any more time on the information process. Nor do they appreciate being told by a machine that they are stupid.

I don't believe that the designers of the information superhighway, who understand machines and what they can do, understand people anywhere nearly as well as we do. And yet, even as we presumably understand the problem and what ought to happen to be able to solve it, we stubbornly cling to obsolete and outmoded concepts. We insist that information users not only ought to do their own information work, but that they ought to want to. In doing this, we place a moral value system on the entire process that is totally irrelevant to the issue. There are conflicting values between wanting to be teachers, to be moralist preachers, or wanting to be information professionals.

At one major Canadian university at which I taught, the library embarked on a massive program of faculty end user training, so that faculty would be able to find what they needed, in their own offices, without coming to the library. I understand that many faculty don't like to come to the library, and perhaps they even enjoy spending time in their own offices, particularly if they have nice furniture. However, what makes us think they want to spend their time sitting at terminals fending off error messages? Certainly they would like to be able to do direct, specific, and simple item lookups of what the library owns, and even to order a document to be delivered to their office. But that is very different from a complex and time-consuming search, the outcome of which is quite problematical.

Of more than 600 faculty members offered the opportunity for end user search training, only 25 responded. Six took the course, the others enrolled their graduate assistants or their secretaries. We shouldn't think of the faculty unkindly. They have a lot of things for which they will be evaluated. If necessary, information searching is something about which they can pretend.

If there is so clearly an opportunity and a need, it continues to puzzle me that librarians are so reluctant to assume that role. If we calculate the number of academic library reference librarians and compare them to the number of faculty members, then their number is much smaller than the comparable staffing in a good corporate library. In public libraries, at least in the United States, reference service is one of the first things to be eliminated in a budget crisis, in the insistence that above all else the doors must be kept open. To do what? And how do these strategies and perceptions of the library as a place for low-key, self-service relate to the new parameters of rapid and up-to-date information, in huge quantities, brought to us over the multiple lanes of the information superhighway?

We already have a superhighway of sorts, in the identification of options for acquiring material from other institutions, as their holdings are displayed for us in online systems. That electronic superhighway leads to a rutted, two-lane, dirt road called document delivery. It still takes weeks and sometimes months to deliver what we have located in seconds and minutes.

A fairly common vision of the future in what is called the academic virtual library involves transferring from the library to the terminal in the user's office direct access to what is contained in the library, or is available from other sources. All of that material? And without any filtering? Are we certain that is what our clients want or prefer? Have we asked them and given them alternatives? Or is this simply an attempt to disguise library costs by distributing them to the accounts of the end users? The result could well be a greater overall cost, but at least the library will presumably not be blamed. Is this good for the end user? Is it good for the organization that supports both of us? Is it good politically for librarians? In politics it is always unwise to give away your power base, and the control over money represents one of the most obvious power bases. If the end user wants something, is it not wiser as well as cheaper in total to have him come to the librarian, who controls the money and has the wisdom to make decisions?

However, even more important than the political implication for librarians is still the preference of the end user. There is a growing industrial specialization that recognizes the need for information intermediaries, and in an article in the July 26, 1993, issue of the British journal *The Economist*, this enterprise is given an intriguing name.[1] It is called "meatware," and the term can be understood directly in relation to the other two information technology terms, "hardware" and "software." Hardware and software supply us with tools, but those tools demand someone to use them. For those who prefer to delegate the process to others, and the suggestion is that this is a very large group, the meatware represents the human beings hired to use the hardware and software on our behalf.

I have talked to a number of people who work in organizations that contract with meatware specialists. They are grateful for the interaction, but they wish that these far-off meatware specialists, with whom they communicate by telephone, fax, and electronic mail, had a better understanding of what the clients were doing and why they needed information. This suggests that a far better alternative might be an in-house information intermediary. However, the article mentions no alternatives, and suggests that contracted meatware specialists are the only alternative. Whatever happened to reference librarians?

Part of the understanding of why this happens must come from the recognition that often an appearance of economy is more important than economy itself. The process of "downsizing" eliminates positions within the organization, but it does not necessarily eliminate the need for what they do. When librarians are eliminated, the cost of contract meatware specialists to do their job will probably be much greater. It just won't be as obvious.

However, despite all of the efforts to hide and disguise costs, we should be able to count on accountants to tell the truth, and it is my observation that, unlikely as this first appears, financial managers are at least potentially the librarian's greatest allies. This is because we should be able to demonstrate what is most cost-effective. If an organization disavows its need for information, that is rather stupid, but at least consistent. However, when there is both a fervent commitment to the information superhighway and a cutting of the library budget, something doesn't make sense. It is important that we, who know this, stress that linking onto the information superhighway is crucial, but that it is also very expensive, not only in terms of hardware and software, but particularly in human time commitments. Spending more time on the information process for the end user, and therefore less time on the primary task, is not an attractive alternative. Hiring meatware specialists is one option, but there are already better ones in place.

When I speak to medical librarians, I ask for a show of hands of those who think that doctors perform online searches three times as well, or three times as rapidly, or with only one-third the computer-access costs as they do. There are no hands raised. I use the concept of three times the quality or three times the economy because, conservatively, doctors earn three times as much as librarians, and their time is therefore three times as valuable. If their own access to databases does not meet that test, then it seems obvious that they shouldn't be wasting time and money doing detailed searches at all. They should be doing what they presumably do best, and allow information intermediaries such as medical librarians to do this work. I am told that many doctors do not now have access to medical librarians. However, that is a simple problem to solve. All we need is more medical librarians, and then we must hook them to physicians through the terminal access systems the doctors already have if they can do their own searches. The result is both an improvement in quality of searches and in cost-effectiveness. Is the money spent by an end user somehow more "virtuous" as a cost than money spent by a librarian? I hardly think so.

As we move toward the reality of the information superhighway, it is not difficult to predict that early implementations will be imperfect. We already know that the ultimate user will do what is most convenient and most comfortable for him. He always has, and he will continue to. In dealing with information, we are not dealing with exact phenomena that can be measured. Just as the user is free to cross his name off a routing list and pretend that he has read the material, so is he free to delete all of his computer messages if he has a headache, or feels particularly swamped. As the users of Luhn's system at IBM learned very quickly, the odds of finding something useful in this open-ended approach are not in their favor.

When I return to my office from having been away for a period of about two weeks, I usually find about 250 e-mail messages. They are not rank ordered in any way, they are simply chronological. Of these, perhaps 10 or 15 will be of significance for me, another 10 or 15 will contain interesting but not crucial tidbits of gossip and speculation. The remaining 90 percent will be, for me, uninteresting and a waste of time. However, I must look at all of them to find the ones that really do interest me.

I am probably not ready, as Norbert Wiener suggested, to pull the plug, but I will be sorely tempted. I will place a greater reliance on what comes through regular mail, over the telephone, or by fax, because in all of these approaches the originator of the message is making a personal commitment to reach me that involves a financial investment, and that may be for me the best control of all. However, what I would really like is an individual in whom I had absolute trust (and that is neither a secretary nor a meatware specialist I have never met) who will tell me that, based on his or her understanding of what I am working on and what I care about, 225 of the 250 messages have already been deleted, so that I can concentrate on the 25 important ones. Are librarians interested in such an assignment? Do they feel comfortable with it? Others not nearly as competent will have no qualms about taking on the job if we don't.

Information intermediaries not only meet a crucial need, they fit in completely with the shift, as countries develop and mature, from a production and agricultural economy to a service economy. We want this sort of intermediation, so when it comes to information we will certainly be prepared—as a nation, a corporation, or a university—to pay for it. Not only because the alternatives are more expensive, but also because they are more uncomfortable. Peter Drucker has noted that cost becomes irrelevant when a product or a service is considered essential to an individual's own value system. Both librarians and publishers learned as early as the 1970s from studies for the National Science Foundation that the average price of canceled journals was considerably smaller than the price of retained ones.[2] Price is only an excuse for canceling something we really didn't want in the first place. When it comes to a contest between money and value, at least in the professional setting, value will win every time. We should be pleased at knowing this, but only if we know how to use that knowledge.

If there is going to be a large profession of meatware specialists—of information intermediaries—as I am certain there is going to be, who will these people be? Certainly this should be based on an understanding of subject, of need, of the preferences of the users, and of the technology and options available. However, it requires more than that. It requires political and marketing skills, it requires an ability to talk not only about absolute costs but also about alternative costs, about not only the cost of information but also about the cost of ignorance. Perhaps most of all, it requires the ability to generate confidence in our own skills and our own abilities, and getting others to believe in us must begin in believing in ourselves. That may be the greatest challenge and the greatest obstacle of all.

I am neither for nor against technology, because technology is a tool that is often tremendously useful and beneficial, but not automatically so. The potential for benefit is overwhelming, and indeed it can be argued that without the judicious evaluation of our technological options, and the adopting of those that meet our needs and those of our clients, we can accomplish very little. The question of whether or not we use technology is really not germane. The important question is how we use it, how we manage and control it, and how we make it serve us.

Notes

1. "Teltech Tales." *The Economist* 327, no. 7817 (June 26, 1993): 90-91.

2. White, Herbert S. "Factors in the Decision by Individuals and Libraries to Place or Cancel Subscriptions to Scholarly and Research Journals." *Library Quarterly* 50 (July 1980): 287-309.

Librarians in the Cruel World of Politics and Money

Introduction

So much has been written about both the characteristics of the political process and of financial transactions that it might be expected that librarians, who are assumed to read more than most, and who in any case know how to find information, should be well versed in these subjects. That they are not, and most certainly they are not, can be ascribed in part to the misconceptions that society has about librarians, that librarians lead genteel and stress-free lives in which they do good and kind things for people, and get to do a lot of reading. The ghost of the nice, spinster librarian with her hair in a bun who introduces people to the world of books and learning has been invoked by enough politicians to turn all of our stomachs. However, it is likely the same misconception about how librarians function that leads guidance counselors to steer quiet, bookish, and unassuming students into what seems to be a perfect career for wimps may also affect the self-selection process that populates our profession. Recent studies by Jim Carmichael and earlier studies by many others suggest this. However, libraries are nothing like their image. They are intensely organized and bureaucratically structured. Librarians, far from being loners, must interact with many people on many different levels. Most importantly, because those who run libraries have no automatic power base, and no automatic funding, they must depend on the political process to persuade others to support them.

As I teach management to unsuspecting neophytes (perhaps excepting those students who have been in law school), I immediately stress three points. The first is that politics is not a dirty word. It is the process of allocating resources in a competitive environment, and we can be sure that resources, in good years as well as in bad years, will always be inadequate when compared to the demand for resources. The political process then decides who gets money and who does not, and while politics can take place in an environment that is either fair or not, the purpose of any manager is to persuade those in authority (always nonlibrarians) to give money to us rather than to somebody else. Anybody else.

Peter Drucker, whose name comes up frequently in any discussion of management strategies, defines "friend" and "enemy" quite narrowly. A friend is an individual who supports you before any other priorities, including perhaps even the support of his own budget requests. Everyone else is an enemy, and that includes both those who would rather not spend any money at all, and certainly not on you, and those who profess that they would fund you if only they had the money. Drucker lumps all of these as enemies, because he understands that the argument that funds do not exist is a lie. When something must be done, funds are found to do it, and, of course, we have all seen that done to us in our operational settings time and time again. There is no money for the library, but. . . . Why are we still so naive?

The reason may lie in the second point I make to my students. Librarians tend to wrap ourselves in the flag of moral imperativism, and argue that we should be funded because what we do is virtuous. However, the suggestion that we be supported because we are inherently good has never worked well, and has been even less effective lately. Our competitors also wrap themselves in the cloak of virtue, whether deservedly or not. The enemy (and, remember, anyone who wants the same money we do is the enemy) is not just the industrial/military establishment, much as the rhetoric at ALA conferences would like to suggest it. The enemy in terms of funding priority is the war on crime, the war on drugs, medical research, and shelters for the homeless. As California public librarians know full well, their immediate enemy is the public school system that, as a result of poorly thought-out legislation, has siphoned public library money into the school systems. And, of course, the school systems are not going to return any of the money. It is defining the enemy as anyone who wants money from the same people as we do that upsets students. However, they might as well learn the truth early in their careers. The competition does not need to be ugly, but it will be selfish and intense. As dean of the library school at Indiana University I understood that every other dean was my rival—for attention, affection, and money. Any initiative funded from the general university budget for business, music, or education decreased the likelihood that I would get funds. My need was to justify to my bosses why giving me money was more important than giving it to somebody else.

The third and last part of a full opening class lecture was how we persuade these individuals to support our initiatives in preference to those of others, particularly when we are dealing with nonlibrarians whose commitment to us is certainly no greater than to any other subordinate. Individuals, quite simply, make decisions based on what is best for them, or at least what they perceive is best for them. Although this sounds both arrogant and selfish, it really is not. None of us, and that includes librarians, have any problem in persuading ourselves that what is best for us is also, quite coincidentally, what is best for the organization. Engineers call this process of making facts fit conclusions retrofitting, and we all do it without even being aware of it. If we understand this, we can comprehend that when Charles Wilson stated "What is best for General Motors is also what is best for the country," he was simply saying what any General Motors executive has to believe in order to continue to function. Understanding this premise also serves to explain why cooperation, which works so well in principle, works so poorly in practice. We all believe in cooperation, and we know that we are totally cooperative, although we are not as certain of the others. And, of course, cooperation means doing it my way. Not because I am selfish, or stubborn, or manipulative. I know I am none of those things. We should do it my way because I am right! Why are you so stubborn that you can't see that?

If my readers and students find all this strange and perhaps even ugly, let me hasten to assure that there is nothing here that basic management writers have not understood for a long time. In a brief column in the August 1, 1986, issue of the *Wall Street Journal*, Peter Drucker noted that it was imperative for subordinates that they and their bosses were on the same side. Drucker pointed out that in a battle with your boss you will always lose, but that at the same time there was no reason for this to happen. What subordinates need to do is to determine what the boss's priorities are, and how our success can enhance, or our failure endanger, those priorities. Drucker reminds us that while bosses control, they are even more responsible for decisions, and that ultimately they are responsible for both the positives and the negatives that occur. Responsibility can be delegated, but it cannot be abdicated. In other words, what you accomplish is to your boss's credit; what you fail to accomplish is his or her fault even more than yours. With that as a background, and a clear understanding that you and your boss *must* have the same priorities, Drucker concludes that your boss becomes your most important subordinate, because he or she has the power to accomplish what you both have agreed needs to happen.

If this all sounds strange, let me assure the reader that Drucker is absolutely correct, and that nothing else will really work. If librarians have been far less effective in stressing both the good results of support and the disastrous results of a lack of support for those who get to decide than our rivals in the political process, that failure has not been unnoticed by the politicians who are perhaps grateful for the fact that, unlike police chiefs, we do not punish them politically. As former Governor Otis Bowen of Indiana noted in a message to a meeting of the State Library Association (a message that was totally ignored), "The problem for librarians seems to me to be that you have not figured out how to reward your friends and punish your enemies."

In that context, the weakness of our political strategies becomes apparent. We appeal to members of state legislatures, to governors, to Congress, and to presidents for more money for libraries. Sometimes, we even earnestly and disastrously argue that we need the money to buy books or computers. To do what with them? Surely we must understand that an official who has just been threatened with public outrage unless something is done to halt crime will not find that impressive. The point of the message must be that you ought to give us funds to protect yourself from being defeated in the next election. What will happen if we don't get the money? Anything specific? We'd rather not say, in large part because we have created the expectation that, with or without money, we still do what is considered an acceptable job. The essence of management communication is exception reporting, and all of this is part of management by objectives. If you don't give us the money, what terrible things will happen to your career? Do we reward, and do we threaten to punish, those very essential parts of the political quid pro quo? Police chiefs certainly do, and even teachers and nurses are learning.

If all of this seems so outrageous and strange, it is because we have adopted a strategy that is really no strategy at all. We want support for libraries, because libraries do good things. What sort of good things? Well, first, they are there and they are open. Second, they allow people to "read" and to "learn." How, specifically? We can only provide anecdotal evidence. Are we wiping out adult illiteracy? Well, not exactly, but we have taught some people to read, and that's good, isn't it? Is there a crucial role in all of this for properly educated, motivated, and rewarded professionals? Stating that would appear to be self-serving. We focus on the institution, not the people, and the institution is undefined except in the suggestion that more is better.

If all of this seems harsh it is because we fail to understand that our strategies earn us sympathy and warm letters of encouragement, but no support. We want a greater level of support for federal library programs. At what level? At whatever level we can get, although the June 1994 issue of *American Libraries* suggests $146 million. What is correct about that truly trivial amount? What will it accomplish? What problems will it solve? We can only state that it probably would make things slightly less rotten. Politicians, who can easily vote $100 billion for a savings and loan bailout or to put more police on the street, cannot deal with justifications that are so vague, and so trivial.

Many of my writings in this section deal with specific examples of our failed opportunities and our failed strategies. Because, despite all the pleas of poverty, this country will spend a great deal of money on the very issues on which we have a primary interest—education and information. They simply don't plan to spend it on us. They don't even know we have a role to play.

Many of the strategies of government bureaucrats will always center on making us rank order our priorities, to demand that we list what is number 1. If they can get us to do that, it is much easier to ignore everything else, and perhaps just give us a token amount of money to deal with priority number one. What is a token amount of money? Certainly, within the federal context, $146 million is a trivial and token amount. As this essay is being written, we are spending at least that much in sending routine ultimatums to Serbs, North Koreans, Somalians, Rwandans, or whoever happens to be handy to receive ultimatums.

In articles in this section, I deal with specific examples of our trivialization in allowing ourselves to be backed down into accepting a single priority, and thereby forsaking all others. The state of Oregon might give public libraries a dollar per child to spend on services for children, but won't the information superhighway extend into Oregon? Will it stop at the Continental Divide? The Office of Library Programs is also quite good at defining our first priorities. At one time it was adult illiteracy. Now, according to its brochures, it is public library support for education. All of this seems just a bit humorous in terms of federal funding initiatives; it doesn't really matter what our priorities are, because the government is not planning to fund any of them. And if it is not important at the federal level, why would it matter at any other level?

I am not angry at the bureaucrats with whom we deal. They are only doing what works best for them. However, surely we know that it doesn't work for us. As a college varsity tennis player, I still recall the management advice from my coach: "Always change a losing game. Never change a winning game." However, that strategy requires that we know the score. What is the score in our game? As for priorities, we certainly know that we have many, and the expansion of the information world is giving us more. I need not persuade librarians (or apparently the Department of Education) about our role in support of education. But what is that role? Is it simply to teach people to help themselves, so that ultimately they can function without us? Or is it all right to occasionally slip them a reference, or even an answer? If so, whom? High school students, undergraduates, graduate students, full professors, academic administrators, corporate or government administrators? Where do we draw the line between service and self-service? Is it really our concern (as opposed to the teacher's) where that line is drawn? Is our problem simply one of fearing that our resources will be overwhelmed? If so, isn't that an easy problem to fix? All it takes is money, and if we can prove that spending it is worthwhile politically for those who have to spend it, they will.

The increase in information access through technology, the information superhighway that will lead to a virtual library, raises other questions. What do we want our role to be in the process of information intermediation? Do we still only want to be teachers or advisors for what we insist will be a self-service activity, even as the evidence overwhelmingly suggests a need for information analyzers, information forwarders, and information suppressors for those who are drowning in the stuff?

There is obviously an issue of money involved, but why are we so anxious to avoid spending it, preferring instead that it be spent by others? If it is going to be spent anyway, and, of course, it is, then keeping that expenditure level under our control is a key part of our power base. We try very hard to pass along our own legitimate costs to other groups, through strategies that range from end user searching (even when that end user's surrogate turns out to be the end user's secretary or graduate assistant), to asking academic departments to "adopt" a journal, to hoping that the virtual library will stick what used to be library costs into a wide range of academic departments where they will certainly get larger, but will at least hide the librarians' costs.

What is the point of such a strategy, for ourselves, for our employers, or for the nation at large? A tremendous amount of money will be spent in the implementation of new informational access channels, and then perhaps an even greater amount of money will be spent in protecting the end user from drowning in the raw information that comes pouring out of those channels. What is the most effective way for doing this? Could it just possibly involve us?

In an article in this section I differentiate between efficiency, effectiveness, and benefit. Benefit is hard to demonstrate except by hindsight, because ignorance is never admitted. Effectiveness is largely a perception of convenience, and it is based on common sense. When I ask medical librarians whether doctors do MEDLARS searches three times as well or three times as rapidly as they do, I get only laughter in response. But doctors, who earn at least three times as much as medical librarians, are doing their own searches. If this is not a cost-effective solution, as there seems to be clear agreement it is not, then why is the strategy of the National Library of Medicine still the training of more doctors to do their own searching? Specific item lookups I can accept, but that's all. Shouldn't the strategy be to urge doctors to stop doing searches in order to lower the costs of medical care? Has anyone told Mrs. Clinton? If some doctors don't have access to qualified medical librarians, isn't the obvious strategy one of making sure they have such access? Why? Because that approach is cheaper for the taxpayer. Librarians have clung tenaciously to examples of cost-efficiency, internal measurements that have no value for politicians, rather than dealing with cost-effectiveness. We speak of circulation, or holdings, or the number of adults taught to read (without mentioning the growing number who can't read). None of these really matter politically.

What we do is important, and what we do has many sides to it. Education is important, and here the key battle must be one that argues that librarianship is not a subset of what the teacher does, but rather a full and equal partner. The field of education is now somewhat in disfavor, but it will still be important for us, if we clarify our role.

Recreation is the most obvious and evident of our roles, and I am not suggesting we abandon it. I am much too territorial for that. However, it does seem to me that in terms of carving out an urgency for our agenda, this is the least attractive strategy. Funding libraries because they are nice and people like them is not going to work during periods of too little money, and that is always.

Our most obvious opportunity is in the information area, because of its growth, its complexity, and because of a growing realization that the nations, states, universities, and corporations that win the information battle will win everything. Our role here can vary greatly, but it will require that we understand two things. The first is that technology is not the end, it is a means to an end, and therefore the technologists must take orders from the information people. The second is that we understand that what is happening here is not simply another example of our responsibilities as educators. The need here is not for education in self-service, but for information managers, and they should be librarians. Engineers cannot supervise the education of librarians. Perhaps librarians should supervise the education of computer professionals. The strategies for winning the money and political games almost suggest themselves. You do not minimize or hide costs. You centralize them, seek control over them, and make others come to you. The ultimate source of power in any environment is that people have to come to you and ask.

There is no survival in being cheap, because there is no such thing as being cheap enough. Nor is there a good time to get money. Money will always be distributed sparingly and grudgingly. Even if we agree that the early 1990s were particularly bad, there is no assurance that the late 1990s will be any better. And even if they are, we will still not be offered any money, because the list of competitors for funding has grown even more rapidly. We can be certain that competition will become far more stringent. The point is that we can win, but that may require a total reeducation for those who fund us.

The point is that we will not get funds simply by asking for them. We will get them, if we get them, by pointing out the alternatives with or without the money. Politicians understand that there is automatic credit for spending less. They will spend more only when they perceive that the risk for them in spending less is greater than the credit received. Or, alternatively, they can take the money away from someone else and give it to us. That would certainly be nice, because the reverse has happened many times.

The key in management communication, any basic management text will tell you, is exception reporting. All subordinates report the good things, but the whole point of program budgeting is that management needs to hear about problems. If your management is not particularly interested in hearing about problems, it may be that they are under the mistaken perception that nothing but the budget matters to their political advancement and survival.

Our strategies are spelled out clearly for us by management writers like Drucker, Peters, and Pinchot, and by astute political observers like Bowen. We begin not with the discussion of money, but rather with what needs to happen, with program budgeting. Program budgeting ought to be easy, because education, information, and knowledge are "clean" words. Ignorance and stupidity are not acceptable for any politician. If you support the clean words, then your actions must support those words, or we will report your hypocrisy. We would rather not rat on you, so can we make a deal? If the money needs to be spent, and it certainly will be spent, then spending it through librarians is the most cost-effective, and ultimately the cheapest, way to proceed. We should have no difficulty in making this point, and in enlisting the General Accounting Office and other financial professionals on our behalf.

The successful strategy is not one of asking for money for "libraries," it is for demanding support for initiatives that are best carried out by qualified professionals in institutions often called libraries or information centers. It must be apparent that I would not bring an eight-year-old girl to meet the president, with the plea that he give libraries "more money" ($100?) to buy books. I would bring eight Nobel prize winners from eight different disciplines, who before meeting the president would announce at a news conference that they planned to demand that the president properly support the proposals put forth by librarians to avoid destroying the country. Would that make the president angry? I certainly hope so. Sometimes anger can lead to respect. Nothing else we have tried does.

My strategy with the mayor of San Francisco, who not only cut the library budget, but then fired the library board that dared to implement these draconian cuts in a manner that was not cosmetically satisfactory, would be similar. Having created one stupidity, the mayor is now prepared to create a second, by insisting on a pretense that is designed to help him, but hurt the city. Is anyone from ALA prepared to take that initiative? We can hardly expect the staff of the affected public library to do it, because that mayor would fire them just as quickly as he fired his own board for having the temerity to speak the truth. And, incidentally, if we can find reasons to remove conferences from Phoenix and Cincinnati for reasons that have nothing to do with librarianship, might this not be a possible reason for boycotting San Francisco?

The point of this essay, and of the articles that follow, is to note that politics is a process of winning through a range of strategies that include being nice only if it works. Not all librarians can be successful politicians, any more than this would be true in any other field. However, all successful managers must be willing to be politicians, and this is particularly true in our professions, in which we do not control our resources, and in which we must persuade nonlibrarians who will see the issue of supporting or not supporting us as a subset of their own well-rationalized priorities. Management, as Tom Galvin reminded us, is a contact sport.

The Value-Added
Process of Librarianship

Former Secretary of Education William Bennett recently commented that the quality of education is not measured by the number of books in the library. I am not so naïve as to fail to understand the real thrust of the secretary's statement. It was not to propose alternative methods involving the library to improve the quality of education. It was rather to provide some more support for the tenuous argument that this federal government need not spend money in support of libraries.

I am not going to waste the reader's time by attacking that premise, because it was a dishonest exercise from the start. It began with the conclusion that the federal government should not support such "local" activities as libraries (made at the budgetary level by individuals not burdened by any specific knowledge of libraries), and then moved to a search for reasons for decisions already reached. First the verdict, then the trial, as Lewis Carroll would remind us.

The Ultimate Trivialization

Nevertheless, Bennett is correct. The quality of education is not measured simply by the number of books in the library, because such statistics tell us very little. Bigger libraries are not necessarily better libraries or more effectively used libraries. Secretary Bennett prefers to speak in terms of educational outcomes, but when these are expressed as cookbook competencies (can read at the rate of x words per minute, comprehension and an understanding of large scope not required) they become the ultimate in trivialization.

Reprinted, with changes, by permission of the author and *Library Journal* 114, no. 1 (January 1989): 62-63. Copyright © 1989 by Reed Publishing, U.S.A.

The role of libraries, I would argue and the secretary has not yet seen fit to deny, is essential to the quality of the educational process for which he had federal responsibility. It is essential because we are preparing people to think, to evaluate, and to cope in an increasingly information-dependent society.

The most important thing then is not just what people remember (although that is obviously important), but what they can find out by themselves or through others. It is here that the role of librarians is as important as that of the classroom teacher. The quality of education is not measured by the number of books in the library. I agree. I suggest it is measured rather by the quantity and quality of what professionally happens in the school library.

Irrelevant Statistics

Librarians who have criticized Bennett's statement have argued that we do not really measure libraries by their holdings. But we do, of course, by that and by the size of circulation, another largely irrelevant statistic. Readers of this column are already aware of my impatience with the simplistic National Library Week slogans encouraging people to "read" or to "use the library," without bothering to define what a library is and what it should be able to do for us, to be allowed the title of library.

I have noted recently a more serious thematic approach to National Library Week, and that obviously pleases me. It leads me to hope that the next White House Conference (whenever Congress decides it can "afford" it) will also adopt a more serious theme. Such a theme would concentrate on what librarians can contribute, rather than see the theme used as a convenient political football by every possible single-issue pressure group that could be assembled under one roof. That kind of process ultimately uses us rather than serves us.

It is unfortunate that we don't have generally accepted definitions of terms such as "library" and "librarian" to match the clear legal definition of "hospital" and "doctor." To me a collection of books is a collection of books, and if it is organized and managed for optimum use it becomes a library. Librarians select their collections based on their education for the process. Otherwise, the library can become randomly responsive to uncoordinated user requests.

Adequate Programs/Responses

Even the best librarians, and the best selection processes, cannot approach completeness of service. Books are expensive, and any academic librarian can testify how expensive scholarly periodicals have become. What librarians provide, or at least should provide, is not just materials delivery from the shelves of their libraries. It is the unkindest misperception of our profession that librarians concern themselves exclusively with due dates and overdue notices. The misperception continues because that is exactly what happens in some places called libraries. It then becomes logical to assume that all people who work in what are called libraries must be librarians.

We accept that trap in a thousand little ways, most directly by developing programs that meet our resources and then insisting that they are adequate, instead of developing programs that are adequate and then outlining the necessary resources. If that means, at least at the beginning, many of our libraries are labeled unsatisfactory, can our egos stand it? Perhaps not. We now find, in not just public and school but also in special libraries, a negative reaction to the implementation of standards promulgated by some outside body.

Instead, the argument is for internally developed criteria that meet "the unique and specific needs of the community." Sounds good, but that is what we now have because as it turns out the definition of need is captive to the budget. It all becomes an exercise in doublespeak in which what we have "meets the needs" because, after all, it is what we have.

The Effects of Budget Cuts

Budget cuts do affect materials budgets, but more often they affect people who work in libraries, either librarians or clerks. This is because we have accustomed our users to the notion that the quality of a library is primarily its collection instead of primarily its staff. Perhaps some of us even believe it ourselves. We read almost daily of library directors who "protect" their patrons from the harsh reality of a budget cut by saving the materials budget, and instead reducing the staff or eliminating the planned raise.

If, as a result, the better people leave or the clerks are not replaced, whoever is left becomes a clerk because clerical work must be done while professional work is considered optional. The collection returns to a self-service status, and in time we can eliminate the last librarian. Finally, as James Matarazzo's dissertation has told us, we close a library that is already so bad nobody cares or notices. That last action, tragic as it is, at least makes some sense. Money, we must constantly remind ourselves, is certainly the bottleneck but never the real issue.

Corporations, communities, and school systems can afford good libraries, and that means affording good librarians. Peter Drucker has noted that if organizations provide a service that people really want, cost becomes irrelevant. That, of course, is the issue of marketing. Libraries in general do not know how to market. We need to know how to create a desire for services for which there are presently no funds, and for which there will never be funds, until and unless people at least know what they are not getting but should have. But that issue deserves a column of its own.

The Bottomless Pit

Secretary Bennett's words provide an opportunity, and we should take him literally. The issue, according to him, is accountability, of determining what value is received for value spent. Library materials budgets that do not provide a mechanism for properly using the information purchased, libraries that just let the stuff sit there on the off-chance that someone might find and use it, are not very cost-effective given the large and increasing cost of materials.

Moreover, that materials cost has no realistic ceiling, and, of course, that is what bothers Bennett. Libraries are never as large in their holdings as we think they ought to be. It is a phenomenon that the late Robert Munn referred to as a recognition of the "bottomless pit."

Anyone who has traveled in Europe is aware of the value-added concept, the premise that as a product or service is developed and refined, its value increases. The extent to which it increases obviously varies. There is a vast difference between the value of metal ore and the value of a Swiss chronometer, between a bolt of cloth and a designer dress. Books and journals sitting on a shelf are raw materials. Professional librarians not only accelerate and facilitate their use, but, in what are now far too few settings, use them directly to serve the information needs of their clients.

However, the value addition of librarians is even greater than what we do with the things we have bought. Mechanisms of computerized information access and delivery in the hands of a competent librarian open the vistas of library service to the point where local ownership is, although certainly relevant, not crucial. The premise of service offered by the National Library of Medicine is that any doctor, even in the wilds of Alaska, is entitled to a minimum level of information access, regardless of what may or may not be available locally. Can we promise any less to the rest of our citizens?

The only difference in information service between a large city and a small town ought to be the difference between what is available immediately and what will take 48 hours to obtain. We should work toward compressing that time constraint. Certainly Federal Express and other overnight services already have done so for their clients. They would serve us, too, if we paid them.

The Value of Librarians

What is the added value that professional librarians bring to the worth of the library? Does the value increase twofold, fivefold, tenfold? Is it not relatively simple to demonstrate that having a library without a qualified staff (including professionals to do professional work and clerks and aids to do what the professionals should not spend their time doing) is stupid from a cost-effectiveness standpoint?

In fact, is it not confusing and inaccurate to call an amorphous collection of passive materials, whether found in a school, a community, or a corporation, a library at all? We had better find a way to distinguish between these levels of activity. If we don't, Gresham's Law takes hold, and the bad drives out the good because it is seen as cheaper.

If Secretary Bennett is serious in his insistence that education be responsible and cost-effective (and I hope and assume he is), then perhaps he should have taken steps to see that every school is served by a good though not necessarily large library, and that means a proper mix of professional and support staff.

He might have examined the curious premise that while academic and public librarians usually need to be educated in graduate programs accredited by the American Library Association (and readers of this column already know that I consider the present standards for accreditation bare bones minima), school librarians, it can be argued, perform an even more crucial function. School librarians constitute the initial and habit-forming library contact, yet they may receive their library education in programs that do not have to meet this standard of professional library education. They do have to meet other requirements in teacher preparation that are also important for librarians in our schools, but this is not a trade option. Let's not play "Let's Make a Deal" with our own profession.

Secretary Bennett and his replacement in the next administration can best serve the cause of educational effectiveness if they posit that, in addition to collection adequacy, American school children have the right of access to a qualified school librarian, fully qualified both as a librarian and as a teacher. That is the value-added process. That is economy, because schools without proper libraries cost the taxpayers far too much.

Cheapness Through "Fairness":
The Unholy Conspiracy

Biologists tell us that animals do not foul their own nests, regardless of how sloppy and messy they might otherwise be. Years of family pets confirm this observation for me. It is therefore puzzling and disturbing to note that librarians are constantly fouling their own nest, i.e., the library.

We do this by running libraries we know are bad because somebody else did not fund them properly, and then pretending they are really good. We foul them by refusing to place a value on our own species as inhabitants of the nest. Unlike most other animals, we will nurse anybody, and we will even call them fellow librarians. As I watch the territoriality of blue jays in my backyard, I am very much aware that they do not act like librarians.

I have addressed in earlier columns the issue of school librarians who downplay their uniqueness as librarians to try to blend in as teachers; and of academic librarians so desperate to look like teaching and research faculty that they will even undercut their own discipline by making value judgments that indicate that English or sociology are more important fields than library science. I have also noted that such tactics do not work. I agree with Pauline Wilson that we will get credit for our unique contributions as librarians or not at all.

"No Substitute for Courage"

The process extends to public libraries as well. Public librarians and state accrediting bodies are always going to be under pressure to shortcut the process of hiring qualified librarians. Finding someone who is local and handy even if not qualified is simpler and cheaper. That pressure to find cheaper, shortcut

Reprinted, with changes, by permission of the author and *Library Journal* 114, no. 9 (May 15, 1989): 52-53. Copyright © 1989 by Reed Publishing, U.S.A.

solutions exists in any field. I would expect both library directors and state library accreditation officers to resist it with vigor and with courage. There is no substitute for courage. It means that, somewhere, we draw a line in the sand and retreat no further.

It is quite something else when that pressure to avoid hiring librarians for what are supposed to be professional positions comes from other librarians. It is that phenomenon that puts me in mind of the biological comparison. In my consulting and speaking travels I run into pockets of what are usually public librarians who argue that they require a waiver from rules requiring an M.L.S. or even an accredited M.L.S., because of their "special" circumstances. These usually focus on one or more of the following: 1) they can't afford degreed librarians; 2) they can't get them to come to this part of the country; 3) their state, or their corner of the state, has no library education program; or 4) what happens in their library does not require a professionally degreed librarian.

I respond to these arguments with less than the expected sympathy because I accept none of the premises. Their communities can and do afford whatever is important enough to afford, and they can afford librarians. Decent salaries will attract candidates willing to move to their communities. The analogy, for me, is the need to attract a doctor, and communities that think it is important sweeten the pot until they finally get one. They don't settle for a faith healer or snake charmer as a substitute for a degreed M.D. They don't necessarily think having a librarian is as important as having a doctor, but I would argue that it could be considered more important.

Doctors only deal with a small percentage of the population at any one time, but librarians have the power to help everybody all of the time. The argument that the state has no accredited library education program (and 19 states don't) doesn't pose insurmountable problems. Some states have fee courtesy exchange agreements with neighboring states that would permit lower tuition at another library school. Other states, particularly through their state libraries, have made diligent efforts to have schools from other states provide extended education opportunities. Those initiatives could be expanded, but some state agencies don't try at all.

Finally, of course, some states that presently have no accredited library education program did have one, or could have one because they are large enough. The most logical place for them is usually the state university, the seat for graduate education and the institution that can be made to feel responsibility (albeit with some effort) for meeting this need for the citizens. But this can only happen if the need is held up to the glare of public attention.

Watering Down Librarianship

Why would librarians want to participate in a process of diluting their own profession for the sake of economy? Others may want cheap libraries even at the cost of quality, but why would we? There is no simple answer; I will not accept the premise that we are a spineless profession. We are, however, a self-perpetuating profession. Whatever level of assertiveness we now find or fail to find in practitioners will also tend to be replicated in new students who use them as role models.

An excellent article by Nancy Van House in a recent issue of *Library and Information Science Research* (April/June 1988, p. 157) examines the factors that caused library science students at one university to choose this career. It notes that, low as we know salaries to be, the expectation by students of what they would earn was even lower. And yet, at another university that I happened to be visiting as part of an accreditation team, students responded to the suggestion made by a "community leader" that they volunteer their services to offset the personnel cuts in public libraries "required by budgetary shortfalls" by stating that they were not scabs prepared to undermine the jobs of professional librarians.

The community should either fund its libraries properly, or it should close them entirely. It is a stance I see all too infrequently. It underlies my own suggestion that the National Library Week theme employed in past years, that the "library" was the place in which adorable movie stars hugged books, was the ultimate in self-trivialization. The library is the place with the professional librarians. If you don't have one you just may not really have a library, and the sign over the door may be fraudulent. What you may have is a reading room, which has benefits but also clearly limitations, and it is *not* a library.

Cheapness and Trivialization

The thrust for cheapness we have understood all along. The suggestion that we waive the requirement for a library degree because such an action would provide greater professional growth opportunities for women is a new form of mischief. It does not provide more opportunities for women, it trivializes and clericalizes the opportunities they now have. Somehow the judge in the Merwine case, although he had no library background, understood this immediately.

He found the argument that an insistence on an M.L.S. discriminated against women to be absurd, given the fact that the great majority of individuals who do have the M.L.S. are women, and he was, of course, correct. The individuals whom a politically motivated waiver of the M.L.S. discriminates against are those librarians, 80 percent of them women, who took the trouble and expended the effort to obtain a degree. Waiving the degree does not professionalize anyone new; it deprofessionalizes those who up to then had been professionals. It is not a coincidence that this dilution has only been proposed for the so-called women's programs, and not for law, engineering, and so on.

I understand why bureaucrats who hire people for libraries would want to seek waivers for our modest degree requirements. What I fail to understand is why such a strategy could be supported by librarians. I also fail to understand why a waiver of educational requirements for librarianship would be attractive for women's rights organizations, when librarianship is only among a handful of true professions now dominated by women. If it is perceived that a waiver of educational requirements can be of benefit to the employment opportunities of women, then that benefit is in direct relation to the paucity of women already in that field. If nonde-greed women are to replace anyone it shouldn't be already-degreed women, at a lower status and a lower salary.

Broadening Educational Opportunities

There is more that library schools can do to broaden educational opportunities for prospective students. Perhaps, paradoxically, this is already spelled out in the Standards for Accreditation, which state the requirement for "responsiveness to the needs of the constituency which the school seeks to serve." What that constituency is may be in question for a private institution, but it is clearly understood for a public university, particularly a state university. It is all the citizens of the state whose name you bear.

However, that part of the standard has never been enforced. If it were, schools would be asked to demonstrate what they did to meet this require-ment in permitting starts at various times during the year, by accepting part-time students, by teaching at off-campus locations, and by offering courses in the evenings and on weekends. There is a balance between quality and access that must be maintained, and the Committee on Accredi-tation (COA) quite correctly demands proof of the first. It should require proof of both.

The responsibility of schools is to provide both quality of education and a broadened access to that education. For employers it involves a support for educational aspirations of present staff members who do not have the professional degree, e.g., through educational leaves, tuition support, guaranteed jobs, and all the other things that conscientious em-ployers do in other disciplines. It means protecting the educational invest-ment that the students have made, by not giving away to others what they have labored so long to accomplish.

Finally, it means paying decent starting salaries. What sort of salaries? Any statistic becomes immediately dated, but for 1989 the fact that high school students are sneering at jobs that pay "only" $5 per hour suggests that individuals with master's degrees are worth at least several times that. Can those who hire librarians afford it? I have no doubt that they can. In any case we can make it clear that even if they insist they can't afford a proper library we won't let them get away with a pretend pseudo-library. The students mentioned earlier understood this clearly, because they weren't prepared to foul their own nest. By contrast, the students in the Van House survey, who expect low salaries, end up realizing their expectations.

Kicking Women in the Teeth

My point is simple. When public library directors seek waivers so that they can hire individuals without the proper educational qualifications because such candidates are cheaper or more convenient, they are doing nothing for women's rights. They are only giving a kick in the teeth to those women who bothered to get an education; they are sending a message to library schools that they are foolish to bother to try to educate public librarians.

A recent news story in the library literature illustrates the point. A public library director arguing against the implementation of degree requirements notes that in order to run the kind of library she runs one does not need a library degree. She is undoubtedly correct. But just perhaps the citizens of her community have a right to a *better* library than the one she runs because she doesn't know enough to be able to run one or because the budgetary process does not allow it to happen.

Ultimately, which of the two reasons applies doesn't matter, because we are dealing with a self-fulfilling prophecy. Librarians who accept low-quality libraries because that is all the community is willing to fund validate the premise. Eventually it follows that library boards staff such poor libraries with individuals only well enough prepared to run poor libraries, and not with individuals with the ambition to run better ones. In a perverse way, that last action even makes a certain amount of sense, if not for the profession or the clients then at least for the funding agencies who find agreeable drones to carry out their edicts. However, when librarians actively participate in this demeaning process they are only fouling their own nests. And they are fouling ours.

Librarians and Marketing

What is marketing? There is some confusion even in the business literature. By and large, marketing is considered greater than the offering of specific services, which would be considered selling. Marketing subsumes selling; it starts well before the specific identification of the product and service to be provided. It makes a service desirable, and then looks at mechanisms for filling the need it has just created. Filling that need is selling.

Libraries are not adept at selling, let alone marketing. To the extent to which they provide agreed upon services, there may still be lacking the incentive to create greater demands for that service. Frequently the excuse is that we are already too swamped to provide even the things it is agreed we should provide. The death trap opens for us because if we don't supply what we had contracted to supply, users accept that, forgive us, and lower their expectations. And so balance is restored, at what may be an ever lower level. It is sometimes patiently explained to me that the reason that the library does not offer online searches is because it has neither staff nor funds to perform this function. And, of course, it never will have if it does not offer the service first to see if it is worth funding.

Creation of a Need

The provision of agreed upon services, even if we could do it without the need to dilute, is still not marketing. Marketing consists of the *creation* of a need, or at least of the awareness that there is such a need. Marketing constantly seeks to develop imbalances between what is and what should be, in the recognition that only once pressure for satisfying a need is generated will there be action.

Reprinted, with changes, by permission of the author and *Library Journal* 114, no. 13 (August 1989): 78-79. Copyright © 1989 by Reed Publishing, U.S.A.

Perhaps the best example of a marketing-oriented organization is the telephone system. The original marketing target, of supplying a telephone for every American home, was satisfied many years ago, at least in terms of practical fulfillment. AT&T could have closed up shop and gone home. Instead it created in our minds new needs—for multiple phones, colored phones, Mickey Mouse-shaped phones, cordless phones, car phones, call forwarding, and call waiting. If we don't have call waiting, our child stranded in a rain-drenched phone booth might be unable to reach us. Manufacturers of expensive pet foods appeal to that same sense of guilt, by suggesting that if we don't buy their products we don't love our pets. And it all works.

For libraries the scenario is far less startling. There are plenty of things we could suggest that are useful, that are needed, that nobody else provides, and that many individuals don't even know could be provided. We have never attempted to test the need for information services. Sometimes we simply offer what we can afford to offer, and then seek to "prove" retrospectively that it meets the need. Of course we do that by ruling anything claimed as a need that we cannot support as outside the scope of our operation.

Sometimes we seek to determine what we call need by asking people what they want, but that is not a determination of need. Our users can only react within the framework of "reasonableness" as we have trained them. Professionals in my corporate consulting assignments (who may or may not be library users but who are never angry with the library) are asked to hypothesize their personalized ideal information service, regardless of cost or even reasonableness. Many of them simply can't do it.

We have beaten the poverty we wear as a badge into their heads too long and too well. They simply don't expect much from us, and we live up to their expectations. When they want more they look elsewhere, and a whole new generation of information entrepreneurs have awakened them to that want and that need. They consider it outside the role of the library.

The Great Sin of Being Boring

Aside from the beneficial impact on the people we serve, there are certainly advantages for us in both marketing and selling, in creating an unserved information need. Peter Drucker has noted that managers only get credit for two things, innovation and marketing. Doing the same things as before, even if doing them well, creates that greatest of all management communication sins: it is boring. Drucker also assures us that price is never the real issue; if there is something people really want, price becomes irrelevant. If librarians ground down by "no money" propaganda have difficulty believing that, they need only look around at the video market that the society that could not afford libraries has created.

The practice of marketing—involving as it does a destabilizing of historical preconceptions and relationships and the creation of needs and demands for which there are as yet no resources—is, of course, a prime example of entrepreneurship. It is therefore surprising to find an article from so distinguished an academic scholar as James Govan that decries the development of entrepreneurship in our profession ("The Creeping Invisible Hand: Entrepreneurial Librarianship," *Library Journal*, January 1988, pp. 35-38). Surprising because it had not occurred to me that we were exactly awash in entrepreneurs. Govan's concern is valid, but I believe he makes several mistakes of oversimplification.

For one, he equates entrepreneurship (and presumably thereby marketing) with the rising pressure for cost recovery. That pressure is real; it is deplorable when it is applied as a pseudoeconomy without real benefit, real control, or real measurement. However, it has nothing to do with what it is we provide. Cost recovery can rear its ugly head in any setting; no library service is so trivial that somebody might not suggest that we ought to charge for it. Information programs, in their present form and in new forms that innovative entrepreneurial marketers might develop, certainly have a cost. How that cost is to be met is an entirely different question. Crossword puzzles to the contrary, cost and price are not synonyms. In fact, they are at best vaguely related.

Developing a Clientele

Librarians must determine what it is they ought to provide, and then develop a clientele for those services. That is marketing. A service provided must be paid for. We at least have to deal only with issues of cost recovery, and not of profit or return on investment. If it is important to us (and I think it is) that our services be provided to all users without reference to an ability to pay, then it becomes our job to fight for the adequate support funding that makes this possible. For us to adapt an attitude of "free or not at all," and then let our funding bodies determine what we will do, is a good way to edge us toward irrelevancy, because management usually just cares about the money.

It is we, and through our guidance our users, who must focus on what needs to happen as the prime issue. It has not been lost on me in years of management negotiations that if I don't bring to a discussion agenda the additional things I want and need, my management introduces an agenda of budget reduction. I certainly don't get everything I want, but at least I try to keep the discussion focused on the additions we may or may not get, and never let it get around to reductions at all. To repeat for the benefit of the still unconvinced: *there is money for whatever is important enough to do.*

The suggestion that we abdicate our responsibility as a simple reaction to our failure to obtain support funds does not solve any problems for any user group, even if it leaves us with unsoiled hands. The entrepreneurs who are guided by the profit motive and the clear recognition that people are willing to pay for useful information will not provide services to those unable to pay. They won't even care as we would. Insulating ourselves from that painful process of relating services to support funds is nothing more than a cop-out.

Entrepreneurs Indifferent to Service?

Govan makes, without substantiation, the surprising point that entrepreneurs are relatively indifferent to service. It is surprising because we know that without attention to service entrepreneurs fail and, more importantly, they know it. It is also surprising because we have never seen that much commitment to service, particularly in academic research libraries.

Two obvious examples come to mind. In our decisions about cutting materials budgets we have ruthlessly eliminated duplicates in favor of esoteric and perhaps unused single copies. That is clearly collection integrity as a higher priority than service. Our attitude when we are unable to supply something from our collections and must get it from another library is also interesting. Rather than apologizing, or somehow seeking to make it up to the inconvenienced client, we charge them a penalty.

My local supermarket manager is still willing to go back to the stockroom to find me the brand of cereal not on the shelf, or to call another store to have a shipment expedited. He has never suggested I pay extra for this, instead he has apologized for not having what I want on the shelf when I want it. That is service, and we could learn from it.

The Spectrum of Information Service

Libraries find themselves a part of the continuing spectrum of information service. Regardless of what happens to libraries, that activity is perhaps the fastest growing part of the economy. If we are declining in support level as everything around us grows, then clearly we are doing something wrong. We are not gathering the funds necessary for what we need to do, and yet we know those funds are there.

Whether we seek to get the money from our own institutional management, from a government subsidy, or by charging our users is obviously important to our commitment to an unfettered communication process. It is still irrelevant to the determination of what we need to do. They are both crucial, and yet distinct.

The key words that govern the decision process for the foreseeable future will be accountability and fiscal responsibility. If it is important that major research libraries participate in a national resource sharing effort, then our strategy cannot be to hide that cost from the university administration. It must be to specify what that cost is, and why the university needs to include it in the library budget.

The disastrous implications of a failure to budget for cooperation are certainly easy to demonstrate. If it is important for faculty and students to have access to bibliographic databases—and it is, because meaningful research is just about impossible without it—then it is essential that the library offer that service to anyone who needs it. Let the university administrators decide the funding mechanism. We probably even have some recommendations on who should pay for it.

Living in a Fool's Paradise

Libraries, particularly academic libraries, which hope that some other campus organization will take faculty online bibliographic and document needs off their hands because they are really outside the scope of the traditional library are living in a fool's paradise. Academic information use has changed dramatically through the communication linkages computers provide. That is not only true for our internal processing but also for what we provide our clients.

Academic libraries have always changed over time. I suspect that this change is nowhere as traumatic as the one brought about by the printed book. Academic faculty are by nature isolated, suspicious, and slow to change. But change they do, and we have the wonderful opportunity to lead them into new opportunities before they do it without us and assume we don't care. That is innovation. It is entrepreneurship. It is marketing.

If we don't do this, we can be sure that someone else will do it instead of us. It is too important and too obvious to be left undone. And they will find the funds we despair of finding. It will probably cost much more.

What happens to us then is that we are allowed to sit on a large and growing pile of reactive paper, to be used when and as somebody feels like using it. In that function we become simply bookkeepers, and academicians don't like keepers. They remind them of jailers.

The 26-Mile, 380-Yard Marathon

I have long had trouble with the fable of the tortoise and the hare. Granting that this rabbit is smug and supercilious, there is still no need for him to take a nap halfway through a race he could win in just a few minutes. Why not win first and nap later?

The true story I am going to relate is not about animals but intelligent and educated American citizens who run a marathon and quit five yards from the finish line. They quit not because they are tired, but because they feel they have run far enough.

An Investment in Youth

This strange tale concerns our scholarly communication system, and, most particularly, our scientific communication system. Our nation, like any enlightened country, invests heavily in the education of its youth. There are certainly those who would argue that we do not invest enough, but that is not the issue here. Suffice it to say that we spend a great deal of effort and resources on the education of our citizens over a long period of time.

The process can be argued to begin prenatally. It certainly becomes visible in preschool, kindergarten, and Head Start programs, all either funded directly or heavily subsidized through government intervention at the nation, state, and local level. The school lunch program is one of the few initiatives that seems to be immune to partisan attack, because that would alienate both parents and farmers at the same time.

Our concern for the support of education continues through high school and then college, abetted by (again, never enough) scholarships and student loans. As some of these students then go on to graduate school to pursue doctoral and

Reprinted, with changes, by permission of the author and *Library Journal* 115, no. 20 (November 15, 1990): 51-52. Copyright © 1990 by Reed Publishing, U.S.A.

post-doctoral studies, the government provides not only educational stipends and research grants, but, particularly in the physical sciences, comes up with the money for laboratory equipment and research and experimental materials.

Why do we do this? The answer is, of course, complex; one of the reasons is that this represents an investment in our future. At least some and perhaps many of these future scholars and scientists will extend frontiers and produce results eagerly expected by a nation of payers who have been waiting patiently for 20 years or more.

Finally our nest egg is ready to hatch. We can hardly wait for these graduates to put their findings into reports and journal articles so that we can disseminate them as widely as possible to the waiting nation. Right? Wrong!

At the point when our fledgling finally produces a return on investment, we tire of the race. We don't want to pay anymore, and we quit five yards short of the finish line. Having invested in our young (and sometimes not so young) scholars and scientists for all of their lives, we are suddenly disinterested in whether anybody finds out what they did. The scientific lore is full of stories about findings that lay about unnoticed for decades. Scientific research fascinates us; dissemination of that scientific research, by far the lesser cost, interests us not one whit.

Full of Energy and Fury?

The only plausible explanation I can find comes from the writings of C. Northcote Parkinson, who argued that the amount of energy and fury expended on a problem was inversely proportional to its importance. We support education and scientific research fully in part because it is so expensive. We challenge the costs of disseminating the results of that research largely because it is so cheap.

Parkinson knew exactly what he was talking about. Large costs are too massive to permit investigation, let alone challenge. If the savings and loan bailout turns out to cost several hundred billion dollars more than originally anticipated, what does it matter? However, if somebody suggests spending $10 million to support the dissemination of information for which we have already spent billions, some who pretend that they monitor costs find that last expenditure to be somehow outrageous.

Libraries Spend Too Little

The problem for library programs both nationally and locally is not that we spend so much, but that we spend so little. Small programs are always most vulnerable to attack. When I lecture on strategies to library managers, the same lesson is there to be learned. Never submit a request to management for the addition of one clerk, because one clerk is too trivial a request to interest anyone; Parkinson's Law will strike yet one more time. Far better to submit a justification for 10 reference librarians with terminal access, and settle for a compromise of five now and the other five phased serious. What can a nation that spends $50 billion a year on pet food not afford?

Part of the reason for a failure to subsidize information dissemination when we have subsidized everything else is that this is perceived in part as a "library cost," and libraries have proven over and over that they will do whatever has to be done whether they get money or not.

Obviously, nobody ever gives anyone any money in this kind of scenario. However, here the simplistic and smug logic does not work. Communication does not work very well now, through a whole range of factors including lack of planning, naïveté, greed, and simple ignorance. It is most important that those government officials most concerned with the effectiveness of decision processes and expenditures be made to understand that saving money in some cases ends up wasting a great deal more money in others.

When something is cheap it is not therefore necessarily cost-effective or cost-beneficial. I tried to make this point when I wrote about the process of contracting our federal libraries ("What Price Salami?" *Library Journal*, January 1988, p. 58). Contracting out libraries may or may not be a cost-effective action, but we will never know unless we first specify what these libraries are supposed to *do*. Cheap can become very expensive when there are no returns on the investment; the agencies now doing the contracting simply have no way of knowing.

Our Info Dissemination Secret

My indictment is not just bipartisan but multipartisan. While some segments of the political spectrum are perhaps more favorably inclined to support libraries than others, none of them really know why, particularly as we relate the cost of dissemination that is largely the responsibility of librarians to the investment cost of the material now being poorly disseminated.

Even some of our supporters don't know that libraries disseminate. Even some of us don't know. They think we store information in case someone asks for it.

The Large Get Larger

This administration, earlier administrations, and perhaps a number of administrations yet to come are dedicated to the premise of "small" government. The fact that government gets larger as we shrilly insist it really is getting smaller is little consolation; as victims of the Parkinsonian principles, our libraries really do get smaller because we were small to begin with.

Only the large get larger, because they are too large to permit tampering with their size. Try closing obsolete military or naval bases, and see what reaction you get even from local Congresspeople who hate all *other* military expenditures.

One of the premises of this ongoing philosophy is that government should not be competing with industry for things that the private sector can do and is willing to do. As applied to the information process, this is a simplistic argument, if "dissemination" through the private sector is at a price that forecloses use by those of our citizens who need it.

"Information Stamps"

We can, of course, have the best of both worlds if we decide to subsidize the information process on the basis of need, as we have already subsidized the process of producing the information and not even on any needs basis.

We can do this quite easily using the model already developed in the food dissemination program, which is a commercial process dependent on an exchange of money for goods.

We do not tamper with this process by distributing free food. Instead we distribute food stamps so that the recipients can not only participate in the process but can even select what it is that they will "buy" with this distributed purchasing power.

It does not work perfectly, but it is one of our more effective programs, and it is far less dehumanizing than the food lines common in other countries.

If we have maintained the privatization of the food process through food stamps, then does not the privatization of the information process depend equally on information stamps? Or is food only for the body and not for the mind?

If the premise is that all information products and services that *can* be handled by the private sector *should* be handled by the private sector, then it must follow that what remains for government dissemination through the Government Printing Office (GPO) and the National Technical Information Service (NTIS) *must be the things that lose money.*

We must disseminate this information anyway, because we have already produced it, and that is where the real cost has occurred.

Stopping now is the equivalent of the marathon minus the last five yards. If you don't want to subsidize dissemination, then stop the undertaking of all research and save some real money.

Keep What Sells; Trash What Doesn't

Fortunately, there is not yet any publicly elected official who supports this option. The acid test for government information dissemination programs would seem to be that they had better lose a lot of money, because if they make money or break even they presumably destroy their free-market credibility.

The adherence by both political parties to the conspiracy that both NTIS and the GPO should recover their costs makes a travesty of any philosophical semblance to a free enterprise system. If the GPO and NTIS are to be run as businesses, then they must be allowed the freedom of making normal, everyday business decisions. This means, quite simply, keeping and heavily marketing the stuff that sells, and trashing the stuff that doesn't sell.

That is the "business" of information, but the U.S. government is not in the "business" of either disseminating information or of running libraries, but of promoting the national good.

The Final Link

Our libraries are the final and therefore most crucial link in a process of encouraging and supporting education, inquiry, and research that begins in preschool programs or earlier.

Clobbering the agencies innocently stuck with distributing the documents mandated billions of dollars ago, and clobbering the libraries that then try to turn all of these potential boondoggles into a return on investment makes no sense. Parkinson would understand immediately why government officials do it anyway.

Hiding the Cost of Information[1]

As a profession we argue endlessly about the quality of our activities in providing information. From my background as an educator, practicing librarian, and corporate official, I have concluded that while obviously the quality of the service we provide varies with the abilities of the specific librarian, on balance what we do is cost-effective. This must be evaluated with the recognition that there is much in the recent literature, both business and general, to suggest that the availability of information is important, both for decision making and for quality of life. Protagonists such as Daniel Bell and international corporations like AT&T and IBM have convinced all citizens that information is vital. Just to make the point obvious, there is no visible group that champions ignorance as a desired way of life, or as a desirable mechanism for making decisions. The importance of information, and its value in providing for its disseminators a greater level of prestige and remuneration, is now clearly understood both by M.B.A. and computer science graduates, who have concluded that they are, after all this time, suddenly "information professionals." Those of us who have observed the development of these people do know better, but that knowledge will not serve us if we are the only ones who possess it.

Frugality Without Risk

Librarians fall into the grouping that Peter Drucker calls the service professions. Drucker is so fascinated by the characteristics of this group that he plans to spend the rest of his career examining the not-for-profit sector and service professionals, who tend to act as though they were in the not-for-profit sector even when they are not. Drucker characterizes these individuals, including nurses and social workers, as being trapped by their

Reprinted, with changes, by permission of the author and the publishers of *The Bottom Line* 4, no. 4 (Winter 1990): 14-19. Copyright © 1990 by Neal-Schuman Publishers, Inc.

adherence to the "moral imperative." Drucker means that somehow, with or without resources, service professionals accept the premise that they have to do whatever needs to be done. Articles in our literature about burnout in a profession publicly assumed to be low in prestige and salaries but also low in stress confirm the premise that we think we must do everything even if with nothing. The problem for you as service professionals, Drucker notes, is that once management understands that with or without funds you will still do whatever you perceive needs to be done, and that they will not be blamed, you are trapped. You will never get the required resources, since you have shown you don't need them.

Librarians have certainly become more adept at understanding the budgetary process, at being able to read accounting statements and decipher invoices. However, along with the others Drucker describes as service professionals, we have had difficulty in relating programs to budgets. Most specifically we have had difficulty in making the point, crucial in basic Management 101, that in a well-run organization it is the programs that drive budgets and not the other way around. Our bosses understand this as it applies in general, but they fail to see the connection between budgets and programs in libraries, since regardless of budgets we seem to manage to do everything that needs to be done. Nor do we apply concepts either of upward delegation or of forcing higher-level management to recognize that while responsibility can be delegated downward, it can never be abdicated. The premise that librarians need somehow accomplish only two things—stay within the budget and keep the customer from being surly or at least turning surly toward higher management—is something that non-librarian managers above the level of the library gladly settle for, even when they understand that their own responsibilities for monitoring their subordinates vaguely suggest that they should not settle for so little.

For our part, we librarians have developed a variety of strategies for coping in this worst of all possible world scenarios, "Do whatever needs to be done regardless of resources, and by the way resources will be declining." We absorb, by working harder, by developing burnout, by staying late, and by paying each other rotten salaries, even though authors as early as Bo Hedberg noted that nothing can ever be absorbed because an admission of absorption capability is a self-indictment of having been indolent in the past.[2] He notes that we can shift and transfer priorities, but quite simply a cut in budgets means a cut in something, and the ultimate responsibility for that rests with the people who decreed the budget cut. In the political framework credit for frugality must then be weighed against the risk incurred by a decrease in services. If there is no such risk, then frugality is the obvious selection, because it always carries at least some credit.

In addition to absorbing, librarians have also shifted priorities, not so much in terms of users' service needs as in terms of political expediency. Studies as early as the mid-1970s[3] indicated quite clearly that the shift from a monographic to a serials-based acquisition budget in academic libraries was not based on the decision that monographs were relatively worthless, but on the realization that the cut of a serial subscription was a highly visible and confrontational act, while the impact of a cut in monographic funds could be blurred by a delay in purchasing, or by the elimination of monographs selected by the librarians themselves. Our willingness and ability to passively accept 25 percent serials price increases in the framework of 6 percent overall budget increases speaks loudly of our inability or unwillingness to control our own domain, and our reluctance to confront hard issues. All of these are tactics for avoiding problems and confrontation, even though the literature of management reports to us quite confidently that good managers bring their bosses more problems than poor ones, because problems may only be a synonym for opportunities.

Who Will Control Decisions?

However, of particular concern to me in this paper is the tactic adopted by many librarians, when the cost could no longer be deferred or "absorbed" in priority shifting, of transferring a cost to an organization outside the library. This tactic, observed most directly in both academic and corporate settings, is not cost-effective for the parent organization. Indeed, it may incur greater costs if, as is common, with the transfer of funding responsibility comes a transfer of control over decisions. Individuals not educated and trained in the information process will most certainly make worse decisions about how to do things and what to buy, when those decisions involve competencies acquired as part of the library education and training process. They may spend less or they may spend more, but their decisions will be intuitive and uninformed. The pitfall for us, unlike for brain surgeons, is that the unqualified don't necessarily understand that they are unqualified.

It is generally accepted that information is an increasingly important commodity, and assumed that society, even if not libraries, will therefore spend more on the information process in the future than in the past. When, in spite of this, the cost of libraries is kept down while the cost of other information transactions rises, it becomes only natural for executives in any setting to dissociate the process of information management from the process of running libraries, as though the two were unrelated. What organizations then develop is a library policy as separate from a far more important and far more dynamic information policy. Library policy becomes simply a strategy for providing the clerical and routine functions of obtaining things on demand and controlling the whereabouts of the material purchased. That, of course, is nothing more than a classical stockroom function. To make the scenario even worse, these routine functions will become increasingly mechanized on the one hand and decentralized on the other. Even today, our customers do not depend on us either to identify specific documents in a computer file or to order a copy. If that is all librarians plan to do, our customers will no longer need us. Our role, if we have one, is to participate uniquely in the information process, separated as an objective even if not as a mechanism from the document process. The information process contains both the glamour and the money.

The Golden Rule

The funds an organization spends on the information process are obviously always negotiable, but are easy to negotiate because everyone accepts the importance of information, and importance implies cost. We should also understand that, given a scenario in which money is going to be spent in any case, it is politically essential that we control the expenditures. From a political standpoint, one of the observations about the Golden Rule is that those with the gold make the rules. People with large budgets are more important than people with small budgets, and having a small and cheap library carries no advantages, particularly since nobody is in a position to define small or cheap. There is no library that couldn't be made smaller or cheaper, particularly if there is no visible impact or dangerous repercussion. In any case, our bosses will certainly try.

Those are the political ramifications, but there are also ramifications of quality and cost-effectiveness that dictate that librarians should control the budget for the information process. These implications exist for us, for our managers, and for our customers, and that covers just about anyone. Centralizing librarian control over information expenditures is, therefore, a win-win-win scenario.

The Power Base of Service

The importance of all this for librarians is easiest to demonstrate. In any organizational environment, and most certainly in the corporations and universities with which I am most familiar, power comes from the exercise of unique expertise or authority, the control of turf. Purchasing, accounting, legal, personnel, and security departments understand this quite well. They earn no income, and the contribution they provide uniquely may be difficult to prove. What is so hard about hiring somebody if you have money to pay a salary, or what is so complex about calling a vendor and arranging a shipment? Service organizations are not about to get into a discussion over what they know better than you. They simply obtain an organizationally exclusive franchise. Nobody is allowed to do what they are uniquely permitted to do. They understand, probably better than we, that the power base of service professionals is that they control the interaction with their clients. Certainly doctors don't need to have this explained to them.

For librarians, development of an implementation strategy must rest first of all on our belief that we can do what we do professionally more effectively than others and that the alternative will result either in poorer quality or greater cost, or both; all unacceptable in an information society. Is literature searching by librarians more cost-effective for the parent organization than end user searching? Probably in most cases, and the hypothesis can always be tested. We have the skills developed through education and training, and we almost always also have lower salaries. Gaps in subject knowledge that might affect the search can be bridged through a process of interviewing and question negotiation that we understand pretty well. If our users just send in the questions and fail to communicate? Then we refuse to undertake the search, and we point out to management that we are not going to waste organizational funds because others are irresponsible.

The solutions are really quite simple and can be found in lots of executive management handbooks, but we have no interest in applying them. Abdicating library tasks is not a bad strategy when they are boring and trivial things we don't want to do in any case, but abdicating our professional bread and butter makes no sense. We do it because we perceive that being cheap is a preferred strategy to being important, even as we understand that the appearance of economy is not necessarily economy. There is an old corporate saw that comes to mind, but you must be careful to whom you tell it. "We are going to have economy no matter how much it costs." For us, from a political standpoint, it might earn us a temporary respite from being hassled. However, it is a foolish strategy for us over the long term; it is also a total abdication of our responsibilities for spending our management's money wisely.

Displaying the Costs of Information Service

The significance of a process that properly displays rather than hides and scatters the cost of information is almost self-evident. I have served as a consultant in numerous situations in which I was brought in to evaluate the effectiveness and cost of the library. In my very first meeting with top management, I pointed out that such an exercise would be a waste of time. The library and its cost of operation is not an end in itself. It is a means to an end. That end can be discussed or refined, but ultimately it is assumed to be the most cost-effective provision of information to individuals who need it to further the objectives of the parent organization. Understanding that process, and the cost of that process, is essential for management decisions, but I suggest that they do not really know how this process works and what it costs. They only know the cost of managing the library.

If they had mechanisms for assuring that all information costs were properly displayed they would have a basis for deciding not only whether the money should be spent but who should spend it. However, since they have no such mechanism, they understand only the funds spent by the library. Other costs are routinely miscoded; time spent by nonlibrarian professionals on the information gathering and information analysis process is usually not collected at all. Therefore, upper managers run a real risk, particularly if they monitor library costs closely while ignoring all other cost allocations, of driving costs underground and probably increasing them further. In an age of information, no organization can arbitrarily limit information access by economic fiat. It can only seek to determine what it gets for the money it spends on information. It can do this best through the centralization of the information process through the only information professionals they have, their librarians. Others, I point out, were educated in other disciplines, and only adopted information as a means toward personal advancement. I close my argument with one simple question: "Are you interested in the real cost of the information process, or are you interested in some sort of pseudo-analysis that makes *it appear* that information costs have been reduced, whether or not this is true?"

There can only be one answer to this question, at the level of upper management, at least I have encountered no other. Financial managers, I have found, are my most immediate allies. They are interested in the implementation of a very simple agenda, the accurate reporting, control, and if possible reduction of costs. They and librarians are on the same side. Operational professionals—chemists, economists, biology researchers, and historical scholars—have a far more complex value system in which perhaps they don't mind at all that the parent organization spends more money to provide them with additional comforts, as long as they don't have to admit it. Indeed, it is even possible that upper management might consciously decide to spend more money to create this level of professional contentment. If so, that is management's privilege. However, any argument that the library must take particular care to control costs because of an economy wave, can be pointed out as the absurd contradiction it is. These waves, like the surf, are continuous and have no relationship to economic reality; they are decreed simply because they are considered good housekeeping practice.

There is one further point of admonition. The argument that a dollar spent on literature searching is a dollar spent no matter who does it, and the question is not which budget receives the charge but rather where more return is received for the dollar, works with higher level managers. It may not work with the managers directly above the level of the library, who may indeed decide, although never admit, that they would prefer the cost of two economists at a higher salary performing bad literature searches to the cost of one librarian at a lower salary, as long as the higher cost is not in their own budget. They may indeed attempt to force this sort of value system on you. However, it then becomes your responsibility as the resident information professional to point out to the highest level manager that this is an idea that looks good but is in fact dumb.

Is there risk in such an action? Of course there is, but there are ways to minimize and control risks. Librarians, whose activities allow them to communicate with just about everybody in carrying out their work and to bypass the strict organizational reporting lines, as long as the contact is presumably for the purpose of communicating information, should certainly be able to plant a few seeds in the process.

No individual, in any organization, can be perceived as furthering a mechanism that has as its objective personal empire building and aggrandizement. However, if strengthening the library's control over information costs is seen as the most direct way for information cost-effectiveness, it is hardly our fault that we benefit.

Information Ombudsman

The earlier sections of this paper are heavily devoted to strategies of political negotiation that strengthen the role of librarians. In representing our user communities, however, our role of ombudsman becomes most crucial of all. Users, as I have already noted, are not experts in the information process, and that is true even when they don't realize it. Their experience with other librarians may have been one in which the library interaction was passive and reactive. Our own literature is full of the confusion between user need, which we make almost no attempt to determine, and user want, to which we tend to react slavishly, even if it is the wrong want. No doctor would allow himself or herself to be so treated.

The loss in prestige in this process has already been noted. However, the loss for our users is even more serious. Simply put, users have no way of telling a good library from a bad one. They can tell a big one from a small one, a courteous one from a rude one, and they can even evaluate the rapidity with which we obtain information from another outside library, although they tend to forgive us unforgivable delays of several weeks or more. Even when they do evaluate, they can only do so within the framework of what they asked for, and not within the framework of what they needed. Nor, for that matter, can we totally tell. However, we have a better chance at it because we tend to know what information exists and what the access alternatives are. As a minimum, we must assure that information need is not artificially suppressed by a system that concentrates on cost rather than on value.

Information "need" is a fragile flower and it is easily suppressed and sublimated. If management wants a cheap information system, it can perhaps get one. It can certainly get one that looks cheap, if the fascination is only with library costs. However, the risks of ignorance, already noted, are so enormous that few organizations will consciously opt for ignorance just to save the money. What they would prefer is an information system that operates on the basis of cost benefit, but that is probably not possible. What they can get is an information system that operates on the premise of cost-effectiveness, and that involves centralization of both cost collection and spending authority. I recognize that the concept of centralization runs contrary to current trends in management structure, which state, quite accurately in most cases, that a decentralization of decision making also improves the process of evaluating decisions. The premise does not work for libraries, and indeed it needs to be pointed out that some functions remain centralized in all organizations for reasons that are not too difficult to fathom. That almost always includes a centralized approach to legal determinations and decisions. Legal systems are centralized because non-lawyers are seen to lack the knowledge to make decisions. The precedent exists.

Several reasons exist why decentralization of decision making does not work when applied to libraries. First, the cost of individual transactions (one book, one literature search, one interlibrary loan) is too trivial to warrant control. As a general rule of thumb, just about anything that costs less than $100 is more expensive to control than to buy. Second, and as already noted, libraries and librarians rarely have exclusive control over the information process. If getting material or information through the library is too cumbersome or too difficult, the user still has two options. He or she can do it personally or purchase the service from some other source, usually disguising the cost so that even if it is higher nobody knows. Second, and even more dangerously, the user can pretend that the information was never needed in the first place.

Determining the ROI

The reason that cost-benefit comparisons rarely work when applied to libraries is that the savings are almost never recoverable. The research department might agree that the services of the library are worth two laboratory scientists, but it is not willing to cut two laboratory scientists from its own staff. The best it is willing to do is to agree that a wonderful library prevents the need for an increased research staff. However, any accountant will note very quickly that as the additional research scientists were never approved in the first place, the savings are not real. And indeed they are not. We are trading real cost reductions, or at least invisible costs, for the promise that more, better, and timelier information will probably provide a return on investment. It is a risky premise, but if properly constructed, it is a proposal that few managements can turn down. The problem in present scenarios of library budget starvations is that the question is never asked.

It is never asked because users can adapt to poor library service and quickly rationalize that what is difficult to obtain was never needed in the first place. In many years of consulting, I have never found a corporate library or academic library whose users felt that the quality of professional interaction, as opposed to quantity of material and responsiveness of clerical service, was unacceptable. To do this would cast doubt on their own work. Thus a presentation to upper management made on a Monday morning takes place with the confident expression that it is a fully informed presentation, and having made the claim it is not difficult even to believe it. We librarians lack the control to prove the value of information that is readily available in biological experiments. Rats deprived of Vitamin B become sickly and die. What happens to researchers deprived of adequate information? We can't make the case, because we lack the ability to establish the test group and the control group. It is, of course, plausible to uncover specific cost and time savings directly resulting from one exotic piece of information unearthed by a brilliant librarian. However, these actions, even if found, will serve only to defend this year's budget. What will you do for an encore? Effective libraries, properly staffed with an appropriate division of labor between professionals and clerks and between professionals and users can be justified because they make sense. That is probably the best we can do, but it is really all that the personnel and purchasing departments have done to justify their existence, and they manage to do just fine.

Pain Means No Gain

Another phenomenon suggests that nothing should ever be done that makes library use for users difficult or cumbersome. Since information ignorance does not have to be admitted, Mooers' Law, promulgated more than 30 years ago to explain why some information systems are used and others are not, immediately comes into play.[4] Calvin Mooers makes a very simple point. "An information system will tend not to be used whenever it is more painful and troublesome for a customer to have information than not to have it." I have seen this simple premise validated many times. The point for organizations, and for librarians who have the expertise if not always the responsibility and authority to monitor information flow, is never to control and limit the use of information. It is rather to encourage and to enhance it. Cost-effective information systems are obviously better than wasteful information systems, but the existence of information systems is invariably safer than their absence. There are enough built-in constraints in user behavior to assure that a failure to seek information is always a possibility if the system is cumbersome. Suggesting to reluctant users that they really ought to do their own information searches whether they want to or not poses one such risk. They may do it badly, but worse they may not do it at all; there is no organizational process to expose this lapse because it is never reported. Users will also try to avoid an information system if the process is tied down by the red tape of budgetary approvals and cost transfers. It is that danger in allocation mechanisms that I will discuss in the last section of this paper.

Dangerous Allocation Mechanisms

There is nothing necessarily wrong with allocating the cost of the library to user groups, as long as that allocation is made according to a formula that makes sense. The number of professionals in an organization that are presumed to use the library in their work suggests such a formula. This is easy to determine (the personnel department can usually supply the numbers), it seems both fair and reasonable, and it makes the allocation process simple. It does not require detailed record keeping on the part of the library. I have seen examples in which the cost of keeping the records in both the library and in accounting was far greater than even the most optimistically presumed savings. It frees the users from the annoyance of securing approvals from their own managers for things they want the library to do. Approvals rarely work as a control in any case, except for the most junior of library users. Requests for senior users are approved as a matter of routine, but not without a prestige cost to the library that is assumed to have instigated this silly control on its own initiative. We know it to be untrue and unfair, but librarians are assumed to like rules and red tape. Where the control might work, it works to discourage the information work of junior people, who, of course, need the information most of all.

An allocation process, if based on *potential* rather than *actual* use, simplifies record keeping, and should therefore be immediately embraced by hordes of grateful accountants. It also encourages library use and penalizes library nonuse, which is the whole point. Use the library because you are paying for it whether you use it or not! The suggestion that people would use the library just because they are paying for it, putting aside their other work, is really too silly to be taken seriously. If anyone suggests it, research will quickly disprove it. Formula allocation by presumed rather than actual use also has a built-in barometer for either increasing or decreasing library budgets. Librarians are now free to market, and if those services are found desirable, the justifications for an increased budget and increased allocations are already built in. There is no risk of developing an information system that is too good. There is, on the other hand, considerable risk of developing an information system that is either insufficient for the organization's needs, or ineffectively managed in a way that wastes money. If this happens, the fact that the waste is not immediately obvious is little consolation. The risk is magnified by the recognition that all of this can happen without anyone knowing. Ignorance is not bliss. In every consultation assignment I have found that management has no idea whether or not it has an effective or adequate information system. Management only knows what the library part costs.

Proving Uniqueness

Libraries share the lot of almost all overhead organizations in that their contributions to overall organizational goals are more difficult to prove. They do not contribute revenue dollars to the sales total or student tuition income to the Bursar's Office. That problem is unavoidable. We can learn from the way other service organizations have dealt with this issue, invariably by establishing their uniqueness and their role as gatekeepers along the critical path. Safety here comes from establishing a scenario that suggests that: a) it must be done; and b) only we can do it because we do it better, faster, and cheaper.

Information has a value, and it has a cost. There is nothing to be gained in trying to hide or to distribute that cost. It loses control, and loses impact. Let's build our justifications on the triple premise that what we do is important to the point of being crucial, that it may be costly but is nevertheless cost-effective, and that we are the experts who must make all of these determinations. If we don't succeed in doing this, we lose. However, so do the organizations that hired us on the premise that there was something we could do uniquely. It is high time to remind them what a great bargain increased expenditures may be. *If* they are controlled and monitored by experts who know what they are doing. *If* management further has the assurance it now so sadly lacks that the visible expenditure is also the real expenditure. Waste and ignorance are unacceptable. It must be our point that this recognition must supersede comfortable illusions.

Notes

1. This article is based on the presentation, "Paying the Piper: The True Costs of Information," presented at the American Library Association Conference, Chicago, Illinois, June 1990.

2. Hedberg, Bo, et al. "Camping on Seesaws: Prescriptions for a Self-Designing Organization." *Administrative Sciences Quarterly* 21, no. 1 (1976): 41-65.

3. White, Herbert S. "Publishers, Libraries and Costs of Journal Subscriptions in Times of Funding Retrenchment." *The Library Quarterly* 46, no. 4 (October 1976): 359-77.

4. Mooers, Calvin. "Mooers' Law, or Why Some Retrieval Systems Are Used and Others Are Not." *American Documentation* 11, no. 3 (July 1960): 204.

Librarians, Journal Publishers and Scholarly Information: Whose Leaky Boat Is Sinking?

Although I am a librarian and library educator, I think I bring a balanced understanding to the involved and sometimes delicate relationship between librarians and publishers of scholarly journals. I have been in the publishing business, both as a creator of secondary journals, when I was senior vice president for operations of the Institute for Scientific Information, and as an intermediary between publishers and librarians, when I was president of a major American subscription agency. My research into the economic interdependence between publishers of scholarly journals and the librarians, who, in some cases, comprise virtually the entire customer base, has brought me into contact with many representatives of both groups. Neither group is unanimous in its view of their interdependence. For every publisher who sees libraries as docile cash cows to be milked regularly, there is at least another who is genuinely concerned about what may be happening to the scholarly communication process, and to what disasters that might lead. And there are librarians who disagree with my conclusions and my recommendations for future action.

My interest in the subject was originally aroused by research undertaken for the National Science Foundation in the period 1976-80. This was prompted by several trends of that time. Both the amount of dollars and the percentage of the budget spent for periodicals (publishers call them journals—just one indication of difficulty in communication) had increased dramatically during the period 1972-78. United States academic library budgets at that time were growing at the unspectacular, but certainly not disastrous, rate of about 5 percent a year, while the dollars demanded of them by scholarly journal publishers were growing at the rate of over 15 percent in calm years and more than 25 percent in turbulent ones. It was obvious, even at this early stage, that something had to give.

Publishers justified these price increases then, as they do today, by a variety of explanations, some plausible and some simply insulting to the intelligence of their librarian customers. For journals published outside of the U.S., it was pointed out that the dollar had weakened. That had certainly been true for a while. It was equally true that during the early part of the period being researched, the dollar had been remarkably strong. For about the last five years of the 1980s, the dollar has been fairly stable, with governments and international banks making sure that it neither rises nor falls precipitously. We can expect that for the foreseeable future the dollar will remain relatively stable. But none of this really matters. It is irrelevant, first of all, because libraries already commit all available dollars (and some dollars not so readily available) to the purchase of journal subscriptions. If the dollar is strong, they spend more. If the dollar is weak, they still spend more. If you begin to suspect that the laws of economics have nothing to do with this, read on. Exchange rates are irrelevant, secondly, because dollar fluctuations are presumably the problem of the foreign vendor, who must shift strategies and reef sails accordingly. If prices go up automatically because the dollar is weaker, the vendor has to make his products more competitive. Japanese automobile manufacturers understand this. Why don't European journal publishers?

Publishers also pointed to increased costs in labor, printing and paper, but none of this accounts for a 25 percent annual hike in prices. In general, given some good years and some bad years, publishing does not differ dramatically from the rest of the economy. The cost of my daily newspaper has risen, but it hasn't doubled in price every four years. Publishers also argue that while the cost of journals has increased, the *cost per page* is really quite stable because the journal has grown in size, thanks in part to twinning, spin-offs, special issues and *Festschriften* (at jubilee prices). In fact, some publishers have trotted out charts and graphs at library association meetings that show only a modest slant in the curve, but all this does is confirm the old adage that figures lie and liars figure.

Perhaps "liars" is unkind, certainly to those publishers who really do care. However, the statistics of growth in journal size are irrelevant when we recognize that at no time have librarians, who are presumably the customers, asked that journals get larger. It would be equivalent to a motor car manufacturer announcing that doubling in price was quite logical because next year's model would be twice as long. It is just possible that the customers might decide that they did not want a longer car, perhaps even at the same price. No librarians have ever asked for thicker journals at twice the price.

Are librarians seen as customers, or simply purchasing agents who do what they are told to do by the *real* customers—the community of academic scholars (a group to which I also belong)? I think we all know who the presumed real customers are. Simply put, they are the people with all of the authority and none of the responsibility, and they are capable of rigging the game to suit themselves. "Scholarly communication" and perhaps even "academic freedom" are often shields to excuse petty and petulant attitudes. In truth, we are dealing with neither of these principles, but with the issue of academic credit, and here the authors, referees, editors, presumed readers and certainly credit dispensers on tenure and promotion boards are the same individuals with different hats. The refereeing process to control scholarly publication stopped working long ago. I participate in this process on behalf of perhaps half a dozen journals, and I have learned that I cannot keep an article from being published. I can only keep it out of one journal and force it to be published in another. Since the author, or would-be author, is anxious to validate the prestige of his publishing vehicle, purchase by libraries of marginal journals is shrilly demanded, because these represent the safety valve. We already know the journals highly ranked in perception studies and we buy these routinely.

The game is therefore simple and everyone except librarians is on the same side of the ball. Authors/referees/editors/readers/promotion reviewers opt for more and larger journals because this suits their process. The fact that these journals then cost more is an irrelevant inconvenience when confronted by claimed threats to academic freedom and integrity. Publishers and even subscription agents are on the side of greater dollar billings. Subscription agents get their cut as a percentage of the total invoice, and a $500 title generates more revenue for them than a $200 title. Publishers, of course, like higher prices, not only for the obvious reason, but also because of the additional benefit of cash flow. Journals, unlike monographs, represent front-end cash flow. Virtually nothing is spent until everything is collected. Money earns money, and some of this subscription income can earn interest for 6 to 18 months and even longer.

It is of little surprise, then, that the laws of economics, which have worked quite nicely to control monographic publishing (sometimes precisely because of the activities of journal publishers) do not apply to journals. Properly titled, properly positioned, and properly promoted scholarly journals will succeed, and the editorial quality of the publication (or indeed the price) has very little to do with this. It can be argued that some scholarly journals have died, but a close examination will probably show that these are the journals published at the low end of the spectrum by academic departments or small professional societies that do not know how to market. Journals started by the major commercial scholarly publishers almost all succeed. More journals are started, sometimes through the process of twigging, or they get larger. In any case, they get more expensive. And they are hardly ever aborted. Indeed, they need never be, as long as certain simple precautions are taken:

1. Find a small and narrow area not presently covered in the journal literature. Academic fragmentation constantly opens such opportunities. The publisher need only be watchful.

2. Aim this journal at a small group, perhaps represented by only one scholar in a major research university.

3. Find the most prestigious editor and editorial advisory board you can enlist.

4. Target your publicity and literature at each individual enthusiast. Frequency of publication and price do not matter. You are marketing

security. This is his one key journal and the library must subscribe to it. The publisher doesn't even have to tell the library because, if properly prompted, the scholar will.

The members of the editorial advisory board also benefit because they receive both academic credit and a free subscription. All you need do is promise them they have to do very little work. The situation is not dissimilar from fund-raising letterheads that list an honorary chairman or honorary sponsor. Sometimes (to be fair) sincere members of an editorial advisory board reject particularly silly, irrelevant, or repetitive manuscripts, but they will then appear in other journals. The libraries get no relief from referees' rejections.

Major European commercial publishers, with a large part of their market in the U.S., have other devices to improve their profits. One consists of manipulation of the exchange rate, by pegging price equivalents in currencies other than those of the country of publication at conversion rates which favor the vendor. International publishers could, if they wished, hedge their risk by investing, at very low premiums, in foreign currency futures at a pre-set rate. Libraries also, at least in theory, have the option of paying foreign publishers in their own currencies, and subscription agencies use that device as a matter of normal business procedure. Some publishers seek to beat this system by insisting that the U.S. library purchase its subscriptions in U.S. dollars from an American subsidiary at a price that has no relationship to the advertised price in the country of publication. This requirement is sometimes justified on the premise that these U.S. subsidiaries provide "a convenience" for American libraries, which only suggests how far such publishers have trivialized the presumed vendor-customer relationship with librarians. Some publishers treat the feelings of librarians as irrelevant (short of an occasional conference cocktail party because even children must be given a treat now and then) and concentrate instead on cultivating the "real" clients, who have no money but are perceived to have power. If a U.S. subsidiary provides economy and convenience, it does so for the publisher, not the librarian customer.

Following the first National Science Foundation study in 1976, with Bernard Fry as my co-investigator at the Indiana University Research Center for Library and Information Science, we predicted that the process, already apparent, of transferring more and more library funds to journal acquisitions had to end. Indeed, librarians and publishers maintained that it had just about ended and predicted quite confidently that the future was based on a total library community journals budget that would increase by an amount approximately related to normal inflationary growth, or about 5 percent. If it did not, we and they foresaw the start of a death spiral, in which major powerful journals would kill off the weaker ones, and in which some of the more fragile disciplines in the humanities might disappear entirely under the pressure of funding new physical science titles and of price increases that might approach 25 percent a year. We predicted that this simply could not happen. Our report included a cartoon of a librarian and publisher sharing a leaky rowboat, each stating that the other's half of the boat was sinking.

Some of our predictions were proven correct, but others just as obviously were not. We simply could not predict or imagine the willingness, let alone the ability, of librarians to fund an annual extortion of 20 percent and more above the previous year. The dexterity of librarians in finding this money must amaze even the most callous of these publishers. Extortion is not too strong a term to describe an invoice involving a 20 percent increase presented to the customer without consulting that customer or listening to his input. Suggesting that the ultimate clients have been consulted (although, of course, they haven't been, they have only been humored) does not change the case. The ultimate client, lest we forget, has neither money nor responsibility.

Our later studies for the National Science Foundation examined other myths, some perpetuated by librarians and others by publishers. Librarians had argued that interlibrary lending arrangements opened new marketing vistas for publishers by exposing formerly uninformed scholars to attractive new publications. Publishers by contrast were concerned that cooperative arrangements by librarians would cut into their potential sales market. This has not happened, at least not yet. If and when it does, I might wonder why it took so long, except that I also know why. It is because the "ultimate" users are less concerned with access than they are with local ownership. It is a game we librarians taught the scholars in the first place, and now both they and the publishers have learned to play it. It will end only if and when libraries stop reporting holdings either in total volume or in specific titles, and simply deal with requests, as they are generated, whether they have the titles on the shelves or not. The technology to deal with requests on a one-day basis already exists, but the problems are more deep-seated than that. They do not involve copyright laws. Copyright laws are vague at best, cumbersome to enforce, and the needs of the numerous users will always win out over the interests of the few and unpopular publishers if and when the question is brought to public attention. The U.S. Supreme Court case of *Williams & Wilkins v. the National Library of Medicine* should have taught us that. The case preceded the revised U.S. Copyright Law, and under the old law legal precedent clearly favored W&W. However, the Court voted 5-4 in favor of NLM. How could it do otherwise? I am amazed that only five judges agreed that the needs of medical research and the potential for saving lives outweighed the legal rights of an individual publisher. If it ever came to a clear confrontation between the rights of publishers and of scholarly research and communication, publishers would lose. However, there will be no such case. The only possible protagonists are librarians, who have shown neither the power nor the inclination to take on such a task, particularly without support from their parent institutions. The strategy of these worthies is something like "Stay within the budget, but keep the faculty happy." It is not a scenario easily transferred into a management case study.

Our studies in the late 1970s indicated that the claims both by librarians and by publishers of the impact of interlibrary activities were groundless. Librarians borrowed the things they did not own and almost never purchased them. The reason for this is that the journals which the users wanted the library to buy were those they already knew—from their classwork, from their colleagues, and from their conferences. Indeed, our findings suggest a strategy of free student subscriptions, or at least free handouts to the faculty members to wean future readers. Librarians did not cancel the titles that they could obtain from other libraries, but those they could get away with canceling, either because the journal did not have a powerful protector or because the protector had left or retired. All of this, of course, assumes that the journal was little read, if indeed read at all. Libraries know what journals are used, and keeping these is not an issue. However, our study, as well as one at the University of Pittsburgh, suggested that there were journal subscriptions in libraries that faculty wanted placed, but that nobody read (a sort of "storehouse of knowledge" argument). When this is combined with the realization that for some journals, library subscriptions are the only subscriptions, it suggests a scenario of articles written, refereed, published, and unread. Does this matter? Not at all. They still count toward the promotion and tenure dossier.

Price, it turns out, is not a significant factor in subscriber placement and cancellation decisions. Publishers have come to understand that once libraries are down to one subscription, the renewal decision is not price-sensitive. Indeed, we found that the average price of retained subscriptions was greater than that of canceled ones. Journals that are vulnerable are perhaps made more vulnerable by a price increase, but a price increase by a safe journal can only endanger a vulnerable one.

I see no short-term solution. Librarians sit stubbornly in their leaky boats, while initiatives (automation, enhanced bibliographic service) are left undone in the race to find money to pay the journals' renewal invoices. Librarians have not shown any willingness to confront the issue, perhaps because they lack the will or perhaps because they are afraid they are alone and would lose. Those few librarians who have raised the problem with faculty colleagues who serve as editors and as members of advisory boards have found a remarkable lack of interest. University administrators, beset with many problems, would rather browbeat librarians than do battle with the antiquated and inefficient process of determining qualifications for promotion and tenure.

The growth of published research has little to do with *communication for information transfer*. It has, rather, to do with *communication for credit*. Certainly, as new disciplines and new subdisciplines are formed, some areas will grow rapidly. However, the *net* growth of the total publications process is predictable, because it relates roughly to the number of researchers in subdisciplines and disciplines within the universal collegium of scholars. That total has not grown very much. I need look no further than my own discipline to find the example. The number of librarians, the number of library schools, and the number of researchers have not grown very much over the last 20 years. Indeed, there are suggestions that they have declined. The number of journals to report our "research" has grown dramatically. And my discipline is not atypical. I have served on enough university-wide review committees to recognize that every fragment of research is reported over and over. Why? Because counting is still easier than evaluating.

The system will not change unless somebody changes it. In the past few years, a small number of faculty researchers have begun to speak out against this absurdity and some of the international conglomerate publishers have turned on these enemies in recognition of the danger they represent. After all, if somebody starts pointing out that the emperor is not wearing clothes, after a while people will notice. I don't expect the publishers who are the beneficiaries of this charade to change it. Even responsible publishers, who are truly concerned, could not do it by themselves. The writers/reviewers/editors/readers/evaluators have nothing to lose in a conspiracy of silence, as long as they don't have to pay the bill, and as long as nobody makes them face the alternatives to what the library or the university now doesn't do. Librarians, who presumably do know what is wrong, lack the power, and perhaps the will, to enforce their knowledge, and, of course, unscrupulous publishers understand this. That leaves university administrators, and perhaps government officials, who just might learn to understand the enormous price that is being paid for what can best be described as a creature comfort exercise, because there are other and cheaper mechanisms for scholarly communication. There just isn't as much profit in them, and for the authors the alternative would be more rigorous and therefore more dangerous.

Change might happen, but the likelihood in the near future is fairly slim. We have become adept, not at preventing crises or at solving them, but at putting them on back burners for later generations to address. This crisis hasn't even yet begun to be recognized, except by a few whose views are perceived not to matter very much.

The Tragic Cost
of Being "Reasonable"

Library science students (or at least my students) know that the negotiation of their initial salary is the most important salary determination of their careers. Future increases within the same library, and even potential salary offers from other libraries, will be figured as percentages of their present salaries.

Increases based on a percentage of present salary exacerbate the difference between those who earn less and those who earn more. It does not take an understanding of regression analysis to grasp that 5 percent of $40,000 produces twice as many dollars as 5 percent of $20,000.

The same thing holds true when next year's library budget is based on some sort of "reasonable" extension of this year's budget. Reasonable may be interpreted to mean a munificent 5 percent increase, no increase at all, or a cut of "only" 2 percent. It is explained to us that everybody else is also being so treated, but the question of how correct the starting budgets were is never examined. It is assumed.

The Question of Money

It is sort of an obvious and meaningless statement to say that managers are supposed to manage, but there are some glimmers of suggestion that in an era of increasing accountability it may yet come true. If so, it will perhaps come last to libraries, because budgetary discussions involving our field do not start with programs, they start and end with money.

The question for us is often not what we are going to do, or at least what we should do and what that would cost. The question becomes how much money we are going to get from bosses (who may be either kindhearted or possess a heart of

Reprinted, with changes, by permission of the author and *Library Journal* 116, no. 3 (February 15, 1991): 166-67. Copyright © 1991 by Reed Publishing, U.S.A.

stone) who will make their decision based on criteria that are meaningful for them but probably irrelevant for us.

When budgets drive programs rather than program decisions driving budgets, it is recognized as bad management. When budgets are established totally independently of programs, or when it is suggested that programs don't really need money because somehow librarians will find a way, it is not bad management but gibberish.

Losing Budget Ground

For far too long libraries have been "funded" on a percentage relationship to last year's budget. If that produced increments of 25 percent, I would not complain. But it doesn't. The representatives of one large system funded by a political body pointed out to me at a meeting that in the last six years they had received budgets ranging from an increase of 3 percent through flat budgets to a decrease of 1 percent. I was forced to point out that, even assuming an inflation rate of only 5 percent (if you are buying scientific journals it is a lot more), the only question is whether they had lost a lot or a little ground in each year.

That library characteristic projects nationally. My studies of academic library funding for the National Science Foundation show that when we factor in inflation we have lost ground steadily and consistently since 1972. That is a long time to keep betting on a losing hand. Why do we do this? There might be all sorts of possible reasons ranging from the sociological to the physical (Are there such things as human invertebrates?). I suspect the real reason comes from our inability to control our management communication process.

Peter Drucker, whom readers of this column know I quote shamelessly and endlessly, has noted both that the management chain produces an increasing dose of decision responsibility and that your own manager represents your most important subordinate. This is true quite simply because your boss, and particularly your nonlibrarian boss, will decide whether your library succeeds or fails by his or her support or failure to support your initiatives.

The Basis of Success or Failure

That is certainly generally understood. But what these managers may not understand is that since responsibility can be delegated but never abdicated, the success or failure of you and your library is also their personal success or failure. The way I have put this in the shorthand of management seminars is to suggest to bosses that since they are responsible for the library, it must be assumed that they are enthusiastic about it and what it does. If they are not, then they have to turn the job of managing you to somebody else, because you are entitled to a boss who cares and wants to help.

The statement to students is, of course, glib and intended as a slogan, but the point should not be lost. If your bosses do not care, then your bosses will not support you financially. Their financial and political actions are their primary contributions, because they don't personally catalog the backlog. If they do not care, they will not support you because there is always credit for economy, particularly if the results are hazy. If our budget requests and their budget decisions are based on a "reasonable" increase from a number that was irrational to start with, the result will also be irrational. Even an 8 percent increase will not help much if the base number was already 50 percent too low, because percentages applied to smaller bases lead to smaller numbers.

Paying to Lose?

Why don't we report what ought to be happening and is not? Why do we persist in playing a game we cannot win? Perhaps we are just gullible in believing our managers when they tell us they have no money, and, of course, any hard-pressed manager will exploit gullibility. It may or may not be true that they have no money, but even if it is true, it becomes irrelevant. Money has to be found by them for the things that suddenly become priorities. Read your daily paper to see how new needs get funded when there isn't enough money for the old needs.

Librarians in their negotiation with nonlibrarian bosses must therefore not begin with budgets but with proposed programs. If managers agree with the program, it is their responsibility to fund it. If they do not fund it (and the reason doesn't matter because it is a rationalization in any case), then the decision not to have the program, or to abort the program, will be theirs. They can dislike but not really object to our then telling people the truth. If, by contrast, our managers do find the money, we will, of course, broadcast this as well so that credit can be had.

For years I have been telling corporate librarians that their job is running good libraries, and that saving money for the organization is the job of the controller, who gets paid a great deal more for the effort. In any case, librarians, even if so inclined, couldn't squander enough money to make a difference. My illustrative example is to point out that even by spending the entire day in the shower shredding $20 bills, they cannot affect corporate earnings by one cent per share.

Some Reasonable Examples

However, the same problem of living within a "reasonable" extension of the status quo also applies to academic and public librarians. Two recent examples come to mind. In one I was handed an academic library's five-year plan. It was an impressive-looking document, with clear typography and eye-catching graphics.

However, it began with the library's realization that its funding would not increase except very modestly over the next five years. I really didn't want to read any further, but since I was expected to, I did. Starting with the conclusion of flat funding led to the strategy of stressing faculty end user searching to avoid further pressures on an already understaffed reference department that would not grow.

Had the plan argued that faculty end user searching was either better in quality or cheaper for the university, I would have disagreed but accepted the line of reasoning, but that wasn't the point. The point was to make the library look cheaper by pushing the cost elsewhere into the university cost structure. Who gains from this? Certainly the library loses.

If faculty do searches badly, or if they pass the chore along to graduate assistants and secretaries, quality suffers. If the university spends more but the cost is hidden, is that supposed to please the president? Are we hoping that he doesn't find out how un-cost-effective our strategy is?

Self-Canceling Transactions?

Reciprocal borrowing is sort of a more direct version of interlibrary loan (ILL). The user gets the material in person. Both concepts are presented as societal common goods, and indeed they are. They are also presented to us as self-canceling transactions from which all libraries gain. That they are not. In both ILL and reciprocal borrowing it becomes clear that, from the standpoint of serving individuals in the political constituency, some libraries gain financially and others lose.

Those who gain argue that they haven't had the money to start with. If you buy that argument you haven't been reading the beginning of this column. Those who lose in the transactions are beginning to wonder why they should, and more importantly recognize that this is irresponsible to their own clientele.

I predicted some time ago that, with the growing concern for management accountability, the process could be subsidized through a whole range of options, but that it would not, and indeed should not, be subsidized by the supplying library, filling requests outside its service responsibility and tax base. The logical body to fund reciprocal borrowing is the state, because that transaction is usually intrastate; the logical amount is 100 percent of the cost.

ILL Crossing State Boundaries

Interlibrary loan presents greater complexity when it crosses state lines, and here the responsibility becomes logically federal. However, when in one state the directors of large public libraries have suggested state support for what they calculate is the correct amount for reciprocal borrowing, another library leader has suggested a more prudent request strategy, representing not the needed amount but a modest increment over present levels. He acknowledges that this won't solve the problem, but that our requests have to be "reasonable."

I can't predict the likelihood of receiving the total amount. It will, of course, be difficult, but it will depend on how well librarians threaten to blame the culpable legislators and state administrators for the fact that citizens are being deprived of needed information that is available, but not in their own little taxing district.

It sounds like a self-serving boondoggle contrived by bureaucrats, particularly since the alternative of making every small library large is absurd. If librarians state the alternative based not on budget but on program need, it might or might not work. However, the strategy of asking for a little bit of money in the frank admission that this won't solve the problem, will not work at all, because we have been beating that dead horse for decades.

Management Truisms

It all comes back to two management truisms. In the absence of money there is always money for what is important enough to do. And it is easier to get a lot of money than a little bit of money, particularly when a lot of money promises dramatic results and the little bit provides only a virtually invisible change to the status quo and provides credit to no one.

Besides, libraries never could ask for enough to make a major difference in the financial structure of the parent body. Negative reaction to budget requests is not based on poverty, it is based on instinct. Get out your calculators and see for yourselves how little you ask for, even in your wildest dreams.

Playing Shell Games
Without Any Peas

It is always more fun to manage in a time of increasing budgets than of declining budgets. Unfortunately, we have been in a period of declining funding, at least when measured in inflation-adjusted dollars, for the last 20 years. There are strategies that can be used for stemming this bloodletting and for assuring that we are treated no worse than other applicants for public funding, but there are probably none for reversing the trend, at least not over the next 10 years, which is about as far as anyone can see. This reality has nothing to do with the ogre of defense spending or the search for a "peace dividend."

Our competitors for funding are not the military; they are other social programs, unpleasant and uncomfortable as that realization may be. We compete most directly at the local level and with the expressed needs of the school system, police protection, road repair, garbage disposal, and urban blight.

Too Many Goods to Go Around

Almost 14 years ago, I suggested at a meeting of the Canadian Library Association that being "self-evidently good" would not be a successful strategy, because there were too many other good things around. People still like libraries and even like librarians, even if they consider them quaint, but they have also developed an instinctive aversion to higher taxes and that aversion is growing.

This is not because they have lost any sense of innate goodness, but rather because they have come to realize that their support of higher taxes in the past did not provide promised results. Perhaps those promises, made so glibly in the 1960s, could never have been kept. In any case, the present competition

Reprinted, with changes, by permission of the author and *Library Journal* 116, no. 12 (July 1991): 63-64. Copyright © 1991 by Reed Publishing, U.S.A.

for funding among "good" things is ferocious and it should suggest to us an insistence on hard-nosed quid pro quos in building alliances.

If we are to support your causes even to the detriment of funding for our own, will you sometimes support our causes even to the detriment of yours? Not at present. We support education at all levels, literacy programs, service to the elderly and to latchkey children, and many more such worthy initiatives. These advocates accept our support, although they sometimes barely acknowledge it. But there is no quid pro quo, no willingness to support our positions even at some direct cost. That is not how alliances are supposed to work.

Finding Our Repriorities

The one positive result of declining budgets, management writers tell us, is that it forces us to reprioritize and particularly to get rid of the tasks that we never wanted to perform in the first place. Indeed, they tell us that a constant reassessment of priorities is essential to confirm that we are prudent and not just spendthrifts.

I am usually quoted correctly as stating that I don't believe in charging for any library services because that simply suggests charging for more and eventually all library services. There is no logical limit to the process, unless we are foolish enough to be drawn into "traditional" and "nontraditional" service definitions, an approach that automatically makes us the old fogies. However, what is usually left out of the quote is the corollary that this decision then requires effective strategies for increasing public funding support, because a chosen strategy of "free or not at all" is just as disastrous. We need to insist on doing that which we know needs to be done, and that which we can prove we do best.

Defining Our Unique Priorities

What are our unique priorities? It is an obvious and yet a difficult question; historically we have allowed our priorities to be subsumed and diverted by the priorities of others. Some of us keep insisting that we are really simply educators, and indeed Will Manley recently suggested that we abandon specific library education programs and return to being part of Schools of Education (*Wilson Library Bulletin*, February 1991, pp. 79-81). The presumed logic in this is that what worked so disastrously 25 years ago might work perfectly today.

I know that some librarians in academic, public, and school libraries cling to the belief that they are first and foremost educators, and that this subsumes their own professional identity. There is little point in debating the merits of the argument, as long as the "real" educators do not think of us as their fellows and peers, only as support staff to their own work and priorities.

Do we need to go back any further than *A Nation at Risk* (1983), an otherwise superb political document that never acknowledged the existence let alone the importance and role of libraries? We rushed into print with our own addendum to point out what it had forgotten to say, and, of course, our document was neither acknowledged nor was an apology for the oversight tendered. We can insist that educators accept us as equal partners, or we can insist that our groups are related: different but equal. However, it is demeaning and to little purpose to hang around the back door of establishments that won't admit us.

A Department of Libraries?

Where might we fit into the federal bureaucracy? Ideally we ought to have our own cabinet post, and the creation of a Department of Veterans Affairs shows that political clout creates its own priorities. However, I am pragmatic enough to recognize that we can't get a cabinet post when we can't control the makeup of the National Commission on Libraries and Information Science (NCLIS), or of the White House Conference on Library and Information Services, or of the appointment of a Librarian of Congress. We might not find a happier home, but being subsumed under education has done us no favors, precisely because educators have their own certainty about what libraries are and do.

Unfortunately for us, that view is limited and restricted. We had no representation in or funding from the Institute for Education, the body that was supposed to fund educational research identified as needed by educators. When I noted that our placement in education also suggests that our research priorities also fall into that domain, I was met not with animosity but with surprise. It had simply never occurred to these educational worthies that we had research priorities. The National Science Foundation funded information science research. What else was there?

No Doubt About Illiteracy

What sort of issues get transported into our profession, inevitably without a recognition of funding needs? Adult illiteracy is the most obvious and certainly at present the most emotional one. It is a huge and growing problem that does not warrant optimism. Some parts of it have always been in our domain. In the March 1991 issue of *American Libraries*, Deanna Marcum and Betty Stone remind us of the important role that libraries played in teaching newly arrived immigrants the English language and American ways of life.

I am a beneficiary of that process, and these opportunities are still there for our profession. Cultural diversity and bilingualism in no way dilute the continuing reality that in order to succeed here, you have to be able to understand and speak English, as indeed Swedes and Chinese understand the importance of learning English in their native countries.

There is no contradiction here. Bilingualism means two languages. Libraries have been superbly situated and equipped to offer cultural bridges that preserve and cherish old values while introducing eager and willing neophytes to the new—including the tactic of enticing with the old and presenting the opportunity for the new. Nothing works all the time, but this has always worked well. Self-interest and self-motivation have always been key to the process, and the process does not replace, it adds.

Adult illiteracy for those born and presumably educated in this country through years of mandatory school attendance is a much more complex and difficult problem; to a large extent we don't know the implications because we may not want to know. There is a remarkable paucity of research, only a rush to fix. What percentage of adult illiterates now want to learn to read and why? If the initiative is not already there, is there much chance of success? Does this really differ from our experience with alcohol and drug addiction, where the solution must start with a personal commitment?

What is the rate of recidivism, a process almost inevitable unless people once taught to read continue to read? If people made it through the seventh grade without learning to read, what caused this, quite aside from the question of how they made it to the seventh grade? What are the changing factors that would motivate an adult today, when the process is more difficult? There is no educational research, and I suspect educators may not want to find out.

How Libraries Contribute

The same thing applies in librarianship. I looked forward to the report of a recent study of the role of libraries in combating adult illiteracy not only because the question is important but because I have respect for the researchers (Jane Robbins and Douglas Zweizig, University of Wisconsin-Madison). I was disappointed to find that the study never even touched on the question of whether, but only of how and how better.

As I try to fight my way through this euphoric mist, there are two things that concern me. The first is that we have never determined what we can specifically contribute to this process of teaching adults to read their own language, except perhaps space and resources. This issue is quite different from that of people who are literate, but not in English, and who are moreover eager. Any extrapolation from the Marcum-Stone article breaks down at this point. My second concern is for funding, assuming that it is agreed that our answer to the first question is positive. If we don't receive additional funding for this, and normally we don't, then we inevitably do this instead of something else. What is that? When did we make that decision to swap priorities, and whom have we told?

Where Will the Money Come From?

If we are willing to continue to play shell games without peas and are willing to accept without question the burden of adult domestic illiteracy not only without funds but at a time of decreasing funds, the results are not hard to predict. Local funding bodies continue to assume that library funding and what libraries do are not necessarily related.

They might allow us to cut programs, but they always seem hurt and bewildered when we do, as though we had betrayed them and the citizens. The time to spell out budget alternatives is before budget decisions are made. Once they are made there can be lots of newspaper reports or protests and placards, but it is too late, because the money has already been allocated.

The federal scenario suggests an even more dangerous variation. The administration has recommended that only one library program be funded in the federal budget: the fight against adult illiteracy. It is Mrs. Bush's first priority, and as we have warmly commended her for it, it is assumed that this is also our priority and perhaps even our first priority.

Even as we are reluctant to prioritize, government leaders do it all the time. Is this indeed our first priority, even at the risk of losing everything else we have secured over the years? Or have we been misunderstood, and our euphoria only means that we would like to help if we can, but only if there is additional funding for this process? If so, we had better tell them that they have misunderstood our meaning.

In any case, we must understand that if we are not willing to prioritize, and to reprioritize as funding changes, others will do it for us. I have never in all of my management experience refused to take money to implement somebody else's first priority, provided that this effort was not contradictory to my own concerns. *Additional* money. My own program proposals reflected my own priorities, and it went without saying that these were tied to my own goals and objectives. If one has no programs or priorities, those who have them will impose their own. It was certainly true in corporate libraries, but it is true for public libraries as well, because political decision makers remain the same, even as we fail to understand them.

Hewers of Wood
and Drawers of Water

The title phrase, at least vaguely familiar to most of us, comes from Joshua 9:21, and it describes the presumably merciful decision to let the vanquished Gibeonites live, rather than put them all to death, commonly the lot of a conquered people. "Let them live, but let them be hewers of wood and drawers of water unto all of the congregation."

The decision may have been merciful, but it also may have resulted from the practical realization that there was a need for hewers of wood and drawers of water. The Old Testament does not tell us, but there may have even been a shortage of such unskilled labor then.

What happens in the information process is also, like just about any other process, a mixture of professional and support tasks. There was a time, only a little more than a century ago, when the role of librarians was clearly "professional." They presided over their collections, like the dragon guarding the Rheingold, and decided who might or might not be worthy of access.

That arrangement is now almost universally gone, certainly in this country, and we don't regret its passing. There was even, and there may yet be, an opportunity to extend the recognition of the professional importance of librarians, particularly as we grow to understand that literacy, understanding, knowledge, and information access are key to success in just about everything. Those are the cards that have been dealt to us.

How We Play the Game

That we have not played our hands well results from several circumstances. We have lost sight of the uniqueness and primacy of our role and mission and allowed ourselves to become bit players and spear carriers to the scripts of others.

Thus when we talk of "building coalitions," we find very little quid pro quo, only our support for the priorities of others, without any return. Even that might be tolerable, particularly if these other priorities are perceived as "worthwhile," but limited funds require harsh rank ordering.

If we willingly give up our unique priority list to support others', ours automatically sinks in importance. Peter Drucker has taught us that the political process permits no neutrals. Individuals either support us as a prime priority, or they support someone else or something else that demands money from the same source. That makes them our rivals, and their supporters our enemies.

Why Numbers Fascinate Us

We have also developed a fascination with counting the cords of wood and pails of water we have accumulated. In our vernacular, these are called holdings and circulation, and even the ancient Hebrews knew that wood and water were for a larger purpose, and that counting them was only a protection against a shortage.

Why are we so willing to count and proudly report quantities without the more professional concerns about what happens as a result of our having it available? "Give people what they want" may sound democratic, although it is also the rationale for Roman circuses. It isn't much of a professional rallying cry. "Give people what they need and ought to have" sounds much better and implies a professional role.

Even as we insist on ignoring the valuable territory that fell to us, others understand it quite well and develop plans for converting it to their own condominiums and shopping malls.

I first became aware of the strategy of separating libraries from information when I served as executive director of the contract-operated NASA Scientific and Technical Information Facility in the 1960s. Government information programs, including not only NASA but also the Defense Documentation Center, the National Technical Information Service, and the National Library of Medicine (NLM), filled an important role by providing bibliographic access both in printed and in computer form to local librarians who served individual clients, and then in backing up bibliographic services with a strong document delivery system.

The Role of National Libraries

The process worked better with some programs than with others, but it did emphasize support of local library service to clients, in this case largely scientists, engineers, and doctors. The national program to legitimize, formalize, and assure subsidized document delivery developed by NLM in the mid-1960s was a landmark activity we still teach in library education, even if as a historical footnote. It recognized clearly what the roles of national libraries were. The most important was to support the activity of local libraries.

While that role was and is appropriate, it was also recognized as politically disastrous by any good bureaucrat seeking to build an empire. Service to librarians carries few political bonus points. Service to doctors, engineers, and scientists—who are seen as directly contributing to the public good—does. So national information programs began to deemphasize what they did for librarians and stress what they did directly for the people in the space suits and the lab coats.

What was initially a mirage was turned rather quickly into a reality, and the tool was the enhanced development of decentralized searching of online databases. Databases can be searched by anyone with equipment and resources. While it continues to stand to reason that they can be searched most effectively by the professionals prepared for the purpose, they can also be searched sloppily and expensively by end users who may not even know what they have done is sloppy and expensive.

Database vendors understood quite rapidly that there was more money to be made by marketing to rich and sloppy end users than to poor and careful librarians.

NLM and Its Doctors

NLM, which has always had more freedom and flexibility because of the understood importance of its product, has moved aggressively from its support of medical libraries to a direct relationship with doctors, through marketing approaches called Grateful Med and Lonesome Doc.

Lonesome Librarian wouldn't sound nearly as catchy in testimony before Congressional committees. Occasionally, in enthusiasm for building one-to-one bridges with doctors, NLM administrators overstep the bounds of courtesy by forgetting to mention the role of the good old local medical librarian. When that happens, and the medical library community protests, NLM sends emissaries to explain and even apologize.

These corrections never reach those who received the original misinformation. Maintaining good relations with medical librarians is still important even if secondary for NLM because it does need their support when budget hearings get sticky. However, the entire process of the NLM-doctor interface concentrates on bibliographic access, on the sizzle.

The meat of the program, the document delivery, is still left to the strained and largely unsupported resources of the local medical librarian. The program needs its hewers of wood and drawers of water, and it is perhaps an indication of the trivialization of the relationship to note that NLM tries to sell its initiatives to medical librarians as a benefit for them, because "use of the library" through document requests will go up. More water pails, anyone?

Medical Librarians and Power

I have no animosity toward the management of NLM. Indeed, I can admire a successful political ploy to seize the high ground of information communications. What I fail to understand is the passive willingness of medical librarians to allow themselves to be so manipulated.

Perhaps they do not realize that they hold potential power over the agenda of the National Library of Medicine. The key word here is potential, because it would require two activities. It would mean first summoning the director of NLM (and not just emissaries) to a meeting of reckoning, to determine the price of librarian support for the initiatives of their own national library.

The value of that process is limited, although it should nevertheless be done. The greater potential power is in persuading the medical researchers and administrators with whom librarians should have built up a relationship of trust and mutual respect that the arrangement so carefully being engineered by NLM is not cost-effective; it wastes the money of the local hospital as well as that of the national budget. In fact, the arrangement is backwards from the standpoint of national objectives. It works only narrowly and politically, and I will grant that it certainly works there.

Searching and Logic

The logical people to undertake complex literature searches are not the end users, be they doctors or university professors. The complexity of the files, the unfamiliarity with search protocols, the frequent impatience of the neophyte searcher, the lack of concern for resources expended all indicate that higher-priced and less knowledgeable end users should only be doing searches in the absence of lower-priced (unfortunately) and more skilled bibliographic searchers.

That in turn suggests a fairly obvious management strategy. In the absence of enough bibliographic searchers or reference librarians, it is to management's advantage to get some more, as a cost-effective decision. Ultimately the question of whether information is important has only one answer, and the only remaining question concerns who is best qualified to find it.

Why are we, in medical as well as academic libraries, so reluctant to make this point and to demand the research studies that would so clearly prove what database vendors already know without studies? Do doctors who are paid twice as much do searches that are twice as cheap or twice as effective? When we are all through laughing, let's do some simple studies to prove it. Or are there people who have already made up their minds and can't be bothered with facts, particularly as they spend other people's money?

Twofold Library Service Role

NLM had its priorities straight the first time, before it assessed the political fallout, and we have a stake in making what works best also worth NLM's while. The library's service role is twofold, and it has already shown it can perform both superbly.

The first is to provide bibliographic access to medical librarians. No, not primarily to doctors. If we find doctors and medical researchers unserved by medical librarians (and, of course, there are some), then let us work together to devise a strategy to make sure they are served.

Geographic proximity here is no more crucial than it is for NLM. The existence of 800 telephone numbers provides an obvious potential. Leave the doctors to bibliographic specialist librarians who can best understand their needs, separate them from their sometimes naïve requests (and there is no disgrace in this), and serve them far more effectively than NLM can. NLM, as its name recalls, is a national library. It serves local libraries.

The second service role? National libraries are superb vehicles for the supply of documents from centralized, regionalized, but in any case convenient storehouses. The British National Lending Library demonstrated this long ago. In the final analysis, national libraries are superbly qualified as hewers of wood and drawers of water. Why not do it, and do it well?

Assessing the White House Conference: Two Chances to Miss the Brass Ring

Enough time has now elapsed since the conclusion of the 1991 White House Conference on Library and Information Services (WHCLIS) to permit some evaluation of what did and didn't happen. The tons of used paper have found their way into biodegradable recycling, and the delegates have returned home to regale colleagues with their war stories of all-night sessions and the fight to overcome monumental bureaucratic stupidity.

What is left, after all the clamor has subsided, are the recommendations. There is certainly no need here to repeat or even summarize them, because they are readily available. Instead, I would prefer to begin by stating my largely intuitive reactions.

Libraries as Pivotal Players

The first is that these recommendations look similar to the recommendations of WHCLIS I, updated only to reflect changes in jargon. Libraries are expected to play a pivotal role, particularly in the education of our citizens and in the search for a better quality of life.

Specific references are made to the needs of particular groups, because any large conference with an uncertain delegate selection process will include some who come specifically to make sure that a particular recommendation is included. There is also a counter effort to avoid such fractionalization, but some one-cause advocates inevitably succeed.

Reprinted, with changes, by permission of the author and *Library Journal* 117, no. 7 (April 15, 1992): 66-67. Copyright © 1992 by Reed Publishing, U.S.A.

The second observation is that these are "Motherhood and God" recommendations with which it is impossible to quarrel. Missing are implementation mechanisms and strategies and, most of all, specifics of funding. There are neither cost estimates nor time frames. In the reality of a government process that rank orders among finite resources, this suggests rank ordering these goodies against each other and against other worthwhile nonlibrary purposes.

Wish Lists Ad Nauseam

We are left with a long wish list, and in the political arena such lists become useful primarily for embarrassing incumbents, although with an executive branch controlled by one party and a legislative branch controlled by the other even this becomes difficult. Let's be fair.

There might be public servants who want to take these recommendations seriously, but they can't. They haven't even been told what constitutes an acceptable solution level, only that the problems are large. The normal process is then to accept such recommendations "in principle," and that's obviously cheaper than funding them.

Old Recommendations Are New Again

The third observation is how pedestrian these recommendations are, and perhaps this can be inferred from their similarity to past recommendations. Much has changed in the last 10 years—in technology, in resource sharing options, in networking. A part of this observation is my recognition that they focus primarily on one aspect of our profession—education—with perhaps a sideswipe at social programs.

The conference theme promised more, but I fail to find any references to productivity enhancement that economists would understand. Libraries do, or at least should do, a lot more than educate and amuse. If the majority of the delegates didn't know or care, it is undoubtedly because their own knowledge is restricted to personal experience.

For some rather strange reason offered in the interest of democratic participation, ignorance is an important qualification in the selection of delegates. I am not suggesting an application of the old observation that it isn't what people don't know that causes problems. It is what they do know, except that it is wrong. Academic librarians dealing with full professors who pontificate about library values know exactly what I mean.

Quality Librarians = Quality Libraries

Related to all of this is my fourth and most concerned observation. This conference dealt with libraries without bothering to define them, but we know better than that. What is a real library, what is a pseudo-library, and can anyone tell them apart? Do libraries depend on librarians, or is that incidental? And what is it that librarians know and that others, including both classroom teachers and secretaries of the Department of Education, should realize they don't know? Can we have an agenda for quality libraries without an agenda for quality librarians—properly selected, properly educated, properly paid, properly respected?

Sounds silly to even have to mention it, doesn't it? And yet the conference fastened primarily on the geographic widening of library education access opportunities. There is nothing wrong with that, but does this relate to the quality of what might be taught at these geographically accessible sites? No connection is even attempted. Just do it!

They Want Our Support, Not Our Advice

If I seem more churlish and irritable than my usual unflappable and charming self, it is because I am tired of hearing individuals who stress the virtue of libraries, frequently invoking the ghost of Carlyle, without even mentioning librarians. This includes university presidents, who have opened conferences at which I was about to speak with that assurance, but then immediately departed, claiming pressing other business, and who, after having spoken, listened to nothing else.

It is not then surprising that the budgets they present to us stress the building and the collection, but never the people. Isn't this a bit incongruous, particularly since the emphasis on networks and resource sharing depends directly on what qualified people can accomplish? Can we adopt the tactic of the football coach who informed the alumni that he would appreciate their support but not their advice?

WHCLIS Report Card

Did this White House Conference do any good? We can have opinions, but we can't know, because we can't even tell whether the first White House Conference did any good. Some good things have happened in the last 10 years, but on balance we have almost certainly lost ground. Would we have lost even more ground without a White House Conference? Would we have done better if we had concentrated our energies on promulgating our own agenda, and then finding friends in the Congress and in the community for our own initiatives? Speculation is all that is available to us, because any researcher would recognize the absence of a control group.

What disturbs me far more than this speculation is the realization of what might have been possible if this profession focused first of all on issues of empowering itself, with the explanation that only the empowerment of librarians, and really nothing else, can bring about good library service. However, it must also be understood that good library service encompasses a whole range of activities and not just whatever a particular pressure group can identify. In other words, we have our own unique agenda.

Are we so easily assuaged that we can "celebrate" the day on which the president, the secretary of education, and the wife of the vice president all came over to provide a photo opportunity? What they told us was probably from their hearts. I happen to believe that these are all basically nice people. They are just woefully uninformed. Is this ignorance their fault? I suspect it is ours.

Nurses Lead the Way

Our friends and colleagues in nursing can perhaps show us the way. In large part through their efforts, TV has replaced a situation comedy that featured nurses as sex objects with one that promises to deal with them seriously and professionally. Nurses have also developed an advertising campaign that stresses the professional things nurses do, why they are important, and most significantly why educational preparation of top recruits is fundamental for all of this. Their slogan is "If caring were enough, anyone could be a nurse."

I don't know if the nurses can pull this off, but I am rooting for them, and certainly if they can do it, we can. They have to contest their turf with doctors who sometimes seem to trivialize just about everything else. By contrast, we deal with individuals who instinctively care about what librarians do and who usually want to help. If they meddle and become difficult, it is because we haven't properly trained them. Puppies don't instinctively use paper, either.

Please don't misunderstand my meaning. Some of the WHCLIS recommendations are indeed important and even eloquent. Others appear narrower and more selfish. Still, there are so many of them! We were weaned at the time of the first White House Conference by a presidential advisor in an administration in sympathy with conference objectives that we should concentrate on perhaps four or five recommendations. We should make them hard-hitting and specific and then indicate implementation strategies.

In other words, we were asked to prioritize. We were told that a smorgasbord of recommendations would be useless. When I look at the large number of recommendations for the second conference I am perhaps being unkind, because there are fewer than the last time. I know that but for the work of many diligent librarian delegates, there would have been far more. Still, there were far too many. For me, any number over five is too many.

What Stays, What Goes?

Our unwillingness to prioritize—to state what we will do instead of something else—is clearly understood by outsiders, and this causes us endless grief. The concern is not whether we will have programs for latchkey kids, but rather, in an unchanging or declining total budget, what will we not have and why? This also applies to our organizational deliberations within the American Library Association (ALA), but that issue is large enough to deserve an entire column by itself.

The White House Conference recommendations include some that would fit into any kind of prioritized agenda for the profession and others that would be at best secondary. And if they are secondary, they are dangerous. As any operations researcher will tell you, the things you aren't going to stress or emphasize get in the way of the things you would like to emphasize.

If our theme is "Your Right to Know: Librarians Make It Happen," any recommendation that assumes that librarians will always be there—and that totally ignores quality in favor of activity—dilutes our focus. It is easy to see that their appearance at the White House Conference meant absolutely nothing of substance to the administration bigwigs who attended. The proposed federal library support budget still includes only one item: the support of adult literacy programs. And that one, while libraries can be additionally funded to participate in it, isn't even ours. It belongs to the educators, but I suspect primarily Barbara Bush.

I have a little dream scenario about the next White House Conference. In my dream, the delegates assemble and immediately decide that they are unqualified for any meaningful discussion of detailed issues, because that is the expertise of professional librarians. They therefore pass only one resolution, which urges the proper recruitment and selection of professional librarians, their quality education, their proper salaries, their adequate clerical support, and their empowerment to run libraries. Then the delegates vote to adjourn, thereby saving the taxpayers the cost of lunch, let alone a banquet. The president, too late for a photo opportunity here, decides he'd better attend the next ALA conference and say something meaningful about programs, priorities, and money. The dream will work equally well with any of the current presidential candidates.

Coalition-Building
and the Image of Power

According to my unabridged dictionary, an alliance is an association or union formed for the furtherance of common interests and aims of the members of the allying groups. A coalition, by contrast, is only a temporary alliance of distinct parties for joint action or to achieve a common purpose.

All of this assumes that each of the parties has a set of unique priorities that it brings to the negotiating sessions with its would-be coalition partners, and this results in an active and healthy quid pro quo based on the existence of different but complementary agendas and priorities. If the agendas are the same, there is no need for coalitions. If one group forgoes its priorities for the other, it is simply subsumed.

It obviously helps in planning political strategy if we understand from whom we want what. Federal funds will not support local library operating expenditures in the near future. We ought to be able to get federal funds for the things for which there is an agreed-upon federal role, at least in principle. Even an agreement in principle may not lead to funding, but at least it offers a chance. At the federal level this may include pilot and start-up costs, research, educational grants for minority recruitment, and cooperative activities that cross state lines.

From state agencies we should expect funding for any activities that are statewide. This includes educational support for state universities and library networks and most particularly statewide bibliographic access and resource sharing. State legislatures should pay for these things, because the cost of fragmenting such activities is absurdly high, and that is a point we don't make nearly well enough.

Reprinted, with changes, by permission of the author and *Library Journal* 118, no. 1 (January 1993): 69-70. Copyright © 1993 by Reed Publishing, U.S.A.

Coalition Rivals

The local agency—be it a school district, municipality, college, hospital, or corporation—pays the operational costs of running its own library. I have not mentioned affordability. Nothing is usually admitted as affordable, and yet everything that has to be done is affordable. The federal government will continue to pay for the savings and loan bailout without even knowing what the final bill will be.

Where does this leave us in our relation to presumed coalition partners? Not in very good shape, because these groups all have massive funding proposals of their own. If you want to argue that they deserve the money, you may be right, but you will have missed my point.

When two groups compete for the same money from the same source, they are not partners. They are rivals. Compromise is, of course, possible, but nobody has yet offered any sort of compromise to us. In looking at our so-called coalition partners, I see no quid pro quo.

Instead, what happens is that we are willing to support their priorities, and they are willing to let us. In talking to us, they rarely even bother to modify their set speeches to include the needs of the specific audience they are addressing.

The Kozol/Snyder Connection?

When Jonathan Kozol speaks at national and state library conferences, as he frequently does, he speaks with the sincere commitment to his cause and the practiced eloquence he has developed, but I fail to find the direct connection to our agendas. Since there will always be a variance of wealth in local school districts and even in states, I assume that Kozol is advocating some sort of national funding guarantees.

I am sure that Kozol hopes that this will improve the quality of the nation's schools, but will it necessarily improve the funding and quality of school libraries and media centers? I doubt that Kozol has thought at that level of micromanagement, and we haven't been crass enough to ask him.

However, we do know that the federal government does not resemble Santa Claus, and that with federal programs we get federal rules and controls. Is there reason to expect that a federal imposition of school library standards would lead to a greater appreciation of school librarians? Where would that wellspring of love come from? The Department of Education, or the Office of Management and Budget? They might even decide to contract out all school libraries to the private sector.

There is a more garish example. The late Mitch Snyder, self-appointed spokesperson for all the complex and multifaceted community of homeless, was invited to speak at an American Library Association (ALA) conference. That talk, which never mentioned libraries or librarians (read it for yourself), was somehow published in the September/October 1989 *Public Libraries* and then selected for inclusion for the *Best of Library Literature for 1989*.

Are we really that desperate for articles to select something that was simply a political diatribe (even if an eloquent one) without either references to or a mention of our profession? What do we tell those who already question the state of academic rigor in our profession, or do we just hope they don't notice?

Coalitions with Senior Citizens

This column may spark letters that argue the saintly virtues of Kozol and Snyder, but they will miss my point that ALA conferences should not be love-ins but meetings at which we talk about the cares and concerns of libraries and librarians and strategies of what to do about them. Are there then groups with which we can negotiate agreements of mutual benefit and convenience, as true coalition partners?

It goes almost without saying that the first requirement is that they be groups not after the same money we are after. The workers at the closing GM assembly plant in Ypsilanti, Michigan, may yet come to realize that their most immediate rivals were not the Japanese, but the GM plant in Arlington, Texas. If you have rivals, at least know who they are.

The most attractive coalition candidate for us might be the American Association of Retired Persons (AARP). It is generally acknowledged to be the most powerful political lobby in the United States, and one whose enmity is never sought by any politician. Yet AARP has taken no stance in support of public library funding, despite the fact that we know we play a significant role in enhancing the quality of life for senior citizens. When I mentioned this at a state conference of public library trustees, one trustee commented that the situation was even worse than I had pictured it.

Senior citizens were, as a group, particularly opposed to any and all tax increases, including those that might benefit or save libraries. Senior citizens who do use libraries have not demanded that their fellow senior citizens support us even as they perhaps oppose something else. Perhaps this is because we have never made the case that the quality of service to them is related to and perhaps even dependent on their activity and vocal support.

I guess we just don't like taking hostages, but once the library budget cut is already announced it is usually too late, because in addition to pleading for funds, you have to identify alternative victims. In any case, we make no demands on any of the citizens as a precondition for quality library service. Ours is only an outpouring of unconditional and perhaps unrequited love.

Power and the Image of Power

Robert L. Strauss, U.S. ambassador to what is left of the Soviet Union, is a Democrat who has exercised political power under the administrations of both parties without ever being elected to anything. He describes his strategy as the cultivation of the "image of power." As trade representative for President Carter, he refused to provide a briefing paper for the secretary of State to use in Moscow trade negotiations. He insisted on representing the country personally in these negotiations and ultimately stated that the only "paper" he would deliver would be his resignation. He prevailed, and his explanation for insisting is direct and simple. He had to represent the country, or he would have lost all future credibility as a trade negotiator. And having lost that image of power, he would no longer be taken seriously.

What is our self-image of power, or are we just unconditional lovers? The issue is not whether Kozol or Snyder are right or virtuous. The point is that all they can really ask is that we let them into line ahead of us. Has anyone noticed that the longer we stand in line, the longer it gets in front of us? Is our image of power simply the process of saying "yeah, me too!" whenever someone says something we deem virtuous? Or would we be better off concentrating on those images that are both important and in our unique area of expertise? I suspect that Ambassador Strauss would know the answer to that question.

We are not going to establish any coalitions that work for us if we invite pleaders for special causes just because some of us think the cause is just, and particularly if, as reported, those eloquent and practiced speakers make us weep. In our saline outpourings we may even forget why we came to the professional conference. Mark Antony noted that "ambition should be made of sterner stuff." What are our ambitions, specifically for ourselves, our profession, and our institutions?

We Are Still a Bargain

Perhaps, paradoxically, the results of a recent Gallup Poll (News, *Library Journal*, August 1992, p. 16) suggest that we really have more political power than we think. According to Gallup, public and community leaders would be willing to more than double the present level of support for public libraries. Despite all of our efforts at self-effacement, people can see what a fantastic bargain we are. The Gallup pollsters did not hear that these people were willing to pay higher taxes, only that they were willing to support libraries. That means support them instead of supporting something else.

Are we prepared to use such leverage in the negotiation of our coalitions, by positing that our agenda comes first because we have more support? Not unless and until we first embrace our own self-image of importance and power. It is not difficult to predict that, in the absence of specific initiatives by our profession, the recent election will make very little difference.

Our profession has not fared particularly well under a Republican executive agenda, but we will do no better in a Democratic environment in which taxes must be kept down but social program expectations are allowed to rise. If anything, competition with our "coalition partners" could become more ferocious, assuming we decided to compete at all. It is more likely that the line in front of us will just get still longer.

Still Unanswered Questions

There are many unanswered questions. If we have the strength for elbowing our way to the head of the line, do we have the stomach for it? Is the phrase "ruthless librarian" an oxymoron? When I say ruthless I obviously mean ruthless in a good cause—ours.

Election winners probably make little difference for us because we don't just lose ground during the bad years. We lose ground during the good years, too. Do the issues that surround libraries and librarians really interest the association leaders who attend ALA conferences, or are they there for some other purpose to which their professional affiliation is at best incidental? There are reasons to wonder.

Fee vs. Free: A Catchy But Not Very Meaningful Option

Fee vs. free has a clever ring to it, but when applied to public library services, it is not merely misleading, it is actually harmful. Why is it misleading? Because public libraries *never* provide any free services. It's simply a matter of who pays and how. Rather than relating the fee vs. free comparison to a service offered to users from within the same taxing district, the more realistic question posed should be "Would you prefer to pay as part of your tax bill or separately?"

In that framework it becomes no different from the option of paying taxes as part of an annual tax bill or as part of a sales tax collected daily. The property tax vs. sales tax option provides at least the mirage of choice, since we can presumably avoid sales tax by not buying anything. As some wise person surely must have said: "Money is money no matter what denomination you pay it in." Libraries cost money. The point we must make is that they are worth it. "Fee or free" creates the impression of an option that does not exist.

The tactic is also dangerous precisely because it stresses the free aspect of the library service instead of its quality. Individuals who write advertising copy know better than to stress that their product is cheaper than their competitor's, because they know instinctively that people will shy away from such a product on the assumption that if it is cheaper, it must be inferior.

Stressing Freeness over Goodness

Two of three competing long-distance telephone companies stress their low rates, but the third remains number one by a comfortable margin because it stresses its dependability. The advertising of discount chains represents the only instance

Reprinted, with changes, by permission of the author and *Library Journal* 118, no. 15 (September 15, 1993): 55-56. Copyright © 1993 by Reed Publishing, U.S.A.

when it is preferable to stress cost over quality, a strategy that succeeds only because customers know what is being sold is brand-name merchandise. When the product is the same, then price does matter. However, we're not in the discounting business.

Why do we stress freeness rather than our goodness as our primary attribute? Perhaps the letters etched over the entrances of our institutions should be changed from "Free Public Library" to "Valuable Public Library." Peter Drucker notes in *Managing the Non-Profit Organization: Principles and Practices* (HarperBusiness, 1992. pap. $12), his most recent book on managing in the nonprofit sector, that any conman can tell you it is easier to sell the Brooklyn Bridge than to give it away. If it is offered for free, there must be a catch.

Destructive Semantics

Having argued the fact that "free" library service is a game of semantics, and a destructive one at that, I would nevertheless posit that library services should always (and I am aware of the dangers of that word) be provided without additional charge to customers and that funding should come from the normal operating budget provided by the municipal agency that realizes what a bargain it has in us.

While charging our customers for any library service is a shell game within the community, the process does discriminate against those unable to pay, as any sales price does. Not paying taxes does not bar people from essential municipal services, and that is what we are. It was determined long ago that those with grown children and no children still pay for schools, and that argument applies to libraries. Librarians cannot discriminate against one kind of library user or favor one user over another—for any reason. That is the essence of our profession, and that is why we are librarians and not bankers. Bankers prefer wealthy people.

This process, once started in conspiracy with public officials happy to be let off the hook, has no logical end to it. If we charge for service A today, why not charge for services B and C tomorrow and sell tickets to the public library the day after tomorrow, as some museums already do? Why not make the library self-supporting? It is not far-fetched to suggest that there is no end to such a process. It has been fairly common practice to use Library Services & Construction Act (LSCA) funds as a way to reduce local funding, or to suggest that public libraries beg for funds from charitable donors to offset public funding cuts.

There are huge dangers in all of this. "How much have you raised on your own?" is a dangerous question, and the only safe, even if impolite, answer is "None of your business!" We see similar dangers in the national bipartisan injunction that federal information services recover their costs. What is affected is merely the tip of the iceberg in a long process: we educate people able to create information, then pay them to create it in a chain that costs hundreds of billions of dollars; shortchanging the dissemination of all that investment would be silly. However, in the formation of government policy, silly is not necessarily a deterrent. If we are reluctant to subsidize dissemination of research, how much cheaper it would be not to undertake the research in the first place. However, that's too dangerous to suggest. Somebody might find that idea attractive as well.

Traditional vs. Nontraditional

The process forces us to distinguish between "traditional" and "non-traditional" services. What are nontraditional services? They are usually the newer ones placing us in a straightjacket from which there is no escape. Anything done with a computer must be nontraditional, since we weren't doing it 20 years ago. Some librarians may be conservative, but that conservatism doesn't compare to the values favored by some customers and politicians who think fondly of their libraries as their grandmothers described them.

When asked to identify a nontraditional activity, the one that comes immediately to mind is online searching. Terminal searching is an option in reference work with the relevant question being: Is the library supposed to do this? Not how. How is an internal management judgment. "Should the library do this" is easy to answer in today's cost-effective environment. Helping people by making our collections useful to them is the most obviously cost-effective service we can offer in validating the money spent on operations, collection, and staff salaries; it is the service local bookstores do not offer. Providing best-sellers is something bookstores can do better than we can. If we are not going to help people make the library more useful in their lives, then what is the point?

Searching for Cost-Effectiveness

The primary reason we fret over the cost of online searching is because of the way we budget. Online searches may be more or less costly than manual reference, depending on several factors that we have already evaluated, although we have rarely told others. However, any valid cost comparison must allow the reference librarian to spend as much time on the question as finding the answer requires. Limiting reference service to five minutes per question means that the game is over even before it begins. It means that we have tailored library programs to budgets dictated by others without ever pointing out the gaps that remain. The point regarding inadequate reference service would be made far more clearly if there were a long wait at the reference desk and virtually all callers were on hold for 15 minutes. However, the point only works if we learn to stop blaming ourselves. Answering a reference question takes as long as it takes.

Online searches look more expensive because we have set aside little or no funds for it. In contrast, searches by reference librarians using material for which we have already paid are presumed to cost nothing. The argument is transparently absurd to any accountant, but why was no money set aside for this task, or why was this activity so badly underestimated? Is online searching trivial or peripheral in library activities, as we look beyond the 1990s?

Can We Get What We Don't Have?

The same problem surfaces when we talk about the service that we refer to, rather simplistically, as interlibrary loan—though for journal articles we don't lend, we photocopy. No library can expect to be complete, and what we already have as compared to what we obtain on the outside, is our management decision, based on the likelihood of repeated use vs. infrequent use vs. probably no use at all; cost and convenience also enter into the equation.

Fortunately, the decision is made less traumatic by the development of ever-improving bibliographic access and document delivery services. The customer, whose interest is in obtaining a copy, need not be involved in the decision of how we obtain it and must not be involved in paying a penalty because of our decisions.

However, perpetuating customer satisfaction can only work if our budgets recognize the certainty that some things are bought in anticipation of repeated use and some things are acquired later in reaction to what may be only one-time use. Unless our basic library service provides at least these options for both documents and reference, we promise our customers service only *if* we decide to purchase it and *if* someone else doesn't beat them to it.

"There Really Is Money"

There is no escaping the reality that programs depend on funding, but it seems that we don't spell out those options very well for those who are responsible for anteing up. When neither the funding entities nor customers are aware of the implications of budgetary decisions, the cuts become easier; they also become easier when costs are shifted out of the budget because they are not "traditional."

What are considered perfectly normal library services in 1993 and will they be the same in 2003? This is not the same question as it was in 1950 or even in 1980. If we introduce user fees for such services, we engage in a strategic abdication that, once it starts, becomes endless. If we can be drawn into a discussion of what is normal and traditional, we can eventually be drawn back 150 years, when there were no free public libraries. The definition of "adequacy" in libraries changes, and it should not surprise us that this frequently means more and faster.

However, there is a catch. If we stress that library services must be offered to our customers without additional charge, we must also recognize that this places upon us the great responsibility of assuring that the services are indeed offered. In the final analysis, "Free or Not at All" is not a very heroic statement when the result is "Not at All." Those who are responsible for funding public libraries are responsible for the quality of that service. Politicians have options. They can transfer funds from priority A to priority B, they can increase taxes, they can decrease taxes. Of course, they would rather not increase taxes, and unless they have a strong reason for doing so, they don't.

The point is that they *could* if the reason were compelling enough, even in 1993. Frankly, they will never volunteer to increase our funding. There are no "good times" in our future.

I am not unsympathetic to the pressures that public library directors face, but I find it disturbing to read where some of their rationalization leads them (Wendy Smith, "Fee-Based Services: Are They Worth It?" *Library Journal* 118, June 15, 1993, pp. 40-43). When it is suggested that without fees we will get something to you in due course, but if you want special treatment (relevant service), you have to pay for it, I am reminded that the 911 number for emergency calls imposes no such restraint (911 for paying police customers; 912 is for nonpayers, but don't expect a patrol car any time soon). Funding options are never simple, but let us not justify the freeness of library service by its lack of speed, or perhaps by its irrelevancy to the needs of the customer. "The library is free and worth every cent of it" is not a good slogan for National Library Week.

Electronic Resource Sharing: It May Seem Obvious, But It's Not as Simple as It Looks

There can be no doubt that electronic resource sharing provides great opportunities for libraries in permitting the library's clientele a much wider access to information. There can also be little if any doubt that these opportunities will enhance both awareness and demand. They will therefore tend to be both cost-effective and cost-beneficial, but certainly not cheaper than earlier alternatives, and this is particularly true if faculty and researchers are permitted simply to add these new opportunities to their more traditional methods of demanding full-sized copies in their libraries. The unwillingness of academic administrators to recognize and deal with the issue of these additional costs suggests the danger that librarians will be expected simply to "absorb" these additional costs through reallocation. The paper argues the need for total and comprehensive budget planning instead of the piecemeal approach of considering only specific technological options, and the need to include organizational management in these decisions and responsibilities.

At last year's conference at which I was honored to be invited and recognized, I ventured some predictions about the opportunities and dangers in serving library users beyond the year 2000. I am further honored to be asked to make additional comments at this conference. This conference, as you know, deals with the possible use of new technologies for resource sharing and universal availability. As I look at the titles of some of the papers I look forward to hearing, I am struck by the fact that they deal in large part with practical applications, and I have no doubt that they will be informative and helpful. Nor, of

Speech presented at the 16th International Essen Symposium, "Resource Sharing: New Technologies as a Must for Universal Availability of Information." University of Essen, Germany, October 18, 1993.

384

course, do I have the slightest doubt of the impact that technology can and should play in the way we access and share information, or of the certainty that this provides tremendous opportunities for improving the communication of information in a world whose thirst for knowledge will probably never be slaked.

My concern is, though, with the political implications of all of this, and most particularly with the lack of clear understanding that surrounds the phrase "virtual library." I must confess that much of the thinking that went into this paper was triggered by last year's presentations by Barbara von Wahlde, Dick Dougherty, and Maureen Pastine. It struck me then, and to an even greater extent now, that "virtual library" has become for many outside our own profession, and perhaps from some inside it, a buzzword slogan. Everyone is in favor of it; nobody is prepared to pay for it (insisting that somehow the costs can be absorbed or shifted); and few people outside our own field have the vaguest idea of what this means. My alarm is then triggered by recalling the old saying variously attributed to Mark Twain, Will Rogers, and Josh Gibbons. "It isn't what we don't know that causes all the trouble. It's what we do know for a certainty, except that much of what we know for a certainty is wrong."

I have attempted no literature survey, but my own observations lead me to conclude that there are many assumptions about the virtual electronically shared library that, if not wrong, are at least simplistic. They assume basic changes in human behavior patterns for which we have very little indication. If there is one thing we understand, it is that individuals will try very hard, whenever possible, to adapt their environment to their own preferences, rather than adapt themselves to their environment. And, indeed, they should. Sometimes technologists, or those subsumed by their awe of technologists, make assumptions about people that are simply not valid. We now find increasingly that certain online capabilities are not being used, or at least by far fewer users than projected. It was assumed that if a service were available, everyone would want to use it. We forget that people prefer to do what is convenient for them, and that they will continue to do this. Librarians working with time-dependent clienteles in industry have known for some time that when information is not available either in a convenient format or within the time frame demanded, we are perfectly capable of denying that any such information exists at all, even when we know it does.

My first concern about the assumptions that come with the technological library is the assumption that it will somehow require less space for the library itself. I have seen that argument put forward in such diverse settings as the planning for a new public library in my home community, and in library building discussions now taking place on several University of California campuses. The future library, it is argued, will not need to be nearly as large, because it will require far less physical materials on site. All we will need, for the most part, are some self-service terminals and screens on which information can be displayed—anything from anywhere.

It is, of course, an exaggeration, but something like this is at least possible, but only if that is what people want. We will recall Wilfrid Lancaster's predictions for a paperless society.[1] Lancaster was correct in stating what *could* happen, but he was totally wrong in predicting what *would* happen. We now all know that computers are huge producers of paper, in part because they can do so easily, rapidly, and relatively cheaply, but in large part because it turns out that we like the safety and security of paper. Just about all of the faculty terminals in our offices have printer attachments, and I know of individuals who routinely print out all of their e-mail messages, so that they can scan them later at their leisure. Then they throw them away.

As architects and the public and academic administrators who plan for library needs (frequently without asking the librarians) plan for smaller buildings, they perhaps do so on the shaky premise that what is possible is therefore going to happen. The attraction in the presumed reduction in costs, or at least the transfer of costs from acquisition to resource sharing, is something about which I will speak in greater detail later. However, the premise is at best dubious, because we have been extremely careful not to disturb faculty in particular by suggesting that libraries will perhaps not have large collections of several million volumes as we switch the emphasis from physical to electronic storage and that we will substitute additional electronic availability. There is nothing necessarily wrong with not telling them, but it makes both the premise of space and cost reductions highly dubious. We are already in a position to transfer much of what we call interlibrary loan from hard copy to electronic display. However, the quantity of physical documents continues to increase, even as everything else also increases. Indeed, technology has given us new and improved ways to produce paper, for storage or perhaps later disposal. I am talking about the fax machine, simply another technology that produces paper.

If it is assumed, therefore, that technology will reduce the physical space requirements of libraries, nobody has yet discussed that issue with library users, and my concern is that the space will be reduced without anyone talking to them, with librarians then left with the unpleasant task of explaining someone else's bad decision regarding the library. Has it happened before? Countless number of times. There is still, to this day, a great reluctance to discuss unpleasant news with academic faculty members, and if the examples I am about to cite for you sound nasty, please remember that I am talking about a group of which I am myself a member.

In 1992 the Mellon Foundation reported the results of a three-year comprehensive study in a volume titled *University Libraries and Scholarly Communication*, published by the Association of Research Libraries.[2] As the researchers looked at the various implications of both technology and resource sharing, it would not have been an unreasonable hope that they would make some significant recommendations to their fellow academicians. Instead, they noted that scholarly publication is tied to prestige, and that this tends to make scholars more conservative. The study warned against unwarranted automation, without really defining what that meant, and after noting a wide range of ways in which scholars use information from their academic libraries, left the matter simply there, without suggesting alternatives that might or might not be reasonable.

It is this continued unwillingness to choose among alternatives that leads to my second concern—that the virtual library we are about to create will probably not substitute *electronic costs* for *publication costs*, but rather substitute them for the publications costs we are no longer paying in any case, because we can no longer afford to do so. If there is going to be a faculty willingness to *voluntarily* forego ownership for access, to forego physical possession of the journal in which I have published or might someday perhaps like to publish, there has been no indication of this. It is therefore essential, I think, that librarians make sure that administrators understand that the massive electronic resource sharing which is not only possible, but indeed desirable, will be cost-effective, but that it will not be cheap. It will require additional funds, considerable additional funds, and, of course, it is the responsibility of the university president, not the librarian, to either find the money or explain why the opportunity will have to be missed.

Before I return to this theme, let me just posit my third concern, and this is one that I addressed here last year—that somehow all of this technology will be easy for the end user, when, of course, we know, or at least should know, that the world of information intermediaries is growing with tremendous rapidity. An article in June 1993 in the British journal *The Economist*, after noting the tremendous growth of the information service sector (without once mentioning libraries) even uses a term to describe this specialization I had not seen before.[3] In addition to hardware and software, customers are able, and are increasingly willing, to acquire a third commodity. The article calls this *meatware*, the purchase of the intellectual labor with which to use the hardware and the software. I recall hearing at last year's conference of the emerging strategy within the Association of Research Libraries (ARL) of seeking a role of information advisors, who will counsel the end user in how to do his or her own information searches. However, human behavior studies would suggest that before we seek or accept advice, we would like some assurance that the individual providing the advice is qualified to do so. Symphony conductors do not emerge from thin air, they have paid their dues as recognized and respected instrumentalists. If advisers emerge, they will do so from honored and trusted intermediary meatware specialists, not from thin air.

My concern, then, is not that we will lack the technological opportunities to create true access and resource sharing networks. In our business the technology has always been well ahead of our opportunities to use it. There will, of course, be issues that require adjustment, and particularly these are issues of ownership, copyright, and downloading. These are only economic issues, and I use the word "only" because I believe, with Peter Drucker, that of all of the resources, money is still the easiest to obtain, provided that we deal with products and services that people really want. In such an environment cost becomes irrelevant, and the money is found, perhaps at the expense of something else. In the United States alone, the annual level of expenditures for video games is more than $65 billion, and video games are hardly as important to the health, safety, and economic prosperity of our nation as the issues we are discussing here.

It is my concern that the technology will move us forward too fast, before the issues of the economics of this process have been discussed and the responsibilities allocated. And the responsibility is not that of the librarian, but of the individuals to whom both the librarians and the faculty members at least nominally report. There are choices here, and they must be carefully spelled out and priced, so that decisions can be made.

We should certainly understand that issues of economics are usually more of a process of style than of reality. About a month ago, a plan was unearthed in the United States that promised to reduce the federal work force by over 200,000 employees.[4] How this was to be done was left vague, with suggestions of attrition and retirements, and that was wise, because none of this will ever happen. It will never happen because it can't happen politically. All administrations rail against waste and high taxes, but they also rail against unemployment, and perhaps wasted labor is the price of high employment. Certainly, if there had been a real desire to reduce the federal work force by 200,000 people, it could have been done easily enough. Let me try a sample announcement to show you how simple, and yet how impossible, this is. "We are reducing the government work force by 200,000 people. The individuals have been selected, and termination notices to each are in the mail. They will be gone within the month. We selected these individuals by the simple expediency of doing computer searches on their job descriptions, and eliminating all employees who ostensibly had roles as coordinators or facilitators. We have done this because we know from the work of Tom Peters, Gifford Pinchot, and Peter Drucker that facilitators and coordinators don't really do anything except create more work for other people."

Why have I told you this rather fanciful tale? In part to point out that the promise of economy in a political environment is enough, and that there is no real need to ever produce any economies. People forget. However, this issue of living in a never-never world is particularly significant for the academic environment in which so many of us live. In 1986 Howard Bowen and Jack Schuster published another study, based on four years of data gathering, this time sponsored by the Carnegie Corporation, under the provocative title *American Professors: A National Resource Imperiled*.[5] I will not do the eloquence of the study justice when I tell you that the basic conclusion was that professors were found to be intelligent, well-educated, hard-working, productive and honorable, and that they were also unappreciated and underpaid. If academic and government library administrators are also so treated, nobody has yet been willing to undertake a study to tell our bosses.

My point in this paper is very simple. In the sessions that follow we will learn about many new and exciting opportunities. In talking about these, let us not forget about the money without which none of this can happen. If we talk about the opportunities and not about the price tag, then we will somehow be saddled with the job of finding a way to finance something that cannot and should not be funded through reallocation. Economies in the process of scholarly communication are, of course, possible, but those economies depend largely on the activities of two other bodies, scholarly publishers and academic researchers and whatever inconveniences or changes in work style they might be willing to adopt for the sake of economy. At this point I see virtually no willingness to do this. Could we be left holding the bag? It has happened before.

Let me suggest a simple mini-tutorial of the management process. It is the responsibility of subordinates, and certainly this includes us, to examine options and alternatives, to spell out the pros and cons of each of the alternatives, and to make recommendations. It is the job of our bosses, and we all have bosses, to make decisions based on those alternatives, and then to take responsibility for those decisions. What this means is that if there is faculty insistence on procedures and value systems that cost money, then the president gets to decide whether to find more money or to discipline the faculty. Either alternative, but only those alternatives, can be acceptable to us. "You figure out a way, because I don't know how," is not an acceptable phrase of downward management communication.

Costs of information access systems can be considered high, although the word high is relative. Compared to what? Most certainly the overall cost will go up, because opportunities increase, and with opportunities expectations also increase. We now insist on having what before we did not even know was possible. The advantage that technological resource sharing and access brings to us is not greater economy, or even cost-efficiency, but cost-effectiveness. If something costs twice as much but produces five times as much, and if we need and want it, then it is a bargain. The organizations that sell us things understand that well enough. That is why products can be bought by the case, or at least by the large bottle, and why wine is not sold by the mouthful.

Everyone is in favor of cost-effectiveness, but we have not been particularly competent in making the case for the value of what we do instead of simply the activity itself. For libraries, both circulation and holdings are poor justifications because they deal with the activity rather than with the purpose of the activity. As budget crunches continue, the problem can get worse. All of my examples come from my own country, but I suspect the application is universal. In one public library setting it has been suggested that the library should charge clients for reference service, but why did we purchase the collection in the first place, unless we planned to maximize its use? In a report issued by the Urban Libraries Council, it is stated that the pressure is on libraries to forego education and training to allow the doors to be kept open longer. And what is supposed to take place inside those open doors? Doesn't that matter?

Peter Drucker has suggested that service professionals are addicted to the moral imperative, to the belief that somehow with or without money we have to do everything or it will be our fault.[6] Drucker does not mention librarians, but I suspect that the description fits. Astute manager that he is, Drucker also notes that the strategy of moral imperativists is self-defeating, because if they assume the blame, nobody will ever give them any money.

If I see reasons for concern in this for our own field, I think there is good cause. And that is the message I bring to this conference. By all means let us examine the opportunities and economies of effectiveness that resource sharing and automation bring us. Let us make our recommendations based on what, in our professional judgment, would be best for our parent institutions. However, let us not forget about the money. This process will cost more, and it is not money that can be totally reallocated, even if we were free to make all kinds of reallocation decisions. So by all means talk about the cost. But identify it as an opportunity cost, and as a fantastic bargain. Ultimately, if you manage them properly, your bosses really have no option but to pay for this, because it makes sense.

We cannot promise to bring proposals that cost no additional money. We can only promise to bring proposals that we believe make sense in terms of the mission of the institution as it has been articulated. Implementing that mission requires, in our professional judgment, that the things we are proposing must be done, and must be funded. If that ends up costing more, we can only state that we can demonstrate that it is worth it, and that there is really no choice unless this institution wants to condemn itself to obsolescence.

If academic administrators are concerned about money, and, of course, they are, there are probably even some economies we can suggest for their consideration that would save money without a significant deterioration of the academic institution. However, they involve decisions we cannot make and authority we do not possess. They involve a reassessment of ingrained values and ingrained habits, and for these the only virtue may be that they are old and comfortable. Certainly, when Bowen and Schuster dismiss the discussion of academic ineffectiveness with the argument that this is just the way professors are, they leave very little room for any further debate.

None of this would be particularly significant for us, because after all, others can be inefficient if they want to be as long as it does not affect us, except that it does affect us. Funding agencies, in part because of genuine money shortages, and in part because of disenchantment with what the academic sector has long promised but rarely delivered—quality of life and high employment—are making things still more difficult for the academic institution. Even during the so-called good times, which we now historically know to be the 1960s and 1970s, there was a tendency to think of the library as a place and as a collection, or if you prefer to be eloquent, the heart of the university. Librarians themselves, their selection, qualification, pay, continuing education and training, and support for needed equipment, have all taken a back seat. If we now find the opportunity for electronic resource access, the so-called virtual library, defined simply as nothing more than an even larger collection without any other sort of adaptation of research and information use style, then it is not difficult to see that in the future the pressures on all of the things that librarians do that are not directly connected with the acquisition of material, whether in hard copy or electronically, will increase. Incentive supporting this strategy is seen in the abdication of administrators who a) want expanded electronic access for their institutions, b) don't want to find the funds for this exciting new development, and c) don't even want to hear about it. Any student of management knows that the statement "you figure out a way to absorb and reallocate" is an ultimate management abdication, because if there is one thing that our bosses are supposed to do it is to decide—decide on the basis of options we spell out and recommendations we make, and if the decision involves choosing between expanded service at a greater cost and an obsolete and irrelevant service at a lower cost, then this is precisely what their own job descriptions demand that they do. They must decide.

I have, in many of the writings that were so generously recognized last year, noted that we were far better at working hard, and even working effectively, than in getting credit or in understanding the political environment, and I won't bother you with those arguments today. However, there is plenty of evidence that the trend to trivialize both the cost of the library and the role of the professionals who presumably make its policies continues, with the greater emphasis on "the place" or "the thing," and that can grow into "the terminal." In a branch of our profession somewhat different from that represented by this group, Eleanor Jo (Joey) Rodger of the Urban Libraries Council reports in the September 1, 1993, issue of *Library Journal* that there has been a drastic shift of public library funding from continuing education and training, but also from all other activities, in favor of a strategy of "just keep the doors open."[7] I think that Rodger reports accurately, but I disagree with her when she concludes that these changes, implemented by management above the level of the library, are therefore not the fault of librarians. It is librarians' fault, in the failure to plan, to point out alternatives, and to make others responsible for the disastrous consequences that can result from management's bad decisions.

It is only a short step from "just keep the doors open" to "just keep the terminals wired for self-service" and never mind everything else, because we have a shortage of funds. If this is the future for academia, then all our strategies for enhancing access electronically, essential as this certainly is to the effectiveness of doing our jobs, will have become a Pyrrhic victory. Planning for resource sharing in the electronic environment must be large-scale and of multiyear dimensions, and not micromanagement, because this is an area that cannot be funded one year at a time. It is important that we develop these plans and projections, because if we don't somebody else will, and because they only know money or only know machines but don't know the information process, their projections and conclusions will certainly be incompetent. As we develop our plans and documentation, it should not be surprising if a number of strategies emerge that, quite coincidentally, also serve us. It should not surprise us because only candidates for sainthood do anything else. Everyone else, in a management setting, proposes what is best for them because they can certainly convince themselves that what is best for them is also best for the organization. Having convinced ourselves, we then need to convince others.

Some, although by no means all, of the pieces of this strategy that we present to our administrators would include the following:

1. Electronic resource sharing and access are absolutely essential if this is to remain a significant institution for research, scholarship, and teaching.

2. Electronic access and resource sharing will be cost-effective and even cost-beneficial, but they will not be cheap. They will require additional money. Finding that money is the job of the administrators at the highest level, because finding money has always been their most important job. Professors, and for that matter librarians, really need them for little else.

3. How much cost-effectiveness and how much money depends in part on changes in academic behavior that we can only suggest, but that we cannot enforce. Administrators then have a choice of either attempting some review of how the information-use process takes place, or of finding even more money.

4. Of course, the planning and implementation of such a significant undertaking will require technical support from many people, particularly technologists and computer specialists. However, there is only one group of people that can effectively manage the effort. Guess who that is?

As I face the prospects of enhanced electronic access and resource sharing I am, of course, exhilarated by the potential opportunities. I worry about the many vacuums that can be left in a piecemeal planning process. I recall enough from my study of physics to know that nature abhors a vacuum. If we leave vacuums, somebody else will fill them. I am also reminded of Napoleon's advice about the three important elements in building an army. The first important element, he stated, was money. The second was money. And the third was money.

And those are my cautions as we begin this conference.

Notes

1. Lancaster, F. Wilfrid. *The Dissemination of Scientific and Technical Information: Toward a Paperless Society.* Champaign-Urbana, IL: University of Illinois Occasional Paper 127. 1977.

2. Andrew W. Mellon Foundation. *University Libraries and Scholarly Communication.* Washington, DC: Association of Research Libraries, 1992.

3. "Teltech Tales." *The Economist* 327 (June 26, 1993): 90-91.

4. Gore, Albert. *Reinventing Government.* Report of a task force chaired by the Vice President of the United States. Washington, DC: Government Printing Office, 1993.

5. Bowen, Howard R., and Jack H. Schuster. *American Professors: A National Resource Imperiled.* New York: Oxford University Press, 1986.

6. Drucker, Peter F. *Managing the Non-Profit Organization.* New York: HarperCollins, 1990.

7. St. Lifer, Evan, and Michael Rogers. "Urban Libraries Council Study Finds Libraries Invest Little in Staff Development." *Library Journal* 118 (September 1, 1993): 112-113.

The Leader as Decision Maker: When Centralized Decisions Become Imperative

My title requires at least some definition. I am not an advocate for authoritative decision making just for the fun of it, or simply to fuel the manager's ego. Of the four ranges of management styles I identify—authoritative, consultative, participatory, and abdicative—I stress that the most appropriate for any situation is the one that manages least, given the constraints under which the manager is operating, and, of course, managers always operate under constraints. These include time, money, space, and the expectations of others outside his or her management sphere. In lecturing on this point to my students, I stress that frequently managers make decisions they need not make or should not make, and perhaps as frequently, they refuse to make decisions that they alone can make.

Inevitably, I am pressed for examples. I suggest that library directors do not need to decide—indeed it is a decision they can totally abdicate—where to hold the library picnic, or what color to paint the staff lounge, and I am met with howls of protest. Those aren't really important decisions for the staff, I am assured. I can only state that, as they gain management experience, the students will learn that these are very important decisions, in terms of staff morale. I think we all know that it is not the big things that destroy the confidence and will of an organization, it is the cumulation of little things. We can understand and accept the reality that there isn't much money for salary increases, even as we wish there were more. By contrast, we become furious when somebody else gets the desk near the window; that somebody else is getting to attend that L.C. committee meeting in Washington; or conversely, that I am stuck once again by having to go to Washington. Either negative reaction can occur, and the

Speech presented at the 35th Allerton Institute on "Critical Issues in Library Management: Organizing for Leadership and Decision-Making." University of Illinois, Monticello, October 24-26, 1993.

sensible manager understands that, when selecting someone to go to Washington, or to chair a committee, or even to be a member of a committee, if possible select someone who thinks the appointment would be an honor, or at least fun.

To do this you have to know your staff as individuals, and understand what motivates them. And what motivates them is not necessarily what you think ought to motivate them. It is the cumulation of little decisions, particularly when they are perceived as arbitrary and unreasonable, that tend to destroy the morale of an organization. The manager does not need to pick either the picnic site or the color of the staff lounge. Managerial competence is no stronger in this area than anyone else's. It is, of course, possible that the decision, once reached democratically, will still cause some unhappiness, but that unhappiness is directed at a process (I am surrounded by people without taste), and not at the organization itself. If students think that "minor" decisions are not important for staff morale, they will just have to take my word for it until they can discover it for themselves.

My example of an autocratic decision comes with the question of what I might do if the fire alarm bell rang. Would we discuss, and perhaps vote on, whether or not to leave? After all, we know that most library fire alarms are false alarms. No, there would be no discussion. I would tell them to pick up their coats and notebooks and leave the building, now!

I am sure that other speakers will tell you it is desirable to permit the staff to participate in the decision-making process, and I agree. Delegation, that much revered and little practiced concept, is a valuable management tool that we don't employ nearly enough. However, delegation is not abdication, the tactic I suggested in selecting a picnic location. It is not even participation, except in a very narrow and limited sense.

The Japanese have far more delegation than we do, but that delegation is specifically focused on the individual's or the group's own job. Japanese workers do not make automotive company policy with regard to whether to open a new U.S. production plant, what prices to charge for cars, or whom to promote to director of the factory. Japanese workers are given a great deal of responsibility (which they translate into freedom) in determining how *they* will do *their* work more effectively to achieve the desired results—greater output, lower cost, fewer errors. They accept this willingly because they understand the contract between the employer and themselves—loyalty returned for loyalty offered. That may change as the Japanese work force is faced with layoffs, but that is an issue for the future. For the present, it should be noted that these Japanese tactics of individual and team empowerment work even, albeit with modifications, for American employees of Japanese corporations. And this is because of one very simple characteristic of delegation—it concentrates on results and not on methods.

Being judged by results is something we generally consider fair, as long as we understand what those expected results are—in advance. The way to deal with this is through specific job descriptions that relate to unit and larger group plans and strategies, and, of course, these are based on goals and objectives. Individuals must know *why* a product has to be of certain quantity, cost, and quality. Understanding this is for them more important than the question of how the decision was made—participatorily or consultatively if possible, authoritatively if necessary. Human beings, unlike robots, need to know why. It is a question we begin asking almost as soon as we learn to talk, and it demands an answer.

Once we understand the why, the how is a territory that individual workers, and teams of workers, cherish as their own domain. Where authoritative managers fail most abysmally is not so much in edicting what should result, but in how it should be accomplished. That how is usually totally unnecessary, and as the Japanese have found, it can be totally counterproductive. Workers usually know their own jobs better than the boss knows them. If encouraged and rewarded to participate in this process, they will improve quality and quantity, and in doing this also enhance their own morale. It is the classic example of the win-win phenomenon. The problem, I would argue, is not just that managers make too many decisions, it is that they make the wrong decisions. Some of the things they are supposed to decide they often refuse to decide. What is at fault here is the existence of needless rules and needless decisions—what we so fondly call red tape bureaucracy. Whether these needless and intrusive rules were introduced by managers or by a committee matters very little, because the committee process also can lead to intrusive and unnecessary regulations. My concern, in this paper and in my management teaching, is far less with the issue of who makes certain decisions (although I have already expressed my preference for decentralization whenever appropriate), but rather with whether needless decisions are being made, and on whether needed decisions are not being made. Both problems can occur, and they can occur simultaneously in the same organization.

Managers have many roles, but probably the most significant of these can be identified as the need for control, and the need for decisions. For the control process we now have a great deal of help, from computer programs that instantly spot deviations from the financial plan, and from "helpful" staff organizations within the library and, most frequently, outside it. I am thinking in particular of the accounting department, which reminds us that we have spent 57 percent of the funds in only 48 percent of the time. Control, while obviously an essential part of management, is a process that can, to a large extent, be abdicated to others and even to machines. It is by far the easiest part of management.

However, we get very little help with decisions, and here I would define the managerial role as one of either making decisions or of seeing to it that decisions are made. There are certainly authoritative managers who make decisions that should be left to subordinates, to committees, and to individual workers, or for that matter who make decisions that need not be made at all, by anyone. Loren Belker refers to these as octopus managers,[1] and it is my own sad observation that these individuals may not be trainable and, as in dealing with an octopus, we may simply have to squish them.

Of greater concern to me are managers who refuse to make decisions, and who refuse to see to it that others make decisions. My observations, in libraries but not necessarily exclusively in libraries, is that decision-avoidance managers are far more likely to be found than authoritative and octopus managers. Most specifically, when we reach the level above the library, we find that the nonlibrarians above us who are supposed to make decisions as part of their jobs—university presidents and chancellors, mayors, presidents of library boards, corporate directors of research or of administrative service, principals and superintendents of schools—won't decide at all. We also find managers within libraries who are reluctant to decide what they are supposed to decide, or at least to make sure others decide. As we know from management precepts, the absence of a decision is a decision. When I tell you I can't or won't decide whether we will let you attend the next ALA conference, which is now only four weeks away, I send one of several messages, all of which are unhappily received, unless I can also tell you *why* I can't yet decide and *when* I will be able to decide. Those messages may include: 1) you are trivial and don't matter to me; 2) I have no guts; or 3) a combination of the two. I think everyone who has been caught in this trap would agree that, at some point, even a negative decision is preferable to no decision. Nature abhors a vacuum, and organizations abhor a lack of decisions, a lack of direction, a lack of focus. Managers are responsible for seeing to it that decisions are made—by themselves if necessary—by others if possible. That is, if a decision needs to be made. If no decision needs to be made, then that conclusion that no decision is required, and you can do whatever you want, is in itself also a decision. My concern here is less with fixing percentages on who makes what decisions, but rather to insure that the process takes place at all. In general, I don't care for authoritative managers, particularly where authoritarianism is not called for. However, not only I, but just about everybody else, would prefer a predictable authoritarian to someone who is paralyzed by the need to do anything.

Why do individuals avoid making decisions? The answer may be nothing more than a lack of interest, or a lack of awareness that decisions matter, at least for the individual charged with making the decision. That could well apply to nonlibrarians who have responsibility for libraries as part of their domain. We understand that such a situation cannot be acceptable for the library. As Peter Drucker[2] notes, any subordinate has the right to expect that his or her boss is fascinated with what is done by subordinates, because it is the manager's responsibility to care.

That reason is less likely to apply to library managers. Their reason for failing to react may be a decision paralysis related either to lack of confidence, a fear of offending, or a whole range of other reasons. Unfortunately, decision-avoidance managers have become very good in the process of avoiding decisions. Some of the tactics are a claim of being too busy, which can lead to a failure to read supplied documentation, or a failure to schedule meetings or return telephone calls. It should be noted that a claim of being "too busy" is a selective claim, because it simply means that they are too busy to deal with *you*. In other words, it is really a lie, although a polite lie. The process of decision avoidance through endless delay by asking for more information, even when it is not needed, is also well known to those who have suffered from its effects. However, some tactics designed to encourage greater participation, and I would state that this is an appropriate tactic where applicable, can also serve the decision-avoidance manager. The appointment of committees where no committee is really required is such a tactic, and we should note that those named to pointless committees almost always know what has been done to them. The misuse of the committee process as a dodge against decision making is so well understood even by the general public that cartoonists are safe in using it.

I recall one cartoon of tourists examining a historical marker proclaiming, "On this spot the leaders of all the world powers convened to face the crises facing the world, and decided to appoint a committee."

It may be useful to reexamine, very briefly, some of the characteristics that define managers and leaders, and particularly the differences between the two, and I attempted to do this in one of my own articles[3] that drew heavily on the work of Tom Cosgrove.[4] Management can be taught, although it requires, in its successful application, a number of characteristics. The most important of these, I would argue, is courage. Because if it is important that managers empower their subordinates, it is at least equally important that they protect them—against unfairness, against unreasonableness, against abuse. There are some very courageous library managers, but there are also some who are not. I find it discouraging that, in an in-basket exercise I give to my students, some acting in the assigned role of an academic library director, they respond to a demand for an apology by a faculty member for the presumed rudeness of a staff member by simply apologizing. Is anything known at this point, even, for example, who it was who was rude? Managers are by necessity pragmatists, but they must also understand their obligation to others, and particularly to the members of their staff. Management is not perceived as fair and predictable. Since we rarely appoint managers because of their perceived stellar qualities as future managers, but more likely because of their success as workers, it should not be surprising that some managers lack courage, and that some will dive headlong into a search for compromise and consensus. It should be noted that such senior management writers as Peter Drucker and Mary Parker Follett[5] caution against the easy search for agreement and consensus. Drucker notes that when consent appears to be too easily reached, it may simply be because some people don't care, or because others are intimidated. The decision could well turn out to be wrong, and Drucker argues that we should back away from consensus too quickly reached and talk some more. Follett stresses that we should encourage rather than squelch dissent, and Thomas Watson of IBM meant the same thing when he urged his managers to protect the "wild ducks," those whose opinions differed markedly from the majority. They might be misguided pests. On the other hand, they might be right.

If it is the job of the manager not just to find, through a variety of techniques, *an* answer to the problem but also the *best* answer, the appropriate and inappropriate use of the committee process comes into focus. Managers can be arbitrary and tyrannical, but so can committees in squelching dissent. I have long been worried about the phrase "gets along well with others" as a virtue in the performance evaluation process, because it never seems to add "in the reaching of good decisions."

It is here that the characteristics of managers and leaders can differ. If managers seek a consensus, even if the decision is not necessarily their own (and that may not be bad if the group's is better), leaders are rarely so lacking in confidence. Leaders do not seek consensus, they try to persuade others to accept their view of the world. Positive leaders accomplish great things, but we can't really judge until after the fact, and certainly not all leaders are beneficial. If they were, we would not have had Nazi Germany, Jonestown, or Waco. Leadership as a character trait, I would insist, cannot be willed into existence, and even basketball coaches have learned that the only senior is not necessarily the best team captain. Sometimes it is a freshman. It is certainly even a bad idea to force unwilling managers to manage, with such exhortations as "sure you can do it, anybody can." It is probably even more mischievous to suggest that anybody can be somehow taught to be a leader. We can perhaps empower leaders, or show them how to be more effective, but the suggestion that anybody can lead (or for that matter manage) simply perpetuates the problems documented by Laurence Peter,[6] who noted that, despite all of our good will, personnel selection still seems aimed at finding for everyone a job they can't do. We do this in large part because we promote people to management as a reward for work well done in another dimension. Parallel career lattices are still not common in libraries. How many superb reference librarians are able to earn more than the individual who is merely an adequate head of the Reference Department? And yet, what's wrong with that, if the reference librarian makes a greater contribution?

Instinctively, we look for individuals who will both lead and manage us, but in a recent column, Tom Peters[7] points out this is not simple. Leaders deal with large concepts, managers deal with detail. While it is desirable to appoint our leaders as managers, it is also important for these individuals to understand the discipline that this now imposes on them. If leaders seek followers, management automatically hands them some, and power can become an aphrodisiac. Peters recalls the observation by Admiral Hyman Rickover, the father of the nuclear submarine and a leader by any standards, that when he moved from conceptualizing the project to having to manage it, he was immediately faced with thousands of annoying little decisions that took up most of his time. Countries that operate under a parliamentary system usually have two designated officials—a prime minister who runs the country, and a ceremonial president or monarch who cuts ribbons, graciously receives the championship hog, and welcomes the winning soccer team. In America, we expect one individual to carry out both the leadership and the ceremonial functions, and it is difficult. Our founding fathers abhorred royalty, but royalty has its management uses in doing what real managers are too busy to do.

On a much less dramatic scale, I can attest to the limitation of freedom I encountered when I served as dean of a library school, or when earlier I had served as president of two national societies. Contrary to what we are shown on television situation comedies, management roles do not enhance power, they form barriers and limitations. As dean I understood that when I walked down the hall to the cafeteria, I had to be pleasant to any student I encountered, even if I had a toothache. The student, not knowing about my toothache, would assume she was about to be expelled from school if I frowned at her. Similarly, as a dean I also had to be polite to everyone in the administrative hierarchy, because if I made them angry, they might punish my school as a way of getting even with me. They shouldn't do that, but they might, and I simply could not take that chance. Now that I have no administrative responsibilities, but serve as a tenured faculty member, I can afford to pick fights with anyone I choose and write anything I like. This is a newfound freedom, and I understand the trade-offs between freedom and authority. I am not sure that all charismatic leaders, who may seek managerial status because it conveys prestige and money, necessarily understand what they are giving up, or at least should be giving up. Leaders who seek appointed power as a manipulative tool should, of course, worry all of us.

What does all of this mean for the management of libraries? I would agree that there are managers who should be more open, more sharing, and at least more consultative if not participatory. In many cases, such a blustering style covers incompetence and insecurity, although there are managers who make all the decisions because they think they are smarter than their subordinates. Even when they are right, the price for this management style is too high, because the prophecy becomes self-fulfilling. Managers who treat their subordinates as incompetents will eventually have a staff of incompetents, who are perfectly willing to let the boss make all of the decisions. Individuals with even a modicum of self-respect and competence will have left as soon as they could.

However, while I agree that managers should be as open and democratic as possible, I must again remind you that style is not nearly as important as substance. Are good decisions being made? Committees, I would stress, can be incompetent, and more importantly, can be viciously intolerant of dissent from the group. In an article in a recent issue of *Fortune*, Assistant Managing Editor Walter Kiechel[8] argues that tough times for managers (and there is general consensus that times are tough) do not improve management, they simply strengthen the manager's primary attribute. Good managers get better, but bad managers get worse. More specifically to the point, Kiechel warns against a rapid increase in what he calls "wimp" managers, individuals who see survival as their primary goal. That is, survival for them, and not necessarily for the organization that employs them. The musical *How to Succeed in Business Without Really Trying* had a song that captured that mood completely, "No Matter Whom They Fire, I Will Still Be Here." If we measure managers by their rate of success in achieving their objectives, it becomes clear that for success they will have to employ a range of management styles, from the autocratic to the abdicative. If there is a generalization in all of this, it is that good managers, regardless of the range of styles, must be approachable, fair, predictable, willing to communicate, and particularly willing to answer questions and explain. Finally, they must be courageous. If we want to add to that the unique characteristics of a leader—vision, communication skills, and charisma—we must remember that the leaders who would also be managers must learn self-discipline, and must understand and consider the impact on others of what they do. Turning good leaders into good managers is not a simple process.

If management writers such as Drucker and Gifford Pinchot[9] are correct, the changes that are coming to the management structure may make much of this discussion moot in the long run, although we must remember that management changes made in industry may take a decade to reach libraries, because it isn't just librarians who tend to be conservative but also those who control their direction. When we add librarian conservatism to user conservatism to the conservatism inherent in the university environment, it may take more than 10 years.

We already see a ruthless weeding in the corporate sector of layers of middle managers, and most particularly of those who carry such staff titles as facilitator or coordinator. These individuals, it has been noted, don't really do anything, and perhaps many managers don't either. If we move, as has been suggested, to self-directed work teams, we will have far fewer managers, and they will not be able to meddle nearly as much. Managers will be responsible for selecting the right people, setting overall goals and objectives, negotiating and defining resources and time scales, and then getting out of the way.

I think this is positive news for us because, unlike a lot of people, librarians really do a lot. It is also at least potentially positive news for those who want to empower individuals to the maximum of their potential and their effort. Because, in this process, at least as I understand it, it is individuals and not just groups whom we will be empowering. Those individuals will undoubtedly form themselves into work teams and temporary task forces, and they will monitor the contributions of their fellow team members far more closely than management ever did. If this turns out to be a true meritocracy, I for one have no problems with it. It will require excellent if fewer managers, and it will both reward and punish on the basis of merit far more effectively than we have ever done. There is risk in this process, as there has always been in a situation that can be subjective, that we not allow biases against individuals and groups who are different (and perhaps different because they are better) to take hold. We used to label those biases rather blatantly—preconceptions about women, about men, about minority members, about young people, about older people. We hide those biases more carefully—in terms such as "fits the model of the group," and "acts collegially toward other staff members." We will have to guard against such labels, because they can be every bit as discriminatory. It doesn't really matter that you match the others, because the others can be told to adjust.

In the future, will successful managers be expected to practice centralized decision making, consultation, participation, abdication? The answer to all of those is yes. The primary concern is that they had better know why they are doing what they are doing. We should have demanded this all along. Perhaps now we will.

Notes

1. Belker, Loren B. *The First-Time Manager.* New York: American Management Association, 1978.

2. Drucker, Peter F. "How to Manage the Boss." *Wall Street Journal*, August 1, 1986.

3. White, Herbert S. "Managers and Leaders: Are There More Differences Than Similarities?" *Library Journal* 115, no. 11 (1990): 51-53.

4. Cosgrove, Tom. "Cleaning Up Our Language About Leadership," *Campus Activities Programming* 21, no. 3 (September 1988): 40-45.

5. Follett, Mary Parker. *Dynamic Administration.* New York: Harper, 1942.

6. Peter, Laurence J. *The Peter Principle.* New York: Morrow, 1969.

7. Peters, Tom. "Even the Most Mundane Work Can Become a Source of Pride." *Bloomington Herald-Times.* May 12, 1993, (B6).

8. Kiechel, Walter. "The Problem Boss." *Fortune.* August 12, 1986.

9. Pinchot III, Gifford. *Intrapreneuring: Why You Don't Have to Leave the Corporation to Become an Entrepreneur.* New York: HarperCollins, 1986.

Would You Like to Rank Order the Importance of Your Children?

Librarians face multiple priorities. In that regard, I have been particularly interested in the issues raised by the differing needs of the customer communities served by public libraries.

Special and school librarians serve communities that are largely limited by who has building access. Academic libraries serve faculty and students, with the emphasis shaped by the type of institution, primarily research or teaching. Academic libraries should also serve the information needs of administrators, like any good special library, in the recognition that serving them successfully has many rewards. However, they rarely do.

The missions that converge on the public library—educational support and information provision—are particularly complex because they have very different and sometimes antithetical emphases. Public libraries have at least three clienteles with very different expectations, with a political payoff in serving each. The first involves the recreational support role of libraries, sometimes simplistically seen as the provision of best-sellers or books plugged by Donahue or Oprah.

It is the mission most directly assumed by that part of the public that never uses libraries, and it is the easiest to measure. You simply count circulation, on the premise that the greater the circulation totals, the better. It should be noted that "reading more" is an immediate virtue only in recreation and, perhaps partially, in education. Circulation has negative value in the provision of information, and special librarians understand that circulation statistics impress no one.

They may even suggest that people are spending a great deal of time reading when they could be working if someone would just tell them what the article says and whether it is

Reprinted, with changes, by permission of the author and *Library Journal* 118, no. 19 (November 15, 1993): 50-52. Copyright © 1993 by Reed Publishing, U.S.A.

important. Library service in support of recreation is easiest to explain, but it also has the weakest support rationale during the tough times that are always with us. It is considered nice but hardly as crucial as some of the other municipal priorities.

Convince the Chamber of Commerce

Library service in support of individual and group decision making by business and industry users is perhaps the most difficult to plan for and provide, particularly because it is rarely expected, let alone demanded. It is, at the same time, the safest in terms of political clout. If you can get the Chamber of Commerce to agree that without strong public library service the city will deteriorate, employers will leave, unemployment will increase, and the tax base will shrink, politicians will be inclined to listen.

It is my impression that we do less of this now than when John Cotton Dana and a nucleus of librarians, including many public librarians, founded the Special Libraries Association (SLA) to serve business and industry better. The reasons for the present reluctance to serve business needs from the public library are open to speculation, but could result from the allure of moral imperativism (reprinted in this book on pages 273-277). The business community, already assumed to be rich and powerful, and perhaps rapacious to boot, "needs" us least.

Politically Weak Constituencies

We are instinctively drawn to serving the third group, consisting largely of three components. We couldn't have done better in selecting three politically weaker constituencies. Helping to stamp out adult illiteracy is a monstrous problem, and it may be getting worse: It is largely older people who read newspapers, while younger people watch TV news.

Yet, we refuse to evaluate and quantify this problem, to assess the many reasons why people might suddenly want to know how to read, to measure literacy, or to try to get a handle on why people who once knew how to read well enough to graduate from school no longer know how to read. It isn't even primarily our problem, but we may be able to help.

However, we should be able to secure funds for this from the educators who created this mess in the first place. Otherwise we will continue to transfer funds from other library programs to literacy programs without identifying the real losers in the process. While there are some grant funds for library literacy programs, they pay for a small part of the cost; we are not willing to limit our activities to what is paid for by that funding.

Service to senior citizens could create political power if we could just get that most powerful of political lobbies, the American Association of Retired Persons (AARP), to adopt us, as it has adopted health insurance and Social Security benefits as primary concerns. We now serve senior citizens on a large scale, even though they tend to vote against our bond initiatives.

Serving the Children

The group we really love to serve is children, and many M.L.S. students choose to become librarians for no other reason. We will get very little political mileage out of what we do for children, however, including preschool children, simply because the professional educators insist on hogging the spotlight.

As a generalization, educators see us at best as loyal helpers for their greater and more glorious purposes. We need look no further than *A Nation at Risk*, in which our role was never mentioned, or note that school librarians must fight not only for their professional identity within the school, but must also defend themselves against the assumption that they are the most convenient layoff target during budget cutting.

Teachers will always agree that it is preferable (regretfully) to get rid of the librarians, although perhaps we can staff the library with volunteers. Their contracts make sure we don't staff classrooms with volunteers. Ultimately, we will never get much recognition or credit from local educators or the Department of Education. In the educational household, we will always be the despised Cinderella, and, unfortunately, we have no fairy godmother.

Watch Your Priorities

All managers understand instinctively that a priority rank order made public is a very dangerous exercise. What we announce as our *most* important priority is immediately interpreted by others as the *only* worthwhile priority. Salary minimums are understood to be hiring maximums, and they are helpful only if your salaries are now lower. They are disastrous if pay is higher. As a dean I knew that my university administrators were never to learn that the average faculty size for library schools was 10, because ours was 16, and I had been stressing how small that was.

It was therefore disturbing to read (Hotline, *Library Journal*, May 10, 1993) that the state of Oregon had decided to target all of its public library aid to serve children and that the bill to do so was supported by both the State Library and the Oregon Library Association. The message this sends is that all of the other services provided by public libraries are at best nonessential and, perhaps, even trivial. At the same time, Oregon's Multnomah County Public Library (Portland) is trying to defend itself against a local edict that it should charge for telephone reference service. The state's action comes as a validation of that decision. Obviously, if public service to adults is not worthy of state support, why should it receive local support?

Exchanging Apples for Oranges?

There is no other setting in which either a professional association or an official charged with protecting that profession would allow the creation of such a hopeless dilemma. Would the mayor argue that police protection is more important than fire protection, or vice versa? Would any academic library administrator suggest that serving the English department is more important than serving chemistry? All of these needs are important and deserve funding, and all of the things Oregon public libraries do deserve state support. Next question!

There is little in the way of good tidings from Oregon. Per capita support for libraries (according to a recent issue of *Statistical Abstracts*), and indeed for education, as compared to other states, is miserable. For library support, Oregon ranks well below some of the New England states, though those librarians will never volunteer that information. Their secret is safe with me.

General educational support is much greater in some of the upper Midwest states. Why is it so low in Oregon? Probably tradition and habitual budgets that are hard to modify. We can't blame this on the spotted owl, because the pattern predates the decline in the lumber industry. The funding being offered, in return for a pledge that it will all be used for children, simply moves the Oregon ranking from miserable to terrible. These "solutions" are not worthy of the praise they have been receiving.

Not So Praiseworthy

Here are quotes from the State Librarian and the project consultant: "We want to position public libraries as the lead agency for preschool education in Oregon," and "We expect these funds will result in improved children's collections and an increase in outreach." Are we then talking about a lot of money? No. The potential annual amount is $693,000.

That represents .009 of 1 percent of the total state budget, and 0.26 of 1 percent of the total state education budget. It represents about $1 annually for every child below the age of 15. And they expect to accomplish all that? Do even the governor and state legislature believe it? Why do we let public servants off with praise for giving us so little now, on top of the little they gave us in the past? Why are we willing to sacrifice all of our other public library priorities as candidates for state funding support so easily? Is it because we have no faith in our power to persuade or frighten, or because we don't even believe we deserve more money?

Indecent Is Right!

The $693,000 promised is less than the offer Robert Redford made to Woody Harrelson in *Indecent Proposal* for spending one night with Demi Moore. One dollar is less than I spend on a given afternoon (despite my doctor's advice) on snacks. And that is supposed to provide excellent library service for the children of Oregon? I would prefer to reject such an offer and either get some more funds, or campaign against any public official who doesn't support giving us more.

We have apparently forgotten, or perhaps never noticed, what Peter Drucker has said all along: it is hardest of all to get a little bit of money. How much money would it take to place Oregon first in the nation in public library state support? What's wrong with that objective? There's no doubt it would still be a small part of the state general budget and of the state education budget. In other words, if Oregon found it important enough to do, it could afford to do it.

I have been to Oregon a number of times to speak to library groups, and I have friends and Indiana alumni in the state library community. It is a beautiful state, and I hope to be invited back. Perhaps I risk losing another invitation when I observe that what Esau received from his brother Jacob in return for his birthright (Gen. 25:29-34) was probably a better deal.

Is There More Yellow Brick Road Beyond This Poppy Field?

Wizard of Oz fans will recognize this title—and that includes all librarians. Like Dorothy and her friends, academic librarians made good progress in the 1950s and 1960s, skipping toward the Emerald City on a well-marked path. When the film travelers are entrapped in the sleep-inducing poppy field, we know that somehow help is not far away. Academic librarians, by contrast, have been asleep in their own poppy field for more than 20 years.

Dorothy was accompanied by supportive friends, but we must remember that the Scarecrow, Tin Man, and Cowardly Lion all had their own strong personal reasons for reaching the Wizard. Our supporters obviously follow their own agendas, too; after 20 years of inaction there is now a good deal of yelling, shoving, and finger pointing from people who were our friends as long as the path was paved and well marked. Finally, and unlike us, Dorothy had the support of a good witch to counterbalance the wicked witches we encounter daily.

Since the 1960s, academic librarians have produced much literature to explain the problem, which is really only a conflict between unlimited expectations (those of scholars and publishers) and very limited resources (our own). Both publishers and faculty have ignored just about everything we have said; in fact, faculty have begun to find us shrill and annoying. The academic value system may be a restatement of the old office joke: There are two options: 1) The faculty are always right. 2) If the faculty are wrong, please see option 1. As you consider this assessment, please don't lose sight of the fact that I am also a card-carrying faculty member. Perhaps I know too much about my own egomaniacal fraternity.

Reprinted, with changes, by permission of the author and *Library Journal* 119, no. 1 (January 1994): 68-70. Copyright © 1994 by Reed Publishing, U.S.A.

407

The Expectations/Resources Dilemma

I have argued for some time that librarians have neither the power nor the authority to do anything about solving this expectations/resources dilemma. Only faculty and the academic administrators who are faculty members temporarily residing in large corner window offices can deal with it but would prefer not to. Publishers know all this.

That is why publication of *University Libraries and Scholarly Communication* (Association of Research Libraries [ARL], 1992) was eagerly anticipated. It is the result of a comprehensive three-year study funded and undertaken by the Mellon Foundation. It consists basically of scholars telling other scholars what they ought to know about what is happening in the university library. Since they pay so little attention to what we tell them, there was at least some potential.

Telling Us What We Know

We librarians already know much of what is included in this careful collection of data; indeed, it is largely extracted from library reports, librarian articles, and interviews. It is useful, and perhaps credible, to have someone else write it down. The report shows that—perhaps contrary to administrative assumption—academic libraries have not been receiving an increasing percentage of the university budget but a decreasing one. It also notes that the materials budget has remained a consistent share of the overall library budget, and that the lack of enough materials dollars does not result from there being too many high-priced librarians.

The shifts have been within the materials budget—from monographs to serials. However, when we finally do cancel serials, the price for remaining subscribers increases further to recover lost revenue—despite all we know about economic models that suggests that in the face of cancellations the price ought to go down. *University Libraries* does not specifically make this last point; it is unfortunate that it is left to the reader to infer.

It is also too bad that the report states observations but draws no conclusions and makes no recommendations. Finally, it is particularly unfortunate that the publisher is ARL. Librarians did not write this report or draw its conclusions, but it now runs the risk of being ignored as another document of complaint from the library community.

Electronic Publishing and Automation

The book explores the premises of electronic publishing and library automation but concludes little about these phenomena. However, it does caution against unwarranted automation costs and notes that the potential of electronic publishing has to be balanced against the reality that scholarly publishing is tied to prestige and that tends to make scholars more conservative. The study examines the factors that trigger the sharp and continuing increase in the cost of scholarly publishing but then simply leaves the argument there as though the explanation provided the justification.

Finally, the book notes a wide range of ways in which scholars use information from their academic libraries. That's true, but one would hope for some recommendations from these distinguished researchers as to what might or might not be reasonable in terms of future alternatives. Can this process simply remain open-ended, allowing all alternatives regardless of what they might cost?

Because the book lacks any sort of focus and conclusion, we must be grateful for the very useful synopsis provided by Ann Okerson of ARL, which was written after the report was completed. The synopsis is not just a historical summary and at least provides some clues about possible future directions for those inclined to seek them. Any such work supported and undertaken by the prestigious Mellon Foundation cries out for publication in places likely to be frequented by university faculty and administrators— perhaps *Change* and *The Chronicle of Higher Education*—because the usefulness of this document hinges on what happens next.

That the book does not even suggest a next step is its greatest disappointment. It leaves us in our poppy field, unless someone other than librarians reads and reacts to it. It is not the librarians who faithfully read ARL monographs whom we need to reach. We need to reach those who just might be willing to do something about the problem.

Bowen/Schuster's Potential

The reluctance of academicians to deal with issues in real time frames is well documented and, more importantly, strongly perceived by those outside academia. It is that perception that costs us dearly. In 1986, Howard Bowen and Jack Schuster published a study that resulted from four years of data gathering and analysis. That study, sponsored by the Carnegie Corporation, carries the provocative title *American Professors: A National Resource Imperiled* (Oxford University Press), and it had the potential for spelling out the problems and suggesting possible solutions for other academicians as well as politicians and the general public.

Unfortunately, the book is simply a collection of important information leading to a psalm of self-praise for the beleaguered academic community; it concentrates heavily on attacking the niggardliness of the philistines who fail to appreciate us. Faculty are described as intelligent, well educated, hard-working, productive, and honorable, with an emphasis on autonomy, academic freedom, and collegiality. They are found to be underpaid but willing to suffer that indignity for their principles.

The study acknowledges that faculty have perhaps unusual ways of approaching their work, tenure, retirement, evaluation of the work of others, and their potential for outside earnings, but that these attitudes can neither be questioned nor changed because this is simply how faculty are. The book concludes that what is needed is primarily the infusion of a great deal of additional money. We have all seen how seriously those 1986 recommendations have been taken.

The "Library Problem"

The Mellon study will not be seriously considered either if it is simply left to sit on library shelves. If we can first get academic faculty and administrators to read the Mellon report, can we then get them to accept the premise that the "library problem" is really a problem of a scholarly communication system that no one has attempted or dared to examine, validate, or revise, even when so many things that impact on that process have changed?

Are they willing to make such hard choices between spending more money and indulging the faculty? Or are we still dealing with strategies of increasing tuition and decreasing student support services without a willingness to open that larger Pandora's Box? Are we willing to deal in academia with the even greater reality that those outside our hallowed groves simply no longer trust us to set our own priorities? Is this growing estrangement automatically their fault? Even if it is, is such a shrill proclamation that we are fine and everyone else is wrong helpful?

What Are the Alternatives?

Academic librarians are beset by a problem they did not create and that they cannot solve. It can only be solved if the larger academic community is willing to reconsider the time-honored rituals of scholarly communications.

What does that mean when we deal with resource sharing, with ownership/access alternatives, with different formats for storage and delivery? Alternatives mean choices, not simply a linear addition of more options and more costs. Don't worry about the copyright implications because the law will, as always, adapt to what people want. One hopes that the solution will be fair to all, as the present approach is certainly not fair to those who are asked to pay more and more.

The Texaco decision cannot stand because it is an absurd interpretation (see News, *Library Journal*, September 1, 1992, p. 110). It will either be overturned by the appellate process or corrected through further legislation. If fair use is defined to exclude economic gain, there is no such thing as fair use. Even in academia, scholars research and photocopy in the hope of recognition, tenure, promotion, and salary increase. The economic model for corporations and academia is ultimately the same model. Students photocopy to get As, which they hope will lead to better job offers.

Getting the Rusty Wheel to Turn

The rusty academic decision-making wheel does turn but only when action is unavoidable. It turned when confronted by the explosive issue of academic standards and athletic eligibility and by unfavorable articles in the press and interviews on television. University administrators do make decisions when they perceive that they face a problem that can no longer be avoided. Is there such a perception about libraries and the scholarly communication process? Not yet.

It would have been helpful if the Mellon Foundation had trumpeted such a call for action, because a message such as this would have received attention, perhaps even coverage on the evening newscasts and television talk shows. Sportswriters helped create the sense of outrage about athletes who never attend classes, and that outrage created a sense of urgency. Who will do this for us and our problem if not the major foundations that have not only funds but also credibility? How do we get out of the poppy field and back on the road to the Emerald City?

Our Retreat to Moscow, and Beyond

After the indecisive battle of Borodino, Russian General Kutuzov withdrew his largely still intact army beyond Moscow. Napoleon quickly followed, assuming that once he had captured the enemy capital, the war would be over and the Russian government would sue for terms of surrender. He was mistaken. He found Moscow largely deserted, soon in flames and ruins, and completely depleted of all food. After waiting in vain for an enemy smart enough to know it had lost the war, Napoleon was forced into a retreat that turned into a rout, in which he lost the great majority of his army to cold, starvation, and ambush.

We know so much about this period because Tchaikovsky wrote the stirring "1812 Overture," which is always played at our own July 4 celebrations. It might be more appropriate to have it played during National Library Week. We librarians have been in a steady retreat for some time. Kutuzov had a strategy, but what is ours? If Napoleon had entered the city of Moscow to a welcome from the mayor, plans for a gala ball, and reassurances that Muscovites bore him no ill will, the war might have ended differently. We librarians honor mayors, governors, and presidents who dishonor us by trashing our budget requests. Our capacity for forgiveness is certainly worth examination in doctoral dissertations.

Scorched Library Policy?

Are we prepared to practice Kutuzov's scorched earth policy? Perhaps someone has a better strategy for winning this war for us than Kutuzov's, but I wish they would tell us what it is. Examples of our ongoing losses are so plentiful it takes only a few illustrations from the pages of our own journals. Continuing education funds for public library staff are a casualty of the

Reprinted, with changes, by permission of the author and *Library Journal* 119, no. 13 (August 1994): 54-55. Copyright © 1994 by Reed Publishing, U.S.A.

pressure to keep the doors open. We see a whole range of planning documents, from *A Nation at Risk* to National Research and Education Network (NREN) to electronic superhighways, that never mention us in their recommendations except perhaps as repositories and never include us in a major role on planning committees.

We see a national administration that is ostensibly friendlier and warmer and that argues a commitment to information but nevertheless proposes all of our research and education programs for zero funding, just as its predecessor did. If these are friends, who needs enemies? We see catchy phrases such as "virtual library" bandied about in academia, without anyone noting that this process cannot be implemented piecemeal; that it will cost a great deal of additional money though it will be worth it; and that it must be under the planning control of the only real information experts the campus has—its librarians.

Following Library Generals

I'm sure you get the idea. Any army must be led into battle by generals. I've mentioned Kutuzov and Napoleon, but who are ours? They are those people who, because of their visibility and prestige, are assumed to speak for us. The group automatically includes directors of major academic and public libraries. It includes state librarians, deans of major library education programs, and the elected officers of our professional societies.

That cluster includes some brave and articulate people. It includes others whose sole battle strategy would appear to be a series of strategic retreats without end, and some who think that appointing a long-range planning committee substitutes for action. However, that mixture can probably be found in any army.

Our leaders (some might not feel comfortable with the tag, but they are stuck with it) provide both the appearance by which the profession is judged and the examples for the rest of us to follow. My own management students know that of all of the attributes of a successful manager, the most important is courage. Good bosses expect assertiveness from their subordinates even as weak bosses might send signals indicating a preference for silence and obedience—please don't confuse blind obedience with loyalty. It is a well-known management truth that good subordinates make more trouble than bad ones, but they are worth it.

If that doesn't hold for what is expected from librarians, it may be because our bosses have trouble telling the difference between a good or a bad library, only distinguishing a cheap from a more expensive one. How else, therefore, can some managers allow themselves to be pressured out of the most fundamental of all subordinate rights, that of telling the truth in their statements, news conferences, and formal reports?

What happens to the process of rewarding support and chastising or punishing nonsupport when individuals ask only for what they are told to ask for, presumably to spare management the unpleasantness of having to say no? Why, when the politicians who slashed our budgets finally retire or are put out to pasture, do we then honor them for their "support"? Are we grateful that they didn't slash our budgets even more?

The job of generals, and of the library leaders who by rank of position are our generals, is to win. While generals protect countries, we presumably protect our profession because we fervently believe it is worth protecting.

Can Military Strategy Help?

It might help us in planning our strategy against the enemy (and anyone who doesn't want to fund us—either because they would rather fund something else or nothing at all—is an enemy) if we recalled some of the premises stated in military textbooks. Clausewitz told us that war is the continuation of diplomacy by other means. We would prefer not to fight, but if you fail to give us what we need, we will be forced to get nasty. Basil Liddell Hart suggested that the ideal battle strategy is the creation of a situation so overwhelmingly disadvantageous to the enemy that he is disinclined to fight.

We do have some weapons should we choose such a strategy, but they require that in the battle against ignorance (and ignorance breeds both crime and poverty), we are a key element and not incidental as we are presently assumed to be. Sun-Tzu, many centuries before Liddell Hart, wrote of ways of winning without ever having to fight at all. In the 1990s, Peter Drucker would put that into the framework of making sure that you and your boss are always on the same side, in opposition to "them." Why? Because your boss, being more powerful than you, becomes your strongest ally and, properly impelled, your strongest subordinate. Kutuzov would have had great difficulties in making his plan work if the czar had not supported him.

Librarians as Bit Players

Why do we have such difficulties in understanding our problems, quite aside from understanding the potential solutions? It may be in large part because of our willingness to accept the status of bit players, not only in dealing with national issues but in the institutions in which we work. We have lots of conference programs, annual themes, and news releases to explain what the library does. Allow me to let you in on a secret. Libraries at 2 A.M. do nothing at all. They just sit there.

Whatever good may happen is never because of the building but because of people and what they do. That has always been true, but it becomes even more true as we deal with enhanced bibliographic access and resource sharing. You can share materials, but you can't share people nearly as easily. Perhaps the response to the priority rating "just keep the doors open" is to respond "Why bother? There are other places with public restrooms. What will happen *after* they come in the door to have made their coming at all worthwhile?"

Will we end up with a library that charges for reference service, or that does not have enough reference librarians to satisfy an honest need that no one has rigged? What is the point of having the collection then? Reference service is the one thing Waldenbooks does not provide—it does provide books.

Reference without terminal access? Are we prepared to put a warning sign on the door alerting people that they are reentering an earlier century? We have computer searching because the technology is available, and because in many cases it provides the most cost-effective approach. If anyone wants to challenge the benefits of online searching, then it must be challenged in all of the other fields that use it. Critics might start with banks and airlines, which are also presumably looking for information cost-effectiveness.

"Building" Doesn't Equal "Library"

What does us in, over and over again, is the perception that we will give up just about anything at all to save the building, the "it." Cut the budget, cut the staff, eliminate our pay raises, let us find the money through charitable donations to pay for what you refuse to pay for. We'll do anything, just don't close the building. Drucker calls that moral imperativism and notes that the strategy always loses.

Let me share a bad news/worse news/worst news story with you. The bad news is that our budgets are being cut, our staffs are being decimated, and initiatives and professional needs are being shelved. The worse news is that, despite all of this, circulation is going up. The worst news is that we tell everyone, even brag about it. If circulation activity is perceived to be the most important thing we do, even by us, then certainly that can be accomplished by just keeping the doors open. It is little wonder the president of Dalhousie University questions a market for educated librarians, and the Urban Libraries Council reports little interest in paying for the continuing education of librarians and other staff members.

Although Napoleon is hardly the hero of this column, some still consider his military tactics worth studying. He stated that there were three essential requirements for building a strong army. The first was money. The second was money. And the third was money. Things haven't changed at all.

Tom Childers ("California's Reference Crisis," *Library Journal*, April 15, 1994, pp. 32-35) informs us that as California public library reference budgets are being slashed, public demand for that service continues to increase. Apparently, some politicians have made a serious miscalculation in assessing public will, an error they are careful not to make in funding police protection. They will presumably now pay with their political careers. Or will they? What is our strategy to capitalize on this error, other than ulcers and burnout for ourselves?

If General Kutuzov had been a librarian, Tchaikovsky would not have been able to write the "1812 Overture," and "Burnout Overture" is not really a satisfactory substitute.

Index

About the Author

Herbert S. White, retired Distinguished Professor at the School of Library and Information Science at Indiana University in Bloomington, is author of the popular column "The White Papers" in *Library Journal* and of the book *Librarians and the Awakening from Innocence* (G. K. Hall, 1989). In all White has written more than 150 books and articles on topics of library administration, supervision, and library automation. He is also widely recognized for his work as a consultant, speaker, and reviewer.

White received his master's degree in library science from Syracuse University. During the 45 years of his involvement in the library and information science profession he has served on a variety of boards and committees, including as a member of the American Library Association (ALA) Council and its Committee on Accreditation, and as Chair of Government Relations Committee of the Association for Library and Information Science Education (ALISE). He has received numerous awards, including the American Library Association's prestigious "Melvil Dewey Medal." He received the "Book of the Year" award from the American Society for Information Science and was given the first Lifetime Professional Award by Syracuse University School of Information Studies.